SCHAUM'S OUTLINE OF

THEORY AND PROBLEMS

OF

INTERMEDIATE ACCOUNTING I

•

BARUCH ENGLARD, M.S., M.B.A., CPA

Associate Professor of
Accounting and Computer Science
The College of Staten Island
The City University of New York

SCHAUM'S OUTLINE SERIES

McGRAW-HILL

New York St. Louis San Francisco Auckland Bogotá Caracas
Lisbon London Madrid Mexico City Milan Montreal
New Delhi San Juan Singapore
Sydney Tokyo Toronto

BARUCH ENGLARD, M.S., M.B.A., CPA is Associate Professor of Accounting and Computer Science at The College of Staten Island of The City University of New York. He holds Masters' degrees in both accounting and computer science.

Professor Englard is the author of *Intermediate Accounting II* in the Schaum's Outline Series and has published numerous articles on accounting and computer topics in professional accounting journals. He has participated in the grading of the CPA examination and is also the founder, director, and teacher of *Professor Englard's CPA Review Course*, in Brooklyn, NY.

Schaum's Outline of Theory and Problems of
INTERMEDIATE ACCOUNTING I

7 8 9 10 VFM VFM 0 9 8 7 6 5 4

ISBN 0-07-019579-X

Sponsoring Editor, John Aliano
Production Supervisor, Paula Keller
Editing Supervisor, Patty Andrews

Library of Congress Cataloging-in-Publication Data

Englard, Baruch.
    Schaum's outline of theory and problems of intermediate accounting
I / Baruch Englard.
        p.   cm. - - (Schaum's outline series)
    Includes index.
    ISBN 0-07-019579-X
    1. Accounting - - Problems, exercises, etc.   I. Title.   II. Title:
Theory and problems of intermediate accounting I.
HF5661.E54   1995
657'.044'076 - - dc20   94-34933
                                                   CIP

McGraw-Hill

A Division of The McGraw·Hill Companies

To Surie, Avrumi, and Esther . . .

With Love.

Preface to the Teacher and Student

This book may be used as a *complete stand-alone text* for the classroom, or as a supplement to a standard intermediate accounting textbook. I have written it with two goals in mind: to provide complete coverage of the material and to present it in a clear and easy-to-read manner.

The book contains broad and in-depth coverage of the Intermediate Accounting I topics. It covers theory and practice and is helpful as a study aid for the CPA examination. The latest pronouncements of the FASB have been woven into the text.

Each chapter thoroughly discusses the topic at hand and then concludes with a summary of the chapter. This is followed by a series of rapid-review questions that require fill-in type answers.

At this point the student should have a good, overall understanding of the material presented. What then follows is a series of solved problems that thoroughly challenge the student's grasp of the material. The student is encouraged to solve these without looking at the answers. The problems are presented in the same order as the chapter material and are keyed to the chapter sections.

Finally, the chapter concludes with approximately fifteen supplemental problems *without answers* for additional practice. *These may be selected by the teacher as assignment material to be done at home or in class, or can be done by students on their own.*

The author wishes to thank John Aliano and Patricia Andrews of McGraw-Hill for their assistance in the editing of the manuscript.

BARUCH ENGLARD
Brooklyn, N.Y.
February, 1995

Contents

Chapter 1

Review of the Accounting Process

1.1 INTRODUCTION

Accounting is often referred to as the ''language of business.'' It is a process whose goals are the recording, summarizing, classifying, and reporting of financial information. The inputs to this process are the transactions that a company engages in; the output is the financial statements. The financial statements of a sole proprietorship or partnership consist of the balance sheet, the income statement, the capital statement, and the statement of cash flows.

The recording aspect of the accounting process is based on a fundamental equation, which states:

$$\text{Assets} - \text{Liabilities} = \text{Capital (Owners' Equity)}$$

or
$$A - L = C$$

To understand this equation, we must first define each element. *Assets* are probable future benefits obtained by a company as a result of past transactions. Thus, anything owned by a company (cash, machines, buildings, land, merchandise, paperclips, etc.) and anything owed to it (accounts receivable) is an asset. Liabilities are debts that the company *owes* to others. Thus, accounts payable, wages payable, expenses payable, and notes payable are all examples of liabilities. *Capital* is the amount left over from the asset ''pie'' to be kept (or ''eaten'') by the owners after the liabilities have been paid.

EXAMPLE 1

If assets are $1,000 and liabilities are $700, capital is $300.

Some people express the accounting equation in a slightly different form, as follows:

$$\text{Assets} = \text{Liabilities} + \text{Capital (Owners' Equity)}$$

or
$$A = L + C$$

This form of this equation says that the asset ''pie'' is claimed by two groups (''eaters''): the liabilities and the owners. Both forms of the equation are correct and will be used interchangeably throughout this book.

In a corporation the owners are the stockholders. Therefore, the equation is expressed in the form

$$\text{Assets} - \text{Liabilities} = \text{Stockholders' Equity}$$

or
$$\text{Assets} = \text{Liabilities} + \text{Stockholders' Equity}$$

1.2 THE NATURE OF ACCOUNTS

In accounting, we keep track of assets, liabilities, and capital by recording them in a special record called an *account* (that's why this subject is called accounting!). These accounts resemble the letter ''T'' and therefore are referred to as *T-accounts*. The left side of the T is called the *debit side*; the right side is called the *credit side*. The word *debit* is simply a synonym for ''left''; the word *credit* is a synonym for ''right.'' Some people think that debits are ''bad'' things and credits are ''good'' things. This is not necessarily true, as we will see later in this chapter.

There are three types of accounts, and they are all kept in a special book called the *general ledger*. The three types of accounts are asset accounts, liability accounts, and capital accounts. The rules of debits and credits are quite simple: Asset accounts are debited for increases and credited for decreases; liability and capital accounts work in the opposite manner. These rules are illustrated by the following T-accounts:

Assets		Liabilities		Capital	
DR.	CR.	DR.	CR.	DR.	CR.
+	−	−	+	−	+

Notice that the word *debit* is abbreviated *DR.*, and the word *credit* is abbreviated *CR.*

All companies have expenses, revenue, and drawings (withdrawals by the owner of assets for personal use). Let's remember an important rule regarding these items: Revenue *increases* capital; expenses and drawings *decrease* capital. Thus it would make perfect sense to record these events in the capital account. However, we do not want to "crowd" the capital account, so they have their own separate T-accounts, as follows:

Expenses		Revenue		Drawings	
DR.	CR.	DR.	CR.	DR.	CR.
+	−	−	+	+	−

These accounts are by nature of the capital type, and are considered to be branches of the main capital account. Accordingly, under the rules of debits and credits mentioned earlier, expenses and drawings (which decrease capital) are debits, while revenue (which increases capital) is a credit.

Here is a fundamental rule of bookkeeping to which there are *no exceptions*: Every transaction will have a debit and an equal credit. That is why this system is called the *double-entry bookkeeping system*. This does not mean that there will be *one* debit and *one* credit, but, rather, the total *dollar value* of the debits will always equal the total *dollar value* of the credits. Thus a transaction may have one debit and several credits or vice versa, provided the dollar values are equal. This is called a *compound entry*.

1.3 TRANSACTION ANALYSIS

Let's look at several transactions and see how they are entered in the T-accounts. We will first analyze the transaction in terms of the accounting equation, because this will make it easier for us to determine what T-accounts to use, and how to make the debits and credits.

EXAMPLE 2

The owner invests $30,000 of his personal funds in the company.
Analysis:

$$A = L + C$$
$$+ \quad NC \quad + \qquad \text{(NC means ``no change'')}$$

Entry:

Cash		Capital	
30,000			30,000

Under the rules of debits and credits, the asset Cash is debited because it increased, while Capital is credited for the same reason. Notice that this transaction is consistent with the important rule mentioned earlier: It has a debit of equal dollar value to the credit.

EXAMPLE 3

The company purchases a machine for $5,000, paying $3,000 down and agreeing to pay $2,000 later.
Analysis:

$$
\begin{array}{ccccc}
A & = & L & + & C \\
+5{,}000 & & +2{,}000 & & \text{NC} \\
-3{,}000 & & & &
\end{array}
$$

Entry:

Machine	Cash	Accounts Payable
5,000	3,000	2,000

Note that this is a compound entry.

EXAMPLE 4

The company performs services of $2,000 for cash.
Analysis:

$$
\begin{array}{ccccc}
A & = & L & + & C \\
+2{,}000 & & \text{NC} & & +2{,}000
\end{array}
\qquad \text{(Remember, revenue increases capital)}
$$

Entry:

Cash	Service Revenue
2,000	2,000

EXAMPLE 5

The company performs services of $4,000 on credit (''on account'').
Analysis:

$$
\begin{array}{ccccc}
A & = & L & + & C \\
+4{,}000 & & \text{NC} & & +4{,}000
\end{array}
$$

Entry:

Accounts Receivable	Service Revenue
4,000	4,000

Notice that revenue is recognized even though no cash has been received, because under the *accrual method* of accounting, revenue is recognized when *earned*, even though it is not yet received.

EXAMPLE 6

The company pays its monthly telephone expense of $700.
Analysis:

$$
\begin{array}{ccccc}
A & = & L & + & C \\
-700 & & \text{NC} & & -700
\end{array}
\qquad \text{(Remember, expenses decrease capital)}
$$

Entry:

Telephone Expense		Cash	
700			700

EXAMPLE 7

The company receives a bill of $600 for use of electricity, but does not pay it at this time.
Analysis:

$$
\begin{array}{ccccc}
A & = & L & + & C \\
NC & & +600 & & -600
\end{array}
$$

Entry:

Electricity Expense		Accounts Payable	
600			600

Notice that the expense is recognized even though no cash has yet been paid. This is due, once again, to the accrual method of accounting, which dictates that expenses are recognized when incurred, not when paid.

EXAMPLE 8

The previous electrical bill of $600 is paid.
Analysis:

$$
\begin{array}{ccccc}
A & = & L & + & C \\
-600 & & -600 & & NC
\end{array}
$$

Entry:

Accounts Payable		Cash	
600			600

EXAMPLE 9

The owner withdraws $1,000 for personal use.
Analysis:

$$
\begin{array}{ccccc}
A & = & L & + & C \\
-1,000 & & NC & & -1,000
\end{array}
\qquad \text{(Drawings decrease capital)}
$$

Entry:

Drawings		Cash	
1,000			1,000

EXAMPLE 10

Supplies of $500 are purchased on account.
Analysis:

$$
\begin{array}{ccccc}
A & = & L & + & C \\
+500 & & +500 & & NC
\end{array}
$$

Entry:

Supplies		Accounts Payable	
500			500

EXAMPLE 11

The company collects $3,000 of the $4,000 receivable for services performed. It expects to collect the remaining $1,000 later.

Analysis:

$$
\begin{array}{ccccc}
A & = & L & + & C \\
+3{,}000 & & NC & & NC \\
-3{,}000 & & & &
\end{array}
$$

Entry:

Cash		Accounts Receivable	
3,000			3,000

1.4 THE ACCOUNTING CYCLE

The *accounting cycle* is a series of steps taken by the accountant to maintain a company's books and prepare its financial statements. These steps are as follows:

1. Transaction occurs.
2. Prepare journal entry.
3. Post to the T-accounts in the general ledger.
4. Prepare a trial balance.
5. Journalize and post adjusting entries.
6. Prepare a worksheet (optional).
7. Prepare the financial statements.
8. Journalize and post closing entries.
9. Prepare a post-closing trial balance.
10. Journalize and post reversing entries (optional).

The following sections discuss each of these steps.

1.5 TRANSACTION OCCURRENCE; JOURNAL ENTRIES; POSTING

We previously discussed a series of transactions and showed how they are entered into the T-accounts in the ledger. However, the T-accounts have a weakness. The entry is in two places, which may be several pages apart and thus difficult to find. For example, the debit may be to Cash on page 1, while the credit may be to Capital on page 10.

To correct this weakness, we *first* enter the transaction in another book called the *general journal*, where each transaction is recorded in its entirety in one place. On a weekly or monthly basis we then transfer (*post*) the entries from the journal to their respective T-accounts in the ledger. At this time we make a reference in the journal that indicates the identification number of the T-account to which we posted; we also make a reference in the T-account indicating the page number of the journal from which we posted. These references are called *posting references* (P.R.).

As mentioned, the T-accounts have identification numbers. Companies may assign any numbers they wish to their accounts, but many companies use the following system:

Assets:	numbered 100–199
Liabilities:	numbered 200–299
Capital and Drawing:	numbered 300–399
Revenue:	numbered 400–499
Expenses:	numbered 500–599

EXAMPLE 12

Company A had the following transactions:

July 1 Purchased a machine for $3,000 cash.
    2 Collected $4,000 on account.
    3 Incurred a $500 telephone bill.

The journal would appear as follows:

	General Journal			Page 1
Date	**Account Title**	**P.R.**	**Debit**	**Credit**
July 1	Machine	140	3,000	
	Cash	101		3,000
2	Cash	101	4,000	
	Accounts Receivable	110		4,000
3	Telephone Expense	510	500	
	Accounts Payable	201		500

Note carefully the following important features of the journal:

(*a*) The titles are *exactly* the same as those used for the T-accounts.

(*b*) The debit *always* comes *before* the credit.

(*c*) A line is skipped between transactions to facilitate reading.

(*d*) The title of the credit is indented slightly.

The T-accounts in the general ledger would appear as follows:

Cash	No. 101		Accounts Receivable	No. 110
July 2 J1 4,000	July 1 J1 3,000		July 2 J1 4,000	

Machine	No. 140		Accounts Payable	No. 201
July 1 J1 3,000				July 3 J1 500

Telephone Expense   No. 510

July 3	J1	500

In the T-accounts the reference J1 means that the entry came from the journal, page 1, while in the journal the references (P.R.) refer to the identification numbers of the T-accounts.

It is important to note that the reference numbers, in both the journal and the T-accounts, are entered only *at the time of posting*. Thus, if you see reference numbers, it means that posting has already taken place and should not be done a second time.

The journal we have been using up to this point is referred to as the *general journal*. Some companies use additional, *special journals* for specific transactions. These journals are:

1. Sales journal—for sales on account
2. Cash receipts journal—for receiving cash
3. Cash payments journal—for paying cash
4. Purchases journal—for inventory purchases on account
5. General journal—for all other transactions

Throughout this book we will assume the use of just one journal—the general journal.

1.6   THE TRIAL BALANCE

At the end of the accounting period, the accountant determines the balances of each T-account and lists all the accounts with their respective balances on a sheet of paper. This list is called a *trial balance* and serves two purposes:

1. It acts as a check on the equality of the debits and credits.
2. It creates a starting point for the preparation of the financial statements.

Typical errors that would be detected by a trial balance would be:

(*a*)   Journalizing or posting one-half of an entry, i.e., a debit without a credit, or vice versa
(*b*)   Recording one part of an entry for a different amount than the other part

Errors that would *not* be detected by a trial balance are:

(*a*)   Omitting entirely the entry for a transaction
(*b*)   Journalizing or posting an entry twice
(*c*)   Using an incorrect account

These errors, while causing the totals of the trial balance to be overstated or understated, would not "unbalance" it, and would therefore not be immediately detectable.

EXAMPLE 13

TB Company had the following accounts and balances in its general ledger: cash, $5,000; Service Revenue, $1,000; Telephone Expense, $500; Accounts Payable, $2,000; Drawings, $1,500; Supplies, $3,000; Accounts Receivable, $4,000; Capital, $10,000; Notes Payable, $1,000. The order of the trial balance is: assets, liabilities, capital, drawing, revenue, and expenses. Thus the trial balance for TB Company would appear as follows:

TB Company
Trial Balance
December 31, 19X1

Account	Debit	Credit
Cash	$ 5,000	
Accounts Receivable	4,000	
Supplies	3,000	
Accounts Payable		$ 2,000
Notes Payable		1,000
Capital		10,000
Drawings	1,500	
Service Revenue		1,000
Telephone Expense	500	
Totals	$14,000	$14,000

1.7   ADJUSTING JOURNAL ENTRIES AND POSTING

The ultimate goal and output of the accounting system is the financial statements. However, these statements cannot be prepared directly from the trial balance, because many of the account balances are outdated and incorrect and must first be adjusted and brought up to date. For example, supplies and other assets may have been partially used up, revenue may have been earned but not yet received, and expenses may have accrued but not yet been paid. The updating process is accomplished via *adjusting* journal entries, which are then posted to the T-accounts.

EXAMPLE 14

On January 1, 19X1, Company A purchased a 3-year insurance policy for which it paid a $6,000 premium in advance, debiting Prepaid Insurance and crediting Cash. On December 31, 19X1, an adjusting entry is needed to record the expired portion of $2,000. The entry is:

Insurance Expense   2,000
      Prepaid Insurance   2,000

EXAMPLE 15

On January 1, 19X1, Company B purchased supplies for $5,000. An inventory of the supplies on December 31, 19X1 shows only $3,500 of supplies remaining. The adjusting entry is:

Supplies Expense   1,500
      Supplies   1,500

EXAMPLE 16

On November 1, Company C received a $300 advance payment for services it will render during November, December, and January. At the time of receipt it correctly debited Cash and credited Unearned Service Fees (a liability account). By December 31, $200 of the fees have been earned and the liability is thus only $100. The adjustment is:

Unearned Service Fees   200
      Service Fees   200

EXAMPLE 17

Assume the same information as in the previous example, except that the original entry credited Service Fees instead of Unearned Service Fees. The adjustment is:

Service Fees	100	
Unearned Service Fees		100

EXAMPLE 18

By December 31, Company D has performed services for $500 which it has not yet collected. Thus revenue has accrued and been earned, but not received. The adjustment is:

Accounts Receivable	500	
Service Fees		500

EXAMPLE 19

Company E receives a telephone bill on December 31 for $700 for December's telephone usage. It does not intend to pay this bill until January. Thus an expense has been incurred but not yet paid. Nevertheless, it must be recognized now. The entry is:

Telephone Expense	700	
Accounts Payable (Utilities Payable)		700

EXAMPLE 20

Company F estimates its bad debts as of December 31 to be $925. The entry is:

Bad Debts Expense	925	
Allowance for Doubtful Accounts		925

This entry will be discussed in greater detail in Chapter 7.

EXAMPLE 21

Company G estimates the depreciation on its machinery at $6,000. The entry is:

Depreciation Expense	6,000	
Accumulated Depreciation		6,000

EXAMPLE 22

By December 31, Company H estimates its income taxes for the year to be $25,000. It must make an entry now, even though it will not pay the taxes until April 15. The entry is:

Income Tax Expense	25,000	
Income Tax Payable		25,000

After the foregoing adjusting journal entries have been made, they should be posted to the T-accounts in the general ledger.

1.8 THE WORKSHEET (optional)

Now that the adjusting entries have been journalized and posted, a second trial balance is taken to ensure the equality of the debits and credits. This is referred to as the *adjusted trial balance*, and it can be used directly to prepare the financial statements.

However, accountants like to use an optional, intermediate step to prepare the statements: the worksheet. A *worksheet* is a large piece of paper that acts as an organizer. It contains everything on one sheet: the original trial balance, adjustments, adjusted trial balance, and the statements themselves. Let's take a look at a worksheet.

EXAMPLE 23

Company J had the following information relating to its accounts on December 31, 19X1:

(a)   Supplies used were $1,000.

(b)   Depreciation expense on the equipment is $2,000.

(c)   Accrued property taxes equals $3,000.

(d)   Service fees earned but not yet collected, $10,000.

Company J is engaged both in the sale of services and the sale of goods. Its physical merchandise inventory at January 1 was $25,000, while on December 31 it is $20,000. The company uses the periodic system of inventory and thus the merchandise inventory account has not been touched since January 1. (The details of the periodic and perpetual inventory systems will be discussed in Chapter 8.)

Here is the worksheet:

Company J Worksheet
For the Year Ended December 31, 19X1

Account	Trial Balance Dr.	Trial Balance Cr.	Adjustments Dr.	Adjustments Cr.	Adjusted Trial Balance Dr.	Adjusted Trial Balance Cr.	Income Statement Dr.	Income Statement Cr.	Balance Sheet Dr.	Balance Sheet Cr.
Cash	10,000				10,000				10,000	
Accounts Receivable	5,000		(d) 10,000		15,000				15,000	
Merchandise (Jan. 1)	25,000				25,000		25,000			
Supplies	8,000			(a) 1,000	7,000				7,000	
Equipment	20,000				20,000				20,000	
Accumulated Depreciation		4,000		(b) 2,000		6,000				6,000
Accounts Payable		26,000				26,000				26,000
Capital		23,000				23,000				23,000
Drawing	5,000				5,000				5,000	
Service Revenue		7,000		(d) 10,000		17,000		17,000		
Sales		40,000				40,000		40,000		
Purchases	10,000				10,000		10,000			
Telephone Expenses	8,000				8,000		8,000			
Rent Expense	9,000				9,000		9,000			
Totals	100,000	100,000								
Supplies Expense			(a) 1,000		1,000		1,000			
Depreciation Expense			(b) 2,000		2,000		2,000			
Property Tax Expense			(c) 3,000		3,000		3,000			
Property Tax Payable				(c) 3,000		3,000				3,000
Totals			16,000	16,000	115,000	115,000				
Merchandise (Dec. 31)								20,000	20,000	
Totals							58,000	77,000	77,000	58,000
Net Income							19,000			19,000
Total							77,000	77,000	77,000	77,000

As you can see, the worksheet starts out with the unadjusted trial balance and continues with the adjustments (which are also journalized and posted) to arrive at the adjusted trial balance. The debit and credit parts of each adjustment entry are tied together via letters.

At this point each account balance is carried forward to its appropriate statement. Assets, liabilities, capital, and drawing go to the balance sheet; expenses, revenue, merchandise (beginning), and merchandise-related accounts (such as purchases) go to the income statement. The beginning merchandise balance is included in the income statement because it is a component of cost of goods sold; the ending merchandise balance is debited at the bottom of the worksheet to the balance sheet because it is an asset and represents the goods on hand on December 31. It is also included as a credit in the income statement because it is a subtraction in the determination of cost of goods sold.

The income statement and balance sheet columns are then added up; the difference between the two sides of each should be exactly the same number—the net income of $19,000. In this case the net income is a positive number because the revenue on the credit side of the income statement is greater than the expenses on the debit side. If the debit side was greater, the difference would be a net loss.

You may recall from an earlier discussion that the capital account is not touched during the period. Any changes in capital go instead to the expense, revenue, and drawings accounts. Thus the $23,000 capital shown in the balance sheet column represents the *beginning* capital and not the *current* capital. This $23,000 will have to be updated in the capital statement to arrive at the current ending capital to be shown in the formal balance sheet. This will be discussed later.

One other note: The drawing of $5,000 appears only on the *worksheet* balance sheet. It will not appear in the *formal* balance sheet.

1.9 THE FINANCIAL STATEMENTS

Now that the worksheet has been completed, we can prepare the financial statements directly from the worksheet. The order of preparation is:

1. The income statement
2. The capital statement (to derive the updated capital)
3. The balance sheet

The income statement for Company J would appear as follows:

Company J
Income Statement
For the Year Ended December 31, 19X1

Service Revenue		$17,000
Sales		40,000
Merchandise Inventory, Jan. 1, 19X1	$25,000	
Purchases	10,000	
Merchandise Available for Sale	$35,000	
Merchandise Inventory, Dec. 31, 19X1	(20,000)	
Cost of Goods Sold		(15,000)
Gross Profit		25,000
Total Revenue		42,000
Expenses:		
Telephone	8,000	
Rent	9,000	
Supplies used	1,000	
Depreciation	2,000	
Property Tax	3,000	
Total Expenses		(23,000)
Net Income		$19,000

Now, the capital statement would appear as follows.

Company J
Capital Statement
For the Year Ended December 31, 19X1

Capital, Jan. 1, 19X1	$23,000
Net Income	19,000
Drawings	(5,000)
Capital, Dec. 31, 19X1	$37,000

Note: The *ending* capital amount of $37,000 will appear on the following balance sheet.

Company J
Balance Sheet
December 31, 19X1

Assets:			Liabilities:	
Cash		$10,000	Accounts Payable	$26,000
Accounts Receivable		15,000	Property Tax Payable	3,000
Merchandise Inventory		20,000	Total Liabilities	$29,000
Supplies		7,000	Capital	37,000
Equipment	$20,000			
Accumulated Depreciation	6,000)	14,000		
Total Assets		$66,000	Total Liabilities and Capital	$66,000

1.10 CLOSING ENTRIES

We mentioned at the beginning of this chapter that even though expense, revenue, and drawings transactions affect capital, we do not record them in the Capital account so as not to "overcrowd" this account. Instead, we record these events in separate accounts which are "branches" of the Capital account. Thus, by the end of the period, Capital, which has not been touched since last period (except for additional owner investments), is out of date and must be updated. All the information in the expense, revenue, and drawings accounts must "come home" to the Capital account. The process of "pouring" the information from these accounts into Capital is called *closing*.

The steps in the closing process are:

1. Close ("empty out") the expense accounts via a credit and transfer the information into an intermediate account called Income Summary.
2. Close the revenue accounts via a debit and transfer the information into Income Summary via a credit.
3. Close Income Summary into Capital. If Income Summary has a credit balance, the balance represents net income; if it has a debit balance, it represents a net loss.
4. Close drawings via credits and transfer the information into Capital via a debit.

EXAMPLE 24

Corporation K has the following capital-type accounts on December 31:

K Capital	Rent Expense	Salary Expense
50,000 Jan. 1	2,000	5,000

Service Revenue	K Drawings
12,000	1,000

The closing entries are:

Income Summary	7,000	
Rent Expense		2,000
Salary Expense		5,000
Service Revenue	12,000	
Income Summary		12,000

Income Summary now appears as follows:

Income Summary

7,000	12,000
	5,000 Bal.

The balance of $5,000 represents the net income.
Now, to close Income Summary:

Income Summary	5,000	
K Capital		5,000

Finally, to close the drawings:

K Capital	1,000	
K Drawings		1,000

The Capital account is now up to date and would appear as follows:

K Capital

1,000	50,000	Jan.1 Bal.
	5,000	
	54,000	Dec. 31 Bal.

EXAMPLE 25

Milstein Corporation has the following Income Summary account after its expense and revenue accounts have been closed:

Income Summary

13,000	10,000
3,000	

In this case, the *debit* balance of $3,000 represents a *net loss*. The closing entry would thus be:

Capital	3,000	
Income Summary		3,000

In a merchandise company that uses the *periodic* inventory system, there are additional accounts that need to be closed. These accounts are: Sales, Sales Returns, and Sales Discounts; Purchases, Purchases Returns, Purchases Discounts; and Transportation In (Freight In). The sales and sales-related accounts are closed into Income Summary; the purchases and purchases-related accounts are closed into a new account, Cost of Goods Sold, which is then closed into Income Summary.

In addition, under the *periodic* system, the Merchandise Inventory account, which has not been used all period, must be updated via two closing entries. The first one gets rid of the old, beginning-of-period balance, while the second one inserts the new, updated balance. Both of these use Cost of Goods Sold.

These procedures are illustrated in the following example.

EXAMPLE 26

S & W Metals Corporation had the following accounts relating to its merchandise operations for 19X5:

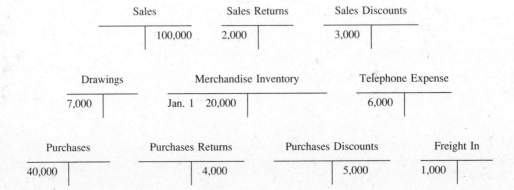

The ending merchandise inventory on December 31 is $23,000. The closing entries are:

Sales	100,000	
Income Summary		100,000
Income Summary	5,000	
Sales Returns		2,000
Sales Discounts		3,000
Cost of Goods Sold	41,000	
Purchases		40,000
Freight In		1,000
Purchases Returns	4,000	
Purchases Discounts	5,000	
Cost of Goods Sold		9,000
Cost of Goods Sold	20,000	
Merchandise Inventory		20,000
Merchandise Inventory	23,000	
Cost of Goods Sold		23,000
Income Summary	6,000	
Telephone Expense		6,000

The Cost of Goods Sold account now appears as follows:

Cost of Goods Sold

41,000	9,000
20,000	23,000
Bal. 29,000	

This is now closed to Income Summary:

Income Summary	29,000	
Cost of Goods Sold		29,000

Income Summary now appears as follows:

Income Summary

5,000	100,000
6,000	
29,000	
	60,000 Bal.

This account, and the drawings accounts, are now closed to Capital:

Income Summary	60,000	
Capital		60,000

Capital	7,000	
Drawings		7,000

In a corporation, there is no account called "Capital" per se. Instead, the net income or net loss from Income Summary is closed to Retained Earnings.

EXAMPLE 27

Corporation C had a net loss of $10,000. The closing entry for Income Summary is:

Retained Earnings	10,000	
Income Summary		10,000

1.11 POST-CLOSING TRIAL BALANCE; REVERSING ENTRIES

Since the time the trial balance was taken several steps back in the accounting cycle, a great deal of activity has taken place in the accounts. Adjusting entries were journalized and posted, and so were closing entries. Thus, to ensure that no mistakes were made in these entries, another trial balance should be taken.

Will this trial balance be larger than, equal to, or smaller than the original one? The answer is smaller, of course, since all the expense, revenue, and merchandise-related accounts that appeared on the first trial balance will not appear now—they have been closed.

The next and last step in the accounting cycle is optional: *reversing entries*. These entries *reverse certain adjustment entries* and are done on the first day of the new accounting period: January 1.

The adjusting entries which the accountant *may* choose to reverse are:

1. Adjustments for accrued revenue
2. Adjustments for accrued expenses
3. Adjustments for the expiration and use of prepaid items that were initially debited to expense accounts
4. Adjustments for unearned revenue that were initially credited to a revenue account

Let's take a look at the optional reversal for adjustments involving accrued revenue.

EXAMPLE 28

Suppose that Corporation P paid its payroll on December 27 and the amount accrued for December 28 through December 31 is $3,000. On January 7, the next payroll date, it will pay this $3,000, plus another $5,000 for the week of January 1–7, for a total of $8,000. If no reversing entries are used, the entries for all these events would be:

Dec. 31	Salaries Expense		3,000	
	Salaries Payable			3,000
	(to record accrued salaries)			
31	Income Summary		3,000	
	Salaries Expense			3,000
	(to close Salaries Expense)			
Jan. 7	Salaries Payable		3,000	
	Salaries Expense		5,000	
	Cash			8,000
	(to pay the current payroll and the accrued payroll from December)			

Notice that under this method, the accountant must remember to apportion the $8,000 payment partially to salaries expense (for this period's portion) and partially to salaries payable (for last period's portion).

If reversing entries are used, the accountant need not bother remembering this information. The entries are:

Dec. 31	Salaries Expense		3,000	
	Salaries Payable			3,000
31	Income Summary		3,000	
	Salaries Expense			3,000
Jan. 1	Salaries Payable		3,000	
	Salaries Expense			3,000
	(to reverse the adjusting entry of Dec. 31)			

Salaries Expense at this point would appear as follows:

Salaries Expense	
	3,000

Notice that it has an unnatural *credit* balance. This will be taken care of with the next entry:

Jan. 7	Salaries Expense	8,000	
	Cash		8,000

Notice that there is no need to apportion the $8,000 into two parts ($3,000 and $5,000). Also notice that the Salaries Expense account now shows the correct *debit* balance for salaries of this period, $5,000.

Salaries Expense

		3,000	Jan. 1
Jan. 8	8,000		
Bal.	5,000		

Whether or not the accountant chooses to use reversing entries, the final results will always be the same. They are just a matter of convenience.

The same type of logic and procedures apply to accrued expenses, as we show in the next example.

EXAMPLE 29

On December 31, Corporation T receives a telephone bill in the amount of $80, which it does not pay at this time. On January 15 it remits $150 to the telephone company, consisting of the $80 accrual for December, plus an additional $70 for January usage. The entries under both systems are:

Reversals Not Used   **Reversals Used**

Dec. 31   Telephone Expense   80   Same Entry
               Accounts Payable   80
            (to record the accrual)

    31   Income Summary   80   Income Summary   80
               Telephone Expense   80   Telephone Expense   80
                  (to close telephone expense)

Telephone Expense

80	80

                                                          Telephone Expense

80	80

Jan. 1   No reversing entry   Accounts Payable   80
                                                   Telephone Expense   80

Telephone Expense

                                                          Telephone Expense

	80 (credit balance)

    15   Accounts Payable   80   Telephone Expense   150
          Telephone Expense   70   Cash   150
               Cash   150

Telephone Expense

70	

                                                          Telephone Expense

	80
150	
70	

As you see, both methods result in the same $70 telephone expense for January.

If prepaid items such as supplies, insurance, and rent were initially debited to an asset account, no reversing entries should be made. However, if the initial debit was to an expense account, then a reversing entry is optional. Similarly, if revenue received in advance was initially credited to a liability account (such as Unearned Revenue), no reversing entries are made. But if the initial credit was to a revenue account, then, again, a reversing entry would be optional. These concepts are illustrated in the following examples.

EXAMPLE 30

On January 1, 19X1, Company K purchases a 3-year insurance policy whose annual premium is $1,000, and pays the entire $3,000 in advance. The initial entry may be debited to Prepaid Insurance—an asset—or to Insurance Expense. The entries under each alternative are:

	If Debited to Prepaid Insurance			**If Debited to Insurance Expense**		
Jan. 1, 19X1	Prepaid Insurance	3,000		Insurance Expense	3,000	
	Cash		3,000	Cash		3,000
Dec. 31	(adjusting entry)					
	Insurance Expense	1,000		Prepaid Insurance	2,000	
	Prepaid Insurance		1,000	Insurance Expense		2,000
31	(closing entry)					
	Income Summary	1,000		Income Summary	1,000	
	Insurance Expense		1,000	Insurance Expense		1,000
Jan. 1, 19X2	No reversing entry			Insurance Expense	2,000	
				Prepaid Insurance		2,000
				(optional reversing entry)		

EXAMPLE 31

On January 1, 19X1, Company R receives a $3,000 advance payment for services of $1,000 to be performed annually over the next 3 years. The initial entry may either be credited to a liability, Unearned Revenue, or to Revenue. The entries for each alternative are:

	If Credited to Unearned Revenue			**If Credited to Revenue**		
Jan. 1, 19X1	Cash	3,000		Cash	3,000	
	Unearned Revenue		3,000	Revenue		3,000
Dec. 31	(adjusting entry)					
	Unearned Revenue	1,000		Revenue	2,000	
	Revenue		1,000	Unearned Revenue		2,000
31	(closing entry)					
	Revenue	1,000		Revenue	1,000	
	Income Summary		1,000	Income Summary		1,000
Jan. 1, 19X2	No reversing entry			Unearned Revenue	2,000	
				Revenue		2,000
				(optional)		

Summary

1. Accounting is a process whose goals are the recording, summarizing, classifying, and reporting of financial information. The inputs to this process are the transactions; the outputs are the financial statements.

2. The *fundamental equation of accounting* states:

$$\text{Assets} - \text{Liabilities} = \text{Capital (Owners' Equity)}$$

In a corporation the equation appears as:

$$\text{Assets} - \text{Liabilities} = \text{Stockholders' Equity}$$

3. *Assets* are probable future benefits obtained as a result of past transactions. *Liabilities* are debts owed to others, while *capital* is the portion of the assets that may be kept by the owners after the liabilities are paid.

4. The left side of the T-account is called the *debit side*, while the right side is the *credit side*. Assets are increased via debits and decreased via credits; liabilities and capital work in the opposite manner.

5. There are three types of accounts: *assets*, *liabilities*, and *capital*. The capital account has several branches: expenses, revenue, and drawings. Expenses and drawings decrease capital; revenue increases capital.

6. In the double-entry bookkeeping system, every transaction has a debit and an equal credit. Entries that have more than one debit or one credit are called *compound entries*.

7. *The accounting cycle* is the series of steps taken to maintain a company's books and prepare its statements. It begins with the occurrence of a transaction and ends with the optional step of reversing entries.

8. Transactions are initially entered in a book called the *journal* and are then transferred or posted to a book called the *general ledger*.

9. In the journal, debits are always entered *before* credits; the titles used are exactly the ones used in the ledger, and the title of the credit is slightly indented.

10. A *trial balance* is prepared at the end of the accounting period. Its purposes are to check for errors and act as a starting point for preparation of the statements.

11. Omitting a *complete* entry or recording a transaction twice will not upset the trial balance.

12. The *worksheet* is an optional, handy organizer that presents everything on one page—the original trial balance, adjustments, adjusted trial balance, and financial statements.

13. The purpose of *closing entries* is to update the capital account (which has not been touched all period) by ''pouring'' into it the information contained in its branches—the expense, revenue, and drawing accounts. This is accomplished via an intermediate account called Income Summary.

14. The steps in the closing process of a nonmerchandise company are:

    (*a*)   Close the expense accounts via Income Summary.

    (*b*)   Close the revenue accounts via Income Summary.

    (*c*)   Close Income Summary into Capital.

    (*d*)   Close Drawings into Capital.

    In a corporation, Income Summary is closed into Retained Earnings.

15. *Reversing entries* are optional, are done on the first day of the *new* accounting period, and reverse *certain* adjustment entries made the day before. The adjustments that may be reversed are:

    (*a*)   Adjustments for accrued revenue

(b). Adjustments for accrued expenses

(c) Adjustments for the expiration of prepaid items initially debited to expense accounts

(d) Adjustments for unearned revenue initially credited to revenue accounts

Rapid Review

1.   The fundamental accounting equation states that Assets = Liabilities + _____ .

2.   Debts owed to others are called _____ .

3.   The portion of the assets that may be kept by the owners is called _____ .

4.   If assets are $10,000 and capital is $6,000, then liabilities are _____ .

5.   The left side of an account is the _____ side; the right side is the _____ side.

6.   Assets are increased via _____ , while liabilities and capital are increased via _____ .

7.   Expense and revenue accounts are branches of the _____ account.

8.   Entries that have more than *one* debit or *one* credit are _____ .

9.   Revenue is recognized when _____ , not when _____ .

10. Expenses are recognized when _____ , not when _____ .

11. The steps taken by the accountant to maintain the books and prepare statements is referred to as the _____ .

12. The accounts are kept in a book called the _____ .

13. To determine from the T-account what page in the journal the entry originated on, one would look at the _____ .

14. The special journal used for sales *on account* is the _____ .

15. The special journal used for *cash* purchases is the _____ .

16. A checking procedure done at the end of the period to ensure the equality of debits and credits is the _____ .

17. Entries made at period end to update the accounts are called _____ .

18. Revenue earned but not yet received is called _____ .

19. A large piece of paper containing all the information needed for the statements is the _____.

20. Entries that update the capital account are called _____.

21. These entries use an intermediate account called _____.

22. In a merchandise company, the merchandise-related accounts are closed into _____.

23. In a corporation, the net income is closed into _____.

24. If Income Summary has a debit balance, the company must have incurred a _____.

25. Optional entries made at the beginning of the new period are called _____ entries.

Answers: **1.** Capital **2.** liabilities **3.** capital **4.** $4,000 **5.** debit; credit **6.** debits; credits **7.** Capital **8.** compound entries **9.** earned; received **10.** incurred; paid **11.** accounting cycle **12.** ledger **13.** posting reference **14.** sales journal **15.** cash payments journal **16.** trial balance **17.** adjusting **18.** accrued revenue **19.** worksheet **20.** closing entries **21.** Income Summary **22.** Cost of Goods Sold **23.** Retained Earnings **24.** loss **25.** reversing

Solved Problems

The Accounting Equation and the Nature of Accounts

1.1. Determine the following:

   (a) If assets are $7,000 and capital is $2,000, what are liabilities?

   (b) If capital is $17,000 and liabilities are $8,000, what are assets?

   SOLUTION

   (a) $5,000

   (b) $25,000   [Section 1.1]

1.2 What must be done to *decrease* the following accounts, and what are their normal balances?

   (a) Accounts Receivable

   (b) Land

   (c) Accounts Payable

   (d) Notes Payable

   (e) Prepaid Insurance

   (f) Unearned Rent

   (g) Service Revenue

   (h) Supplies

SOLUTION

(a)	credit, debit	(e)	credit, debit
(b)	credit, debit	(f)	debit, credit
(c)	debit, credit	(g)	debit, credit
(d)	debit, credit	(h)	credit, debit

[Section 1.2]

Transaction Analysis and Journal Entries

1.3   Englard Realty had the following transactions during 19X1. Show the effect of each transaction on the accounting equation.

(a)   The owner invested $15,000 in the business.

(b)   The owner withdrew $3,000.

(c)   A machine was purchased for $2,000.

(d)   Services were performed for cash of $7,000.

(e)   Services were performed on account for $6,000.

(f)   Land of $8,000 was purchased for $5,000 cash and a note was given for the balance.

(g)   A telephone bill for $65 was received and immediately paid.

(h)   A utility bill for $85 was received and recorded but not paid.

(i)   The $6,000 due from transaction (e) was received.

(j)   The utility bill from transaction (h) was paid.

SOLUTION

	Assets	Liabilities	Capital
(a)	+$15,000	No effect	+$15,000
(b)	−$3,000	No effect	−$3,000
(c)	+$2,000; −$2,000	No effect	No effect
(d)	+$7,000	No effect	+$7,000
(e)	+$6,000	No effect	+$6,000
(f)	+$8,000; −$5,000	+$3,000	No effect
(g)	−$65	No effect	−$65
(h)	No effect	+$65	−$65
(i)	+$6,000; −$6,000	No effect	No effect
(j)	−$85	−$85	No effect

[Section 1.3]

1.4   Prepare journal entries for the transactions in Problem 1.3.

SOLUTION

(a)	Cash	15,000	
	Capital		15,000
(b)	Drawings	3,000	
	Cash		3,000
(c)	Machine	2,000	
	Cash		2,000

| (d) | Cash | 7,000 | |
| | Service Revenue | | 7,000 |

| (e) | Accounts Receivable | 6,000 | |
| | Service Revenue | | 6,000 |

(f)	Land	8,000	
	Cash		5,000
	Notes Payable		3,000

| (g) | Telephone Expense | 65 | |
| | Cash | | 65 |

| (h) | Utility Expense | 85 | |
| | Utilities Payable | | 85 |

| (i) | Cash | 6,000 | |
| | Accounts Receivable | | 6,000 |

| (j) | Utilities Payable | 85 | |
| | Cash | | 85 |

1.5 Prepare journal entries for the following transactions.

(a) Received cash of $15,000 on account.

(b) Paid a liability of $3,000.

(c) Received and paid a gas bill of $500.

(d) Withdrew supplies of $1,000 for personal use.

(e) Performed services on account, $2,000.

(f) Purchased land for a note, $7,000.

SOLUTION

| (a) | Cash | 15,000 | |
| | Accounts Receivable | | 15,000 |

| (b) | Accounts Payable | 3,000 | |
| | Cash | | 3,000 |

| (c) | Utility Expense | 500 | |
| | Cash | | 500 |

| (d) | Drawings | 1,000 | |
| | Supplies | | 1,000 |

| (e) | Accounts Receivable | 2,000 | |
| | Service Revenue | | 2,000 |

| (f) | Land | 7,000 | |
| | Notes Payable | | 7,000 |

[Section 1.5]

1.6   Determine what is wrong, if anything, with the following journal entries, and prepare correction entries if needed.

(*a*)   A building was purchased for $20,000 cash. The entry was:

Building	20,000	
Accounts Payable		20,000

(*b*)   Cash of $7,000 was received on account. The entry was:

Cash	7,000	
Service Revenue		7,000

(*c*)   An account payable of $4,000 was paid. The entry was:

Cash	4,000	
Accounts Payable		4,000

(*d*)   Land was purchased for a $20,000 note. The entry was:

Land	20,000	
Notes Payable		20,000

(*e*)   A telephone bill of $50 was received and immediately paid. The entry was:

Advertising Expense	50	
Cash		50

SOLUTION

(*a*)

Accounts Payable	20,000	
Cash		20,000

(*b*)

Service Revenue	7,000	
Accounts Receivable		7,000

(*c*)   In this case the entry was reversed. The correction is:

Accounts Payable	8,000	
Cash		8,000

(*d*)   This entry is correct.

(*e*)

Telephone Expense	50		
Advertising Expense		50	[Section 1.5]

1.7   Indicate the journal into which each one of the following transactions should be entered.

(*a*)   Cash was received on account.

(*b*)   Sales were made for cash.

(c)   Supplies were purchased for cash.

(d)   Merchandise was purchased on account.

(e)   The adjusting entry for depreciation.

(f)   Sales were made on account.

(g)   The closing entry for service revenue.

SOLUTION

(a)   cash receipts   (e)   general

(b)   cash receipts   (f)   sales

(c)   cash payments   (g)   general

(d)   purchases   [Section 1.5]

The Trial Balance

1.8   Determine the effect that each of the following *independent* errors would have on the trial balance.

(a)   The Accounts Receivable balance of $800 was omitted from the trial balance.

(b)   The Service Revenue balance of $600 was omitted.

(c)   A telephone bill was debited to Advertising Expense.

(d)   Land of $10,000 was listed in the trial balance as a credit.

(e)   A transaction involving the purchase of supplies for $500 was omitted completely.

(f)   A transaction was recorded twice.

SOLUTION

(a)   The credit side will be greater than the debit side by $800.

(b)   The debit side will be greater by $600.

(c)   No effect.

(d)   The credit side will be greater by $20,000. Not only is a debit of $10,000 missing, there is also an incorrect credit of $10,000, resulting in a total error of $20,000.

(e)   The trial balance will balance.

(f)   The trial balance will balance.   [Section 1.6]

1.9   Prepare a trial balance from the following account information.

Accounts Payable	$ 9,000
Telephone Expense	1,000
Cash	10,000
Machine	15,000
Accumulated Depreciation	4,000
Service Revenue	6,000
Capital	9,000
Drawings	2,000

SOLUTION

Trial Balance

	DR.	CR.
Cash	$10,000	
Machine	15,000	
Accumulated Depreciation		$ 4,000
Accounts Payable		9,000
Capital		9,000
Drawings	2,000	
Service Revenue		6,000
Telephone Expense	1,000	
Totals	$28,000	$28,000 [Section 1.6]

Adjusting Journal Entries

1.10 Esther Company has the following information relating to its accounts on December 31, 19X1.

(a) An ending inventory of supplies shows $500 remaining. Supplies of $1,800 were purchased during the year, and there were no supplies in inventory on January 1.

(b) An insurance policy for the next 4 years was purchased on July 1 and the total premium of $4,000 was prepaid.

(c) On December 29, a utility bill of $75 was received.

(d) Revenue for services performed on December 29 in the amount of $2,000 has not yet been collected.

SOLUTION

(a)	Supplies Expense	1,300	
	Supplies		1,300
(b)	Insurance Expense	500	
	Prepaid Insurance		500
(c)	Utility Expense	75	
	Utilities Payable		75
(d)	Accounts Receivable	2,000	
	Service Fees		2,000 [Section 1.7]

1.11 Avrohom Company had the following adjustment data on December 31, 19X1.

(a) On November 1, cash in the amount of $1,200 was *received* as an advance payment for services to be rendered over the next 6 months. The fee per month is $200, and the transaction was initially recorded as a debit to Cash for $1,200 and a credit to Unearned Service Fees.

(b) Bad debts are estimated at $500.

(c) A machine was purchased for $11,000 on January 1. Its estimated life and salvage value are 10 years and $1,000, respectively.

(d) Estimated income tax for the year is $23,000.

Prepare the necessary adjusting entries.

SOLUTION

(a)	Unearned Service Fees	400	
	Service Fees ($200 × 2 months)		400
(b)	Bad Debts Expense	500	
	Allowance for Doubtful Accounts		500
(c)	Depreciation Expense	1,000	
	Accumulated Depreciation		1,000
(d)	Income Tax Expense	23,000	
	Income Tax Payable		23,000 [Section 1.7]

1.12 A 3-year insurance policy with a total cost of $900 was paid for in advance on January 1, 19X1. Prepare the required adjusting entry on December 31, 19X1, if:

(a) The initial entry was a debit to Prepaid Insurance.

(b) The initial entry was a debit to Insurance Expense.

SOLUTION

(a)	Insurance Expense	300	
	Prepaid Insurance		300
(b)	Prepaid Insurance	600	
	Insurance Expense		600 [Section 1.7]

1.13 Service fees in the amount of $1,600 were received in advance on January 1, 19X1. These are for services to be rendered over the next 4 years, at $400 per year. Prepare the required adjusting entry on December 31, 19X1, if:

(a) The initial entry credited Unearned Service Fees.

(b) The initial entry credited Service Fees.

SOLUTION

(a)	Unearned Service Fees	400	
	Service Fees		400
(b)	Service Fees	1,200	
	Unearned Service Fees		1,200 [Section 1.7]

The Worksheet

1.14 Prepare a worksheet from the following trial balance and adjustment information.

	DR.	CR.
Cash	$20,000	
Machinery	16,000	
Accumulated Depreciation		$ 4,000

Merchandise (Jan. 1)	30,000
Accounts Payable	7,000
Capital	44,000
Service Fees	8,000
Sales	20,000
Purchases	9,000
Telephone Expense	8,000
Total	$83,000 $83,000

Adjustment information:

(a) Depreciation for the year is $2,000.

(b) The ending merchandise inventory is $34,000.

(c) Accrued electrical usage is $120.

(d) Service fees earned but not yet collected are $2,000.

SOLUTION

Account	Trial Balance Dr.	Trial Balance Cr.	Adjustments Dr.	Adjustments Cr.	Adjusted Trial Balance Dr.	Adjusted Trial Balance Cr.	Income Statement Dr.	Income Statement Cr.	Balance Sheet Dr.	Balance Sheet Cr.
Cash	20,000				20,000				20,000	
Machinery	16,000				16,000				16,000	
Accumulated Depreciation		4,000		(a) 2,000		6,000				6,000
Merchandise (Jan. 1)	30,000				30,000		30,000			
Accounts Payable		7,000				7,000				7,000
Capital		44,000				44,000				44,000
Service Fees		8,000		(d) 2,000		10,000		10,000		
Sales		20,000				20,000		20,000		
Purchases	9,000				9,000		9,000			
Telephone Expense	8,000				8,000		8,000			
Totals	83,000	83,000								
Depreciation Expense			(a) 2,000		2,000		2,000			
Electrical Expense			(c) 120		120		120			
Utilities Payable				(c) 120		120				120
Accounts Receivable			(d) 2,000	4,120	2,000				2,000	
Totals			4,120	4,120	87,120	87,120	49,120	30,000	38,000	57,120
Merchandise (Dec. 31)								(b) 34,000	(b) 34,000	
Totals							49,120	64,000	72,000	57,120
Net Income							14,880			14,880
Total							64,000	64,000	72,000	72,000

[Section 1.8]

Closing Entries

1.15 On December 31, Bodner Corporation had the following T-accounts relating to its capital:

Utility Expense	Salary Expense	Service Fees
4,000	7,000	12,000

Interest Revenue	Drawings	Capital
4,000	1,000	30,000 (Jan. 1)

Prepare closing entries and also determine the ending balance of capital.

SOLUTION

Income Summary	11,000	
Utility Expense		4,000
Salary Expense		7,000
Service Fees	12,000	
Interest Revenue	4,000	
Income Summary		16,000
Income Summary	5,000	
Capital		5,000
Capital	1,000	
Drawings		1,000

The ending capital balance is $34,000.   [Section 1.10]

1.16 Quinn Company, a *corporation* dealing in the sale of goods, has the following accounts on December 31, 19X1:

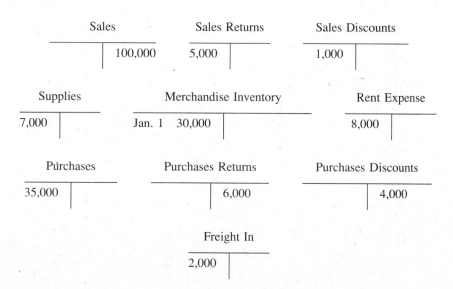

Sales	Sales Returns	Sales Discounts
100,000	5,000	1,000

Supplies	Merchandise Inventory	Rent Expense
7,000	Jan. 1 30,000	8,000

Purchases	Purchases Returns	Purchases Discounts
35,000	6,000	4,000

Freight In
2,000

According to a physical count, the merchandise inventory on December 31 is $40,000. Prepare entries to close the accounts.

SOLUTION

Sales	100,000	
Income Summary		100,000
Income Summary	6,000	
Sales Returns		5,000
Sales Discounts		1,000
Income Summary	8,000	
Rent Expense		8,000
Merchandise Inventory	40,000	
Cost of Goods Sold		40,000
Cost of Goods Sold	30,000	
Merchandise Inventory		30,000
Cost of Goods Sold	35,000	
Purchases		35,000
Purchases Returns	6,000	
Purchases Discounts	4,000	
Cost of Goods Sold		10,000
Cost of Goods Sold	2,000	
Freight In		2,000
Income Summary	17,000	
Cost of Goods Sold		17,000
Income Summary	69,000	
Retained Earnings		69,000

Notice that because this is a corporation, Retained Earnings, rather than Capital, is credited to close Income Summary. Also note that Supplies is *not* closed. [Section 1.11]

1.17 Pathetic Corporation had the following income summary account on December 31:

Income Summary

90,000	70,000

(*a*) Is this a net income or a net loss situation?

(*b*) Prepare the closing entry.

SOLUTION

(*a*) Net loss

(*b*)

Retained Earnings	20,000		
Income Summary		20,000	[Section 1.11]

Reversing Entries

1.18 By December 31, Zinner Corporation has earned service fees of $14,000, which it has not yet received, and has also incurred a gas bill of $850, which it has not yet paid. During January of the next accounting period, it receives $16,000 in cash for services, which includes the $14,000 due from the previous period. In addition, it pays out $1,000 for gas usage, which includes the $850 balance from the last period.

(a) Prepare the required adjusting entries for December 31.

(b) Prepare optional reversing entries on January 1.

(c) Prepare the entries for the January transactions.

(d) If reversing entries were not made on January 1, how would the entries for part (c) be different?

SOLUTION

(a)	Accounts Receivable	14,000		Utilities Expense	850	
	Service Fees		14,000	Utilities Payable		850
(b)	Service Fees	14,000		Utilities Payable	850	
	Accounts Receivable		14,000	Utilities Expense		850
(c)	Cash	16,000		Utilities Expense	1,000	
	Service Fees		16,000	Cash		1,000
(d)	Cash	16,000		Utilities Expense	150	
	Accounts Receivable		14,000	Utilities Payable	850	
	Service Fees		2,000	Cash		1,000

[Section 1.11]

1.19 For each of the following adjusting entries, indicate whether or not reversals are appropriate.

(a) Accrued revenue

(b) Depreciation

(c) Bad debts

(d) Accrued expenses

(e) Insurance expired, where the original entry debited Prepaid Insurance

(f) Unearned revenue, where the original entry credited Revenue

(g) Closing entries

SOLUTION

(a) Reverse

(b) Do not reverse

(c) Do not reverse

(d) Reverse

(e) Do not reverse

(f) Reverse

(g) Do not reverse

Note: Even when appropriate, reversing entries are merely optional, *not* required.   [Section 1.11]

1.20 On January 1, 19X1, Greenfield Corporation purchased a 5-year insurance policy ($4,000 *annual* premium) and prepaid the total premium of $20,000. Prepare the adjusting and reversing entries if:

(*a*) The initial purchase was debited to Insurance Expense.

(*b*) The initial purchase was debited to Prepaid Insurance.

SOLUTION

(*a*)	Prepaid Insurance	16,000		
	Insurance Expense		16,000	
	Insurance Expense	16,000		(optional)
	Prepaid Insurance		16,000	
(*b*)	Insurance Expense	4,000		
	Prepaid Insurance		4,000	

No reversing entry   [Section 1.11]

1.21 On July 1, 19X1, Reliable Furniture Company received an advance payment of $16,000, which it credited to the Service Fees account. This represented services to be performed over the next 4 years. By December 31, $2,000 worth of services have been performed. Prepare the adjusting and reversing entries.

SOLUTION

Dec. 31	Service Fees	14,000		
	Unearned Service Fees		14,000	
Jan. 1	Unearned Service Fees	14,000		(optional)
	Service Fees		14,000	[Section 1.11]

Supplementary Problems

1.22 Company A had the following transactions during 19X3.

(*a*) The owner invested a building in the business.

(*b*) A piece of land was purchased partially for cash and the remainder for a note payable.

(*c*) Services were performed and cash was immediately collected.

(*d*) Services were performed on account.

(*e*) Supplies were purchased for cash.

(*f*) Merchandise was purchased on account (periodic system).

(*g*) The owner withdrew cash.

(*h*) A telephone bill was received but not paid.

(*i*) The merchandise purchased in transaction (*f*) was paid for.

Analyze these transactions in terms of their effects on the accounting equation.

1.23   For the transactions in Problem 1.22, prepare a journal entry (without numbers) for each transaction.

1.24   From the following trial balance and adjustment information of Company B, prepare a worksheet.

	DR.	CR.
Cash	$ 20,000	
Accounts Receivable	7,000	
Merchandise	14,000	
Equipment	40,000	
Accumulated Depreciation		$ 10,000
Accounts Payable		6,000
Notes Payable		2,000
Capital		46,000
Drawings	4,000	
Service Fees		16,000
Sales		20,000
Purchases	12,000	
Purchases Returns		2,000
Telephone Expense	4,000	
Rent Expense	1,000	
Total	$102,000	$102,000

Adjustment data:
(a)   Merchandise on December 31 is $12,000.
(b)   Equipment depreciation is $3,000.
(c)   Interest accrued on the note payable is $80.
(d)   Service fees earned but neither billed nor received are $7,000.
(e)   Advertising expense accrued but not paid is $100.

1.25   Prepare a trial balance from the following account information of Company C and find the missing capital balance:

Accounts Receivable	$10,000
Merchandise	12,000
Accounts Payable	2,000
Equipment	25,000
Notes Payable	8,000
Rent Expense	2,000
Service Fees	7,000
Drawings	4,000
Capital	?

1.26   Prepare adjusting journal entries for the following information relating to Company D.
(a)   Accrued salaries total $12,000.
(b)   Depreciation on machinery is $9,000
(c)   Accrued revenue is $19,000.
(d)   Bad debts are estimated at $3,000.

1.27   Company E has asked you to prepare adjusting journal entries for the following data on December 31, 19X1.

(a)   Unearned service fees, showing a balance of $2,000, has been earned to the extent of $500.

(b)   Accrued utilities fees are $700.

(c)   The physical count of supplies on December 31 shows $500 of supplies remaining. The Supplies account shows a balance of $800.

(d)   A 5-year insurance policy for $5,000 was purchased on January 1 and debited to Insurance Expense.

(e)   Estimated income taxes for 19X1 are $6,000.

1.28   Company F has prepared the following trial balance on December 31, 19X3:

	DR.	CR.
Cash	$ 60,000	
Accounts Receivable	40,000	
Equipment	20,000	
Accumulated Depreciation		$ 5,000
Accounts Payable		10,000
Notes Payable		12,000
Salaries Payable		8,000
Capital		70,000
Drawings	2,000	
Service Fees		25,000
Rent Expense	4,000	
Telephone Expense	4,000	
Total	$130,000	$130,000

Prepare an income statement, capital statement, and balance sheet.

1.29   Company G, a sole proprietorship, shows the following capital-related accounts on December 31:

Salary Expense	$12,000
Rent Expense	18,000
Capital (Jan. 1)	50,000
Service Fees	40,000
Drawings	10,000

Prepare the necessary journal entries to close these accounts and determine the new capital balance.

1.30   Corporation H, a *corporation* engaged in merchandise transactions, has asked you to prepare closing entries for its relevant accounts, as follows:

Merchandise Inventory (Jan. 1)	$50,000
Merchandise Inventory (Dec. 31)	60,000
Advertising Expense	10,000
Service Fees	50,000
Sales	90,000
Sales Returns	4,000
Sales Discounts	2,000
Purchases	40,000
Purchases Returns	2,000
Purchases Discounts	3,000
Freight In	3,000
Equipment	80,000

1.31   Indicate whether or not reversing entries are appropriate for the following adjustment items:

   (*a*)   Depreciation

   (*b*)   Bad debts

   (*c*)   Accrued expenses

   (*d*)   Accrued revenue

   (*e*)   Merchandise inventory

   (*f*)   Supplies originally debited to Supplies Expense

1.32   Prepare adjusting and reversing entries (if appropriate) for the following transactions.

   (*a*)   By December 31, property taxes in the amount of $7,000 have accrued.

   (*b*)   Fees for services performed but not yet billed are $18,000.

   (*c*)   At the beginning of the period, the Supplies account had a balance of $7,000. During the period, supplies of $10,000 were purchased and debited to Supplies Expense. At the end of the period, a physical count of supplies shows $12,000 worth remaining.

   (*d*)   Same as transaction (*c*), except that the purchases were debited to Supplies.

   (*e*)   On October 1, $12,000 in cash was received as an advance payment for services to be rendered *evenly* over the next 6 years. The entry was a debit to Cash and a credit to Service Fees.

Chapter 2

The Income Statement and Retained Earnings Statement

2.1 INTRODUCTION TO THE INCOME STATEMENT

The income statement is a critically important document that is read and carefully analyzed by many diverse groups. These groups include the present owners (or stockholders in a corporation), potential owners, creditors, potential creditors, unions, and various governmental agencies. The purpose of the income statement is to show how well or poorly the company performed during the last accounting period. Its elements or building blocks consist of revenues, expenses, gains, and losses. These have been defined by the Financial Accounting Standards Board (FASB) in *Concepts Statement No. 6* as follows:

Revenues—inflows or other enhancements of assets or settlements of liabilities during a period from delivering or producing goods, rendering services, or other activities that constitute the entity's ongoing *major or central operations.*

Expenses—Outflows or other using-up of assets or incurrences of liabilities during a period from delivering or producing goods, rendering services, or carrying out other activities that constitute the entity's ongoing *major or central operations.*

Gains—Increases in net assets from *peripheral or incidental transactions* of an entity, except for those that result from investments by the owners.

Losses—Decreases in net assets from *peripheral or incidental transactions*, except those that result from distributions to owners.

Thus gains and losses are similar in nature to revenues and expenses, except that the former two result from peripheral or side transactions, while the latter two result from main or central transactions.

What for one company may be a main transaction might be a side transaction for another company. For example, the sale of stocks by an investment company would be classified by it as a main transaction, while the same sale by a manufacturing company would be classified as a side transaction.

The income statement may take two forms: single-step and multiple-step. In the single-step format there are only two groups of items—revenues and expenses—and there is only a single subtraction on the statement—expenses from the revenue to arrive at the net income.

EXAMPLE 1

Fischer Corporation had the following single-step income statement for 19X5:

Revenues:	
Net Sales	$50,000
Dividend Revenue	3,000
Interest Revenue	5,000
Total Revenues	$58,000
Expenses:	
Cost of Goods Sold	$20,000
Selling Expenses	6,000
Administrative Expenses	2,000
Income Tax Expense	9,000
Total Expenses	$37,000
Net Income	$21,000
Earnings per Common Share (10,000 shares)	$ 2.10

The multiple-step income statement contains several groups of items and more than one subtraction. Because this format is more informative and is thus favored by most accountants, we will focus exclusively on this format throughout this chapter and this book.

2.2 THE MULTIPLE-STEP INCOME STATEMENT

The multiple-step income statement consists of several sections. These are the operating section, the nonoperating section, the income tax section, the discontinued operations section, the extraordinary items section, the cumulative effect of a change in accounting principle section, and finally, earnings per share.

The *operating section* reports the revenues and expenses from the company's central or principal operations. It usually has the following subsections:

1. Sales or revenue
2. Cost of goods sold
3. Selling expenses—a list of expenses relating directly to the making of sales. Examples of such expenses are sales salaries, travel and entertainment, advertising expense, delivery expense, telephone expense, depreciation of sales equipment, etc.
4. Administrative expenses—expenses relating to the general administration of the company. Examples of these are officers' salaries, utilities expense, insurance expense, depreciation of building, office expenses, etc.

The *nonoperating section* shows expenses, revenues, gains, and losses resulting from a company's secondary or peripheral activities. This section also includes special gains and losses that are either infrequent or unusual, but not both.

The *income tax* section reports taxes that relate to the income of both the operating and nonoperating sections, while the *discontinued operations* section shows gains and losses, together with the related tax effect, from the disposal of a segment of the company.

The *extraordinary item* section shows gains and losses that are *both* unusual and infrequent, together with their related tax effect.

Let's look at the first three sections in detail.

2.3 THE OPERATING SECTION, THE NONOPERATING SECTION, AND THE TAX SECTION

The operating section, the nonoperating section, and the tax section, as mentioned, show a company's revenue from sales of goods or services, cost of goods sold, selling expenses, administrative expenses, and gains and losses resulting from peripheral operations. These numbers are combined, and the related tax is then shown.

EXAMPLE 2

Ruthie Braunstein Corporation had the following partial income statement for 19X1.

Sales Revenue:		
Sales		$ 50,000
Less: Sales Returns	$3,000	
Sales Discounts	2,000	(5,000)
Net Sales Revenue		$ 45,000

Cost of Goods Sold:			
Merchandise Inventory, Jan. 1, 19X1		$ 60,000	
Purchases	$70,000		
Less Purchases Returns	(2,000)		
Less Purchases Discounts	(4,000)		
Transportation In	1,000		
Net Purchases		65,000	
Merchandise Available for Sale		$125,000	
Less Merchandise Inventory, Dec. 31, 19X1		90,000	
Cost of Goods Sold			(35,000)
Gross Profit			$ 10,000
Selling Expenses:			
Advertising Expenses	$ 1,000		
Delivery Expenses	2,500		(3,500)
Administrative Expenses:			
Officers' Salaries	$ 2,000		
Utilities Expense	3,000		(5,000)
Income from Operating Activities			$ 1,500
Other Revenue and Gains:			
Dividend Revenue	$ 5,000		
Rental Revenue	2,000		7,000
Other Expenses and Losses:			
Interest Expense			(2,000)
Income from Continuing Operations before Taxes			$ 6,500
Income Taxes			(2,000)
Income from Continuing Operations			$ 4,500

Let's discuss the logic involved in the cost of goods sold section. It begins with the merchandise inventory on the shelves at the beginning of the year: $60,000. To this we add the net purchases that took place during the year, $65,000 (purchases of $70,000, plus transportation charges of $1,000, minus returns and discounts of $2,000 and $4,000, respectively). We thus had $125,000 of goods available on the shelves throughout the year. Since on the last day of the year we have only $90,000 left on the shelves, $35,000 must have been sold. This is subtracted from the net sales of $45,000 to yield a gross profit of $10,000.

2.4 DISCONTINUED OPERATIONS, EXTRAORDINARY ITEMS, AND THE CUMULATIVE EFFECT OF ACCOUNTING CHANGES

If a company disposes of a segment of its business, it must show any gain or loss in a separate section of the income statement, together with the related tax effect. In addition, it must also report the results of the operations of that segment from the beginning of the year to the disposal date—again, together with the related taxes.

To qualify as a discontinued operation, the assets of this business segment must be clearly distinguishable from the other assets of the entity. Disposal of assets that do not qualify as disposal of a segment include the following:

1. Disposal of *part* of a line of business
2. Phasing out of a product line or class of service
3. Shifting production activities from one location to another

Thus the sale by a clothing manufacturer of its interest in a computer company would qualify as a disposal of a segment, while the sale of its London clothing manufacturing division, with the retention of its New York division, would not.

EXAMPLE 3

On April 1, 19X2, Company K, a clothing manufacturer, sells its ownership in a football team at a gain of $100,000. From January 1 until April 1, the football team lost $40,000. The income statement for Company K would show the following:

Discounted Operations:	
Loss from Operation of Football Team	$(40,000)
Gain on Disposal of Football Team	100,000
Net Gain before Taxes	$ 60,000
Income Tax (30%)	(18,000)
Net Gain	$42,000

If a company experiences an extraordinary gain or loss, this should be shown in a separate section of the income statement, together with the related tax effect. To do otherwise and mingle this item with the other items on the income statement could mislead the reader. For example, suppose that a company wins $1,000,000 in a lottery. The company's ordinary income, before the extraordinary item, is only $30,000. If the lottery gain was not placed in a separate section, people may think the company did tremendously this year—it made over $1,000,000 in income! In reality, of course, the normal, ordinary income is much less.

In a similar vein, if a company experienced an extraordinary loss from a tornado (in a geographic area where tornados are rare), this must be highlighted by showing it separately, so that the reader does not falsely assume that the company had a bad year.

What does the term "extraordinary item" mean? The accounting profession has defined it as an event that is *both* unusual *and* infrequent. *Unusual* means that the event is not related to normal business activities; *infrequent* means that it is not expected to happen again in the near future.

The environment in which a company operates must be taken into account in determining if an event is extraordinary. For example, an earthquake in New York City would be classified as extraordinary, while one in southern California would not. Similarly, if a company sells the only stock investment it ever owned, the gain or loss would be extraordinary. But if it has a portfolio of securities acquired for investment purposes, such sales would be considered part of ordinary business activities and thus would not meet the criterion of being unusual.

EXAMPLE 4

Pathetic Corporation experienced a flood loss (unusual and infrequent in that geographic region) of $70,000. Its tax rate is 30%. The income statement would show:

Extraordinary Item:	
Flood Loss	$(70,000)
Less Tax Savings	21,000
Net Loss	$(49,000)

Because the flood loss is a tax-deductible expense, Pathetic's net taxable income is reduced by $70,000, thus resulting in a 30% tax savings of $21,000. Thus the loss of $70,000 is somewhat softened by this tax savings.

EXAMPLE 5

Lucky Corporation won $250,000 in the lottery. This gain is unusual and is not expected to recur in the near future (although one woman did win the New York State lottery twice during the mid-1980s!). The income statement would show the following:

Extraordinary Item:		
Lottery Winning	$250,000	
Less Taxes (30%)	(75,000)	
Net Gain	$175,000	

Certain events meet just one criterion. They are either unusual *or* infrequent, but not both. They may not be classified as extraordinary, but, instead, are referred to as *unusual* items. Examples of *unusual* are

1. Write-offs of receivables
2. Write-offs of inventories
3. Write-offs of intangible assets
4. Gains and losses from fluctuation of foreign currencies
5. Gains and losses from the sale of property, plant, and equipment
6. Effects of a strike

If these items are not material in amount, they are shown with the normal recurring expenses and revenues. If they are material, they are shown in the nonoperating section under the caption "Other Revenues and Gains" or "Other Expenses and Losses" and are given the caption, "Unusual Items." Either way, their related tax effect would *not* be shown, so as to distinguish them from extraordinary items.

Companies occasionally change accounting methods from one generally accepted method to another. An example of this would be a change from FIFO to LIFO or a change from one depreciation method to another. Such changes are recognized in the current year by calculating the cumulative effect (net of tax) of the change on a retroactive basis, and showing it in the income statement.

EXAMPLE 6

In 19X1, Corporation D purchased a machine which it depreciated under an accelerated depreciation method during 19X1 and 19X2. In 19X3 it decided to switch to the straight-line method. Had this method been in use during 19X1 and 19X2, depreciation would have been $10,000 lower for both years combined, and thus income before tax would have been larger by this same amount. If we assume a tax rate of 30% for those years, the 19X3 income statement would show the following:

Change in Accounting Principle:		
Cumulative Effect of Depreciation		
Change for 19X1 and 19X2	$10,000	
Less Tax	(3,000)	
Net Change	$ 7,000	

The topic of changes in accounting principles is discussed in greater detail in *Intermediate Accounting II* of the Schaum's Outline Series.

We have seen that special events such as extraordinary items, discontinued operations, and the effect of changes in accounting principles require the disclosure of the related tax effect next to each respective item. This is referred to as *intraperiod tax allocation*, or as some have said, "Let the tax follow the income."

2.5 EARNINGS PER SHARE

Earnings per share (EPS) is a computation made for *common stock*. It determines how much of the net income "pie" has been earned by the common stockholders. Since part of this pie also belongs to the preferred stockholders, we must first subtract their share of the pie in order to determine the EPS on the common stock.

The formula for EPS is:

$$EPS = \frac{net\ income - preferred\ dividends}{average\ number\ of\ common\ shares\ outstanding\ during\ the\ year}$$

If the preferred dividend is cumulative, it is subtracted regardless of whether or not it has been declared; if it is not cumulative, the dividend is subtracted only if declared.

EXAMPLE 7

ABC Corporation had net income of $110,000 during 19X1 and had an average of 10,000 shares of common stock outstanding. It also had 1,000 shares of $100-par, 10% preferred stock. The preferred dividend was not declared; however, the stock is cumulative. Earnings per share on common stock are

$$\frac{\$110,000 - \$10,000*}{\$10,000} = \$10\ per\ share$$

*1,000 shares $\times$ ($100 $\times$ 10%).

If the preferred stock was not cumulative, the $10,000 preferred dividend would *not* be subtracted in the numerator, since it was not declared.

We have seen throughout this chapter that the income statement is divided into several major parts: income from continuing operations, gain or loss on the disposal of a segment, extraordinary items, and the effect of a change in accounting principle. It is customary to show EPS for each of these parts. However, the accounting profession has required EPS disclosure only for the following: income from continuing operations, income before extraordinary items and effects of changes in accounting principles, and net income. These disclosures must be shown on the face of the income statement.

EXAMPLE 8

Perlowitz Corporation has 10,000 shares of common stock outstanding and had the following income groups during 19X1; income from continuing operations, $40,000; loss on disposal of a discontinued operation, $5,000; extraordinary gain, $18,000; cumulative effect of a change in accounting principle, $3,000. Assuming that there are no preferred shares outstanding, we must divide each of these groups by the 10,000 shares of common stock to arrive at the EPS per group. The presentation on the income statement would appear as follows:

Earnings per Share:	
Income from Continuing Operations	$ 4.00
Loss on Disposal of Discontinued Operation	(0.50)
Income before Extraordinary Item and Accounting Change	3.50
Extraordinary Gain	1.80
Cumulative Effect of Change in Accounting Principle	0.30
Net Income	$ 5.60

The topic of earnings per share includes many issues which have not been discussed in this chapter. They are discussed in detail in *Intermediate Accounting II* of this series.

2.6 A COMPLETE MULTIPLE-STEP INCOME STATEMENT

In this chapter we have discussed the various individual groups of income that constitute the income statement. We will now tie all these together by presenting a complete income statement—one that contains all these items. For the sake of brevity, we will omit the computation for the cost of goods sold, and simply show a one-line item for this amount.

EXAMPLE 9

ABC Corporation
Income Statement
For the Year Ended December 31, 19X1

Net Sales		$200,000
Cost of Goods Sold		(50,000)
Gross Profit		$150,000
Selling and Administrative Expenses		(40,000)
Income from Operations		$110,000
Other Revenues and Gains		
Dividend Revenue		10,000
Other Expenses and Losses		
Unusual Charge: Loss on Sale of Investments		(14,000)
Income from Continuing Operations before Income Taxes		$106,000
Income Taxes		(31,800)
Income from Continuing Operations		$ 74,200
Discontinued Operations:		
Income from Operations of Football Team	$ 25,000	
Loss on Disposal of Football Team	(15,000)	
Income from Football Team before Income Taxes	$ 10,000	
Income Taxes	(3,000)	
Net Income from Football Team		7,000
Income before Extraordinary Item and Accounting Change		$ 81,200
Extraordinary Item: Tornado Damage	$(20,000)	
Income Tax Saving	6,000	
Net Extraordinary Item		(14,000)
Cumulative Effect of Accounting Change	$ 7,000	
Income Taxes	(2,100)	
Net Effect of Accounting Change		4,900
Net Income		$ 72,100
Earnings per Share (1,000 common shares):		
Income from Continuing Operations		$ 74.20
Income from Discontinued Operations		7.00
Income before Extraordinary Items and Accounting Change		$ 81.21
Extraordinary Loss		(14.00)
Cumulative Effect of Accounting Change		4.90
Net Income		$ 72.10

2.7   THE RETAINED EARNINGS STATEMENT

The retained earnings statement is a "moving picture" of how the retained earnings changed from the beginning of the period to the end of the period. Its elements consist of the beginning Retained Earnings balance; prior period adjustments that correct this balance; the net income, which increases this balance; and the declaration of dividends, which decreases it. Normally, the balance should be a credit;

a debit balance sometimes occurs and is referred to as a *deficit*. This will usually arise in situations where the company has sustained heavy losses.

It should be noted that it is the *declaration* of dividends, rather than the payment, that affects retained earnings. The declaration involves a debit to *Retained Earnings* and a credit to a payable; the payment debits the payable and credits Cash.

Prior period adjustments are defined as the discovery and correction of errors in the net income of previous periods. These should not appear in the current income statement, since they were not "born" this year, but, instead, should go directly to Retained Earnings, together with the related tax effect. Thus the current year's income statement is "bypassed" with respect to these items.

EXAMPLE 10

Error Company discovers in 19X2 that it understated its depreciation expense in 19X1 by $1,000. If there were no such thing as taxes, net income and the ending 19X1 Retained Earnings account (into which the net income is closed) would be overstated by this amount. Since the beginning 19X2 Retained Earnings is the same as the ending 19X1 balance, it would need to be adjusted by a subtraction of $1,000. In reality, though, there are, of course, taxes. Thus, if the tax rate is 30%, the effect on net income and retained earnings is only $700 ($1,000 − 30%). If the beginning Retained Earnings balance for 19X2 is $80,000, a partial retained earnings statement would show the following:

Retained Earnings, Jan. 1, 19X2		$80,000
Correction of Depreciation Understatement in 19X1	$(1,000)	
Tax Effect	300	
Net Correction		(700)
Adjusted Balance of Retained Earnings, Jan. 1, 19X2		$79,300

EXAMPLE 11

Error Company had a beginning Retained Earnings balance of $100,000, and its net income and dividends declared were $18,000 and $9,000, respectively. During 19X4, Error discovered that it had overstated its advertising expense by $2,000 in 19X2 and 19X3, resulting in an *understatement* in income and retained earnings, before taxes, of this amount. If the tax rate is 30%, we must adjust retained earnings by *adding* to it $1,400 ($2,000 − 30%). The statement of retained earnings would thus appear as follows:

Retained Earnings, Jan. 1, 19X4		$100,000
Correction of Error in Advertising Expense in 19X2 and 19X3	$2,000	
Tax Effect	(600)	
Net Correction		1,400
Adjusted Balance of Jan. 1, 19X4, Retained Earnings		$101,400
Net Income		18,000
Dividends Declared		(9,000)
Retained Earnings, Dec. 31, 19X4		$110,400

The retained earnings account and statement contain other elements in addition to the ones mentioned here. These elements, and further details regarding prior period adjustments, are discussed in *Intermediate Accounting II*.

2.8   CHANGES IN ACCOUNTING ESTIMATES

We have just discussed that mistakes relating to prior periods require a correction to Retained Earnings. Not all mistakes, however, require a correction. Changes involving faulty estimates are not corrected to Retained Earnings and require no corrective journal entry. They merely require us to use the new and corrected estimate from this point on. An example of an error in accounting estimate would be the overstatement or understatement of the life of a fixed asset or its salvage value, or an incorrect amount chosen as the estimate for bad debts.

For mistakes involving fixed assets, a new annual depreciation amount would be determined, based on the revised, corrected life and salvage value. No correcting entries for the past would be made. The formula for the new depreciation would be:

$$\text{New depreciation} = \frac{\text{book value} - \text{new salvage value}}{\text{remaining years}}$$

EXAMPLE 12

Error Company purchased a machine on January 1, 19X1, for $11,000. At that time it estimated the life and salvage value to be 10 years and $1,000, respectively. Thus the annual depreciation is $1,000 ($11,000 − $1,000) ÷ 10. Early in 19X4, Error determines that the salvage value is $2,000 and the *total* machine life is 12 years (thus 9 years remain). No correcting entries or adjustments should be made to Retained Earnings. However, a revised annual depreciation amount should be calculated for 19X4 and all *prospective* years, based on the following:

Machine	Accumulated Depreciation
11,000	1,000
	1,000
	1,000
	3,000

The book value is thus $8,000. The new depreciation is:

$$\frac{\$8,000 - \$2,000}{9 \text{ years}} = \$667 \qquad \text{(rounded)}$$

EXAMPLE 13

Until 19X4, Error Company estimated its bad debts at 5% of net sales. During 19X4, when net sales were $100,000, Error decided that a more accurate estimate would be 6%. Thus, on December 31, 19X4, Error makes the following routine adjusting entry for bad debts:

Bad Debts Expense	6,000	
Allowance for Doubtful Accounts		6,000

Summary

1. The income statement is designed to show how well or poorly a company performed during the last accounting period. Its elements consist of revenues, expenses, gains, and losses. Revenues and expenses relate to a company's major operations; gains and losses relate to its peripheral operations.

2. The income statement may take two possible forms: single-step and multiple-step. We have focused on the multiple-step form throughout the chapter.

3. The multiple-step income statement consists of several sections. The *operating section* reports the

revenues and expenses from the company's central operations, and contains the following subsections: revenue, cost of goods sold, selling expenses, and administrative expenses.

4. The *nonoperating section* reports items relating to the company's peripheral activities and special items called unusual items.

5. The *income tax section* reports the taxes that relate to both the operating and nonoperating sections.

6. The *discontinued operations section* shows the gain or loss, together with the related taxes, of the disposal of a business segment.

7. The *extraordinary items section* shows extraordinary items—gains and losses that are *both* unusual and infrequent—together with the related tax effect.

8. If a company disposes of a segment of its business, it must show any gain or loss in a separate section of the income statement, together with the related taxes. It must also show the results of the operations of that segment from the beginning of the year to the date of disposal, together with the related taxes.

9. *Extraordinary items* are gains and losses that are *both* unusual *and* infrequent. *Infrequent* means that the event is not expected to recur in the near future; *unusual* means that it is not related to normal business activities. These items must be shown in a separate section, together with their related taxes. To do otherwise may mislead the reader of the statements. Items that are *either* unusual *or* infrequent, but not both, should *not* be shown with their related taxes.

10. The write-off of receivables, inventories, and intangible assets, and the effects of a strike, are *not* considered to be extraordinary.

11. If a company changes from one generally accepted accounting method to another, the cumulative, retroactive effect of this change, together with the related taxes, should be shown in a separate section of the statement.

12. The practice of showing the related taxes for each special item, as discussed, is referred to as *intraperiod tax allocation*.

13. *Earnings per share* (EPS) is the amount each share of common stock has earned of the net income "pie." It is determined by taking the net income, subtracting from it the preferred dividends, and dividing the remainder by the average number of common shares outstanding during the year. If the preferred stock is cumulative, the preferred dividends are subtracted regardless of whether or not they are declared. If the preferred stock is noncumulative, they are subtracted only if declared.

14. At a minimum, there must be EPS disclosure for the following: income from continuing operations, income before extraordinary items and the effect of accounting changes, and net income. These disclosures are shown on the face of the income statement.

15. The *retained earnings statement* shows how Retained Earnings changed during the course of the year. It starts with the beginning-of-year Retained Earnings balance, adjusts this for any prior period adjustments, adds the net income, and then subtracts dividends *declared* in order to arrive at the year-end balance.

16. *Prior period adjustments* refer to the discovery and correction of errors in the net income of prior

periods. These bypass the current-year income statement and go directly to retained earnings, net of their tax effect.

17. Certain errors do not require an adjustment to retained earnings. Mistakes involving faulty estimates merely require a future change-of-course; the past is left unchanged. Examples of such errors are mistakes in the estimated life of a plant asset and in its estimated salvage value. In these cases, the new depreciation per period would be determined as follows:

$$\frac{\text{Book value} - \text{new salvage value}}{\text{Remaining years}}$$

Rapid Review

1. The elements of the income statement consist of revenues, expenses, _____, and _____.

2. The two forms of the income statement are the _____ form and the _____ form.

3. The section dealing with a company's income and expense from peripheral activities is the _____ section.

4. Extraordinary items must be *both* _____ and _____.

5. The practice requiring that items be shown together with their related taxes is called _____.

6. Changes in accounting methods require disclosure of the _____ effect of the change on the income statement.

7. If preferred stock is noncumulative, then for EPS calculations, its dividends are subtracted only if _____.

8. Discovery and correction of errors in previous periods are called _____.

9. Errors in _____ do *not* require adjustment to retained earnings.

Answers: **1.** gains; losses **2.** single-step; multiple-step **3.** nonoperating **4.** unusual; infrequent **5.** intraperiod tax allocation **6.** cumulative **7.** declared **8.** prior period adjustments **9.** accounting estimates

Solved Problems

The Operating Section, the Nonoperating Section, and the Tax Section

2.1   Schlesinger Corporation had the following items relating to its income statement for 19X1:

Merchandise Inventory, Jan. 1	$40,000	Sales	$100,000
Merchandise Inventory, Dec. 31	20,000	Sales Returns	2,000
Transportation In	2,000	Sales Discounts	4,000
Purchases Returns	3,000	Purchases Discounts	5,000
Purchases	50,000		

Determine the following:

(a) Net sales

(b) Net purchases

(c) Goods available for sale

(d) Cost of goods sold

(e) Gross profit

SOLUTION

(a) $94,000 ($100,000 − $2,000 − $4,000)

(b) $44,000 ($50,000 − $3,000 − $5,000 + $2,000)

(c) $84,000 (beginning merchandise of $40,000 + net purchases of $44,000)

(d) $64,000 (goods available of $84,000 − ending merchandise of $20,000)

(e) $30,000 (net sales of $94,000 − cost of goods sold of $64,000)   [Section 2.3]

2.2 Fill in the missing number(s) for each one of the following *independent* cases:

	Case 1	Case 2	Case 3	Case 4
Net Sales	$80,000	(c)	$70,000	$90,000
Beginning Merchandise	10,000	$ 9,000	(e)	24,000
Net Purchases	30,000	51,000	20,000	(h)
Merchandise Available	(a)	(d)	50,000	(i)
Ending Merchandise	7,000	14,000	(f)	16,000
Cost of Goods Sold	33,000	46,000	33,000	25,000
Gross Profit	(b)	20,000	(g)	(j)

SOLUTION

(a) = $40,000	(f) = $17,000
(b) = $47,000	(g) = $37,000
(c) = $66,000	(h) = $17,000
(d) = $60,000	(i) = $41,000
(e) = $30,000	(j) = $65,000

[Section 2.3]

2.3 Prepare the operating and nonoperating sections of the income statement from the following information. Assume a tax rate of 30%.

Sales Commissions	$ 24,000
Officers' Salaries	15,000
Interest Revenue	7,000
Dividend Revenue	5,000
Loss on Sale of Investment (unusual)	(8,000)
Net Sales	240,000
Cost of Goods Sold	160,000

SOLUTION

Net Sales	$ 240,000
Cost of Goods sold	(160,000)
Gross Profit	$ 80,000
Selling Expenses:	
Sales Commissions	(24,000)
Administrative Expenses:	
Officers' Salaries	(15,000)
Income from Operating Activities	$ 41,000
Other Revenue and Gains:	
Interest Revenue $7,000	
Dividend Revenue 5,000	12,000
Other Expenses and Losses:	
Unusual Loss on Sale of Investment	(8,000)
Income from Continuing Operations before Taxes	$ 45,000
Income Taxes	(13,500)
Income from Continuing Operations	$ 31,500 [Section 2.3]

Discontinued Operations, Extraordinary Items, and the Cumulative Effect of Accounting Changes

2.4 Food, Inc., a manufacturer of packaged snacks, sells its interest in a computer company at a loss (before taxes) of $17,000. From January 1 of the current year until the date of the sale, the computer company incurred a loss (before taxes) of $8,000.

In addition to the above, Food, Inc., incurred a gain on the sale of its Wisconsin *division* in the amount of $20,000. How much gain or loss should Food, Inc., show on its income statement from discontinued operations? Why? Assume a tax rate of 20%.

SOLUTION

Loss on Sale of Interest in Computer Company	$(17,000)
Loss on Operations of Computer Company	(8,000)
Loss before Taxes	$(25,000)
Tax Savings	5,000
Net Loss from Discontinued Operations	$(20,000)

The gain on the sale of the Wisconsin division is not included, because a division is not considered a business segment.   [Section 2.4]

2.5 A construction company sells a stock investment at a gain of $10,000. The last time it purchased or sold stock was 25 years ago.

(*a*) Is this an extraordinary item, or merely an unusual item? Why?

(*b*) Show how this would be presented on the income statement. Assume a tax rate of 20%.

SOLUTION

(*a*) It is extraordinary, because it is both unusual *and* infrequent.

(*b*)

Extraordinary Item:	
Gain on Sale of Stock $10,000	
Income Taxes (2,000)	
Net Gain $ 8,000	[Section 2.4]

2.6 A company experiences $50,000 damage to its building from a tornado. In this geographic region, tornados are extremely rare. Is this an extraordinary item? Why? Show how this item would be presented on the income statement, assuming a tax rate of 20%.

SOLUTION

It is extraordinary because it is both unusual and infrequent. The presentation would be as follows:

Extraordinary Item:

Loss on Tornado Damage	$(50,000)	
Tax Savings	10,000	
Net Loss	$(40,000)	[Section 2.4]

2.7 Poor Credit Corporation writes off a receivable for $22,000. The last time it did this was 25 years ago.

(*a*) Is this an extraordinary item? Why?

(*b*) How would this be presented on the income statement? Assume a tax rate of 20%.

SOLUTION

(*a*) It is *not* extraordinary, because it is *infrequent* but not *unusual*, since it relates to normal business activities.

(*b*) It would be presented in the nonoperating section called "Other Losses and Expenses" and would be referred to as "Unusual Loss from Write-off of Receivable." The related tax would *not* be shown.

[Section 2.4]

2.8 In 19X1, Feldbrand Corporation purchased a machine which it depreciated under the straight-line method for 19X1 and 19X2. Early in 19X3 it decided to switch to the sum-of-the-years'-digits method. Had this method been in use during 19X1 and 19X2, depreciation for these two years combined would have been $20,000 higher. Assume a tax rate of 20% for 19X1 and 19X2.

(*a*) Under the new method, would the incomes of 19X1 and 19X2 combined be higher or lower than previously reported? Why?

(*b*) What type of change is this?

(*c*) Show how this change would be reported on the 19X3 income statement.

SOLUTION

(*a*) The combined incomes of 19X1 and 19X2 would be lower by $20,000 (before taxes), because the depreciation expense would be higher.

(*b*) A change in accounting principal.

(*c*)

Change in Accounting Principle:

Cumulative Effect of Depreciation Change for 19X1 and 19X2	$(20,000)	
Less Tax Savings	4,000	
	$(16,000)	[Section 2.4]

Earnings per Share

2.9 Reliable Furniture Company earned a net income of $140,000 during 19X1. It had 1,000 shares of $100-par, 10% preferred stock and 20,000 shares of common stock outstanding during the year.

Determine earnings per share if:

(*a*) The preferred stock is cumulative and no dividend was declared.

(*b*) The preferred stock is noncumulative and no dividend was declared.

(*c*) The preferred stock is noncumulative and a dividend was declared.

SOLUTION

(a) $\dfrac{\$140,000 - \$10,000}{\$20,000} = \$6.50$

(b) $\dfrac{\$140,000}{\$20,000} = \$7.00$

(c) $\dfrac{\$140,000 - \$10,000}{\$20,000} = \$6.50$ [Section 2.5]

2.10 Arlene Bodner Corporation had 1,000 shares of common stock outstanding during 19X1 and no preferred shares. Its income groups consisted of the following: Income from Continuing Operations, $50,000; Gain on Disposal of a Business Segment, $10,000; Extraordinary Loss, $12,000; Cumulative Effect of a Change in Accounting Principle, $7,000. All these items are net of taxes.

(a) As a minimum, for which captions must a company present earnings-per-share data?

(b) If this company decides to present EPS for all groups, show what the presentation would be. Assume that there are no preferred shares.

SOLUTION

(a) Income from Continuing Operations, Income before Extraordinary Items and Accounting Changes, and Net Income.

(b) Earnings per Share:

Income from Continuing Operations	$50
Gain on Disposal of Discontinued Operation	10
Income before Extraordinary Item and Accounting Change	$60
Extraordinary Loss	(12)
Cumulative Effect of Change in Accounting Principle	7
Net Income	$55 [Section 2.5]

Complete Multiple-Step Income Statement

2.11 Sheldon Epstein Corporation had the following items relating to its income and expenses for the year 19X1:

Cumulative Effect of Accounting Change	$ 2,000	Sales	$160,000
Error in Accounting Estimate	(14,000)	Sales Returns	14,000
Beginning Merchandise Inventory	85,000	Sales Discounts	5,000
Ending Merchandise Inventory	40,000	Purchases	30,000
Extraordinary Gain (Lottery)	15,000	Purchases Returns	3,000
Income from Operation of Discontinued Segment	7,000	Transportation In	2,000
Loss on Disposal of Discontinued Segment	(22,000)	Selling Expenses	16,000
Administrative Expenses	8,000	Dividend Revenue	12,000
Unusual Gain on Sale of Investment	6,000	Write-off of Inventory	7,000
Purchases Discount	4,000	Income from Discontinued	
Loss on Disposal of Hockey Team	(22,000)	Hockey Team	7,000

Prepare an income statement in good form. *Do not show earnings per share*. Assume a tax rate of 20% on all items, and that all of the above is *before taxes*.

SOLUTION

Sheldon Epstein Corporation
Income Statement
For the Year Ended December 31, 19X1

Sales		$160,000	
Less Sales Returns		(14,000)	
Less Sales Discounts		(5,000)	
Net Sales			$141,000
Merchandise Inventory, Jan. 1, 19X1:	$ 85,000		
Purchases	$30,000		
Less Purchases Returns	(3,000)		
Less Purchases Discounts	(4,000)		
Transportation In	2,000		
Net Purchases	25,000		
Merchandise Available for Sale	$110,000		
Merchandise Inventory, Dec. 31, 19X1	(40,000)		
Cost of Goods Sold			(70,000)
Gross Profit			$ 71,000
Selling Expenses			(16,000)
Administrative Expenses			(8,000)
Income from Operations			$ 47,000
Other Revenues and Gains:			
Unusual Gain on Sale of Stock	$ 6,000		
Dividend Revenue	12,000		18,000
Other Expenses and Losses:			
Write-off of Inventory			(7,000)
Income from Continuing Operations before Taxes			$ 58,000
Income Taxes			(11,600)
Income from Continuing Operations			$ 46,400
Discontinued Operations:			
Income from Operation of Discontinued Hockey Team	$ 7,000		
Loss on Disposal of Hockey Team	(22,000)		
Net Loss from Hockey Team before Taxes	$(15,000)		
Income Tax Savings	3,000		
Net Loss from Hockey Team			(12,000)
Income before Extraordinary Item and Accounting Change			$ 34,400
Extraordinary Item:			
Lottery Winning	$15,000		
Income Taxes	(3,000)		
Net Extraordinary Gain			12,000
Cumulative Effect of Accounting Change	$ 2,000		
Income Taxes	(400)		
Net Effect of Accounting Change			1,600
Net Income			$ 48,000

Note that the error in accounting estimate was ignored; it does not belong on the income statement.
[Section 2.6]

The Retained Earnings Statement

2.12 On January 1, 19X3, the Retained Earnings account of Error Company showed a balance of $100,000. During 19X3, Error Company discovers that it overstated its 19X2 revenue by $10,000. Assume a 19X2 tax rate of 20%.

(a) What type of item is this?

(b) Does this require a credit correction, or a debit? Why?

(c) Determine the corrected Retained Earnings balance of January 1, 19X3.

SOLUTION

(a) Prior period adjustment.

(b) A debit correction, because Retained Earnings is overstated.

(c)

Unadjusted Retained Earnings		$100,000
Prior Period Adjustment	$(10,000)	
Tax Savings	2,000	(8,000)
Adjusted Retained Earnings		$ 92,000

[Section 2.7]

2.13 On January 1, 19X2, the Retained Earnings account of Careless Company showed a balance of $80,000. During 19X2, Careless discovers that it mistakenly recorded depreciation twice—each time for $12,000—during 19X1. Determine the adjusted beginning Retained Earnings balance for 19X2. (Assume a tax rate of 20%.)

SOLUTION

Unadjusted Retained Earnings Balance		$80,000
Prior Period Adjustment	$12,000	
Income Tax	(2,400)	9,600
Adjusted Retained Earnings Balance		$89,600

[Section 2.7]

2.14 ABC Corporation had the following information related to 19X2:

Net Income	$ 50,000
Dividends Declared	7,000
Dividends Paid	4,000
Retained Earnings, Jan. 1, 19X2	100,000
Error in 19X1: Depreciation Omitted	2,000
Tax Rate, 19X1	30%
Error in Accounting Estimate, 19X1	(4,000)
Cumulative Effect of Change in Inventory Method	8,000

(a) Do any of the above items *not* belong on a retained earnings statement? If yes, which ones and why?

(b) Prepare a retained earnings statement.

SOLUTION

(a) The error in accounting estimate does not appear on any statement; we merely revise the future rates. The change in inventory method appears on the income statement.

(b)	Retained Earnings, Jan. 1, 19X2		$100,000	
	Prior Period Adjustment: Depreciation	($2,000)		
	Income Taxes	$ 600	(1,400)	
	Adjusted Retained Earnings, Jan. 1, 19X2			$ 98,600
	Net Income			50,000
	Dividends Declared			(7,000)
	Retained Earnings, Dec. 31, 19X2			$141,600

[Section 2.7]

2.15 Indicate whether each of the following items would appear on an income statement or a retained earnings statement:

(a) Cumulative effect of accounting changes

(b) Prior period adjustments

(c) Dividends paid

(d) Dividends declared

(e) Extraordinary items

(f) Unusual losses

(g) Net loss

(h) Discontinued operations

SOLUTION

(a) Income statement

(b) Retained earnings statement

(c) Neither

(d) Retained earnings statement

(e) Income statement

(f) Income statement

(g) Income statement, retained earnings statement

(h) Income statement   [Sections 2.6 and 2.7]

Changes in Accounting Estimates

2.16 Careless Company purchased a machine on January 1, 19X1, for $21,000 and estimated that its life and salvage value would be 5 years and $1,000, respectively. Early in 19X3, Careless realizes that the *total* life of the machine is 8 years and the salvage value will be $3,000.

(a) What type of change is this?

(b) What correction entries are needed, if any?

(c) What is the book value of the machine as of the beginning of 19X3?

(d) How many years will the machine still be used?

(e) Determine the revised depreciation per year.

SOLUTION

(a) Change in accounting estimate

(b) None

(c) Book value = cost − accumulated depreciation
     = $21,000 − ($4,000* × 2 years)
     = $13,000

   *annual depreciation = $\dfrac{\$21,000 - \$1,000}{5 \text{ years}}$

     = $4,000

(d) Six years (8 − 2)

(e) $\dfrac{\$13,000 - \$3,000}{6 \text{ years}}$ = $1,667   (rounded)   [Section 2.8]

2.17 During 19X2, Careless Company determined that its 19X1 bad debt percentage of 5% of net credit sales was too high.

(a) What correction entry, if any, should Careless make for 19X1? Why?

(b) If Careless feels that a more accurate percentage would be 4%, and its 19X2 net credit sales are $80,000, what entry should it make?

SOLUTION

(a) None; it is an error in accounting estimate.

(b) The normal adjusting entry on December 31 for bad debts, using the new percentage, is:

Bad Debts Expense	3,200	
Allowance for Doubtful Accounts		3,200 [Section 2.8]

Supplementary Problems

2.18 Company A had the following items relating to its income statement for the year 19X3:

Merchandise Inventory (beginning)	$70,000	Purchases	$ 60,000
Merchandise Inventory (end)	55,000	Sales	200,000
Transportation In	3,000	Sales Returns	7,000
Rent Expense	1,500	Sales Discounts	6,000
Purchases Returns	4,000	Purchases Discounts	5,000

Determine:

(a) Net sales

(b) Net purchases

(c) Goods available for sale

(d) Cost of goods sold

(e) Gross profit

2.19 Fill in the missing numbers for each one of the following *independent* cases:

	Case 1	Case 2	Case 3	Case 4
Net Sales	$100,000	(c)	$95,000	$85,000
Merchandise (beginning)	40,000	$60,000	(e)	10,000
Net Purchases	40,000	50,000	60,000	(h)
Merchandise Available	(a)	(d)	90,000	(i)
Merchandise (ending)	30,000	70,000	(f)	5,000
Cost of Goods Sold	50,000	40,000	70,000	65,000
Gross Profit	(b)	50,000	(g)	(j)

2.20 Sheldon Elefont Inc. had the following items relating to its income statement for 19X1:

Extraordinary Loss—Earthquake	$ (20,000)	
Accounting Change—Inventory Method	5,000	(cumulative effect)
Sales Salaries	20,000	
Officers' Salaries	40,000	
Unusual Gain on Sale of Stock	5,500	
Dividend Revenue	9,000	
Net Sales	120,000	
Interest Revenue	4,000	
Cost of Goods Sold	60,000	

Prepare the *operating* and *nonoperating* sections of the income statement from the above information. Assume a tax rate of 30%.

2.21 Company C, a furniture manufacturer, had the following information relating to the sale of a division and of a business segment during 19X1:

(a) Its North Carolina division operated at a gain of $20,000 until March 15, when it was sold at a loss of $30,000.

(b) On April 23 it sold its computer manufacturing operation at a gain of $60,000. From January 1 until April 23, this operation incurred a $23,000 loss.

Determine what Company C should report as its gain or loss from discontinued operations for 19X1. Assume a tax rate of 30%.

2.22 Determine whether the following items are to be considered extraordinary items, unusual items, or neither, and show how they would be presented on the income statement. Assume a tax rate of 30%.

(a) Tornado damage—considered frequent in this state

(b) Lottery winnings

(c) Change in depreciation methods

(d) Crop damage from frost—this occurs only every 25 years or so

(e) Discovery that depreciation expense was omitted 2 years ago

(f) Write-off of inventory

The amounts for these items are:

(a) ($12,000)

(b) $50,000

(c) $6,000

    (d)   ($19,000)

    (e)   ($7,000)

    (f)   ($14,000)

2.23   In early July of 19X1, Corporation D purchased a machine which it depreciated under the double-declining-balance method for 19X1, 19X2, and 19X3. Early in 19X4 it decided to switch to the straight-line method. Had this method been in use during 19X1 through 19X3, depreciation for those years would have been $30,000 lower than it actually was.

       Determine the nature of this change and how it would affect the 19X4 income statement. Assume a 30% tax rate.

2.24   During 19X4, Company E had net income of $120,000, ten thousand common shares, and one thousand $150-par, 10%, preferred shares.

       Determine EPS if:

    (a)   The preferred shares are cumulative

    (b)   The preferred shares are noncumulative.

       Assume in *both* cases that the preferred dividend was *not* declared.

2.25   Company F has 10,000 shares of common stock, no preferred shares, and the following income groups: income from continuing operations, $70,000; loss on disposal of a business segment, ($4,000); extraordinary gain, $9,000; cumulative effect of a change in accounting principle, ($11,000). These items are net of taxes.

       Determine *total* earnings per share.

2.26   Prepare an income statement in good form from the following information. Assume a tax rate of 30%.

Write-off of a Receivable	$ 2,000	Dividend Revenue	$ 9,000
Sales	180,000	Extraordinary Loss—Earthquake	12,000
Administrative Expenses	1,000	Extraordinary Gain—Lottery	9,000
Selling Expenses	8,000	Sales Returns	11,000
Cost of Goods Sold	125,000	Sales Discounts	7,000
Unusual Gain on Stock Sale	10,000	Error in Depreciation Estimate	
Prior Period Adjustment	(5,000)	from 2 Years Ago	4,000
Change in Accounting Principle	8,000		

2.27   Company G has the following information regarding its operations for 19X3. Prepare an income statement in good form and assume a tax rate of 30%. Do not present EPS.

Administrative Expenses	$ 5,000	Purchases	$50,000
Sales Commissions	10,000	Sales Returns	14,000
Advertising Expense	8,000	Merchandise Inventory (beginning)	70,000
Interest Revenue	12,000	Merchandise Inventory (end)	10,000
Sales Discounts	18,000	Purchases Discounts	8,000
Purchase Returns	13,000	Unusual Loss on Stock Sale	(1,000)
Extraordinary Loss—Tornado	(20,000)	Loss on Operation of Segment	(10,000)
Change in Inventory Method	(5,000)	Loss on Disposal of Segment	(15,000)
Sales	200,000		

2.28 On January 1, 19X3, Mistake, Inc., had a Retained Earnings balance of $75,000. During 19X3, Mistake discovered that it had understated its 19X2 revenue by $20,000. Assume a 19X2 tax rate of 30%.

(*a*) Does this require a debit correction or a credit? Why?

(*b*) Determine the corrected January 1, 19X3, Retained Earnings balance.

2.29 Company H had the following information relating to 19X2:

Net Income	$100,000
Dividends Declared	20,000
Dividends Paid	25,000
Retained Earnings, Jan. 1	400,000
Error in 19X1: Understatement of Revenue	28,000
Tax rate, 19X1	30%
Unusual Loss from Sale of Stock	(21,000)
Error in Depreciation Estimate, 19X1 (understatement)	7,000

Prepare a retained earnings statement.

2.30 Mistake, Inc., purchased a machine on January 1, 19X1, for $50,000 and estimated its life and salvage value to be 6 years and $3,000, respectively. Early in 19X4, Mistake realized that the remaining life is only 2 years and the salvage value will be $2,000.

(*a*) What correction entry is needed, if any?

(*b*) What will the revised depreciation be for 19X4 and after?

2.31 For each of the following items, indicate whether it belongs in the income statement, the retained earnings statement, or neither:

(*a*) Dividends declared

(*b*) Unusual gains

(*c*) Net income

(*d*) Error in accounting estimate

(*e*) Cumulative effect of accounting change

(*f*) Patents

(*g*) Prior period adjustment

(*h*) Extraordinary items

(*i*) Long-term investment in stock

(*j*) Gain on disposal of a segment

(*k*) Earnings per share

Chapter 3

The Balance Sheet

3.1 INTRODUCTION

The *balance sheet*, also known as the *statement of financial position*, shows the financial position of the company at a given point in time. Its elements consist of *assets*, *liabilities*, and *capital* (stockholders' equity for corporations). It provides a basis for financial analysts to assess a company regarding its rate of return, liquidity, working capital, and many other ratios.

A fundamental principle on which the balance sheet rests is the cost principle: Assets are reflected at the amount the company paid for their acquisition. *Increases* in the market value of assets are not recorded; *decreases* are occasionally recorded, as we will discuss later in this chapter, and throughout this book.

Subjective items for which it is difficult to assign a monetary value are not presented in the balance sheet. These items include the value of a company's human resources, its managerial skills, and its established customer base. This is a limitation of the balance sheet.

Assets, liabilities, and capital have been precisely defined by the FASB in *Concepts Statement No. 6*. According to those definitions, *assets* are probable future economic benefits obtained by an entity as a result of past transactions or events; *liabilities* are present obligations of an entity to transfer assets or provide services to other entities in the future, as a result of past transactions or events; and *capital*, or stockholders' equity, is the owners' interest in the assets that remains after deducting the liabilities. Capital is also referred to as *net assets*.

To provide clarity and facilitate financial statement analysis, the asset, liability, and capital classifications are broken down into numerous subclassifications. The subclassifications of *assets* are:

Current assets

Long-term investments

Property, plant, and equipment

Intangible assets

Other assets

Liabilities are broken down into current and long-term subclassifications, while *capital* consists of capital stock, additional paid-in capital, and retained earnings.

We will discuss assets first.

3.2 CURRENT ASSETS

Current assets are defined as cash or any other asset that will be converted into cash, or consumed, within 1 year (of the balance sheet date) or the operating cycle, whichever is longer. The *operating cycle* is the span of time during which a company purchases or manufactures its goods, sells them on account, and then collects the receivable. In most companies this can range anywhere from 1 week to 6 months. In some companies, especially those that deal with expensive items such as cars or fur coats, the cycle may take more than 1 year.

The following company has an operating cycle of 10 months:

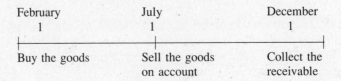

EXAMPLE 1

Glazer Corporation has an operating cycle of 9 months, while Sand Corporation has one of 14 months. Since we must choose the longer of 1 year or the operating cycle, Glazer would use 1 year, while Sand would use 14 months for the current asset classification in the balance sheet.

EXAMPLE 2

Both Glazer and Sand have a machine which they intend to sell and convert to cash in precisely 13 months. For Glazer, this would be beyond its 1-year cutoff period and would thus not be considered a current asset. For Sand, however, it is a current asset, since the conversion will take place *within* its cutoff period of 14 months.

To simplify matters for all future discussion of current assets throughout this chapter, we will assume that the operating cycle of the company is *less* than 1 year and therefore use the 1-year period as our cutoff point.

The assets that meet the criteria to be considered current are as follows: cash, marketable securities (*short-term* investments in stocks and bonds, where the intention is to sell them within 1 year), accounts receivable, short-term notes receivable, merchandise inventory, and prepaid items (prepaid rent, prepaid insurance, supplies).

Prepaid insurance and rent are considered current assets because they are usually consumed within 1 year. If, however, they have been prepaid for longer than 1 year, then only the portion applicable to the first 12 months is current; the rest is long-term.

EXAMPLE 3

Leah Englard purchases an automobile insurance policy and makes a prepayment of $3,000 for 15 months ($200 per month). Of this amount, $2,400 applicable to the first 12 months would be classified as current; the remaining $600 would not.

If cash is restricted and may not be used for current operations, it is not classified as current. For example, cash that is set aside to pay a bond due in 5 years or to fulfill pension obligations in 20 years is not considered current.

For merchandise inventory, a disclosure should be made regarding the method used (FIFO, LIFO, average, etc.) in determining the inventory amount. This may be shown in the body of the balance sheet, or in the footnotes.

Now that we have discussed current assets, we shall turn to the next category of assets: long-term investments. Unlike current assets, the company has no intent to turn these into cash, nor to consume them within 1 year. This category includes:

1. Long-term investments in stocks or bonds
2. Buildings and land not used in operations but held for long-term speculation
3. Sinking funds
4. Pension funds
5. Cash surrender value of life insurance (with no intent to cash in the policy within 1 year)
6. Investment in nonconsolidated subsidiaries

3.3 PROPERTY, PLANT, AND EQUIPMENT; INTANGIBLE ASSETS; OTHER ASSETS

Property, plant, and equipment includes all the various assets a company uses to carry out its operations. Also referred to as *fixed assets*, this category includes buildings, land, equipment, machinery, furniture, and fixtures. Land differs from the other assets in that, unlike the others, land is not subject to depreciation.

As mentioned earlier, if a fixed asset is not being used in operations but is held for speculative purposes, it should be excluded from this category and placed instead into the long-term investment category.

Intangible assets are assets that have no physical substance or form, *and* carry a high degree of uncertainty regarding their future benefits (thus accounts receivable, despite its lack of physical form, is *not* considered an intangible asset).

Examples of intangible assets are patents, copyrights, trademarks, tradenames, franchises, and goodwill. These assets wear out with time, just as tangible fixed assets do, and the "wearing out" process is called *amortization*. The amortization period ranges from 5 years to a maximum of 40 years. Both tangible and intangible assets will be discussed in more detail in Chapters 10–12.

The "other asset" category includes assets that do not fit into any of the above categories. One example is long-term prepayments of insurance. If insurance is prepaid for more than 1 year, the current portion is included in the current asset section, while the portion applicable to the period after 1 year is included in the "other assets" section, and is referred to as a "deferred charge."

EXAMPLE 4

Chaim Tennenbaum purchases a 3-year insurance policy on December 31, 19X1, and prepays the entire $3,000 premium ($1,000 per year) on this date. On the December 31, 19X1, balance sheet, the $1,000 portion applicable to the next year is classified as current; the remaining $2,000 is classified as a deferred charge.

Some companies also include organization costs in the "other assets" category as a deferred charge. Organization costs are costs incurred in creating a corporation and include state charter fees, legal fees, and stock issuance costs. Some companies, however, consider organization costs to be an intangible asset. Another example of a deferred charge is plant rearrangement costs.

EXAMPLE 5

Joel Hochman creates a corporation and in doing so incurs state charter fees and legal fees of $3,000 and $10,000, respectively. The journal entry is

| Organization Costs | 13,000 | |
| Cash | | 13,000 |

This item is classified either under the "other assets" category or as an intangible asset.

EXAMPLE 6

Wenger Corporation has the following assets on its books at the end of 19X1:

Patent	$ 50,000	Plant Building	$300,000
Goodwill	200,000	Sinking Fund	150,000
Land Held for Speculation	80,000	Pension Fund	325,000
Merchandise	25,000	Prepaid Rent (1 year)	38,000
Cash	40,000	Equipment	79,000
Long-Term Bond Investment	70,000	Franchise Fee	142,000
Land Used for Operations	120,000	Organization Costs	22,000
Accounts Receivable	28,000		

Its current asset section would show:

Cash	$ 40,000
Accounts Receivable	28,000
Merchandise Inventory	25,000
Prepaid Rent	38,000
Total	$131,000

Its long-term investment section would show:

Land (held for speculation)	$ 80,000
Long-Term Bond Investment	70,000
Sinking Fund	150,000
Pension Fund	325,000
Total	$625,000

EXAMPLE 7

Referring to Example 6, the property, plant, and equipment section would show:

Land (used in operations)	$120,000
Building	300,000
Equipment	79,000
Total	$499,000

The intangible asset section would show the patent, goodwill, and franchise fee of $50,000, $200,000, and $142,000, respectively, while the organization cost of $22,000 would appear in the "other assets" section.

3.4 CURRENT LIABILITIES; LONG-TERM LIABILITIES

Current liabilities are liabilities that are payable within 1 year or the operating cycle (whichever is longer) and are payable either out of current assets or by the creation of other current liabilities. Examples of current liabilities include accounts payable, wages payable, taxes payable, expenses payable, and short-term notes payable. In addition, unearned items, such as unearned rent representing revenue received in advance, are classified as current liabilities for the portion that will be earned over the next year.

EXAMPLE 8

On January 1, 19X1, Landlord Corporation receives an advance payment of $36,000, representing rentals for the next 3 years (at $12,000 per year). The entry at this time is:

Cash	36,000	
Unearned Rent		36,000

The December 31, 19X1, adjusting entry to recognize $12,000 as earned is:

Unearned Rent	12,000	
Rent Revenue		12,000

At this point $24,000 is still unearned and is thus a liability. Of this amount, $12,000 will be earned over the next year and is therefore a current liability, while the other $12,000 is a long-term liability.

If the company has a long-term liability that is payable in installments, the portion payable over the next year is classified as current, while the remainder is classified as long-term.

The excess of a company's current assets over its current liabilities is referred to as *working capital*. This is often used by financial statement analysts to assess a company's liquidity—its debt-paying ability. If the ratio of current assets to current liabilities is at least 2 : 1, analysts consider this to be a favorable sign. This ratio is called the *current ratio*.

EXAMPLE 9

Liquid Corporation has current assets of $10,000 and current liabilities of $4,000. Its working capital is $6,000 and its current ratio is $10,000/$4,000, which is 2.5 : 1.

Long-term liabilities are liabilities that either:

1. Are payable after 1 year, or
2. are liabilities that are not payable from current assets or the creation of other current liabilities.

Examples of long-term liabilities include bonds payable, long-term notes payable, long-term deferred tax liabilities, and the noncurrent portion of unearned revenues.

For bonds payable and long-term notes payable, the balance sheet should disclose maturity date, rate of interest, and any securities pledged as collateral on the loan.

3.5   CAPITAL (STOCKHOLDERS' EQUITY)

The excess of a company's assets over its liabilities is called *capital* in a sole proprietorship or partnership, and *stockholders' equity* in a corporation. Capital in a corporation consists of three types: capital stock (preferred and common), additional paid-in capital, and retained earnings. Normally, retained earnings has a credit balance; a debit balance resulting from heavy losses is called a deficit.

The additional paid-in capital results from amounts being paid in above or below the par of the stock, treasury stock transactions, donations, and certain kinds of dividends. These are discussed in detail in *Intermediate Accounting II*.

With respect to common and preferred stock, the balance sheet should disclose the number of shares authorized, issued, and outstanding, and the par value. Treasury stock should be shown at the end of the stockholders' equity section as a contra-capital item.

The balance sheet may take two possible forms: the account form and the report form. In the *account form*, the assets are shown on the left side of the page while the liabilities and capital are shown on the right side. This is to demonstrate that the balance sheet follows the accounting equation: Assets = Liabilities + Capital. In the *report form*, assets are shown at the top of the page, followed by liabilities, which in turn is followed by capital.

3.6   CONTINGENCIES

Contingencies are possible future events that may or may not become reality. Gain contingencies are possible future events that may *increase assets* or *reduce liabilities*. Examples of such items are:

1. Possible receipts of gifts or donations
2. Disputes with government tax bodies from which a tax refund may result
3. Pending court cases against other parties that may lead to compensation

Gain contingencies should neither be recorded in the accounts nor be shown in the body of the statements. They should, however, be disclosed in the footnotes, if it is *highly probable* that they will occur.

Loss contingencies are possible future events that may *decrease assets* or *increase liabilities.* Examples are lawsuits against the company or tax disputes that may result in payment of additional tax. If the contingency is *both probable* and *estimable*, a journal entry should be made and its effect reflected in the body of the financial statements. If, however, the contingency is not *probable* but is *reasonably possible*, no entry is made and the event is merely disclosed in the footnotes. If the contingency is not reasonably possible but is only *remote*, then nothing should be done.

Because bad debts and estimated warranty expense meet both criteria, i.e. they are both probable and estimable, we record entries for each and reflect them in the body of the statements.

EXAMPLE 10

Dream Company has the following contingencies on its horizon:

(a) A lawsuit against Mr. Rude for defaming the reputation of the company president. According to the opinion of counsel, it is probable the suit will result in damages of $50,000.

(b) A case pending in tax court which may result in additional taxes of $8,000. According to the opinion of counsel, it is reasonably possible that this will occur.

(c) Dream is dreaming about a donation of $25,000 from Mr. Stingy in memory of his great grandmother. Since Mr. Stingy and all his ancestors have never been known for their generosity, it is remote that Mr. Stingy will actually make this donation.

The first and second contingencies require footnote disclosure, while the third requires no action at all.

3.7   SUBSEQUENT EVENTS

Subsequent events are events that take place after the balance sheet date, but before its issuance. The following diagram illustrates this point:

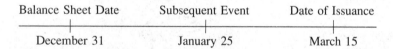

Balance Sheet Date	Subsequent Event	Date of Issuance
December 31	January 25	March 15

There are two types of subsequent events. The first type provides additional evidence about conditions that *existed at the balance sheet date* and retroactively enlightens us that the statements were incorrectly prepared. This type requires an adjustment and correction to the statements before they are issued. An example of this would be the bankruptcy of one of our customers and the resulting write-off of his receivable. We now realize that *at the balance sheet* date, our allowance for doubtful accounts should have been higher.

The second type does *not* provide additional evidence about conditions existing at the balance sheet date, but *involves conditions that arose after that date.* Examples would include the issuance of stock or bonds; stock dividends; fires or floods that damage our plant; and the write-off of a receivable due to the bankruptcy of a customer caused by a fire to his warehouse *after December 31.* In all these cases, the balance sheet was *correctly prepared* as of the balance sheet date; thus no correction or adjustment is required. However, the information should be disclosed in the footnotes for the benefit of the reader.

3.8   MISCELLANEOUS ITEMS

In the introduction to the footnotes of the statements, or in the first footnote itself, the company should provide a ''summary of its significant account policies.'' This summary should disclose depreciation methods, inventory methods, and any other significant accounting policies that were used in the preparation of the statements.

Traditionally, it was customary to use the word *reserve* in the balance sheet, as in "reserve for depreciation" or "reserve for contingencies." The accounting profession has recommended, however, that this term be used only for appropriations of retained earnings.

EXAMPLE 11

S & W Metals, Inc., shows the following on its retained earnings statement for 19X4:

Retained Earnings, Unappropriated	$250,000
Reserve for Plant Expansion	100,000
Total Retained Earnings, Dec. 31, 19X4	$350,000

The accounting profession has also recommended that the traditional usage of the term *surplus* be discontinued entirely.

3.9   A COMPLETE BALANCE SHEET

Now that we have discussed the balance sheet and all its groupings, let's prepare a *complete* balance sheet in account form.

Company B has the following accounts in its general ledger relating to the balance sheet of December 31, 19X4:

Treasury Stock	$ 7,000	Retained Earnings	$69,000
Pension Fund	40,000	Cash	60,000
Accounts Receivable	20,000	Bonds Payable	40,000
Accounts Payable	19,000	Building	60,000
Patents	9,000	Wages Payable	17,000
Organization Costs	4,000	Equipment	8,000
Merchandise Inventory	18,000	Sinking Fund	15,000
Long-Term Stock Investment	12,000	Franchise Fees	9,000
Common Stock	67,000	Paid-in Capital in Excess of Par	50,000

The balance sheet is as follows:

Assets		Liabilities and Stockholders' Equity	
Current Assets:		Current Liabilities:	
Cash	$ 60,000	Accounts Payable	$ 19,000
Accounts Receivable	20,000	Wages Payable	17,000
Merchandise Inventory	18,000	Total Current Liabilities	$ 36,000
Total Current Assets	$ 98,000	Long-Term Liabilities:	
Long-Term Investments:		Bonds Payable	$ 40,000
Pension Fund	$ 40,000	Total Liabilities	$ 76,000
Long-Term Stock Investment	12,000	Stockholders' Equity:	
Sinking Fund	15,000	Common Stock (20,000 shares	
Total Long-Term Investments	$ 67,000	authorized, $10 par; 8,000 shares	
Property, Plant, and Equipment:		issued; 6,700 shares outstanding)	$ 67,000
Building	$ 60,000	Paid-in Capital in Excess of Par	50,000

Equipment	8,000	Treasury Stock (at cost)	(7,000)
Total Property, Plant, and		Total Paid in by Stockholders	110,000
Equipment	$ 68,000	Retained Earnings	$ 69,000
Intangible Assets:		Total Stockholders' Equity	$179,000
Patents	$ 9,000	Total Liabilities and Stockholders'	
Franchise Fees	9,000	Equity	$255,000
Total Intangible Assets	$ 18,000		
Other Assets:			
Organization Costs	$ 4,000		
Total Assets	$255,000		

Summary

1. The *balance sheet*, also known as the *statement of financial position*, shows the financial position of a company at a given point in time. Its elements consist of assets, liabilities, and capital.

2. A fundamental principle on which the balance sheet is based is the *cost principle*: Assets are displayed at the price the company paid for their acquisition. Increases in the market value of assets are not recorded; decreases occasionally are.

3. *Assets* have been defined by the FASB as probable future economic benefits obtained as a result of past transactions or events. *Liabilities* are present obligations to transfer assets or provide services to other entities in the future, as a result of past transactions or events. *Capital*, or *stockholders' equity*, is the owners' interest in the assets that remains after deducting the liabilities. It is also referred to as *net assets*.

4. The asset group consists of the following subgroups: current assets; long-term investments; property, plant, and equipment; intangible assets; and other assets. The liability group consists of current liabilities and long-term liabilities, while stockholders' equity consists of capital stock, additional paid-in capital, and retained earnings.

5. *Current assets* are defined as cash or any other asset that will be converted into cash or consumed within 1 year or the operating cycle, whichever is longer. Current assets thus consists of cash, marketable securities, accounts receivable, merchandise inventory, and prepaid items (rent, insurance, supplies).

6. Restricted cash, such as a sinking fund or pension fund, which may not be used for current operations is classified not as a current asset but as a long-term investment.

7. Other examples of long-term investments are long-term investments in stocks and bonds, buildings and land held for speculation, cash surrender value of life insurance, and investments in nonconsolidated subsidiaries. In all of these, the company has no intent to convert the asset into cash within the current period.

8. *Property, plant, and equipment*, also known as *fixed assets*, refers to the building, land, equipment, and machinery a company uses to carry out its operations. All these assets depreciate with time except for land.

9. *Intangible assets* have no physical substance or form and carry a high degree of uncertainty with regard to their future benefits. Examples of these include patents, copyrights, trademarks, franchises, and goodwill. Their amortization period ranges from 5 years to a maximum of 40 years.

10. Costs incurred in creating a corporation are referred to as *organization costs* and are classified either as an intangible asset or as an other asset.

11. *Current liabilities* are liabilities that are payable within 1 year or the operating cycle (whichever is longer) and are payable out of current assets or through the creation of other current liabilities. Examples of current liabilities include accounts payable, wages payable, taxes payable, expenses payable, short-term notes payable, and the current portion of long-term debt.

12. The excess of current assets over current liabilities is referred to as *working capital*, while the ratio of current assets to current liabilities is known as the *current ratio*.

13. Retained earnings normally has a credit balance; a debit balance is referred to as a *deficit*.

14. The balance sheet may take one of two possible forms: the account form and the report form. In the *account form*, assets are shown on the left; liabilities and capital are shown on the right. In the *report form*, assets are shown at the top, followed by liabilities and then capital.

15. *Gain contingencies* are possible future events that *may* increase assets or decrease liabilities. They should neither be recorded in the accounts nor be shown in the body of the statements; however, if there is a high probability of occurrence, they should be disclosed in the footnotes.

16. *Loss contingencies* are possible future events that *may* decrease assets or increase liabilities. If the contingency is *both* probable and estimable, it should be recorded in a journal entry and be reflected in the body of the statements. If it is not probable but merely reasonably possible, no entry is made but the footnotes to the financial statements should disclose the contingency. If it is neither probable nor reasonably possible, but remote, nothing should be done.

17. *Subsequent events* are events that occur after the balance sheet date, but before the statements are issued. If this event provides evidence about *conditions that existed at the balance sheet date*, then the financial statements must be corrected and adjusted before they can be issued. If, however, the event merely provides evidence about conditions that have *arisen after the balance sheet date*, no adjustments or corrections to the financial statements are required. The correct approach in these cases is footnote disclosure.

18. The accounting profession has recommended that the term *reserve* be used only for appropriations of retained earnings and the term *surplus* be discontinued entirely.

Rapid Review

1. The elements of the balance sheet are _____, _____, and _____.

2. Another name for the balance sheet is _____.

3. Probable future economic benefits are called _____.

4. In a corporation, capital is referred to as _____.

5. Liabilities consists of two subgroups: _____ liabilities and _____ liabilities.

6. Current assets will be consumed within _____ or the _____, whichever is _____.

7. The assets a company uses to carry out its operations are called _____.

8. Assets with no physical form and whose future benefits are highly uncertain are called _____.

9. Costs of creating a corporation are called _____.

10. The current portion of long-term debt is a _____.

11. Current assets minus current liabilities is _____, while one divided by the other is the _____ ratio.

12. A debit balance in retained earnings is referred to as a _____.

13. The two forms of the balance sheet are the _____ form and the _____ form.

14. Possible future events that may increase assets or decrease liabilities are _____.

15. Events that occur after the balance sheet date but before its issuance are called _____.

16. The term *reserve* should be used only for _____.

Answers: **1.** assets; liabilities; capital **2.** statement of financial position **3.** assets **4.** stockholders' equity **5.** current; long-term **6.** 1 year; operating cycle; longer **7.** fixed **8.** intangible **9.** organization costs **10.** current liability **11.** working capital; current **12.** deficit **13.** account; report **14.** gain contingencies **15.** subsequent events **16.** appropriations

Solved Problems

Current Assets; Long-Term Investments

3.1   Company A has an operating cycle of 10 months, while Company B's cycle is 15 months. They each intend to sell a piece of land in 14 months.

   (*a*) What is the cutoff period for the determination of current assets for Company A? For Company B?

   (*b*) Would the land be considered current for Company A? For Company B?

SOLUTION

(a) 1 year; 15 months

(b) Company A, no; Company B, yes.   [Section 3.2]

3.2 Company C prepays its annual rent of $1,000 for 4 years ($4,000). How much of this prepayment is considered a current asset? How should the remainder be classified?

SOLUTION

The current portion is $1,000; the remaining $3,000 is a deferred charge.   [Section 3.2]

3.3 Which of the following are considered current assets?

(a) Pension fund   (e) Merchandise inventory

(b) Accounts payable   (f) Supplies

(c) Accounts receivable   (g) Short-term note payable

(d) Long-term stock investment   (h) Land held for speculation

SOLUTION

Items (c), (e), (f)   [Section 3.2]

3.4 Marketable securities were purchased on November 1 at a cost of $7,000, and their December 31 market value is $9,000. Merchandise inventory was purchased October 8 at a cost of $22,000, and its December 31 market value is $20,000. At what amounts should these items be disclosed on the balance sheet?

SOLUTION

Marketable securities at $7,000; merchandise inventory at $20,000.   [Section 3.2]

3.5 Indicate whether each of the following items is to be classified as a current asset, a long-term investment, or neither:

(a) Cash surrender value of life insurance

(b) Merchandise inventory

(c) Bonds payable

(d) Retained earnings

(e) Accounts receivable

(f) Sinking funds

(g) Short-term investments in stock

(h) Building held for speculation

(i) Organization costs

(j) Investment in nonconsolidated subsidiaries

SOLUTION

(a) Long-term investment

(b) Current

(c) Neither

(d) Neither

(e) Current

(f) Long-term investment

(g) Current

(h) Long-term investment

(i) Neither

(j) Long-term investment   [Section 3.2]

Property, Plant, and Equipment; Intangible Assets; Other Assets

3.6 Company D pays a franchise fee of $80,000 for the use of the McDonald's name and product in its store. Prepare the entries for the acquisition of the franchise and for its annual amortization. (Use the maximum period allowable.)

SOLUTION

Franchise Fee	80,000	
Cash		80,000
Amortization Expense	2,000	
Accumulated Amortization		2,000
($80,000 ÷ 40 years)		[Section 3.3]

3.7 Determine for each of the following items if its classification is current asset; long-term investment; property, plant, and equipment; intangible asset or other asset.

(a) Machinery

(b) Goodwill

(c) Cash surrender value of life insurance

(d) Marketable securities

(e) Long-term portion of prepaid rent

(f) Patent

(g) Merchandise inventory

(h) Land held for speculation

(i) Organization costs

(j) Short-term note receivable

(k) Supplies

(l) Investment in nonconsolidated subsidiaries

SOLUTION

(a) Property, plant, and equipment

(b) Intangible

(c) Long-term investment

(d) Current

(e) Other assets (deferred charge)

(f) Intangible

(g) Current

(h) Long-term investment

(i) Other assets

(j) Current

(k) Current

(l) Long-term investment [Section 3.3]

Current Liabilities; Long-Term Liabilities

3.8 On July 1, 19X1, Company One receives an advance payment of $18,000 representing rent for the next 3 years ($6,000 per year).

(a) Prepare the required entries for July 1 and December 31.

(b) Determine for the December 31 balance sheet how much would be shown as a current liability, and how much as a long-term liability.

SOLUTION

(a)

	July 1	Cash	18,000	
		Unearned Rent		18,000
	Dec. 31	Unearned Rent	3,000*	
		Rent Revenue		3,000

$*6,000 \times \frac{1}{2}$ year.

(b) $6,000 would be a current liability; $9,000 would be a long-term liability. [Section 3.4]

3.9 Liquid Corporation has current assets and current liabilities of $40,000 and $20,000, respectively. Determine its working capital and current ratio.

SOLUTION

$$\text{Working capital} = \$40,000 - \$20,000$$
$$= \$20,000$$

$$\text{Current ratio} = \frac{40,000}{20,000} = 2:1 \qquad \text{[Section 3.4]}$$

3.10 Determine whether each of the following is a current liability or a long-term liability.

(a) Taxes payable

(b) Bond payable in 5 years

(c) Interest payable

(d) Accounts payable

(e) This year's portion of long-term mortgage

(f) Bond due in 8 months, payable from bond sinking fund

SOLUTION

(*a*) Current   (*d*) Current

(*b*) Long-term   (*e*) Current

(*c*) Current   (*f*) Long-term (not payable out of current assets)   [Section 3.4]

Capital (Stockholders' Equity)

3.11 From the following information, prepare the stockholders' equity section of the balance sheet for Corporation Q.

Building	$50,000	Paid-in Capital in Excess of Par	$25,000
Common Stock	70,000	Investment in IBM Stock	19,000
Retained Earnings	(20,000)	Treasury Stock	(8,000)

SOLUTION

Common Stock	$70,000
Paid-in Capital in Excess of Par	25,000
Treasury Stock	(8,000)
Total Paid in by Stockholders	$87,000
Retained Earnings (deficit)	(20,000)
Total Stockholders' Equity	$67,000

[Section 3.5]

Contingencies

3.12 Possibility Corporation has the following contingencies on its horizon:

(*a*) Rough, Inc., is suing Possibility for $23,000 on the grounds that Possibility infringed on one of Rough's patents. According to the opinion of legal counsel, it is *reasonably possible* that Rough, Inc., will win this suit.

(*b*) Possibility is disputing in tax court an IRS ruling that increased its taxes by $18,000. According to legal counsel, it is *highly probable* that Possibility will win and get a tax refund.

(*c*) Sweet, Inc., is suing Possibility for $32,000 on the grounds that Possibility defamed and slandered the good name of Sweet's president, Sir Simon. According to legal counsel, it is probable that Possibility will have to pay this amount.

(*d*) There is a *remote* chance that Possibility will win $20,000 in the lottery.

Determine the nature of each of the above contingencies and state what the proper accounting treatment should be.

SOLUTION

(*a*) Loss contingency; disclose in the footnotes.

(*b*) Gain contingency; disclose in the footnotes.

(*c*) Loss contingency; prepare a journal entry and show in the body of the statements.

(*d*) Gain contingency; do nothing.   [Section 3.6]

3.13 On what theoretical accounting grounds are bad debts expense and warranty expense estimated, recorded, and shown in the body of the financial statements?

SOLUTION

They are loss contingencies that are *both* estimable and probable.   [Section 3.6]

Subsequent Events

3.14 For each one of the following subsequent events, write "Adjust" if the financial statements need an adjustment, and "Do not adjust" if they don't.

(*a*) Issuance of stock

(*b*) Customer bankruptcy due to general economic conditions

(*c*) Customer bankruptcy due to fire after balance sheet date

(*d*) Stock dividends

(*e*) Old CEO retires; new CEO appointed

(*f*) Building collapses from earthquake

(*g*) Building collapses; engineers assure us that at the balance sheet date, the collapse was imminent

SOLUTION

(*a*) Do not adjust   (*e*) Do not adjust

(*b*) Adjust   (*f*) Do not adjust

(*c*) Do not aadjut   (*g*) Adjust

(*d*) Do not adjust   [Section 3.7]

A Complete Balance Sheet

3.15 Lucshin, Inc., has the following selected account titles and balances in its general ledger on December 31, 19X4:

Accounts Payable	$ 13,000	Cash	$ 10,000
Plant Building	120,000	Goodwill	4,000
Sinking Fund	14,000	Accounts Receivable	18,000
Retained Earnings	113,000	Treasury Stock (at cost)	(30,000)
Note Payable (short-term)	32,000	Land (plant)	84,000
Sales	85,000	Machinery	22,000
Merchandise Inventory	17,000	Copyright	9,000
Equipment	48,000	Bond Payable	50,000
Pension Fund	24,000	Common Stock	120,000
Paid-in Capital in Excess of Par	60,000	Note Payable (long-term)	12,000

Prepare a balance sheet in account form.

SOLUTION

Lucshin, Inc.
Balance Sheet
December 31, 19X4

Assets		Liabilities and Stockholders' Equity	
Current Assets:		Current Liabilities:	
Cash	$ 10,000	Accounts Payable	$ 13,000
Accounts Receivable	18,000	Note Payable	32,000
Merchandise Inventory	17,000	Total Current Liabilities	$ 45,000
Total Current Assets	$ 45,000		
Long-Term Investments:		Long-Term Liabilities:	
Sinking Fund	$ 14,000	Bond Payable	$ 50,000
Pension Fund	24,000	Note Payable	12,000
Total Long-Term Investments	$ 38,000	Total Long-Term Liabilities	$ 62,000
		Total Liabilities	$107,000
Property, Plant, and Equipment:		Stockholders' Equity:	
Building	$120,000	Common Stock	$120,000
Equipment	48,000	Paid-in Capital in Excess of Par	60,000
Land	84,000	Treasury Stock	(30,000)
Machinery	22,000	Total Paid in by Stockholders	$150,000
Total Property, Plant, and		Retained Earnings	113,000
Equipment	$274,000	Total Stockholders' Equity	$263,000
Intangible Assets:			
Goodwill	$ 4,000		
Copyright	9,000		
Total Intangible Assets	$ 13,000	Total Liabilities and	
Total Assets	$370,000	Stockholders' Equity	$370,000

[Section 3.9]

Supplementary Problems

3.16 Company X has an operating cycle of 15 months, while the operating cycle of Company Y is 11 months. They each intend to sell a stock investment in 14 months. Would this investment be considered a current asset for Company X? For Company Y?

3.17 On December 31, 19X1, Company Z purchases a large quantity of supplies for $9,000 which it expects to use *evenly* over the next 3 years. How much of these supplies are considered current? How would the remainder be classified?

3.18 During 19X1, Company Q purchased merchandise inventory and marketable securities for $10,000 and $16,000, respectively. On December 31, the fair market values of these items are $9,000 and $18,000, respectively. At what amounts should these assets be shown on the balance sheet, and in which group?

3.19 Indicate whether each of the following items is to be classified as a current asset, a long-term investment, or neither.

(a)	Supplies	(e)	Common stock
(b)	Retained earnings	(f)	Building (plant)
(c)	Patent	(g)	Prepaid rent
(d)	Marketable securities	(h)	Furniture

3.20 Determine the proper balance sheet classification for each of the following items. Make your choice from the following groups: current assets; long-term investments; property, plant, and equipment; intangible assets; and other assets.

(a)	Land (plant)	(g)	Furniture
(b)	Marketable securities	(h)	Accounts receivable
(c)	Investment in nonconsolidated subsidiaries	(i)	Cash surrender value of life insurance
(d)	Trademarks	(j)	Copyrights
(e)	Notes receivable (in 3 years)	(k)	Equipment
(f)	Building (held for speculation)	(l)	Organization costs

3.21 On October 1, 19X1, Service Corporation receives an advance payment of $3,600 for services to be performed *evenly* over the next 3 years.

(a) Prepare the necessary entries for October 1 and December 31.

(b) For the December 31, 19X1 balance sheet, determine how much of this amount should be considered a current liability, and how much should be considered long-term.

3.22 Tight-Fist, Inc., has current assets and current liabilities of $80,000 and $60,000, respectively. Determine its working capital and current ratio.

3.23 For each of the following, determine if its status is that of a current liability or a long-term liability.

(a)	Bond maturing in 5 years	(e)	Wages payable
(b)	Note payable due in 10 months	(f)	Note maturing in 11 months, payable via conversion into common stock
(c)	Dividends payable		
(d)	Interest payable		

3.24 Prepare the stockholders' equity section of the balance sheet from the following information:

Total Assets	$80,000	Common Stock	$30,000
Total Liabilities	20,000	Preferred Stock	20,000
Investment in Xerox Stock	19,000	Treasury Stock	30,000
Paid-in Capital in Excess of Par— Common Stock	10,000	Retained Earnings	?
Paid-in Capital in Excess of Par— Preferred Stock	20,000		

3.25 Contingent Corporation has the following contingencies on its horizon:

(a) A lawsuit by Corporation Z, for which a light probability exists that Contingent will have to pay $20,000

(b) A reasonable possibility that Contingent will win a tax court case, resulting in a tax refund of $19,000

(c) A remote chance of hurricane damage to its building, resulting in a $17,000 loss

(d) A reasonably possible chance that Contingent will win a $10,000 lottery (Contingent's chief executive officer may be able to "rig" the drawing!)

Determine the correct accounting treatment for each of the above.

3.26 State whether or not each of the following *subsequent* events requires an adjustment of the financial statements.

(*a*)　Bond issuance

(*b*)　Merger with another company

(*c*)　New sales marketing campaign

(*d*)　Appointment of new CEO

(*e*)　Revision of depreciation rates

(*f*)　Customer bankruptcy due to warehouse fire after balance sheet date

(*g*)　Unusually high warranty costs; engineers discover hairline fracture in the company product

3.27 Prepare a balance sheet in *report form* from the following account information on December 31, 19X5:

Organization Costs	$14,000	Marketable Securities	$33,000
Building	80,000	Inventory	22,000
Patent	19,000	Accounts Payable	39,000
Cash	25,000	Accounts Receivable	24,000
Investment in GM Stock (long-term)	42,000	Land	46,000
Equipment	18,000	Notes Payable (long-term)	15,000
Notes Payable (short-term)	70,000	Bonds Payable	50,000
Treasury Stock	?	Common Stock	90,000
Sinking Fund	31,000	Paid-in Capital in Excess of Par	50,000
Retained Earnings	60,000		

3.28 Prepare a balance sheet in *account form* from the following account information on December 31, 19X2:

Plant Rearrangement Costs	$ 7,000	Accounts Payable	$28,000
Machinery	36,000	Bond Payable	63,000
Land (held for speculation)	85,000	Common Stock	70,000
Copyright	17,000	Taxes Payable	20,000
Cash	21,000	Building	65,000
Bond Investment (long-term)	5,000	Accounts Receivable	12,000
Marketable Securities	9,000	Treasury Stock	26,000
Notes Payable (in 19 months)	40,000	Organization Costs	3,000
Paid-in Capital in Excess of Par	40,000	Retained Earnings	?

Examination I

Chapters 1, 2, 3

A. True–False Questions. Place the letter T or F next to the question.

1. _____ The fundamental accounting equation states: $A = L - C$.

2. _____ The left side of the T-account is the credit side.

3. _____ Revenue increases capital.

4. _____ Entries with more than one debit or credit are called complex entries.

5. _____ Permanent accounts are closed every period.

6. _____ Reversing entries are a *required* step in the accounting cycle.

7. _____ Drawings are closed into Income Summary.

8. _____ The operating section of the income statement deals with peripheral operations.

9. _____ Gains and losses that are *either* unusual *or* infrequent are classified as extraordinary.

10. _____ The effect of a strike is not considered to be extraordinary.

11. _____ The separation of taxes on the income statement by section is known as intraperiod tax allocation.

12. _____ For EPS purposes, if the preferred stock is cumulative, its dividend is subtracted only if declared.

13. _____ Mistakes of previous periods appear on the income statement.

14. _____ Capital is also referred to as net assets.

15. _____ The cutoff period for the measurement of current assets is 1 year or the operating cycle, whichever is *shorter*.

16. _____ The cash surrender value of life insurance is an intangible asset.

17. _____ Current assets less current liabilities equals active capital.

18. _____ Gain contingencies should not appear in the body of the statements.

19. _____ The current portion of a long-term debt is classified as long-term.

20. _____ Events that occur after the balance sheet date but before its issuance are called subsequent events.

B. Completion Questions. Fill in the blanks.

21. The fundamental accounting equation states _____.

22. Probable future benefits obtained as a result of past transactions are _____.

23. Revenues are increased via entries on the _____ side.

24. The system whereby the recording of a transaction always involves two entries is known as the _____ system.

25. Transactions are initially entered in the _____ and then posted to the _____.

26. At period end, the starting point for financial statement preparation is the _____.

27. The special account used in the closing process is _____.

28. The financial statement that discloses how well or poorly a company did last period is the _____.

29. The two forms of this statement are the _____ step and the _____ step.

30. A blizzard in Hawaii would be classified as a(n) _____ item.

31. If a company switches accounting methods, the _____ effect of the change must be shown.

32. To determine EPS, take the net income and subtract the _____.

33. On the retained earnings statement, the beginning balance is corrected by _____.

34. Mistakes due to faulty estimates require a change for the _____, but not for the _____.

35. The _____ principle requires that assets not be disclosed at their fair market value.

36. In a corporation, capital is referred to as _____.

37. Assets that will quickly be consumed or turned into cash are known as _____ assets.

38. Intangible assets have no _____ substance and carry a high degree of _____.

39. The two forms of the balance sheet are the _____ form and the _____ form.

40. The term *reserve* may only be used for _____.

C. Problems

41. Prepare journal entries for the following transactions of Company A.

    (*a*) The owner invested $3,000 cash in the company.

    (*b*) Performed services on account for $500.

(c)   Purchased office supplies on account for $100.

(d)   Collected $200 on account for transaction (b).

(e)   The owner withdrew a $250 furniture piece.

(f)   On December 31, there is an accrued phone bill for $80.

(g)   Depreciation on the building is $4,000 for the year.

42.   Company B, a corporation, has the following account balances on December 31, 19X2:

Accounts Receivable	$5,000	Service Revenue	$ 9,000
Salary Expense	1,000	Dividend Revenue	3,000
Advertising Expense	3,000	Building	80,000

Prepare the necessary closing entries

43.   Indicate which of the following *adjustment* items requires reversing entries (if reversing entries are used).

(a)   Adjustments for accrued revenues

(b)   Adjustments for the expiration of prepaid items initially entered as expenses

(c)   Adjustments for accrued expenses

(d)   Adjustment for bad debts

(e)   Adjustment for depreciation

(f)   Adjustment for unearned revenue initially credited to a liability

44.   Company C had net income during 19X3 of $160,000. During the year it had 5,000 shares common stock outstanding, and 1,000 shares of $100-par, 10%, *noncumulative* preferred shares.

(a)   Determine EPS if the preferred dividend was *not* declared.

(b)   Determine EPS if the preferred dividend *was* declared.

45.   Company D had the following items relating to its retained earnings for 19X2:

(a)   Jan. 1, 19X2, balance, $80,000

(b)   Net income during 19X2, $30,000

(c)   Dividends declared, $10,000

(d)   Dividends paid, $7,000

(e)   Discovery of 19X1 understatement of depreciation, $2,000

Based on the above information, prepare a statement of retained earnings. Assume a tax rate of 20%.

46.   On January 1, 19X1, Company E purchased a machine for $44,000 with an estimated salvage value and life of $2,000 and 7 years, respectively. Early in 19X4, Company E revises the salvage value and life to $1,000 and 10 years (total life), respectively. Determine the annual depreciation for 19X4 and thereafter.

Answers to Examination I

A. True–False Questions

1. F **2.** F **3.** T **4.** F **5.** F **6.** F **7.** F **8.** F **9.** F **10.** T **11.** T **12.** F **13.** F **14.** T **15.** F **16.** F **17.** F **18.** T **19.** F **20.** T

B. Completion Questions

21. $A = L + C$ **22.** assets **23.** credit **24.** double-entry bookkeeping **25.** journal; ledger **26.** trial balance **27.** Income Summary **28.** income statement **29.** multiple; single **30.** extraordinary **31.** cumulative **32.** preferred dividend **33.** prior period adjustments **34.** future; past **35.** cost **36.** stockholders' equity **37.** current **38.** physical; uncertainty **39.** account; report **40.** appropriations

C. Problems

41. (*a*)

Cash	3,000	
Capital		3,000

(*b*)

Accounts Receivable	500	
Service Fees		500

(*c*)

Office Supplies	100	
Accounts Payable		100

(*d*)

Cash	200	
Accounts Receivable		200

(*e*)

Drawings	250	
Furniture		250

(*f*)

Telephone Expense	80	
Accounts Payable		80

(*g*)

Depreciation Expense	4,000	
Accumulated Depreciation		4,000

42.

Service Revenue	9,000	
Dividend Revenue	3,000	
Income Summary		12,000

Income Summary	4,000	
Advertising Expense		3,000
Salary Expense		1,000

Income Summary	8,000	
Retained Earnings		8,000

43. (*a*), (*b*), (*c*)

44. (*a*)

$$\frac{\$160,000}{\$5,000} = \$32$$

(*b*)

$$\frac{\$160,000 - \$10,000}{\$5,000} = \$30$$

45.

Retained Earnings, Jan. 1, 19X2		$80,000
Prior Period Adjustment—		
Depreciation	($2,000)	
Tax Effect	$ 400	(1,600)
Adjusted Retained Earnings,		
Jan. 1, 19X2		$78,400
Net Income		30,000
Dividends Declared		(10,000)
Retained Earnings, Dec. 31, 19X2		$98,400

46.
$$\frac{\$44,000 - 3(\$6,000) - 1,000}{7 \text{ years to go}} = \$3,571 \qquad \text{(rounded)}$$

Chapter 4

The Conceptual Framework of Accounting Theory

4.1 INTRODUCTION

It is essential that the discipline of accounting be based on a solid theoretical foundation. This foundation, referred to as a *conceptual framework* and consisting of philosophical objectives, interrelated concepts, precise definitions, and rationalized rules, enables the FASB to:

1. Issue a coherent and consistent set of rules, all built on the same foundation
2. Solve new and emerging accounting problems by reference to the conceptual framework

In 1976 the FASB issued a three-part Discussion Memorandum entitled "Conceptual Framework for Financial Accounting and Reporting: Elements of Financial Statements and Their Measurement." This memorandum set forth the major issues to be addressed in establishing the conceptual framework. Since that time, the FASB has issued five *Statements of Financial Accounting Concepts (SFACs)* relating to financial reporting for *business enterprises*. They are as follows:

1. *SFAC No. 1*, "Objectives of Financial Reporting by Business Enterprises." This statement sets forth the goals and purposes of accounting.
2. *SFAC No. 2*, "Qualitative Characteristics of Accounting Information." This statement discusses the characteristics of useful accounting information.
3. *SFAC No. 3*, "Elements of Financial Statements of Business Enterprises." This statement provides definitions of the items ("building blocks") that comprise the financial statements, such as assets, liabilities, expenses, revenue, and others.
4. *SFAC No. 5*, "Recognition and Measurement in Financial Statements of Business Enterprises." This statement provides guidance on what information should be included in the financial statements and when.
5. *SFAC No. 6*, "Elements of Financial Statements," which replaces *SFAC No. 3* and expands its scope. (The FASB has also issued *SFAC No. 4*, which discusses the objectives of financial reporting for *nonbusiness* organizations).

These statements, which constitute the conceptual framework, will be discussed in detail in the following sections.

4.2 OBJECTIVES AND QUALITATIVE CHARACTERISTICS OF FINANCIAL REPORTING

The objectives of financial reporting are threefold:

1. To provide information that will be useful to people making investment and credit decisions
2. To provide information that will be helpful to present and potential investors and creditors in assessing the amounts and timing of future cash flows
3. To provide information about economic resources, claims to these resources, and changes in these resources

In order for these objectives to be accomplished, accounting information must have certain qualitative characteristics. The FASB has identified two *primary* characteristics necessary to make accounting information useful for decision making: *relevance* and *reliability*. The ingredients of relevance are predictive value, feedback value, and timeliness; the ingredients of reliability are verifiability, neutrality, and representational faithfulness.

By definition, for accounting information to be *relevant*, it must be important enough to influence decisions made by the user. If it has no bearing on a decision, it is irrelevant to that decision. Information may be relevant by helping the user predict future events (predictive value), or confirm or correct prior expectations (feedback value). In all cases it must be available to the user before it loses its significance (timeliness). Thus, for information to be relevant, it should have predictive or feedback value and be presented on time.

For accounting information to be *reliable*, it should be reasonably free of error and bias. It thus must possess three important characteristics: verifiability, neutrality, and faithfulness. Verifiability is manifested when a consensus can be reached among independent evaluators using the same measurement methods (for example, several independent auditors coming to the same conclusions about the statements). Neutrality means that information cannot be subjectively selected to favor one party over another. Faithfulness means that the numbers listed in the statements are neither materially understated nor overstated.

EXAMPLE 1

The statements of Company A show that sales during 19X3 were $80,000, when in reality they were $8,000. The statements of Company B fail to disclose that Company B is being sued for a large sum and the probability is high that the outcome will be unfavorable. Company A's statements lack faithfulness; Company B's statements lack neutrality.

In addition to the *primary* qualities of relevance and reliability, there are two *secondary* qualities: *comparability* and *consistency*. *Comparability* means that information should be reported and measured in a similar manner for all companies in order to facilitate comparisons. *Consistency* requires a company to apply the same accounting treatment from period to period for similar events. Companies may switch accounting methods only if it can be demonstrated that the new method is preferable to the old one. In such cases, the nature, effect, and justification for the change must be disclosed.

EXAMPLE 2

Company C, without justification, changes its depreciation method from straight-line to sum-of-the-years'-digits. This is a violation of the consistency requirement and thus its statements could not pass "inspection" by the auditors.

4.3   ELEMENTS OF THE FINANCIAL STATEMENTS

The financial statements are composed of several "building blocks" or elements. These have been precisely defined by the FASB in *SFAC No. 6*, as follows:

Assets—probable future economic benefits obtained as a result of past transactions or events.

Liabilities—probable future sacrifices of economic benefits arising from present obligations to transfer assets or provide services to other entities in the future, as a result of past transactions or events.

Equity—the residual interest in the assets of an entity that remains after deducting its liabilities.

Investments by Owners—increases in the net assets (assets minus liabilities) of an entity resulting from transfers of value by other entities to obtain an ownership interest (equity). Transfers usually involve assets but may also include services or the settlement of liabilities.

Distributions to Owners—decreases in the net assets of an entity resulting from the transfer of assets to owners, or the incurring of liabilities by the entity to owners. The result is a decrease in ownership interest (equity) in the entity.

Revenues—inflows of assets or settlement of liabilities during a period, from delivering or producing goods, rendering services, or performing other activities that constitute the entity's *major or central operations*.

Expenses—outflows of assets or incurrences of liabilities during a period, from delivering or producing goods, rendering services, or performing other activities that constitute the entity's *major or central operations*.

Gains—inflows of assets or settlement of liabilities resulting from *peripheral or incidental transactions* of the entity. These have the same effect on the financial statements as revenue.

Losses—outflows of assets or incurrences of liabilities resulting from *peripheral or incidental transactions* of the entity. These have the same effect on the financial statements as expenses.

EXAMPLE 3

Company D sells washing machines as its principal activity. It also occasionally purchases short-term stocks with its idle cash and sells these stocks for a quick profit when the market goes up. The profit on the sale of the washing machines is classified as revenue; the profit on the sale of the stocks is classified as a gain.

EXAMPLE 4

Company E spends $1,000 on uprooting and rearranging the machinery in its factory. It is expected that this will streamline factory operations and thus save the company money in the future. Since this transaction will provide probable future economic benefits, it meets the definition of an asset and should be debited to an asset account, rather than to an expense account. The entry is

Machine Rearrangement Costs	1,000	
Cash		1,000

4.4 BASIC ACCOUNTING ASSUMPTIONS AND PRINCIPLES

Four basic assumptions form the underpinnings of the financial accounting system: economic entity, going concern, monetary unit, and periodicity.

The *economic entity assumption* assumes that the activities of a business entity can be kept separate and distinct from those of the owners and of other business entities. For example, if the activities of Zenith were highly intertwined with those of RCA, it would not be possible to account separately for each. A similar result would occur if the assets and liabilities of the company owner were mixed with the assets and liabilities of the company itself.

The entity assumption does not necessarily refer to a *legal* entity per se, but rather to an *economic unit*. Thus, while a parent and its subsidiary are separate legal entities, they may be considered one economic unit for the purpose of consolidating their financial statements, and this would not violate the entity assumption.

EXAMPLE 5

Company F lists as an asset on its balance sheet the home of its owner. This home is used solely for the personal needs of the owner, and the title is in her name. This violates the entity assumption.

The *going concern assumption* assumes that the company will have a long life and is not on the verge of liquidation. If liquidation, however, appears to be imminent, the assets must be shown at their net realizable values, rather than at historical cost less accumulated depreciation.

EXAMPLE 6

Company G shows a building on its balance sheet at $120,000 (cost, $160,000; accumulated depreciation, $40,000). Company G is on the verge of being liquidated, and when this happens, the sale of the building minus related disposal costs will net $100,000. The building must be written down by $20,000, and a loss must be recognized for this amount.

The monetary unit assumption assumes that money (in the United States it is dollars) provides an appropriate basis for the measurement of assets and liabilities, despite the fact that due to inflation, today's dollars are not worth the same (have less purchasing power) than yesterday's dollars. Only if the United States were to experience *high* inflation would the FASB once again consider "inflation accounting," as it did in the 1970s.

The *periodicity assumption* assumes that the activities of a company can be accurately measured and reported by dividing them into artificial time periods, such as the month, quarter, and year.

There are four basic principles of accounting used to record transactions: historical cost, revenue recognition, matching, and full disclosure.

The *historical cost principle* requires assets to be recorded and reported at the price paid to acquire them. Generally, fair market values are ignored. (There are some exceptions to this principle, and they will be discussed at their appropriate places in this book). The advantages of using cost are quite simple: Cost is objective and verifiable. Fair market values, on the other hand, are subjective (five appraisers of a building will usually give five opinions on the building's value) and not easily verifiable.

EXAMPLE 7

Ten years ago a building was purchased at a cost of $150,000. Because the neighborhood has improved, it has a market value today of $190,000. The building may *not* be written up on the books by the $40,000 increase in value.

EXAMPLE 8

A machine was recently purchased at a "good deal" of $5,000. This machine sells in all the stores for $5,500. The machine should be debited for the *cost* of $5,000, not the *market value* of $5,500.

The *revenue recognition principle* states that revenue should be recognized when realized *and* earned, rather than when the cash is received. Revenues are *realized* when goods or services are exchanged for claims to cash; revenues are *earned* when the company has substantially accomplished what it must do to be entitled to the benefits arising from the sale. Normally, realization and earning take place at the point of sale. For the sale of goods, this is when the goods are delivered (or at shipment when they are sent F.O.B. shipping point); for the sale of services, this is when the services are performed.

EXAMPLE 9

Company H performed services in late December 19X1 but did not get paid until January 19X2. The revenue would be recognized on the income statement of 19X1.

EXAMPLE 10

Company I and Company J each sent goods to customers late in December 19X1 and the goods arrived in early January 19X2. Company I sent the goods F.O.B. shipping point; Company J sent the goods F.O.B destination. Company I recognizes the revenue in 19X1; Company J recognizes it in 19X2.

There are several exceptions to the revenue principle. For long-term construction contracts, revenue may be recognized during the construction period despite the fact that the contract has not been fully completed and a transfer of ownership has not occurred. For installment sales that carry a high degree of uncertainty regarding ultimate collections, it is permissible to defer revenue recognition until the cash comes in. Both of these situations are discussed in detail in *Intermediate Accounting II* of this series.

The matching principle requires that expenses be matched with their related revenues whenever it is possible to do so. Thus expenses should be recognized when incurred, not when paid for—when they make their contribution to revenue. Some accountants have stated this quite succinctly: "Let the expenses follow the revenues."

EXAMPLE 11

A saleswoman makes sales of $100,000 late in December 19X1 for which she is entitled to a $5,000 commission. She does not actually receive the commission, however, until February 19X2. The matching principle dictates that since the sales revenue was recognized in 19X1, the commission expense must also be recognized at that time.

EXAMPLE 12

Company K makes sales of $100,000 in 19X1 and offers a 5-year warranty. It is reliably estimated that claims under the warranty will trickle in gradually over the 5 years and total $7,000. This warranty expense of $7,000 must be recognized *completely* in 19X1 since the revenue is recognized at that time.

The *full disclosure principle* requires the financial statements to disclose all matters that might influence the judgment of an informed user. This information may be disclosed in the body of the statements, in the footnotes to the statements, or as supplementary information.

4.5 CONSTRAINTS ON THE FINANCIAL STATEMENTS

In striving to make the financial statements as informative and useful as possible, several overriding constraints must be considered. They are: cost versus benefits, materiality, industry practices, and conservatism.

It would seem that the more information provided by the financial statements, the better. Information, however, is not a free commodity: It costs money to obtain and provide. Thus the *costs* of providing information must be weighed against the *benefits* resulting from the use of the information. Only if the benefits exceed the costs should information be provided.

The *materiality constraint* requires that items be included in the statements only when material. *SFAC No. 2* defines material items as items whose inclusion or omission from the statements would influence or change the judgment of a reasonable person. If a piece of information is immaterial, it may be omitted from the statements.

Relative size plays a key role in determining materiality. What for one company may be material may be immaterial for another company, as the following example illustrates.

EXAMPLE 13

Company L and Company M report net incomes of $1,000,000 and $100,000, respectively. During 19X3, each company neglected to record a $25,000 expense. For Company L, this omission, representing a mere 2.5%, is immaterial; for Company M, the omission represents 25%, which is definitely material.

Another constraint on financial reporting is that of the peculiar *nature* of certain industries. For example, banks will often report short-term investments at market value instead of at lower of cost or market because they believe the market price is more useful to the readers of the statements.

Such industry variations from generally accepted accounting principles are permissible provided that they can be supported with a logical and rational explanation.

The constraint of *conservation* states that, *when in doubt*, choose the accounting principle or method that will be least likely to overstate assets and net income. It is safer to understate than to overstate.

Summary

1. The theoretical foundation of accounting, known as the *conceptual framework* and consisting of objectives, concepts, definitions, and rules, enables the FASB to solve new and emerging accounting problems by referring to this framework.

2. The FASB has issued five *Statements of Financial Accounting Concepts* for business enterprises, which discuss the following: the goals and purposes of accounting, the characteristics of useful accounting information, definitions of the elements of financial statements, and guidance as to the nature and timing of information to be included in the statements.

3. Accounting information must have two *primary* characteristics to be useful: relevance and reliability. The ingredients of *relevance* are predictive value, feedback value, and timeliness; the ingredients of *reliability* are verifiability, neutrality, and representational faithfulness.

4. Accounting information should also have two *secondary* characteristics: comparability and consistency. *Comparability* facilitates comparisons from company to company; *consistency* facilitates comparisons from year to year.

5. The elements of the financial statements, known as building blocks, consist of: assets, liabilities, equity, owner investments, distributions to owners, revenues, expenses, gains, and losses. *Revenues* and *expenses* involve a change in assets or liabilities resulting from a company's major or central activities. *Gains* and *losses* involve a change in assets or liabilities resulting from peripheral activities.

6. Four basic assumptions form the underpinnings of the accounting system: the *economic entity assumption*, the *going concern assumption*, the *monetary unit assumption*, and the *periodicity* assumption.

7. Four basic principles of accounting are used to record transactions: historical cost, revenue recognition, matching, and full disclosure. The *historical cost principle* requires that assets be recorded and reported at their acquisition cost. The *revenue recognition principle* requires revenue to be recognized when realized and earned, not when cash is received. The *matching principle* requires expenses to be recognized when incurred, not when paid for—when they make their contribution to revenue. The *full disclosure principle* requires the financial statements to disclose all matters that might influence a user's judgment.

8. A number of overriding constraints must be considered in the preparation of financial statements. These are: *cost versus benefits*, *materiality*, *industry practices*, and *conservatism*.

Rapid Review

1. The theoretical foundation of accounting is referred to as the _____.

2. The elements of the financial statements are also known as _____.

3. The two *primary* characteristics of accounting information are _____ and _____.

4. The two secondary characteristics of accounting information are _____ and _____.

5. The ingredients of relevance are _____, and _____, and _____.

6. The ingredients of reliability are _____, and _____, and _____.

7. If information is subjectively presented to favor one party over another, it violates the _____ characteristic.

8. If the numbers on the statements are materially overstated, the statements are not _____.

9. If a company changes its accounting methods without justification, the statements lack the characteristic of _____.

10. Probable future economic benefits are known as _____.

11. Probable future economic sacrifices are known as _____.

12. The owners' interest in a company's assets is known as _____.

13. Revenues entail an inflow of _____ or a settlement of _____.

14. Expenses entail an outflow of _____ or an incurrence of _____.

15. Peripheral or incidental transactions may result in _____ or _____.

16. The _____ assumption assumes that a company's assets and liabilities may be accounted for separately from the assets and liabilities of its owners.

17. The assumption that a company will continue indefinitely is known as _____.

18. If a company is on the verge of liquidation, its assets should be written down to _____.

19. The _____ assumption assumes that money is the best yardstick for measuring assets and liabilities.

20. The _____ principle requires assets to be reported at acquisition price.

21. Under the revenue recognition principle, revenue is recognized when _____ or _____.

22. Recognizing expense when incurred instead of when paid illustrates the _____ principle.

23. The _____ constraint requires information to be included in the statements only if it is important enough to influence the judgment of the user.

24. The _____ constraint requires the use (when in doubt) of the accounting method that will minimize assets and net income.

Answers: **1.** conceptual framework **2.** building blocks **3.** relevance; reliability **4.** comparability; consistency **5.** predictive value; feedback value; timeliness **6.** verifiability; neutrality; faithfulness **7.** neutrality **8.** faithful **9.** consistency **10.** assets **11.** liabilities **12.** equity **13.** assets; liabilities **14.** assets; liabilities **15.** gains; losses **16.** economic entity **17.** going concern **18.** net realizable value **19.** monetary unit **20.** historical cost **21.** realized; earned **22.** matching **23.** materiality **24.** conservatism

Solved Problems

4.1   Following is a list of the qualitative characteristics of accounting discussed in this chapter:

1.	Relevance	6.	Verifiability
2.	Reliability	7.	Neutrality
3.	Predictive value	8.	Representational faithfulness
4.	Timeliness	9.	Comparability
5.	Feedback value	10.	Consistency

Match these characteristics with the following information:

(*a*)   Makes statements of one company comparable to another company

(*b*)   One of the ingredients of this characteristic is feedback value

(*c*)   Prohibits changing accounting methods arbitrarily from year to year

(*d*)   An ingredient of this characteristic is verifiability

(*e*)   Prohibits the selection of information favoring one party over another

(*f*)   Helps the user predict future outcomes

(*g*)   Helps the user confirm or correct prior expectations

(*h*)   Requires the numbers of the statements to be accurate

(*i*)   Requires information to be available before it becomes obsolete

(*j*)   Enables several independent evaluators of the statements to arrive at the same conclusions

SOLUTION

(*a*)	9	(*d*)	2	(*g*)	5	(*j*)	6
(*b*)	1	(*e*)	7	(*h*)	8		
(*c*)	10	(*f*)	3	(*i*)	4		[Section 4.2]

4.2   Match the following financial statement elements with the definitions provided below

1.	Assets	4.	Owner investments	7.	Expenses
2.	Liabilities	5.	Distribution to owners	8.	Gains
3.	Equity	6.	Revenues	9.	Losses

(a) Increases in assets from peripheral transactions
(b) Increases in liabilities from central operations
(c) Assets minus liabilities
(d) Contribution of cash by stockholders
(e) Withdrawals of merchandise

SOLUTION

(a) 8   (d) 4
(b) 7   (e) 5
(c) 3   [Section 4.3]

4.3   Match the following information with the elements listed in Problem 4.2.

(a) Future economic benefits
(b) Decreases in liabilities from peripheral transactions
(c) Increases in assets from central operations
(d) Cash dividends paid
(e) Obligations to transfer assets in the future
(f) Net assets
(g) Decreases in assets arising from central operations
(h) Decreases in assets arising from peripheral operations

SOLUTION

(a) 1   (d) 5   (g) 7
(b) 8   (e) 2   (h) 9
(c) 6   (f) 3   [Section 4.3]

4.4   Identify accounting assumption, principle, or constraint associated with each of the following definitions and statements.

(a) Accounting information can be broken into time units of a year, a half-year, or a quarter-year.
(b) "Let the expenses follow the revenue."
(c) The gold industry values its inventories at net realizable value.
(d) The owner's assets are not mixed with the company's assets.
(e) Revenue on services is recognized when the services are performed.
(f) Statements should disclose everything of sufficient importance to the user.

SOLUTION

(a) Periodicity assumption   (d) Economic entity assumption
(b) Matching principle   (e) Revenue recognition principle
(c) Industry practice constraint   (f) Full disclosure principle   [Sections 4.4, 4.5]

4.5   Identify the accounting assumption, principle, or constraint associated with each of the following statements.

(a) Money is the best way of expressing accounting information.

(b) If unsure which accounting method is appropriate, choose the one that understates assets.

(c) Assets should not be increased to reflect higher market values.

(d) Companies are expected to continue indefinitely.

(e) Information may be omitted if this would not change the impressions of the user.

(f) Bad debts are recognized in the year of the sale rather than when they actually take place.

SOLUTION

(a) Monetary unit assumption

(b) Conservatism constraint

(c) Historical cost principle

(d) Going concern assumption

(e) Materiality constraint

(f) Matching principle [Sections 4.4, 4.5]

4.6 Discuss the appropriateness of each of the following situations in terms of accounting assumptions, principles, and constraints.

(a) Company K got a good deal on a machine. The market value was $5,000; it paid only $4,000. The entry it made was:

Machine	5,000	
Cash		4,000
Gain on Purchase		1,000

(b) Company L bought a car solely for the personal use of its president. The entry was:

Car Expense	10,000	
Cash		10,000

(c) Goods originally costing $800 and recorded as such have gone up in value by $300. The following entry was therefore made:

Merchandise Inventory	300	
Income		300

(d) Company M uses the direct write-off method for bad debts. When a $500 receivable became bad, the entry was:

Bad Debts Expense	500	
Accounts Receivable		500

SOLUTION

(a) This violates the historical cost principle and the revenue recognition principle.

(b) By definition, this is an owner withdrawal rather than an expense.

(c) This violates the revenue recognition principle.

(d) This violates the matching principle. [Sections 4.3, 4.4]

4.7 Discuss the appropriateness of each of the following in terms of accounting principles and assumptions.

(a) Company N purchased a $5 wastebasket with an estimated 5-year life and depreciated the entire cost over just 1 year.

(b) Company P purchased a brand new truck and depreciated it over just 1 year.

(c) The owner of Company R purchased a house from personal funds for personal use. The entry was:

House	80,000	
Capital		80,000

(d) Company S, a thriving concern, wrote its buildings down to liquidation values.

(e) Company T sold goods to Company V with terms of F.O.B. shipping point. As soon as the goods were shipped, Company T made the following entry:

Accounts Receivable	1,000	
Sales		1,000

SOLUTION

(a) Since the amount involved is not material, this procedure was appropriate.

(b) This violates the matching principle.

(c) This violates the entity assumption.

(d) This violates the going concern assumption.

(e) This is correct.   [Sections 4.3, 4.4]

Chapter 5

The Time Value of Money

5.1 INTRODUCTION

The concept of the time value of money plays a very important role in accounting. According to generally accepted accounting principles (GAAP), assets and liabilities must be presented on the balance sheet at their "present values." Long-term notes receivable and payable, leases, pensions, and amortization of bond premiums and discounts all must take into consideration the value of time. If they do not, they violate GAAP.

What exactly do we mean by the "time value of money" and "present value"? This chapter answers these questions by presenting a detailed description of these concepts together with practical examples.

To begin with, the time value of money involves interest calculations. There are two types of interest: simple interest and compound interest. Under *simple interest*, interest is earned only on the principal; under *compound interest*, interest is earned on the interest as well as on the principal. We will assume the use of compound interest throughout this book, since that is the way it is done in the "real world."

The actual computation of future and present values is done through the use of complex formulas. We will not need to apply these formulas, since interest tables exist that quickly and easily provide the amounts. These tables are presented at the end of this chapter. The tables are:

Table 1. Future Value of $1

Table 2. Present Value of $1

Table 3. Future Value of an Ordinary Annuity of $1

Table 4. Present Value of an Ordinary Annuity of $1

We shall now examine each of these tables and see how they are used.

5.2 THE FUTURE VALUE OF $1

Table 1 answers the following question: "If I deposit $1 today in the bank (or in some other investment), how much will it be worth in the future?" Naturally, it will be worth more than $1 because of the interest factor. But exactly how much will it be worth? Table 1 gives us the answer very quickly. The left-hand column specifies the number of periods involved, while the remaining columns specify the interest rate.

EXAMPLE 1

If I deposit $1 today for 6 years and the interest rate is 5% compounded annually, the table tells us that this will grow into 1.340 ($1.34) in 6 years.

Naturally, nobody makes deposits of just $1. Although this table deals only with $1 deposits, we can easily adapt it for any deposit by simply multiplying the table value by the amount of the deposit.

EXAMPLE 2

If I deposit $1,000 for 10 years and the rate is 10% compounded annually, the table yields a value of 2.594. Multiplying this by the deposit of $1,000 yields a future value of $2,594.

In the previous examples, the interest was compounded annually. However, if it is compounded semiannually, we must look up half the rate in the table and double the number of periods. Notice that the table does not use the word *years*; it uses *periods*.

EXAMPLE 3

If I deposit $1,000 for 10 years and the rate is 10% compounded semiannually, I must look up 5% for 20 periods in the table; the table value is 2.653. Multiplying this by $1,000 results in $2,653 for the future value.

If the compounding is quarterly, then we must look up one-fourth the rate in the table and quadruple the number of periods.

EXAMPLE 4

If a deposit of $1,000 for 10 years at the rate of 12% is compounded quarterly, find the table value at the 3% mark for 40 periods; the table value is 3.262. Multiplying this by $1,000 yields $3,262.

Notice from the above examples that the rate is always given on an annual basis. This must then be converted to one-half or one-quarter if the compounding is not on an annual basis.

5.3   THE PRESENT VALUE OF $1

The present value of $1 answers the following question: "How much do I have to deposit today to receive $1 in the future?" This is the opposite side of the coin of the future value of 1. There the question was what will be the amount of the future withdrawal. Here the question is what is the amount of the present deposit.

To answer this question we use Table 2.

EXAMPLE 5

If I wish to withdraw $8,000 seven years from now and the interest rate is 12% compounded annually, Table 2 yields a value of 0.452; multiplying this by $8,000 yields $3,616. This means that to receive $8,000 seven years from now, I must deposit $3,616 today.

EXAMPLE 6

Using the same facts as in Example 5 except that the 12% rate is compounded quarterly requires that we look up the table for 28 periods at 3% (12% ÷ 4). The table value is 0.437; multiplying this by $8,000 yields $3,496 for today's deposit.

The concepts of the future amount of $1 and the present amount of $1 can also be used to answer other questions, such as the number of periods needed to accumulate a certain sum, or what interest rate to invest at.

EXAMPLE 7

If I deposit $21,545 today, how many years will it take to grow into $90,000 (with which I intend to purchase a summer cabin), assuming that the rate of interest is 10% compounded annually? This problem can be solved with either Table 1 or Table 2. Let's first use Table 1. We know that $21,545 multiplied by some table value (which we will call X) should yield $90,000. Thus,

$$\$21,545X = \$90,000$$
$$X = 4.17730$$

Looking at Table 1 in the 10% column, we find at the 15-period mark a value that is very close to 4.17730 (4.177). Therefore, the answer is approximately 15 years.

We can also use Table 2 for this problem. In this case, however, the equation has to be set up in reverse:

$$\$90{,}000X = \$21{,}545$$
$$X = 0.23939$$

Looking at Table 2 in the 10% column for 0.23939 yields the same answer of 15 years.

EXAMPLE 8

What rate of interest is needed for a deposit today of $42,241 to grow into $100,000 in 10 years assuming annual compounding?
Using Table 1,

$$\$42{,}241X = \$100{,}000$$
$$X = 2.36737$$

Searching horizontally across Table 1 at the 10-year mark yields a rate of approximately 9%.

5.4 THE FUTURE VALUE OF AN ANNUITY OF $1

The future value of an annuity of $1 answers the following question: "If I make a series of equal deposits of $1 each over several periods, how much will they accumulate to in the future?" Notice the key difference between this situation and the two previous situations. In the previous situations, I made just one deposit; here I am making a series of deposits.

There are two types of annuities: ordinary annuities and annuities due. In the case of an *ordinary annuity*, the deposits are made at the end of each interest period; in the case of an *annuity due*, they are made at the beginning of each interest period. In other words, for ordinary annuities, the deposits begin one period into the future, while for annuities due, they begin immediately today.

EXAMPLE 9

If today is January 1, 19X7, and I plan to make a series of three deposits over the next 3 years with each deposit being made at the end of each year (December 31, 19X7, December 31, 19X8, December 31, 19X9), this is an example of an ordinary annuity. Notice that the deposits do not begin immediately.

However, if each deposit will be made at the beginning of the year (January 1, 19X7, January 1, 19X8, January 1, 19X9), then we are dealing with an annuity due. Notice that the deposits begin right away.

In both cases the withdrawal takes place on December 31, 19X9. In the first case, therefore, the last deposit is made and withdrawn on the same day.

To find the future value of an ordinary annuity, we use Table 3.

EXAMPLE 10

If I make a series of $5,000 deposits at the end of each of the next 5 years and the interest rate is 12% compounded annually, the future value of these deposits will be:

$$\begin{array}{r} 6.353 \quad \text{(5 deposits, 12\%)} \\ \times \$\ 5{,}000 \\ \hline \$31{,}765 \end{array}$$

EXAMPLE 11

Assume that I plan to make a series of $1,000 deposits at the end of each 6-month period for the next 5 years and interest is 12% compounded semiannually. In this case, the total number of deposits will be 10 (two per year for 5 years), and each interest period earns 6% ($12\% \times \frac{1}{2}$).

The table value at 10 deposits and 6% is 13.181. Multiplying this by $1,000 yields a future value of $13,181.

Using some elementary algebra, the table can also be used to calculate the value of each deposit, or the number of deposits that need to be made.

EXAMPLE 12

If I wish to accumulate $20,000 five years from now (in order to make a down payment on a Mercedes) by making a series of deposits at the end of every 3 months, and the interest rate is 12% compounded quarterly, the amount of each deposit can be computed as follows.

The rate per period is 3%, and the number of deposits is 20 (four deposits per year for 5 years). Looking at Table 3 at 20 periods and 3% yields a value of 26.87. Let's call the amount of each deposit X. Then

$$26.870X = \$20,000$$
$$X = \$744.32 \qquad \text{(rounded)}$$

Therefore, if $744.32 is deposited every 3 months for 5 years, the result will be a total of $20,000.

EXAMPLE 13

Suppose that the future desired value is $117,332, the annual deposits are $20,000 each at the end of each year, and interest is compounded annually at 8%. How many deposits have to be made?

Let X = table value. Therefore,

$$\$20,000X = \$117,332$$
$$X = 5.867 \qquad \text{(rounded)}$$

Looking at the table in the 8% column for 5.867 yields five deposits.

Table 3 will work only for an ordinary annuity. It cannot be used directly for an annuity due. However, by using a conversion formula, we can adapt the table value and then use it for an annuity due. The formula involves two steps:

Step 1. Look up the table for one additional deposit.

Step 2. Take this value, subtract 1 from it, and then proceed as if you were calculating an ordinary annuity.

EXAMPLE 14

To find the future value of an annuity due of 10 deposits of $1,000 each, with a 10% rate compounded annually, we would look up the table for 11 deposits and find:

	18.531
Subtract 1	− 1.000
	17.531
Multiply by $1,000	× 1,000
Yielding a future value of	$17,531

5.5   THE PRESENT VALUE OF AN ANNUITY OF $1

The present value of an annuity of $1 answers the following question: "How much do I have to deposit today to be able to make several equal withdrawals, of $1 each, over equal periods, in the future?" Note carefully the difference between this and the future value of an annuity. In that situation there were several deposits and one withdrawal. In this situation there is one deposit and several withdrawals.

Once again, we have two types of annuities: ordinary annuities and annuities due. In the former case the first withdrawal is made one period after the deposit, while in the latter case it is made immediately (i.e., right after the deposit is made).

EXAMPLE 15

If today, January 1, 19X7, I made one big deposit with the intention of making three withdrawals starting one period after today (December 31, 19X7, December 31, 19X8, December 31, 19X9), then it is an ordinary annuity situation.

However, if the first withdrawal takes place immediately (i.e., the withdrawal dates are January 1, 19X7, January 1, 19X8, January 1, 19X9), then it is an annuity due.

For the ordinary annuity, we use Table 4. For the annuity due, however, we must adapt Table 4 by the following conversion formula:

Step 1. Look up the table for one less withdrawal.

Step 2. Add 1 to that value, and then proceed as if you were calculating an ordinary annuity.

EXAMPLE 16

How much must one deposit now to be able to withdraw $1,000 per year at the end of each of the next 5 years if the interest rate is 14%? Since the first withdrawal does not take place immediately, this is an ordinary annuity. Table 4 shows a value of

$$
\begin{array}{ll}
3,433 & \text{for 5 periods, 14\%} \\
\underline{\times \$1,000} & \\
\$3,433 & \text{is the present value}
\end{array}
$$

EXAMPLE 17

Assume the same facts as in Example 16 except that the first withdrawal takes place immediately. This is an annuity due. Looking up four withdrawals in the table yields:

$$
\begin{array}{ll}
& 2.914 \\
\text{Add 1} & \underline{1.000} \\
& 3.914 \\
& \underline{\times \$1,000} \\
& \$3,914 \qquad \text{is the present value}
\end{array}
$$

Table 4 can also be used to determine the interest rate.

EXAMPLE 18

Assume that you owe $634.52 on your credit card and you have a choice of either paying it now or paying $60 a month for 12 months, starting at the end of the first month. You wish to determine the interest rate involved. The calculation is:

$$
\begin{array}{l}
60X = \$634.52 \\
X = 10.575 \qquad \text{(rounded)}
\end{array}
$$

Searching through Table 4 for this amount brings you to the 2% column. This is the rate per month. On a yearly basis the rate is 24% (2% × 12).

5.6   INTERPOLATION OF INTEREST TABLES

Thus far, when we used an algebraic equation to help us find a table value, we were lucky to be able to find approximately that value in the table. But this is not always the case. Sometimes the result will be between two table values, and a technique called *interpolation* must be used to calculate the exact value.

EXAMPLE 19

Assume that we deposit $1,000 today and it accumulates to $2,900 after 20 years. We wish to know the annual rate of interest being earned. Using the method discussed previously, we have

$$
\begin{array}{l}
\$1,000X = \$2,900 \\
X = 2.900
\end{array}
$$

Searching through Table 1 at the 20-period mark, we do not find precisely 2.900. However, we find 2.653 at the 5% mark and 3.207 at the 6% mark. We therefore conclude that the rate is between 5% and 6%. But if we want more precision, we must interpolate, and that is done as follows:

Let's call the actual rate i, and let's call the difference between i and 5%, d. Now we set up a table showing all these relationships:

Rate	Table Value
5%	2.653
i	2.900
6%	3.207

The difference between 5% and 6% is 1%.

The difference between 5% and i is d.

The difference between 2.653 and 3.207 is 0.554

The difference between 2.653 and 2.900 is 0.247

We now express these differences as a proportion:

$$\frac{1\%}{d} = \frac{0.554}{0.247}$$

Cross-multiplication yields

$$0.554d = 0.00247$$
$$d = 0.0044$$

Since $i = 5\% + d$, by substitution we get:

$$i = 5\% + 0.0044$$
$$= 0.0544$$
$$= 5.44\%$$

Summary

1. Under generally accepted accounting principles, the reporting of assets and liabilities must take into account the concept of interest. In this chapter we discuss four interest concepts: the future value of $1, the present value of $1, the future value of an annuity of $1, and the present value of an annuity of $1.

2. The *future value of $1* answers the following question: "If I deposit $1 today, how much will it be worth in the future?" To answer this question, we use Table 1.

3. The *present value of $1* answers a different question. That question is: "How much must I deposit today in order to receive $1 in the future?" For this we use Table 2.

4. An *annuity* is a series—either of deposits or of withdrawals. The future value of an annuity of $1 deals with a series of *deposits* and answers the following question: "If I make a series of $1 deposits over several equal periods, how much will they accumulate to in the future?"

5. The present value of an annuity of $1 deals with a series of *withdrawals*, and answers the following question: "How much do I have to deposit today to be able to make several withdrawals, of $1 each, over equal periods in the future?"

6. The interest tables deal with deposits and withdrawals of just $1 each. Naturally, nobody deposits and withdraws in such small amounts. Nevertheless, by using multiplication we can adapt the table for any amount.

7. Annuities come in two forms: ordinary annuities and annuities due. For an *ordinary annuity*, the series of deposits or withdrawals begins one period from today; for an *annuity due*, it begins immediately.

8. The annuity tables presented in this chapter are for ordinary annuities, but they can be adapted to annuity due situations by the use of conversion formulas. To adapt the future value of annuity table for annuity due situations, take the following steps:

   1. Look up the table for one additional deposit.
   2. Subtract 1.00 from this table value.

9. To adapt the present value of ordinary annuity table to an annuity due situation, take the following steps:

   1. Look up the table for one less payment.
   2. Add 1.00 to this table value.

10. The concepts of future and present value can also be used to answer other questions, such as the number of periods needed to accumulate a certain sum, or what interest rate to invest at.

11. A technique called *interpolation* is used when an algebraic equation provides a result that is between two table values.

Rapid Review

1. If I make one deposit today and wish to know how much it will accumulate to in the future, that value is called _____.

2. If I want to know how much to deposit today in order to be able to make a certain one-time withdrawal in the future, today's deposit is called _____.

3. The concept of making a series of deposits for the purpose of making one withdrawal at the end is called _____.

4. Making one deposit today in order to be able to make several withdrawals later is called _____.

5. If the interest rate is 10% compounded semiannually and deposits will be made for 10 years, then the table should be looked up at the _____ rate and at the _____ period mark.

6. If the rate is 16% compounded quarterly and deposits will be made for 5 years, the table rate is _____ and the number of periods is _____.

7. If the first deposit of an annuity is made after one period goes by, it is called an _____.

8. If the first deposit of an annuity is made immediately, it is called an _____.

9. The conversion formula for Table 3 requires looking up the table for _____ period(s) and then _____ 1.000.

10. The process of finding a precise value that lies between two table values is called _____.

Answers: **1.** the future value of $1 **2.** the present value of $1 **3.** the future value of an annuity of $1 **4.** the present value of $1 **5.** 5%; 20 **6.** 4%; 20 **7.** ordinary annuity **8.** annuity due **9.** one extra; subtracting **10.** interpolation

Solved Problems

5.1 For each of the following cases, indicate what interest rate and number of periods should be looked up in a table for the future value of $1:

(*a*) 10%, 10 years, compounded annually

(*b*) 12%, 10 years, compounded semiannually

(*c*) 16%, 8 years, compounded quarterly

SOLUTION

(*a*) 10%, 10 periods

(*b*) 6%, 20 periods

(*c*) 4%, 32 periods   [Section 5.2]

5.2 Buck Greenfield deposited $13,000 in a money market account that provides interest at 8% compounded quarterly. How much will he have after 3 years?

SOLUTION

Since we want to know the future value of $1, we use Table 1.

At 2%, 12 periods	1.268
	× $13,000
Future value	$16,484

[Section 5.2]

5.3 If I invest $2,000 at 10% compounded annually, how much will I have after 10 years?

SOLUTION

Again referring to Table 1, we get

At 10%, 10 periods	2.594
	× $2,000
Future value	$5,188

[Section 5.2]

5.4 Paula Hirsch will receive $20,000 four years from now from a trust fund established by her rich uncle. Assuming that the rate is 10% compounded semiannually, how much must her uncle deposit today?

SOLUTION

We want to find the present value of $1 and therefore must use Table 2.

At 5%, 8 periods	0.677	
	× $20,000	
Present value	$13,540	[Section 5.3]

5.5 What is the present value of $3,000 due in 6 periods, discounted at 12%?

SOLUTION

The word *discounted* is often used in accounting and simply menas ''at an interest rate.'' Using Table 2, we get:

At 12%, 6 periods	0.507	
	× $3,000	
Present value	$1,521	[Section 5.3]

5.6 If a series of deposits of $8,000 each is made at the end of each period for the next 10 periods at 8%, what will be the total accumulation?

SOLUTION

Since we are dealing with a series, this is an annuity situation. Because this question involves the future, and the deposits are made at the end of each period, we use Table 3 (future value of an ordinary annuity). According to the table:

8%, 10 periods	14.487	
	× $8,000	
Future value	$115,896	[Section 5.4]

5.7 What is the future value of 10 deposits of $2,000 each made at the beginning of each period, if the rate is 10%?

SOLUTION

This, again, involves determining the future value of an annuity. However, since the deposits are made at the beginning of each period, it is an annuity due and we must use the conversion formula on the value listed in Table 3. In the table, we look up the value for 11 deposits and 10%.

	18.531	
Subtract 1	− 1.000	
	17.531	
	× $2,000	
Future value	$35,062	[Section 5.4]

5.8   What is the future value of $3,000 deposited quarterly for the next 3 years, if the interest rate is 12% compounded quarterly? Assume that the deposits are made at the beginning of each quarter.

SOLUTION

This again is a future value of an annuity due, with a rate of 3% and 12 deposits. We check the table for 13 deposits:

$$
\begin{array}{r}
15.618 \\
-\ \ 1.000 \\
\hline
14.618 \\
\times\ \$3,000 \\
\hline
\end{array}
$$

Future value $43,854   [Section 5.4]

5.9   What is the present value of $4,000 to be received at the end of each of the next 16 periods and discounted at 12%?

SOLUTION

This is a present value of an ordinary annuity; hence, we use Table 4.

$$
\begin{array}{r}
6.974 \\
\times\ \$4,000 \\
\hline
\end{array}
$$

Present value $27,896   [Section 5.5]

5.10   Assume the same information as in Problem 5.9, except that the withdrawals will be made at the beginning of each period. What is the present value?

SOLUTION

Since this is an annuity due, we must apply the conversion formula to Table 4, by looking at one less period and adding 1.

At 15 periods and 12%
$$
\begin{array}{r}
6.811 \\
+1.000 \\
\hline
7.811 \\
\times\ \$4,000 \\
\hline
\end{array}
$$

Present value $31,244   [Section 5.5]

5.11   If I deposit $1,845 today at 10% interest compounded annually, how many years will it take for it to accumulate to $20,000?

SOLUTION

Using Table 1 and letting X = the table value:

$$\$1,845X = \$20,000$$
$$X = 10.8401$$

Searching through the table at 10% yields approximately 25 years.   [Section 5.2]

5.12 If I deposit $25,331 at annual compounding for 6 years, and this results in $50,000, what is the interest rate?

SOLUTION

Using the value listed in Table 1, we get:

$$\$25,331X = \$50,000$$
$$X = 1.97386$$

This yields approximately 12% in the row for 6 years.   [Section 5.2]

5.13 If a deposit of $18,000 results in $36,000 after 6 periods, what is the rate?

SOLUTION

Again, we use Table 1:

$$\$18,000X = \$36,000$$
$$X = 2.0$$

We must interpolate:

12%	1.974
i	2.0000
14%	2.195

where i is the rate, d is the difference between 12% and i, 2% is the difference between 12% and 14%, and 0.221 is the difference between the table values at 12% and 14%.

$$\frac{2\%}{d} = \frac{0.221}{0.026}$$
$$0.221d = 0.00052$$
$$d = 0.0024$$
$$i = 12\% + d$$
$$= 0.1224$$
$$= 12.24\%$$ [Sections 5.2, 5.6]

5.14 How much do I have to deposit each year for the next 7 years if the rate is 8%, the deposits are made at the end of each year, and I wish to accumulate $200,000?

SOLUTION

Here we have several deposits and one withdrawal, making this a future value of an annuity. Since the deposits are at the end of each year, it is an ordinary annuity and we use Table 3:

$$8.923X = 200,000$$
$$X = \$22,414 \qquad \text{deposited each year (rounded)} \qquad \text{[Section 5.4]}$$

5.15 Assume the same facts as in Problem 5.14 except that it is an annuity due. How much must be deposited each year?

SOLUTION

Using the conversion formula and 8 years, we refer to Table 3.

$$10.6370$$
$$\underline{-1.0000}$$
$$9.6370$$

$$9.637X = \$200,000$$
$$X = \$20,753 \quad \text{deposited each year (rounded)} \qquad \text{[Section 5.4]}$$

5.16   If a bank lends me $61,940 today and I have to pay back $10,000 at the end of each year for the next 12 years, what interest rate am I paying?

SOLUTION

This is a present value of an (ordinary) annuity, because the bank is making one ''deposit'' (by lending me $61,940) and several ''withdrawals'' (by my paying the bank $10,000 each year). We use the values listed in Table 4 to calculate the interest rate:

$$\$10,000X = \$61,940$$
$$X = 6.194$$

Searching the table for 6.194 at the 12-period mark yields 12%. 　　　　　　　　　　　　　[Section 5.5]

5.17   Greco Corporation owes $600,000. It has a choice of paying the $600,000 now or paying $100,000 at the end of each of the next 10 years. The interest rate is 9%. Which method of payment should Greco Corporation use?

SOLUTION

We must compare the present value of each method and choose the lower one. Using Table 4, the present value of an ordinary annuity at 10 years and 9% is $641,800 (6.418 × $100,000).

The present value of paying $600,000 now is, naturally, $600,000.

Therefore the company should pay $600,000 now. 　　　　　　　　　　　　　[Section 5.5]

5.18   On June 1, 19X8, Berel Wenger borrowed $50,000 from his girlfriend, promising to pay her in 10 equal annual installments of $6,000, starting on June 1, 19X9. What is the rate of interest?

SOLUTION

Here we have one big deposit ($50,000) and several withdrawals ($6,000 each), making this a present value of an annuity. Since the payments are being made at the end of each period, it is an ordinary annuity, and we use Table 4:

$$\$6,000X = \$50,000$$
$$X = 8.333$$

We must interpolate:

3%	8.530
i	8.333
4%	8.111

Then

$$\frac{1\%}{d} = \frac{0.419}{0.197}$$
$$0.419d = 0.002$$
$$d = 0.005$$
$$i = 3\% + d$$
$$= 3\% + 0.00469$$
$$= 0.035$$
$$= 3.5\%$$ [Section 5.6]

Supplementary Problems

5.19 For each of the following cases involving the future value of $1, determine the interest rate and the number of periods.

(*a*) 14%, 12 years, compounded semiannually

(*b*) 8%, 6 years, compounded quarterly

(*c*) 9%, 7 years, compounded annually

(*d*) 15%, 5 years, compounded every third of a year

5.20 Buck Greenfield deposited $10,000 in a savings account that earns 10% compounded semiannually. How much will he have after 5 years?

5.21 Esther Englard deposited $20,000 in a certificate of deposit maturing in 7 years. The interest rate is 8% compounded quarterly. How much will she have at the end?

5.22 Avrohom Englard deposited $20,000 in a savings account paying 12% compounded every 4 months. How much will he have after 12 years?

5.23 Eli Englard wants to receive $50,000 ten years from now. If the interest rate is 10% compounded semiannually, how much must he deposit today?

5.24 What is the present value of $30,000 due in 7 years, if the interest rate is 16% compounded quarterly?

5.25 Today is January 1, 19X1. Sarah Englard makes a series of five $20,000 annual deposits starting January 1, 19X2. The interest rate is 12%, compounded annually.

(*a*) Is this an annuity situation?

(*b*) If it is, does it involve the future value of an annuity, or the present value? Is it an ordinary annuity or an annuity due?

(*c*) What will the total accumulation be at the end?

5.26 Assume the same information as in Problem 5.25, except that the deposits begin immediately. Answer parts (*a*), (*b*), and (*c*) of Problem 5.25.

5.27   If I deposit $1,000 today at 8% interest compounded annually, how many years will it take me to accumulate $1,360?

5.28   If I deposit $20,000 today and leave the money untouched for 48 periods, what rate of interest must the fund earn for me to have $82,640 at the end?

5.29   What is the future value of $8,000 deposited quarterly for the next 6 years, if the interest rate is 12% compounded quarterly? Assume that the deposits begin immediately.

5.30   If the information is the same as in Problem 5.29, except that the deposits begin in one period from now, find the future value.

5.31   Esther Feiner wishes to receive $30,000 at the end of each of the next 10 years. Assume an annual rate of 10%.

   (*a*)   Is this the future value of annuity or the present value of annuity?

   (*b*)   Is it ordinary annuity or annuity due?

   (*c*)   How much must she deposit today?

5.32   Assume the same information as in Problem 5.31, except that withdrawals are to begin immediately. Answer parts (*a*), (*b*), and (*c*) of Problem 5.31.

5.33   How much do I have to deposit each year for the next 8 years if the interest rate is 10%, the deposits begin 1 year from now, and I wish to accumulate $11,436?

5.34   How many deposits must be made to accumulate $23,205 if each deposit is $5,000, and the interest rate is 10% per period? Assume an ordinary annuity.

5.35   If I deposit $83,840 today and the interest rate is 6% compounded annually, for how many periods will I be able to withdraw $10,000 per period? Assume an ordinary annuity.

5.36   If a deposit of $10,000 results in a $30,000 accumulation after 16 periods, what is the interest rate? Use interpolation.

TABLE 1 Future Value of $1

Periods	0.5%	1%	1.5%	2%	3%	4%	5%	6%	7%	8%	9%	10%	12%	14%	16%	18%	20%
1	1.005	1.010	1.015	1.020	1.030	1.040	1.050	1.060	1.070	1.080	1.090	1.100	1.120	1.140	1.160	1.180	1.200
2	1.010	1.020	1.030	1.040	1.061	1.082	1.103	1.124	1.145	1.166	1.188	1.210	1.254	1.300	1.346	1.392	1.440
3	1.015	1.030	1.046	1.061	1.093	1.125	1.158	1.191	1.225	1.260	1.295	1.331	1.405	1.482	1.561	1.643	1.728
4	1.020	1.041	1.061	1.082	1.126	1.170	1.216	1.262	1.311	1.360	1.412	1.464	1.574	1.689	1.811	1.939	2.074
5	1.025	1.051	1.077	1.104	1.159	1.217	1.276	1.338	1.403	1.469	1.539	1.611	1.762	1.925	2.100	2.288	2.488
6	1.030	1.062	1.093	1.126	1.194	1.265	1.340	1.419	1.501	1.587	1.677	1.772	1.974	2.195	2.436	2.700	2.986
7	1.036	1.072	1.110	1.149	1.230	1.316	1.407	1.504	1.606	1.714	1.828	1.949	2.211	2.502	2.826	3.185	3.583
8	1.041	1.083	1.126	1.172	1.267	1.369	1.477	1.594	1.718	1.851	1.993	2.144	2.476	2.853	3.278	3.759	4.300
9	1.046	1.094	1.143	1.195	1.305	1.423	1.551	1.689	1.838	1.999	2.172	2.358	2.773	3.252	3.803	4.435	5.160
10	1.051	1.105	1.161	1.219	1.344	1.480	1.629	1.791	1.967	2.159	2.367	2.594	3.106	3.707	4.411	5.234	6.192
11	1.056	1.116	1.178	1.243	1.384	1.539	1.710	1.898	2.105	2.332	2.580	2.853	3.479	4.226	5.117	6.176	7.430
12	1.062	1.127	1.196	1.268	1.426	1.601	1.796	2.012	2.252	2.518	2.813	3.138	3.896	4.818	5.936	7.288	8.916
13	1.067	1.138	1.214	1.294	1.469	1.665	1.886	2.133	2.410	2.720	3.066	3.452	4.363	5.492	6.886	8.599	10.699
14	1.072	1.149	1.232	1.319	1.513	1.732	1.980	2.261	2.579	2.937	3.342	3.797	4.887	6.261	7.988	10.147	12.839
15	1.078	1.161	1.250	1.346	1.558	1.801	2.079	2.397	2.759	3.172	3.642	4.177	5.474	7.138	9.266	11.974	15.407
16	1.083	1.173	1.269	1.373	1.605	1.873	2.183	2.540	2.952	3.426	3.970	4.595	6.130	8.137	10.748	14.129	18.488
18	1.094	1.196	1.307	1.428	1.702	2.026	2.407	2.854	3.380	3.996	4.717	5.560	7.690	10.575	14.463	19.673	26.623
20	1.105	1.220	1.347	1.486	1.806	2.191	2.653	3.207	3.870	4.661	5.604	6.727	9.646	13.743	19.461	27.393	38.338
22	1.116	1.245	1.388	1.546	1.916	2.370	2.925	3.604	4.430	5.437	6.659	8.140	12.100	17.861	26.186	38.142	55.206
24	1.127	1.270	1.430	1.608	2.033	2.563	3.225	4.049	5.072	6.341	7.911	9.850	15.179	23.212	35.236	53.109	79.497
26	1.138	1.295	1.473	1.673	2.157	2.772	3.556	4.549	5.807	7.396	9.399	11.918	19.040	30.167	47.414	73.949	114.475
28	1.150	1.321	1.517	1.741	2.288	2.999	3.920	5.112	6.649	8.627	11.167	14.421	23.884	39.204	63.800	102.967	164.845
30	1.161	1.348	1.563	1.811	2.427	3.243	4.322	5.743	7.612	10.063	13.268	17.449	29.960	50.950	85.850	143.371	237.376
32	1.173	1.375	1.610	1.885	2.575	3.508	4.765	6.453	8.715	11.737	15.763	21.114	37.582	66.215	115.520	199.629	341.822
34	1.185	1.403	1.659	1.961	2.732	3.794	5.253	7.251	9.978	13.690	18.728	25.548	47.143	86.053	155.443	277.964	492.224
36	1.197	1.431	1.709	2.040	2.898	4.104	5.792	8.147	11.424	15.968	22.251	30.913	59.136	111.834	209.164	387.037	708.802
40	1.221	1.489	1.814	2.208	3.262	4.801	7.040	10.286	14.974	21.725	31.409	45.259	93.051	188.884	378.721	750.378	1469.722
44	1.245	1.549	1.925	2.390	3.671	5.617	8.557	12.985	19.628	29.556	44.337	66.264	146.418	319.017	685.727	1454.817	3047.718
48	1.270	1.612	2.043	2.587	4.132	6.571	10.401	16.394	25.729	40.211	62.585	97.017	230.391	538.807	1241.605	2820.567	6319.749

Reprinted with the permission of the NAA.

TABLE 2　Present Value of $1

Periods	0.5%	1%	1.5%	2%	3%	4%	5%	6%	7%	8%	9%	10%	12%	14%	16%	18%	20%
1	0.995	0.990	0.985	0.980	0.971	0.962	0.952	0.943	0.935	0.926	0.917	0.909	0.893	0.877	0.862	0.847	0.833
2	0.990	0.980	0.971	0.961	0.943	0.925	0.907	0.890	0.873	0.857	0.842	0.826	0.797	0.769	0.743	0.718	0.694
3	0.985	0.971	0.956	0.942	0.915	0.889	0.864	0.840	0.816	0.794	0.772	0.751	0.712	0.675	0.641	0.609	0.579
4	0.980	0.961	0.942	0.924	0.888	0.855	0.823	0.792	0.763	0.735	0.708	0.683	0.636	0.592	0.552	0.516	0.482
5	0.975	0.951	0.928	0.906	0.863	0.822	0.784	0.747	0.713	0.681	0.650	0.621	0.567	0.519	0.476	0.437	0.402
6	0.971	0.942	0.915	0.888	0.837	0.790	0.746	0.705	0.666	0.630	0.596	0.564	0.507	0.456	0.410	0.370	0.335
7	0.966	0.933	0.901	0.871	0.813	0.760	0.711	0.665	0.623	0.583	0.547	0.513	0.452	0.400	0.354	0.314	0.279
8	0.961	0.923	0.888	0.853	0.789	0.731	0.677	0.627	0.582	0.540	0.502	0.467	0.404	0.351	0.305	0.266	0.233
9	0.956	0.914	0.875	0.837	0.766	0.703	0.645	0.592	0.544	0.500	0.460	0.424	0.361	0.308	0.263	0.225	0.194
10	0.951	0.905	0.862	0.820	0.744	0.676	0.614	0.558	0.508	0.463	0.422	0.386	0.322	0.270	0.227	0.191	0.162
11	0.947	0.896	0.849	0.804	0.722	0.650	0.585	0.527	0.475	0.429	0.388	0.350	0.287	0.237	0.195	0.162	0.135
12	0.942	0.887	0.836	0.788	0.701	0.625	0.557	0.497	0.444	0.397	0.356	0.319	0.257	0.208	0.168	0.137	0.112
13	0.937	0.879	0.824	0.773	0.681	0.601	0.530	0.469	0.415	0.368	0.326	0.290	0.229	0.182	0.145	0.116	0.093
14	0.933	0.870	0.812	0.758	0.661	0.577	0.505	0.442	0.388	0.340	0.299	0.263	0.205	0.160	0.125	0.099	0.078
15	0.928	0.861	0.800	0.743	0.642	0.555	0.481	0.417	0.362	0.315	0.275	0.239	0.183	0.140	0.108	0.084	0.065
16	0.923	0.853	0.788	0.728	0.623	0.534	0.458	0.394	0.339	0.292	0.252	0.218	0.163	0.123	0.093	0.071	0.054
18	0.914	0.836	0.765	0.700	0.587	0.494	0.416	0.350	0.296	0.250	0.212	0.180	0.130	0.095	0.069	0.051	0.038
20	0.905	0.820	0.742	0.673	0.554	0.456	0.377	0.312	0.258	0.215	0.178	0.149	0.104	0.073	0.051	0.037	0.026
22	0.896	0.803	0.721	0.647	0.522	0.422	0.342	0.278	0.226	0.184	0.150	0.123	0.083	0.056	0.038	0.026	0.018
24	0.887	0.788	0.700	0.622	0.492	0.390	0.310	0.247	0.197	0.158	0.126	0.102	0.066	0.043	0.028	0.019	0.013
26	0.878	0.772	0.679	0.598	0.464	0.361	0.281	0.220	0.172	0.135	0.106	0.084	0.053	0.033	0.021	0.014	0.009
28	0.870	0.757	0.659	0.574	0.437	0.333	0.255	0.196	0.150	0.116	0.090	0.069	0.042	0.026	0.016	0.010	0.006
30	0.861	0.742	0.640	0.552	0.412	0.308	0.231	0.174	0.131	0.099	0.075	0.057	0.033	0.020	0.012	0.007	0.004
32	0.852	0.727	0.621	0.531	0.388	0.285	0.210	0.155	0.115	0.085	0.063	0.047	0.027	0.015	0.009	0.005	0.003
34	0.844	0.713	0.603	0.510	0.366	0.264	0.190	0.138	0.100	0.073	0.053	0.039	0.021	0.012	0.006	0.004	0.002
36	0.836	0.699	0.585	0.490	0.345	0.244	0.173	0.123	0.088	0.063	0.045	0.032	0.017	0.009	0.005	0.003	0.001
40	0.819	0.672	0.551	0.453	0.307	0.208	0.142	0.097	0.067	0.046	0.032	0.022	0.011	0.005	0.003	0.001	0.001
44	0.803	0.645	0.519	0.418	0.272	0.178	0.117	0.077	0.051	0.034	0.023	0.015	0.007	0.003	0.001	0.001	<.001
48	0.787	0.620	0.489	0.387	0.242	0.152	0.096	0.061	0.039	0.025	0.016	0.010	0.004	0.002	0.001	<.001	<.001

Reprinted with the permission of the NAA.

TABLE 3 Future Value of an Ordinary Annuity of $1

Periods	0.5%	1%	1.5%	2%	3%	4%	5%	6%	7%	8%	9%	10%	12%	14%	16%	18%	20%
1	1.000	1.000	1.000	1.000	1.000	1.000	1.000	1.000	1.000	1.000	1.000	1.000	1.000	1.000	1.000	1.000	1.000
2	2.005	2.010	2.015	2.020	2.030	2.040	2.050	2.060	2.070	2.080	2.090	2.100	2.120	2.140	2.160	2.180	2.200
3	3.105	3.030	3.045	3.060	3.091	3.122	3.153	3.184	3.215	3.246	3.278	3.310	3.374	3.440	3.506	3.572	3.640
4	4.030	4.060	4.091	4.122	4.184	4.246	4.310	4.375	4.440	4.506	4.573	4.641	4.779	4.921	5.066	5.215	5.368
5	5.050	5.101	5.152	5.204	5.309	5.416	5.526	5.637	5.751	5.867	5.985	6.105	6.353	6.610	6.877	7.154	7.442
6	6.076	6.152	6.230	6.308	6.468	6.633	6.802	6.975	7.153	7.336	7.523	7.716	8.115	8.536	8.977	9.442	9.930
7	7.106	7.214	7.323	7.434	7.662	7.898	8.142	8.394	8.654	8.923	9.200	9.487	10.089	10.730	11.414	12.142	12.916
8	8.141	8.286	8.433	8.583	8.892	9.214	9.549	9.897	10.260	10.637	11.028	11.436	12.300	13.233	14.240	15.327	16.499
9	9.182	9.369	9.559	9.755	10.159	10.583	11.027	11.491	11.978	12.488	13.021	13.579	14.776	16.085	17.519	19.086	20.799
10	10.228	10.462	10.703	10.950	11.464	12.006	12.578	13.181	13.816	14.487	15.193	15.937	17.549	19.337	21.321	23.521	25.959
11	11.279	11.567	11.863	12.169	12.808	13.486	14.207	14.972	15.784	16.645	17.560	18.531	20.655	23.045	25.733	28.755	32.150
12	12.336	12.683	13.041	13.412	14.192	15.026	15.917	16.870	17.888	18.977	20.141	21.384	24.133	27.271	30.850	34.931	39.581
13	13.397	13.809	14.237	14.680	15.618	16.627	17.713	18.882	20.141	21.495	22.953	24.523	28.029	32.089	36.786	42.219	48.497
14	14.464	14.947	15.450	15.974	17.086	18.292	19.599	21.015	22.550	24.215	26.019	27.975	32.393	37.581	43.672	50.818	59.196
15	15.537	16.097	16.682	17.293	18.599	20.024	21.579	23.276	25.129	27.152	29.361	31.772	37.280	43.842	51.660	60.965	72.035
16	16.614	17.258	17.932	18.639	20.157	21.825	23.657	25.673	27.888	30.324	33.003	35.950	42.753	50.980	60.925	72.939	87.442
18	18.786	19.615	20.489	21.412	23.414	25.645	28.132	30.906	33.999	37.450	41.301	45.599	55.750	68.394	84.141	103.740	128.117
20	20.979	22.019	23.124	24.297	26.870	29.778	33.066	36.786	40.995	45.762	51.160	57.275	72.052	91.025	115.380	146.628	186.688
22	23.194	24.472	25.838	27.299	30.537	34.248	38.505	43.392	49.006	55.457	62.873	71.403	92.503	120.436	157.415	206.345	271.031
24	25.432	26.973	28.634	30.422	34.426	39.083	44.502	50.816	58.177	66.765	76.790	88.497	118.155	158.659	213.978	289.494	392.484
26	27.692	29.526	31.514	33.671	38.553	44.312	51.113	59.156	68.676	79.954	93.324	109.182	150.334	208.333	290.088	405.272	567.377
28	29.975	32.129	34.481	37.051	42.931	49.968	58.403	68.528	80.698	95.339	112.968	134.210	190.699	272.889	392.503	566.481	819.223
30	32.280	34.785	37.539	40.568	47.575	56.085	66.439	79.058	94.461	113.283	136.308	164.494	241.333	356.787	530.312	790.948	1181.882
32	34.609	37.494	40.688	44.227	52.503	62.701	75.299	90.890	110.218	134.214	164.037	201.138	304.848	465.820	715.747	1103.496	1704.109
34	36.961	40.258	43.933	48.034	57.730	69.858	85.067	104.184	128.259	158.627	196.982	245.477	384.521	607.520	965.270	1538.688	2456.118
36	39.336	43.077	47.276	51.994	63.276	77.598	95.836	119.121	148.913	187.102	236.125	299.127	484.463	791.673	1301.027	2144.649	3539.009
40	44.159	48.886	54.268	60.402	75.401	95.026	120.800	154.762	199.635	259.057	337.882	442.593	767.091	1342.025	2360.757	4163.213	7343.858
44	49.079	54.932	61.689	69.503	89.048	115.413	151.143	199.758	266.121	356.950	481.522	652.641	1211.813	2271.548	4279.546	8076.760	15233.592
48	54.098	61.223	69.565	79.354	104.408	139.263	188.025	256.565	353.270	490.132	684.280	960.172	1911.590	3841.475	7753.782	15664.259	31593.744

Reprinted with the permission of the NAA.

TABLE 4   Present Value of an Ordinary Annuity of $1

Periods	0.5%	1%	1.5%	2%	3%	4%	5%	6%	7%	8%	9%	10%	12%	14%	16%	18%	20%
1	0.995	0.990	0.985	0.980	0.971	0.962	0.952	0.943	0.935	0.926	0.917	0.909	0.893	0.877	0.862	0.847	0.833
2	1.985	1.970	1.956	1.942	1.913	1.886	1.859	1.833	1.808	1.783	1.759	1.736	1.690	1.647	1.605	1.566	1.528
3	2.970	2.941	2.912	2.884	2.829	2.775	2.723	2.673	2.624	2.577	2.531	2.487	2.402	2.322	2.246	2.174	2.106
4	3.950	3.902	3.854	3.808	3.717	3.630	3.546	3.465	3.387	3.312	3.240	3.170	3.037	2.914	2.798	2.690	2.589
5	4.926	4.853	4.783	4.713	4.580	4.452	4.329	4.212	4.100	3.993	3.890	3.791	3.605	3.433	3.274	3.127	2.991
6	5.896	5.795	5.697	5.601	5.417	5.242	5.076	4.917	4.767	4.623	4.486	4.355	4.111	3.889	3.685	3.498	3.326
7	6.862	6.728	6.598	6.472	6.230	6.002	5.786	5.582	5.389	5.206	5.033	4.868	4.564	4.288	4.039	3.812	3.605
8	7.823	7.652	7.486	7.325	7.020	6.733	6.463	6.210	5.971	5.747	5.535	5.335	4.968	4.639	4.344	4.078	3.837
9	8.779	8.566	8.361	8.162	7.786	7.435	7.108	6.802	6.515	6.247	5.995	5.759	5.328	4.946	4.607	4.303	4.031
10	9.730	9.471	9.222	8.983	8.530	8.111	7.722	7.360	7.024	6.710	6.418	6.145	5.650	5.216	4.833	4.494	4.192
11	10.677	10.368	10.071	9.787	9.253	8.760	8.306	7.887	7.499	7.139	6.805	6.495	5.937?	5.453	5.029	4.656	4.327
12	11.619	11.255	10.908	10.575	9.954	9.385	8.863	8.384	7.943	7.536	7.161	6.814	6.194	5.660	5.197	4.793	4.439
13	12.556	12.134	11.732	11.348	10.635	9.986	9.394	8.853	8.358	7.904	7.487	7.103	6.424	5.842	5.342	4.910	4.533
14	13.489	13.004	12.543	12.106	11.296	10.563	9.899	9.295	8.745	8.244	7.786	7.367	6.628	6.002	5.468	5.008	4.611
15	14.417	13.865	13.343	12.849	11.938	11.118	10.380	9.712	9.108	8.559	8.061	7.606	6.811	6.142	5.575	5.092	4.675
16	15.340	14.718	14.131	13.578	12.561	11.652	10.838	10.106	9.447	8.851	8.313	7.824	6.974	6.265	5.668	5.162	4.730
18	17.173	16.398	15.673	14.992	13.754	12.659	11.690	10.828	10.059	9.372	8.756	8.201	7.250	6.467	5.818	5.273	4.812
20	18.987	18.046	17.169	16.351	14.877	13.590	12.462	11.470	10.594	9.818	9.129	8.514	7.469	6.623	5.929	5.353	4.870
22	20.784	19.660	18.621	17.658	15.937	14.451	13.163	12.042	11.061	10.201	9.442	8.772	7.645	6.743	6.011	5.410	4.909
24	22.563	21.243	20.030	18.914	16.936	15.247	13.799	12.550	11.469	10.529	9.707	8.985	7.784	6.835	6.073	5.451	4.937
26	24.324	22.795	21.399	20.121	17.877	15.983	14.375	13.003	11.826	10.810	9.929	9.161	7.896	6.906	6.118	5.480	4.956
28	26.068	24.316	22.727	21.281	18.764	16.663	14.898	13.406	12.137	11.051	10.116	9.307	7.984	6.961	6.152	5.502	4.970
30	27.794	25.808	24.016	22.396	19.600	17.292	15.372	13.765	12.409	11.258	10.274	9.427	8.055	7.003	6.177	5.517	4.979
32	29.503	27.270	25.267	23.468	20.389	17.874	15.803	14.084	12.647	11.435	10.406	9.526	8.112	7.035	6.196	5.528	4.985
34	31.196	28.703	26.482	24.499	21.132	18.411	16.193	14.368	12.854	11.587	10.518	9.609	8.157	7.060	6.210	5.536	4.990
36	32.871	30.108	27.661	25.489	21.832	18.908	16.547	14.621	13.035	11.717	10.612	9.677	8.192	7.079	6.220	5.541	4.993
40	36.172	32.835	29.916	27.355	23.115	19.793	17.159	15.046	13.332	11.925	10.757	9.779	8.244	7.105	6.233	5.548	4.997
44	39.408	35.455	32.041	29.080	24.254	20.549	17.663	15.383	13.558	12.077	10.861	9.849	8.276	7.120	6.241	5.552	4.998
48	42.580	37.974	34.043	30.673	25.267	21.195	18.077	15.650	13.730	12.189	10.934	9.897	8.297	7.130	6.245	5.554	4.999

Reprinted with the permission of the NAA.

Chapter 6

Cash and Temporary Investments

6.1 DEFINITION OF CASH

Cash is generally a current asset, although—as we will soon see—it occasionally is classified as long-term. For an item to be recorded as "cash," it must be readily available for the payment of current obligations and be free from any contractual restrictions that limit its use.

Therefore, cash consists of coins, petty cash, currency, checking account balances, checks, money orders, certified checks, and bank checks. Savings account balances are considered cash even though banks have a legal right to demand notice before withdrawal, since they rarely exercise this right.

Money market funds and short-term certificates of deposit (CDs) should be classified not as cash but as short-term investments, since they usually contain restrictions or penalties on their early conversion to cash. However, money market funds that have checking account privileges without penalty are considered to be cash.

Postdated checks and IOUs should be considered as receivables; postage stamps are considered office supplies. The treatment of travel advances to employees depends on whether or not they must be repaid to the employer. If yes, they are receivables; if not, they should be considered as prepaid expenses.

Short-term, highly liquid investments that are *both* readily convertible to known amounts of cash *and* so close to maturity that they bear an insignificant risk of losing value due to changes in the marketplace are considered cash. Generally, only investments with original maturities of 3 months or less meet these criteria. Some companies classify these as cash; others place them under the caption "Cash and Cash Equivalents."

Some banks require their checking account customers to maintain a certain minimum balance in their accounts. These are referred to as *compensating balances*. Banks require this arrangement from customers to whom they have lent money, since it results in a higher effective interest rate than the stated rate.

The Securities and Exchange Commission (SEC) recommends that compensating balances held against short-term borrowings be stated separately in the current asset section, while those held against long-term borrowings be stated separately in the non-current asset (investments) section.

Cash that is restricted and cannot be used for regular operating needs should be segregated from unrestricted cash. Examples of this would be cash set aside for plant expansion or retirement of debt. If the cash is to be used within 1 year, it is classified as current; if not, it is classified as noncurrent.

Some banks offer overdraft privileges on their checking accounts. This means that if a customer writes a check in excess of the checking account balance, the bank will advance the required funds to "cover" the check, rather than have the check "bounce." Such advances are considered to be current liabilities.

If a company has a positive checking account balance in one bank and a negative balance (overdraft) in another, they may not be offset against each other but must be separately disclosed on the balance sheet. If both accounts are at the same bank, however, offsetting is permitted.

EXAMPLE 1

Feldbrand Corporation has a positive $500 checking account balance at Bank A and a negative $300 balance at Bank B. Its balance sheet would show a current asset (cash) of $500, and a current liability of $300. Offsetting the $300 against the $500 to yield a net of $200 is prohibited.

EXAMPLE 2

Poverty Corporation has a positive $150 balance in one checking account at Bank A and a negative $70 balance in another checking account, also at Bank A. It may offset the two and show the net amount of $80 as a current asset.

6.2 PETTY CASH

While most companies pay their bills by check, it is customary to keep a small cash fund on hand to cover minor expenditures that occasionally arise. This fund is referred to as the *petty cash fund*, and is administered by an employee called the *custodian* of the fund. Each time someone needs money from the fund, he or she goes to the custodian and fills out a receipt which states the date, the amount being disbursed, the reason for the disbursement, and to whom the money is being disbursed.

The following transactions are typical of petty cash funds:

1. *Establishment of the petty cash fund*—Cash is drawn out of the checking account and placed into the hands of the custodian. An entry is made at this time debiting Petty Cash and crediting Cash (cash in the bank).

2. *Usage of the fund*—Employees draw money out of the fund for various expenditures and fill out a petty cash receipt. No entry is made at this time (to require an entry each time cash is disbursed from the fund would be too time-consuming).

3. *Replenishment of the fund*—The fund is replenished when it reaches a low level, and an entry is made at this time to record the various expenditures, based on the petty cash receipts.

4. *Raising the fund level*—The fund level is raised above its originally established amount in order to handle a large volume of transactions. Once again, as was done originally, an entry is made debiting Petty Cash and crediting Cash.

These transactions are illustrated in the following example.

EXAMPLE 3

Petty Coat Corporation decides to establish a petty cash fund of $400. The entry is:

Petty Cash	400	
Cash (in bank)		400

During the first month of the fund's existence, employees draw cash from the fund for the following purposes:

Postage	$110	
Office Supplies	30	
Freight In	125	
Office Food	120	
Total	$385	Total cash remaining: $15

No entries were made for these disbursements; however, petty cash receipts were filled out. At this point, Petty Coat decides to replenish the fund to its original level of $400. The entry is:

Postage	110	
Office Supplies	30	
Freight In	125	
Office Food Expense	120	
Cash (in bank)		385

Notice that Petty Cash is neither credited at the time of disbursement nor debited at the time of replenishment. The only time we "touch" Petty Cash is when we originally establish the fund, and when we raise the fund level, as we will soon see.

Petty Coat now decides to raise the fund level from $400 to $500. The entry is:

Petty Cash	100	
Cash		100

If the petty cash fund balance is smaller or greater than what it should be, the difference goes to an account called Cash Short or Over. This account has a dual nature: If its balance is a debit, it is an expense account; if its balance is a credit, it is a revenue account.

EXAMPLE 4

A company's petty cash fund, which started out with a $700 balance, now contains $297. The petty cash receipts show that $170 was spent on food and $230 was spent on postage. Thus a total of $400 was spent altogether, which should leave a balance of $300 in the fund. Since the balance is only $297, we have a $3 *shortage*. The entry to replenish the fund is:

Cash Short or Over	3	
Postage Expense	230	
Food Expense	170	
Cash		403

The fund is now back to its $700 level.

EXAMPLE 5

During the next period the receipts show that $510 was spent on office supplies. The fund should now contain $190. However, when we count the fund, we find $200. We thus have an *overage* of $10. The replenishment entry is:

Office Supplies	510	
Cash		500
Cash Short or Over		10

The Cash Short or Over Account now appears as follows:

Cash Short or Over

3	10
	7 Bal.

Since the balance is a *credit*, it is considered revenue, and appears as such on the income statement.

EXAMPLE 6

At the end of its accounting period, Company P has the following T-account for Cash Short or Over:

Cash Short or Over

29	26
13	10
Bal. 6	

Since the balance is a debit, it appears on the income statement as an expense.

6.3 BANK RECONCILIATIONS

If you have a checking account, you know that once a month, the bank sends you a statement together with the cancelled checks that cleared during the month. The statement shows all the transactions that took place in the account during the month: beginning balance, deposits and other credits, withdrawals and other debits, and ending balance.

Very often the ending balance will not agree with your checkbook (or, for a business, with the Cash T-account). There are several possible reasons for this disparity.

1. *Outstanding checks*—checks that you wrote, which you subtracted on your books, but which have not yet cleared the bank. Thus the bank is unaware of them at this point.

2. *Deposits in transit*—deposits that you made which have not yet been received and recorded by the bank. This often occurs when you mail deposits to the bank, or place them in an overnight depository. Thus, while you are aware of these deposits, the bank is not.

3. *Special charges (debits)*—the bank charged your account for various reasons (service charges, bad checks, collection fees, etc.) and you were unaware of these charges until now and have thus not yet recorded them on your books.

4. *Special credits*—the bank increased your account for various reasons (collection of notes receivable, interest, etc.) and you were unaware of these transactions until now.

5. *Errors*—either you or the bank committed an error.

A *bank reconciliation* is a form that tries to reconcile the bank statement balance with the book balance in order to arrive at the correct, updated balance. Once this is done, special journal entries usually have to be made to bring the books up to date. Let's take a look at an example.

EXAMPLE 7

On November 30, 19XI, the Cash T-account (after all postings have been made) for Company AA shows a balance of $4,200. The bank statement, however, shows a balance of $5,000. After an examination of the bank statement, the books, and the returned checks, the accountant noted the following:

1. Check no. 482 for $1,200 and check no. 491 for $800 are still outstanding.

2. A check for $200 that was received from Mr. Poor has "bounced." It has been returned with the bank statement and marked "NSF," for "not sufficient funds." This check was in payment for services performed by us on account for Mr. Poor.

3. A deposit we made on November 29 for $3,000 does not appear on the bank statement.

4. The bank charged us a $10 service fee to handle the NSF check.

5. The bank also charged us a $15 monthly checking account fee.

6. Check no. 474 for $85 was mistakenly charged by the bank for only $58.

7. The bank collected a $2,000 note for us and deposited the proceeds into our account.

8. The checking account earned $30 interest during the month.

9. The bank mistakenly charged us for a check of $32 which we never wrote; it was written by Company AB.

The bank reconciliation appears as follows:

Company AA
Bank Reconciliation
November 30, 19X1

Balance per Bank Statement		$5,000	Balance per Books:	$4,200
Outstanding Checks			NSF Check	(200)[§]
No. 482	$1,200		Service Fee on NSF Check	(10)
No. 491	800	(2,000)*	Monthly Fee	(15)
Deposits in Transit		3,000[†]	Collection of Note	2,000
Error in Check No. 474;				
Difference of		(27)	Interest Earned	30
Check of Company AB Charged				
in Error to Us		32[‡]		
Adjusted Bank Balance		$6,005	Adjusted Book Balance	$6,005

*This amount must be subtracted because checks reduce the account balance and these checks have not yet been subtracted by the bank.

[†]The logic for deposits in transit is precisely the opposite of that for outstanding checks.

[‡]The bank never had a right to reduce our balance by this check, since we never wrote it. Therefore, we add it back.

[§]When we originally deposited this check, our balance went up. Now that the check has bounced, our balance goes down.

Once the bank reconciliation is done, it is necessary to prepare journal entries to update the books. Is it necessary to prepare entries for *every item* in the bank reconciliation? The answer is no. Entries are needed only for items on the *book* side of the reconciliation, not for those on the *bank* side. Items on the *book* side represent events that need to be recognized on the books but have not yet been recognized; thus entries are needed. Items on the *bank* side, however, represent events that either do not need to be recognized on the books, or have already been recognized. Therefore, no further entries are needed.

EXAMPLE 8

Let's go back to the previous example and prepare journal entries for the *book* side:
For the NSF check Mr. Poor gave us for services:

Accounts Receivable	200	
Cash		200

When Mr. Poor originally paid us, we debited Cash and credited Accounts Receivable. Now that the check has "bounced," we must reverse that entry.
For the service fee on the NSF check:

Bank Service Fees	10	
Cash		10

For the monthly checking fee:

Bank Service Fees	15	
Cash		15

For the collection of the note:

Cash	2,000	
Notes Receivable		2,000

For the interest earned:

Cash	30	
Interest Income		30

A different form of bank reconciliation, referred to as a *proof of cash* and often used by auditors, is discussed in Appendix 6A at the end of this chapter.

6.4 TEMPORARY INVESTMENTS: MARKETABLE EQUITY SECURITIES

Temporary investments consist of marketable equity securities (preferred and common stock) and marketable debt securities (government and corporate bonds). In order for an investment to be classified as temporary, it must meet both of the following conditions:

1. It must be readily marketable.
2. It must be intended for conversion into cash within 1 year or the operating cycle (whichever is longer).

Readily marketable means that the item can easily be sold. If the stock is not publicly held, there may exist only a limited market for its purchase, thus making it difficult to sell. If this is the case, condition 1 has not been met and the stock is not classified as a temporary investment.

When marketable equity securities are purchased, an asset account should be debited for the purchase price plus any broker's fees or taxes incurred in this transaction. Broker's fees and taxes are not expenses; they are an addition to the cost of the stock. When the stock is later sold, such fees are considered to be a reduction of the selling price. If the selling price is higher than the purchase price, the difference is a gain and it is credited to a gain account; if it is lower it is a loss and it is debited to a loss account.

EXAMPLE 9

A corporation buys 100 shares of IBM stock for a total price of $1,000 and pays a broker's fee of $100. It later sells these shares for $2,000 and pays a broker's fee of $200. Assume that the shares meet both of the above-mentioned conditions. The entries are:

Investment in Short-Term Equity Securities	1,100	
Cash		1,100
Cash	1,800*	
Investment in Short-Term Equity Securities		1,100
Gain on Sale of Securities		700

*$2,000 − $200.

EXAMPLE 10

If in Example 9 the selling price was $900 and the broker's fee was $90, there would be a loss of $290 [($900 − $90) − $1,100].

If dividends are received on short-term shares of stock, an entry is made debiting Cash and crediting Dividend Revenue.

At the end of the accounting period a comparison must be made between the cost of the stock portfolio and its market value. The procedures to be followed, as discussed in FASB *Statement No. 115*, are discussed in Appendix 6B at the end of this chapter.

6.5   TEMPORARY INVESTMENTS: MARKETABLE DEBT SECURITIES

Marketable debt securities are investments in bonds and other debt instruments that meet the two conditions mentioned earlier, namely:

1. They are readily marketable.
2. The intention is to sell them within 1 year or the operating cycle (whichever is longer).

If these securities are purchased above or below par, a discount or premium situation arises. The discount or premium should not be amortized, since the intention is to hold the securities for only a short time. Accordingly, the investment account is debited for the net amount paid, and no use is made of a discount or premium account.

EXAMPLE 11

A $100,000 bond is purchased as a short-term investment at 98 on January 1, 19XI. The entry is:

Investment in Short-Term Debt Securities	98,000	
Cash		98,000

Notice that the investment account is debited at the net price of $98,000 and no discount account is used. The $2,000 reduction from par is not amortized.

Since debt securities pay interest, an entry must be made crediting Interest Revenue. If the interest has been received, then Cash is debited. If it has not, the interest must be accrued on December 31 by debiting Interest Receivable.

EXAMPLE 12

If the bond in Example 11 paid interest of 10% annually and the payment date is December 31, 19XI, the following entry is made on that date:

Cash	10,000	
Interest Revenue		10,000

If the interest payment date is not until the next day (January 1, 19X2), then an adjusting entry for the accrual is made on December 31, 19XI, as follows:

Interest Receivable	10,000	
Interest Revenue		10,000

If a bond is purchased between interest dates, its price is increased by the amount of accrued interest thus far. This increase should be debited to Interest Revenue, since its effect is to reduce the amount of interest earned.

EXAMPLE 13

A short-term bond dated January 1, 19X1, is purchased on April 1, 19X1, at its par of $100,000. The interest rate is 10% and is payable on December 31. The accrued interest thus far is $2,500 ($100,000 $\times$ 10% $\times \frac{1}{4}$). The selling price will therefore be $102,500. At the time of purchase the entry is:

Investment in Short-Term Debt Securities	100,000	
Interest Revenue	2,500	
Cash		102,500

On December 31, the entry for the interest is:

Cash	10,000	
Interest Revenue		10,000*

*(10% $\times$ $100,000)

Thus the net interest revenue is $7,500 ($10,000 − $2,500).

Summary

1. If funds are readily available for the payment of current obligations and free from contractual restrictions, they are classified as "cash" on the balance sheet. Therefore, coins, currency, checking account balances, checks, money orders, certified checks, and bank checks are all considered cash. Savings account balances are also considered cash, since banks rarely exercise their right to demand prior notice for withdrawals.

2. Money market funds and certificates of deposit (CDs) are classified as temporary investments, since they carry penalties for early withdrawals. However, money market funds that have checking account privileges *without penalty* are considered to be cash.

3. Postdated checks and IOUs are considered receivables, while stamps are office supplies. Travel advances to employees that must be repaid to the employer are receivables; others are a prepaid expense.

4. Short-term, highly liquid investments that are *both* readily convertible to cash *and* have original maturities of no more than 3 months are considered cash and referred to as *cash equivalents*.

5. The SEC recommends that checking account compensating balances held against short-term or long-term borrowings be stated separately in the current or non-current asset section, respectively.

6. Restricted cash (such as cash set aside for plant expansion or retirement of debt) should be segregated from unrestricted cash on the balance sheet.

7. Overdrafts in checking accounts are considered current liabilities. They may be offset against positive balances of other accounts in the same bank, but not against those in other banks.

8. Typical transactions of petty cash funds are: establishment of the fund, usage of the fund, replenishment of the fund, and increasing the level of the fund. The Petty Cash T-account is touched only when the fund is established or increased.

9. Shortages or overages in petty cash are debited or credited to the Cash Short or Over account. This account has a dual nature.

10. There are several reasons why the bank statement balance may not agree with the book balance. They include outstanding checks, deposits in transit, special charges and credits, and errors. The process of making these balances agree with each other is called a *bank reconciliation*.

11. As a result of the bank reconciliation, journal entries must be made to update the books for items on the *book* side of the reconciliation. No entries are made for items on the *bank* side of the reconciliation.

12. Temporary investments consist of stocks and bonds that are *both* readily marketable *and* intended to be converted into cash within 1 year or the operating cycle. Brokers' fees are not expenses but are an addition to the cost of the investment.

13. If marketable debt securities are purchased above or below par, a discount or premium situation arises. The discount or premium is *not* amortized.

14. If a bond is purchased between interest dates, its price is increased by the accrued interest. This increase should be debited to interest revenue.

Rapid Review

1. Savings account balances are classified as _____.

2. Certificates of deposit are classified as _____.

3. Postdated checks and IOUs are classified as _____.

4. Short-term, highly liquid investments that have original maturity dates of less than 1 year are called _____.

5. Restrictions against checking accounts as collateral for borrowings are called _____.

6. Checking account overdrafts are classified as _____.

7. Journal entries must be made for the _____ side of the bank reconciliation, but not for the _____ side.

Answers: **1.** cash **2.** temporary investments **3.** receivables **4.** cash equivalents **5.** compensating balances **6.** current liabilities **7.** book; bank

Solved Problems

Definition of Cash

6.1 Determine the proper balance sheet classification for each of the following.

(a) Money orders

(b) Stamps

(c) Bank checks

(d) Certificates of deposit (short-term)

(e) Savings accounts

(f) Highly liquid investments maturing in 2 months

(g) Long-term plant expansion fund

(h) Overdrafts

(i) IOUs

SOLUTION

(a) Cash

(b) Office supplies

(c) Cash

(d) Short-term investments

(e) Cash

(f) Cash equivalents

(g) Long-term investments

(h) Current liabilities

(i) Receivables

[Section 6.1]

Petty Cash

6.2 Prepare journal entries for the following transactions involving petty cash:

(a) Establish the petty cash fund in the amount of $500.

(b) Disburse $100 for postage stamps.

(c) Disburse $85 for office snacks.

(d) Replenish the fund. The petty cash receipts show the following:

Postage Stamps	$100
Office Food	85
Freight In	40
Loan to Vice President	255
Total	$480

The coins and currency remaining in the petty cash box total $25.

(e) Raise the fund level by $90.

SOLUTION

(a)	Petty Cash	500	
	Cash		500

(b) No entry

(c) No entry

(d)	Office Supplies	100	
	Office Food	85	
	Freight In	40	
	Receivable from Vice President	255	
	Cash Short or Over		5
	Cash		475

(e)	Petty Cash	90		
	Cash		90	[Section 6.2]

6.3   A petty cash fund originally containing $300 is now being replenished. The petty cash receipts disclose the following disbursements:

Travel advances to employees (reimbursable)	$180
Entertainment of clients	110

The petty cash box physically contains only $6. Prepare the required entry to replenish the fund.

SOLUTION

Receivable from Employees	180		
Entertainment Expense	110		
Cash Short or Over	4		
Cash		294	[Section 6.2]

6.4   (a)   What do debits to the Cash Short or Over account signify?

(b)   What do credits to the Cash Short or Over account signify?

(c)   How would a debit balance in the Cash Short or Over account appear on the income statement? What about a credit balance?

SOLUTION

(a)   Shortages

(b)   Overages

(c)   Debits would appear as an expense (usually miscellaneous expense); credits would appear as revenue (usually miscellaneous revenue).   [Section 6.2]

Bank Reconciliation

6.5   Show how the following items would be treated on a bank reconciliation:

    (*a*) NSF check from Mr. Honest, $120

    (*b*) Outstanding checks, $250

    (*c*) Monthly charges, $15

    (*d*) Interest earned, $19

    (*e*) Bank charged us for a check we did not write, $42

    (*f*) We journalized a check for $83; the actual check was for $38, payable to the telephone company

    (*g*) Deposits in transit

Use the following key for your answers:

1. Add to the *bank* balance
2. Subtract from the *bank* balance
3. Add to the *book* balance
4. Subtract from the *book* balance
5. Do nothing.

SOLUTION

(*a*)	4		(*e*)	1
(*b*)	2		(*f*)	3
(*c*)	4		(*g*)	1
(*d*)	3			

[Section 6.3]

6.6   For the items in Problem 6.5, indicate which require a journal entry and prepare the necessary entries.

SOLUTION

Items (*a*), (*c*), (*d*), and (*f*) require entries. The entries are:

(*a*)	Accounts Receivable (Mr. Honest)	120	
	Cash		120
(*c*)	Bank Service Fees	15	
	Cash		15
(*d*)	Cash	19	
	Interest Income		19
(*f*)	Cash	45	
	Telephone Expense		45

[Section 6.3]

6.7   Prepare a bank reconciliation from the following information

Balance per Bank Statement	$2,000
Balance per Books	1,500
Interest on Checking Account	50
Outstanding Checks	800
Note Collected by Bank as Our Agent	500
Deposits in Transit	1,000
Bank Charged Us for a Check Written by Another Company with a Similar Name	150
Check No. 564 Was Journalized on Our Books as Repair Expense for $700; Actual Check was $400	

SOLUTION

Balance per Bank Statement:	$2,000	Balance per Books:	$1,500
Outstanding Checks	(800)	Interest	50
Deposits in Transit	1,000	Collection of Note	500
Other Company Check	150	Error in Check No. 564	300
Adjusted Bank Balance	$2,350	Adjusted Book Balance	$2,350

6.8   Prepare any required journal entries for the bank reconciliation in Problem 6.7.

SOLUTION

Cash	50	
Interest Income		50
Cash	500	
Notes Receivable		500
Cash	300	
Repair Expense		300 [Section 6.3]

6.9   A check of $490 received from Mr. Brown for a sale on account became NSF. The sale was for $500 with terms of 2/10 net/30

   (*a*)   What was the original entry for the receipt of this check?

   (*b*).   How would this item affect the bank reconciliation?

   (*c*)   Prepare any required adjusting entry for the new status of this check.

SOLUTION

(*a*)

Cash	490	
Sales Discount	10	
Accounts Receivable		500

   (*b*)   It would be a subtraction of $490 on the *book* side.

(c)   The original entry would now have to be reversed, as follows:

Accounts Receivable	500	
Sales Discount		10
Cash		490

[Section 6.3]

Temporary Investments: Marketable Equity Securities

6.10   A corporation purchases 1,000 shares of Xerox stock as a short-term investment. The cost per share is $100 and there is a broker's fee of $2,000. It later sells these shares at $110 each and incurs a $3,000 broker's fee. Prepare entries for these transactions.

SOLUTION

Investment in Short-Term Equity Securities	102,000	
Cash		102,000

Cash	107,000	
Investment in Short-Term Equity Securities		102,000
Gain on Sale of Securities		5,000

[Section 6.4]

Temporary Investments: Marketable Debt Securities

6.11   A $1,000 bond paying 10% interest annually on December 31 is purchased at 110. Prepare all the entries for the first year if:

(a)   The bond was purchased on January 1.

(b)   The bond was purchased on April 1.

In addition, compute the annual premium amortization using the straight-line method. Assume the bond is a short-term investment.

SOLUTION

(a)

Investment in Short-Term Debt Securities	1,100	
Cash		1,100

Cash	100	
Interest Revenue		100

(b)

Investment in Short-Term Debt Securities	1,100	
Interest Revenue	25*	
Cash		1,125

* $1,000 \times 0.10 \times 3/12$.

There will be no premium amortization, since the investment is short-term.   [Section 6.5]

Supplementary Problems

6.12   Determine the proper balance sheet classification for each of the following.

    (a)   Certified checks

    (b)   Compensating balances

    (c)   Travel advances to employees (reimbursable)

    (d)   Highly liquid investments maturing in 5 months

    (e)   Petty cash

    (f)   Coins

6.13   Prepare journal entries for the following transactions involving the petty cash fund.
    (a)   Withdraw $800 from the checking account to establish the petty cash fund.

    (b)   Raise the fund level by $100.

    (c)   Disburse $200 for merchandise purchase.

    (d)   Disburse $400 for client entertainment.

    (e)   Disburse $50 for delivery charges on merchandise and $80 for office food.

    (f)   Replenish the fund, which now contains $175 in coins and currency.

    (g)   Raise the fund level by $150

6.14   A petty cash fund that originally contained $600 is now being replenished. The fund now contains $95 in coins and currency and also the following petty cash receipts:
    (a)   A receipt for $105 spent on client entertainment

    (b)   A receipt for $200 spent on office food

    (c)   A receipt for $150 spent to purchase office supplies

    (d)   A receipt for $45 spent to pay delivery charges

Prepare the entry to replenish the fund.

6.15   Company P has the following T-account for Cash Short or Over:

Cash Short or Over

100	200
80	90
20	17
10	22

On what statement would this account appear, and what would be its proper classification?

6.16   Show how the following items would be handled on a bank reconciliation.

    (a)   Deposit in transit, $48.

    (b)   Interest earned on checking account, $23.

    (c)   Outstanding checks, $55.

    (d)   Bank collected a note receivable for us, $600.

    (e)   NSF check from Mr. Green, $150.

    (f)   Check no. 628 for $514 was charged by the bank for $415.

    (g)   Check no. 624 for $225, debited to Advertising Expense, was entered on our books as $522.

Use the following key for your answers:

1. Add to the *bank* balance
2. Subtract from the *bank* balance
3. Add to the *book* balance
4. Subtract from the *book* balance

6.17 Indicate which items in Problem 6.16 require journal entries, and prepare the entries.

6.18 Prepare a bank reconciliation from the following information.

Balance per Bank Statement	$5,000
Balance per Books	7,000
Outstanding Checks	2,000
NSF Check	400
Deposits in Transit	4,000
Check No. 229 Was Recorded on the Books as $300 Instead of $200	
Failed to Record on the Books a Deposit of $300	

6.19 Prepare any necessary journal entries for the bank reconciliation in Problem 6.18.

6.20 Mr. Green sent us a check for $441 which "bounced." The check was in payment of an invoice of $450 less a discount of 2% for early payment. Prepare the entry for the "bouncing" of this check.

6.21 Use the following information to prepare a bank reconciliation.

(*a*) Balance per bank statement, $8,000.
(*b*) Balance per books, $7,200.
(*c*) Interest earned on checking account, $800.
(*d*) Outstanding checks, $1,200.
(*e*) NSF check from Mr. Green, $185.
(*f*) Deposits in transit, $2,600.
(*g*) Bank charged us for a check we did not write, $500.
(*h*) Monthly bank charges, $15.
(*i*) Error on the books regarding check No. 251—recorded as $1,000 instead of as $300. The debit was to Salary Expense.
(*j*) Forgot to record a deposit on the books for $600.
(*k*) Bank acted as our agent to collect note of $800.

6.22 Prepare any necessary journal entries for the bank reconciliation in Problem 6.21.

6.23 Corporation A purchases 70 shares of General Motors stock at $50 per share as a short-term investment, and pays a broker's fee of $350. It later sells these shares at $80 per share and pays a broker's fee of $550. Prepare entries for the purchase and the sale.

6.24 A short-term bond dated January 1, 19X1, is purchased on May 1, 19X1, at its par of $80,000. The bond pays interest on December 31 of 10%. Prepare the entries for May 1 and December 31.

Proof of Cash

A different form of the bank reconciliation is often used by auditors when a company has weak internal control over its cash. This form is referred to as a *proof of cash*, and it assists auditors in identifying unauthorized disbursements of cash.

The proof of cash actually consists of four reconciliations in one. The first column reconciles the *beginning-of-the-period* cash balances per the bank statement and books, while the fourth and last columns reconcile the *end-of-period* cash balances. The second column reconciles the *cash receipts* per the bank statement to the *receipts* recorded on the books, while the third column reconciles the *cash disbursements* per the bank statement to the *disbursements* per the books. Thus the first and last columns are simply the regular bank reconciliations for the end of the prior month and the end of the current month, while the two center columns tie the first and last columns together.

Let's take a look at an example.

EXAMPLE 1

On August 21, 19X1, Cash Corporation has the following information relating to its cash balance.

(a) Its July 31 bank balance was $5,000; its book balance was $6,000.

(b) The July 31 bank statement showed a service charge of $600 for July. This was not recorded on the books until August.

(c) Outstanding checks at July 31 were $700; deposits in transit were $1,200.

(d) The bank balance on August 31 was $7,000; the book balance was $7,700.

(e) Deposits and withdrawals per the August bank statement were $3,000 and $1,000, respectively. The withdrawals included a service charge of $300 that was not recorded on the books until September.

(f) Deposits in transit on August 31 were $900; outstanding checks were $500.

(g) Receipts per the books for August were $2,800; withdrawals were $1,100.

(h) The July 31 bank statement showed the collection of a note of $100. This was not recorded on the books until August. The proof of cash is as follows:

Proof of Cash

	(a) July 31	(b) Aug. Receipts	(c) Aug. Disbursements	(d) Aug. 31
1. Per Bank	$5,000	$3,000	$1,000	$7,000
Outstanding Checks:				
2. July 31	(700)		(700)	
3. Aug. 31			500	(500)
Deposits in Transit:				
4. July 31	1,200	(1,200)		
5. Aug. 31		900		900
Correct Balance	$5,500	$2,700	$ 800	$7,400
6. Per Book	$6,000	$2,800	$1,100	$7,700

(*continued*)

	Service Charges:				
7.	July	(600)		(600)	
8.	Aug.			300	(300)
9.	Note Collection	100	(100)		
	Correct Balance	$5,500	$2,700	$800	$7,400

Here is an explanation of the proof of cash. Row 1 shows the bank statement activity for August. The balance on July 31 was $5,000; receipts and disbursements were $3,000 and $1,000, respectively, yielding an August 31 balance of $7,000. In a similar manner, row 6 shows the activity per the *books* during August. The beginning balance was $6,000; receipts and disbursements were $2,800 and $1,100, respectively, yielding an ending balance of $7,700.

Column (*a*) is the standard bank reconciliation on July 31; column (*d*) is the standard bank reconciliation on August 31. The middle columns, (*b*) and (*c*), represent the needed adjustments and tie together columns (*a*) and (*d*). (Note that two columns are always affected for each adjustment.) The adjustments reconcile the receipts and disbursements during August for both the bank and the books, to the correct amounts. Let's take a look at some of these adjustments:

1. The $700 of outstanding checks on July 31 must be *subtracted* from the August disbursements per *bank*, since they were written in July and recorded on the *books* in July. Using similar reasoning, the $500 of outstanding checks on August 31 must be *added*.

2. The deposit in transit of $1,200 on July 31 must be subtracted from the *bank* receipts for August, since the actual deposit was made in July and was so recorded on the books. Using similar reasoning, the $900 outstanding deposit on August 31 must be added to the bank receipts for August.

3. The $600 service charge for July must be subtracted from the *book* disbursements for August, since it was paid in July and was so recorded by the bank. Similar reasoning applies to the $300 August service charge.

4. The $100 note collection during July must be subtracted from the August receipts per the books, since the actual receipt took place during July, and was recorded as such by the bank. Note that the proof of cash reconciles both horizontally and vertically.

Solved Problems

6A.1 BR Corporation has the following information relating to cash for April 30 and May 31 of 19X1.

	Per Bank	**Per Books**	
Cash Balance, Apr. 30	$12,000	$10,200	
Apr. Service Charge	500	—	(recorded in May)
Cash Balance, May 31	9,000	10,400	
May Deposits	3,000	5,300	
May Disbursements	6,000	5,100	
May Service Charge	400	—	(recorded in June)
Outstanding Checks—Apr. 30	4,000	—	
Outstanding Checks—May 31	3,000	—	
Deposits in Transit—Apr. 30	2,000	—	
Deposits in Transit—May 31	4,000	—	
Interest Earned—Apr.	300	—	(recorded in May)

Prepare a proof of cash for May

SOLUTION

	Apr. 30	May Receipts	May Disbursements	May 31
Bank Balance	$12,000	$3,000	$6,000	$ 9,000
Outstanding Checks:				
Apr. 30	(4,000)		(4,000)	
May 31			3,000	(3,000)
Deposits in Transit:				
Apr. 30	2,000	(2,000)		
May 31		4,000		4,000
Correct Balance	$10,000	$5,000	$5,000	$10,000
Book Balance	$10,200	$5,300	$5,100	$10,400
Service Charges				
Apr.	(500)		(500)	
May			400	(400)
Interest Earned	300	(300)		
Correct Balance	$10,000	$5,000	$5,000	$10,000

Supplementary Problem

6A.2 Zebra Corporation has the following information regarding its bank account for August 19X1.

(a) Bank balance July 31, $14,000; August 31, $16,000

(b) Bank receipts during August, $10,000; disbursements, $8,000

(c) Outstanding checks July 31, $5,000; August 31, $3,000

(d) Deposits in transit July 31, $7,000; August 31, $9,000.

(e) Book balance July 31, $18,000; August 31, $23,700

(f) Book receipts during August, $11,800; disbursements, $6,100

(g) Service charge for July, $1,500; for August, $2,900

(h) Interest earned for July, $1,000; for August, $1,200

(i) NSF check in July, $1,500

Prepare a proof of cash.

Appendix 6B

Evaluation and Reporting of Investments

This appendix deals with the end-of-period treatment for both debt and equity securities.

Until 1993, the procedure to be followed was lower of cost or market (LCM). Thus, at period-end a comparison was made between a portfolio's cost and market value, and the lower figure was chosen.

However, this changed with the introduction of FASB *Statement No. 115* in 1993. Let's discuss debt securities first. These securities are divided into the following categories:

1. Held-to-maturity securities

2. Trading securities

3. Available-for-sale securities

Held-to-maturity securities are instruments which the company has *both* the positive intent *and* the ability to hold until they mature. If the intention is to hold the securities merely indefinitely, they do not qualify for this category.

Held-to-maturity securities are reported on the balance sheet at amortized cost (acquisition cost adjusted for premium and discount amortization). They are *not* adjusted up or down to fair market value.

Trading securities, on the other hand, are held with the intention of selling them in the near term. A typical example is securities held by dealers. Discounts and premiums are *not* amortized, and the securities *are* adjusted to fair market value, *both* up *and* down. The difference, whether a gain or loss, is reported on the income statement as such.

Available-for-sale securities are securities being held for an indefinite time period. There is neither a definite intention to hold them to maturity nor to sell them in the short run. These, like trading securities, *are* adjusted up or down to fair market value, with one major difference. Any gains or losses go *directly* to stockholders' equity (capital); they are not reported as income or loss. In short, they *bypass the income statement.*

EXAMPLE 1

Company Green has debt securities with an amortized cost of $5,000. These are classified as held-to-maturity. In this case, the securities are reported on the balance sheet at $5,000; their market value is ignored.

EXAMPLE 2

Assume the same information as in Example 1, except that the securities are of the trading type. If the market value is $6,000, the following entry is made:

Valuation Allowance	1,000	
Unrealized Holding Gain—Income		1,000

The Valuation Allowance account is an adjunct account to the investment account, and the balance sheet would thus show a total investment of $6,000 ($5,000 + $1,000). On the income statement, a gain of $1,000 would appear in the "other revenue" section.

EXAMPLE 3

Assume the same information as in Example 2, except that the market value is only $4,000. The entry is:

Unrealized Holding Loss—Income	1,000	
Valuation Allowance		1,000

In this case, Valuation Allowance is a contra to the investment account, and the balance sheet would show $4,000 ($5,000 − $1,000), while the income statement would show a $1,000 loss.

EXAMPLE 4

Brown Corp. has available-for-sale securities with amortized cost of $5,000 and market value of $6,000. The entry is:

Valuation Allowance	1,000	
Unrealized Holding Gain—Equity		1,000

Notice that the gain does not go to an income account but directly to stockholders' equity. Thus the income statement does *not* show this gain.

If the market value was $4,000, the entry would be:

Unrealized Holding Loss—Equity	1,000	
Valuation Allowance		1,000

Once again, the income statement is bypassed.

Up to this point, we've been discussing debt securities. Equity securities receive the same treatment, except that they are divided into only *two* categories:

1. Trading securities
2. Available-for-sale securities

There is no held-to-maturity category, since stocks do not have a maturity date.

If securities (whether debt or equity) are transferred to *or* from the trading category, they are transferred at market value and a gain or loss is recognized in income. If they are transferred to the available-for-sale category from the held-to-maturity category, they are also transferred at market value, but, once again, the gain or loss bypasses the income statement and goes directly to stockholders' equity.

EXAMPLE 5

White Corp. transfers securities from the trading category to the available-for-sale category. These securities have a cost and market value of $5,000 and $6,000, respectively. The entry is:

Valuation Allowance	1,000	
Unrealized Holding Gain—Income		1,000

EXAMPLE 6

Assume the same information as in Example 5, except that the transfer is from the held-to-maturity category to the available-for-sale category. The entry is:

Valuation Allowance	1,000	
Unrealized Holding Gain—Equity		1,000

Solved Problems

6B.1 Cooper Corp. has investments in debt securities with cost and market values of $9,000 and $10,000, respectively. Prepare the appropriate journal entry for each of the following cases:

(a) The securities are of the held-to-maturity-type.

(b) The securities are of the trading type.

(c) The securities are of the available-for-sale type.

SOLUTION

(a) No entry required.

(b)

Valuation Allowance	1,000	
Unrealized Holding Gain—Income		1,000

(c)

Valuation Allowance	1,000	
Unrealized Holding Gain—Equity		1,000

6B.2 For the securities in Problem 6B.1, show the balance sheet presentation for each case.

SOLUTION

(a)

Investment in Debt Securities	$ 9,000

(b)

Investment in Debt Securities	$ 9,000
Valuation Allowance	1,000
Total	$10,000

(c)

Investment in Debt Securities	$ 9,000
Valuation Allowance	1,000
Total	$10,000

    In this case, the stockholders' equity section would show the $1,000 gain as an increase in stockholders' equity.

6B.3 Assume the same information as in Problem 6B.2, except that the market value is $7,000. Prepare an appropriate journal entry for each case.

SOLUTION

(a) No entry required.

(b)

Unrealized Holding Gain—Income	2,000	
Valuation Allowance		2,000

(c)

Unrealized Holding Gain—Equity	2,000	
Valuation Allowance		2,000

6B.4 For Problem 6B.3, prepare the balance sheet presentation for each case.

SOLUTION

(a)	Investment in Debt Securities	$9,000
(b)	Investment in Debt Securities	$9,000
	− Valuation Allowance	(2,000)
	Total	$7,000
(c)	Investment in Debt Securities	$9,000
	− Valuation Allowance	(2,000)
	Total	$7,000

In this case, the stockholders' equity section would show the $2,000 loss as a decrease in stockholders' equity.

6B.5 White Corp. Transfers securities from one category to another. The cost of the securities is $20,000; the fair market value is $22,000. Prepare an entry if:

(a) The securities are transferred from the trading category to the available-for-sale category.

(b) The securities are transferred from the available-for-sale category to the trading category.

(c) The securities are transferred from the held-to-maturity category to the available-for-sale category.

SOLUTION

(a)	Valuation Allowance	2,000	
	Unrealized Holding Gain—Income		2,000
(b)	Same entry as above		
(c)	Valuation Allowance	2,000	
	Unrealized Holding Gain—Equity		2,000

Examination II

Chapters 4, 5, 6

A. True–False Questions. Place the letter T or F next to the question.

1. _____ The future value of $1 tells us how much to deposit today in order to receive $1 in the future.

2. _____ The present value of an annuity of $1 tells us how much to deposit today in order to receive a series of $1 payments in the future.

3. _____ Despite the fact that the tables deal with $1, they can be used for any amount by dividing the table value by the amount desired.

4. _____ For annuity due situations, the series of deposits or withdrawals begins one period from today.

5. _____ To adapt the future value of an ordinary annuity table for use with annuity due situations, look up the table for one less deposit.

6. _____ The future value of an annuity involves several deposits and one withdrawal.

7. _____ The present value of $1 deals with one deposit and several withdrawals.

8. _____ Saving accounts are not considered cash.

9. _____ Postdated checks and IOUs are considered cash.

10. _____ Checking accounts with negative balances may be offset against those with positive balances if they are in the same bank.

11. _____ Entries are made in the Petty Cash T-account at the time petty cash is disbursed.

12. _____ No entries are made for the items appearing on the bank side of the bank reconciliation.

13. _____ Brokers' fees on stock transactions are an expense.

14. _____ If the market value of stock investments is higher than the cost (on December 31), a loss is recognized.

15. _____ If an equity security is transferred from long-term status to short-term status, the transfer should be made at market value.

16. _____ Discounts and premiums on marketable debt securities are not amortized.

17. _____ The going concern assumption assumes that the company is on the verge of liquidation.

18. _____ Under the revenue principle, revenue is recognized when cash is received.

19. _____ A primary characteristic of accounting information is comparability.

20. _____ Increases in assets arising from a company's central activities are called gains.

21. _____ The entity assumption emphasizes the legal status of a company rather than its economic status.

B. Completion Questions. Fill in the blanks.

22. "If I deposit $1 today, how much will it grow into in the future?" is the question dealt with by the concept of _____.

23. A series of deposits or withdrawals is an _____.

24. The future value of an annuity involves a series of _____ and one _____.

25. The present value of an annuity involves a series of _____ and one _____.

26. To use the tables for values other than $1, simply take the table value and _____.

27. In a future value of ordinary annuity situation, the first deposit begins not immediately, but _____ from now.

28. To adapt the future value of an ordinary annuity table to annuity due, look up the table for one _____ deposit and then _____ 1.

29. To adapt the present value of an ordinary annuity table to annuity due, look up the table for one _____ payment and then _____ 1.

30. A technique called _____ is used when an algebraic equation produces a result that is between two table values.

31. Certified checks are classified as _____ on the balance sheet.

32. Travel advances to employees that must be repaid are classified as _____.

33. Short-term, highly liquid investments with original maturities of less than 3 months are referred to as _____.

34. Overdrafts are considered to be _____.

35. The Cash Short or Over account has a _____ nature.

36. Outstanding checks would cause the bank balance to be _____ than the book balance.

37. The process of making the bank balance agree with the book balance is called _____.

38. Comparing the cost of stock to its market price and choosing the lower value is referred to as _____.

39. If a bond is purchased between interest dates, its price will be increased by the _____.

40. "Let the expense follow the revenue" is the essence of the _____ principle.

41. The requirement to understate assets and net income when in doubt, is required under the _____ constraint.

42. A characteristic of accounting information that it be available to the user before it loses its significance is _____.

43. If a company is on the verge of liquidation, the _____ principle is abandoned and the assets are written down to _____.

C. Problems

44. (a) The present value of $2,000 to be received in 4 years if the interest rate is 8% compounded annually is _____.
    (b) Assume the same information as in part (a), except that the rate is compounded semiannually. The present value is _____.
    (c) Once again assume the same information as in part (a), except that the rate is compounded quarterly. The present value is _____.

45. (a) The future value of an ordinary annuity of $7,000 to be deposited over 4 years (one per year) at an interest rate of 10% is _____.
    (b) Assume the same information as in part (a), except that the annuity is an annuity due. The future value is _____.

46. (a) The present value of an ordinary annuity of $9,000 to be received over 6 years (one per year) at a rate of 10% is _____.
    (b) Assume the same information as in part (a), except that the annuity is an annuity due. The present value is _____.

47. How many deposits of $1,800 each must be made at 6% annual interest to achieve a future value of $17,814.60?

48. Prepare journal entries for the following transactions involving petty cash.
    (a) Establish the petty cash fund with $100.
    (b) Spend $70 on office supplies.
    (c) Replenish the fund, which contains a petty cash receipt for $70, and $28 in coins and currency.
    (d) Raise the fund level to $150.

49. On December 31, 19X1, trading securities with a cost of $4,000 have a market value of $3,500. By December 31, 19X2, the market value has risen to $3,800. Prepare the necessary entries for each date.

Answers to Examination II

A. True–False Questions

1. F **2.** T **3.** F **4.** T **5.** F **6.** T **7.** F **8.** F **9.** F **10.** T **11.** F **12.** T **13.** F **14.** F **15.** F **16.** T **17.** F **18.** F **19.** F **20.** F **21.** F

B. Completion Questions

22. future value of an annuity **23.** annuity **24.** deposits; withdrawal **25.** withdrawals; deposit **26.** multiply **27.** one period **28.** additional; subtract **29.** less; add **30.** interpolation **31.** cash **32.** receivables **33.** cash equivalents **34.** current liabilities **35.** dual **36.** higher **37.** bank reconciliation **38.** lower of cost or market (LCM) **39.** accrued interest **40.** matching **41.** conservatism **42.** timeliness **43.** going concern; net realizable value

C. Problems

44. (*a*) $0.735 \times \$2,000 = \$1,470$

    (*b*) $0.731 \times \$2,000 = \$1,462$

    (*c*) $0.728 \times \$2,000 = \$1,456$

45. (*a*) $4.641 \times \$7,000 = \$32,487$

    (*b*) $5.105 \times \$7,000 = \$35,735$

46. (*a*) $4.355 \times \$9,000 = \$39,195$

    (*b*) $4.791 \times \$9,000 = \$43,119$

47. $\$1,800X = \$17,814.60$

        $X = \$9.897$

The table shows 9.897 at the 8-payment mark.

48. (*a*)

Petty Cash	100	
Cash		100

   (*b*)   No Entry

   (*c*)

Office Supplies	70	
Cash Short or Over	2	
Cash		72

   (*d*)

Petty Cash	50	
Cash		50

49.   December 31, 19X1:

Unrealized Holding Loss-Income	500	
Valuation Allowance		500

December 31, 19X2:

Reverse the December 31, 19X2 entry for $300.

Chapter 7

Receivables

7.1 INTRODUCTION

Receivables are claims against third parties. If they are collectible within 1 year or the operating cycle, they are current; if not, they are long-term. They may be classified under two broad categories: trade receivables and non-trade receivables.

Trade receivables are due from customers for goods and services provided to them. If the customer's promise to pay was an oral one, the receivable is referred to as *accounts receivable*; if it was written, it is referred to as *notes receivable*. Both accounts receivable and notes receivable may be current or long-term.

Non-trade receivables arise from other transactions. These include advances to officers and employees, deposits given to other parties, dividends receivable, and interest receivable. All of these should be disclosed on the balance sheet separately from the trade receivables.

7.2 ACCOUNTS RECEIVABLE: GENERAL

As mentioned, accounts receivable are claims against third parties arising from oral promises to pay for goods and services. While the prices of the goods and services are usually printed in the seller's catalog, there often are discounts from these prices in order to increase sales. Rather than print up a new catalog, the seller will simply attach a piece of paper to the old catalog stating the discount. For accounting purposes, the old price is moot; all entries and calculations are based on the new, marked-down price. This type of discount is referred to as a *trade discount*.

EXAMPLE 1

A catalog shows a price of $50 for Product X. A piece of paper attached to the catalog states that all prices are reduced by 10%. Thus the real price for Product X is $45; the old price of $50 is ignored, and all entries are based on $45.

Another type of discount is the *cash discount*. This is a discount for early payment. For example, if the terms of the sale say 2/10, N/30, a 2% discount will be given for payment within 10 days. No discount will be given after that, and the latest date for payment is 30 days from the date of the sale.

There are two methods of accounting for sales that offer cash discounts. The *gross method* requires the original sale to be recorded at the gross selling price (the full amount before the discount). If the customer pays early, the discount is recorded in a special account called Sales Discounts, which is a contra to the Sales account.

Let's look at an example.

EXAMPLE 2

Company A sells Company B goods for $100 with terms of 2/10, N/30. The entry for the sale is:

Accounts Receivable	100	
Sales		100

Notice that the entry is for the full, gross amount of $100.

If Company B pays within 10 days, it will only have to pay $98. The entry by Company A is:

Cash	98	
Sales Discounts	2	
Accounts Receivable		100

The sale has "shrunk" by the contra of $2.

If Company B pays *after* 10 days, the entry is:

| Cash | 100 | |
| Accounts Receivable | | 100 |

In this case, the sale remains at the original, full $100.

The *net method* records the original sale at the net amount (gross price minus the discount). If the customer pays *after* the discount period, the extra amount goes to a revenue account called Sales Discounts Forfeited.

EXAMPLE 3

Let's continue with the previous example. Under the net method, the original entry would be at the net amount of $98:

| Accounts Receivable | 98 | |
| Sales | | 98 |

For payment within 10 days the entry is:

| Cash | 98 | |
| Accounts Receivable | | 98 |

For payment after 10 days the entry is:

Cash	100	
Accounts Receivable		98
Sales Discounts Forfeited		2

The logic supporting the net method is:

1. Because the customer has the right to pay early and pay only $98 (in the previous two examples), that is proof that the true sale is really only $98. Therefore the sale should be recorded at this amount.

2. If the customer does not take advantage of this discount, the extra payment should not "enlarge" the sale, but should be treated as revenue—a charge the customer is paying for the use of the seller's money (similar to interest revenue).

The accounting profession prefers the net method on the theoretical grounds just discussed. Nevertheless, since the total annual amount of discounts forfeited is immaterial, many companies use the easier and more practical gross method.

EXAMPLE 4

Refer once again to Examples 2 and 3. Under the gross method, if the customer pays the full $100 *after* the 10 days, sales are reported on the income statement as $100. Under the net method, however, sales are reported at $98, while another kind of revenue—Sales Discounts Forfeited—is reported at $2.

If there are any sales returns, the cash discount is based on the amount remaining *after* the discount was taken, not *before*.

EXAMPLE 5

If the sale was for $100 with terms of 2/10, N/30, and there was a return of $10, the discount is 2% of $90 = $1.80, not 2% of $100.

We will see later on in this chapter that *long-term* receivables are measured at their present values. However, for *current receivables*, the accounting profession has specifically stated that present value computations are not to be made. This is because the amount of any "hidden" interest in the receivable is immaterial, since the time period involved is a short one.

7.3 ACCOUNTS RECEIVABLE: BAD DEBTS

Quite often, unfortunately, receivables are not collected: The customer simply walks away without paying. These are called *bad debts*, and there are two methods of accounting for them: the direct write-off method and the allowance method.

The *direct write-off method* makes an entry for bad debts *at the time they take place*. The entry is:

> Bad Debts Expense   xxx
>   Accounts Receivable   xxx

In terms of the accounting equation, the effect is:

$$\text{Assets} \quad = \quad \text{Liabilities} \quad + \quad \text{Capital}$$
$$\text{decrease} \qquad \text{no change} \qquad \text{decrease (expense)}$$

This method makes sense but is deficient on theoretical grounds. According to the matching principle (discussed in Chapter 4), expenses should be recognized in the same accounting period as their related revenue. Under this method, however, this often will not be the case. For example, if a sale is made late in 19X1, bad debts will not arise until January and February of 19X2. Thus the revenue has been recognized in 19X1 but the expenses are recognized in 19X2—an improper matching of the two. Therefore, since this method violates generally accepted accounting principles, it is unacceptable and will not be used in this book.

The second method, the *allowance method*, uses *estimates* to recognize bad debts *before they happen*. Since bad debts are both probable and estimable and thus fulfill the criteria required of loss contingencies discussed in Chapter 3, they cannot be ignored. They are recognized via an adjusting journal entry on December 31, as follows:

> Dec. 31   Bad Debts Expense   xxx
>   Allowance for Doubtful Accounts   xxx

Allowance for Doubtful Accounts is a contra account to Accounts Receivable and is presented on the balance sheet in the following manner:

> Accounts Receivable   xxxx
> Allowance for Doubtful Accounts   (xxx)
> Net Receivable   xxxx

The Bad Debts Expense account, like all other expense accounts, is closed each year into Income Summary, and thus begins each new year with a zero balance. The allowance account, an asset account, is not closed but accumulates from year to year. It is increased each December 31 via the adjusting entry for bad debts, and is occasionally decreased for *write-offs*, as will be discussed later on.

Why is it necessary to use a contra account? Why can't we make things simple and credit accounts receivable *directly*? The answer is as follows: Recall from Accounting I that there is an accounts receivable subsidiary ledger containing a T-account for each individual receivable. The total of these accounts must equal the *controlling* accounts receivable account in the general ledger. Thus, whenever the controlling account is touched, its related individual account in the subsidiary ledger must also be touched as well. But in this case we have a problem: We cannot touch the subsidiary account because we don't know who the person is! (Remember, this is only an estimate; nothing has actually happened!) So what should we do?

The solution to the problem is: Touch neither the controlling account nor the subsidiary account, but use a contra instead. We are thus able to reduce the receivable without having to worry about the subsidiary accounts.

EXAMPLE 6

On December 31, 19X1, Company A estimates its bad debts at $5,000. The adjusting entry is:

Bad Debts Expense	5,000	
Allowance for Doubtful Accounts		5,000

On January 20, 19X2, Mr. X defaults on his $1,000 balance. Thus, part of the original estimate of $5,000 has now come to fruition. Should we debit Bad Debts Expense for this $1,000? The answer is definitely no—we already did so on December 31! The entry for now is:

Allowance for Doubtful Accounts	1,000	
Account Receivable (and Mr. X)		1,000

This is called a *write-off entry*. What is the logic behind this entry? The answer is that until now, as explained earlier, we couldn't credit Accounts Receivable directly because we didn't know who the person is, and we thus could not go to the subsidiary ledger. Now, however, we know it is Mr. X, so we remove his portion from the allowance account, and directly credit *both* the controlling account *and* the subsidiary account.

EXAMPLE 7

Refer to Example 6. Assume that on February 1, Mr. X feels guilty and decides to pay the $1,000. We, therefore, must first reverse the write-off entry:

Accounts Receivable	1,000	
Allowance for Doubtful Accounts		1,000

We then make the regular, routine entry for the collection, which is:

Cash	1,000	
Accounts Receivable		1,000

We mentioned that on December 31 an adjusting entry is made to estimate bad debts. There are two ways of coming up with this estimate:

1. Taking a percentage of credit sales for the year.
2. Taking a percentage of the Accounts Receivable balance. This is often done via a procedure called *aging*.

Let's look at how the aging procedure is done.

EXAMPLE 8

Company D has the following outstanding receivables on December 31:

Age Group	Amount	Probability of Noncollection	Uncollectible
1–30 days	$10,000	1%	$100
31–90 days	5,000	2%	100
91–180 days	6,000	4%	240
181–365 days	2,000	10%	200
More than 1 year	1,000	20%	200

We multiply each age group by its probability percentage, yielding a total of $840.

There is a critical and subtle difference between the two estimation methods. The percentage-of-sales method does not concern itself with any amounts already in the allowance account; the aging method does. Let's look at an example.

EXAMPLE 9

On December 31, 19X1, the first year of operations for Happy Corporation, Happy estimated its bad debts at $5,000. Its allowance account on that date thus appeared as follows:

Allowance for Doubtful Accounts
	5,000

During 19X2, Happy had credit sales of $100,000 and write-offs of $1,000. The allowance account now shows $4,000:

Allowance for Doubtful Accounts
1,000	5,000
	4,000 Bal.

Happy estimates that 6% of its credit sales ($6,000) will go bad. By coincidence, the aging procedure also yields this amount. However, the entries will not be the same. The percentage-of-sales method *does not concern itself* with the $4,000 balance already in the account. Thus the entry is:

Bad Debts Expense	6,000	
Allowance for Doubtful Accounts		6,000

The allowance account will now have a $10,000 balance ($4,000 + $6,000). The percentage-of-receivables method, however, *does concern itself* with the account balance. Since the estimate is $6,000 but we already have $4,000 in the account, the entry will be for only $2,000:

Bad Debts Expense	2,000	
Allowance for Doubtful Accounts		2,000

The allowance account will thus now have a $6,000 balance.

Occasionally the write-offs to the account may exceed the original estimate, thus resulting in a *debit* balance in the account. This is illustrated in the next example.

EXAMPLE 10

On December 31, 19X1, the allowance account has a credit balance of $10,000. During 19X2, write-offs total $12,000, resulting in a $2,000 *debit* balance, as follows:

Allowance for Doubtful Accounts

12,000	10,000
2,000	

Under the percentage-of-receivables method, if on December 31, 19X2, we estimate $7,000 to go bad, the entry would have to be made for $9,000 in order to achieve the desired $7,000 balance. The entry is:

Bad Debts Expense	9,000	
Allowance for Doubtful Accounts		9,000

The T-account would now show the following:

Allowance for Doubtful Accounts

12,000	10,000
	9,000
	7,000 Bal.

7.4   ASSIGNMENT OF ACCOUNTS RECEIVABLE

Companies often borrow money and pledge their receivables as collateral on the loan. They pay the bank an initial finance charge, plus interest for the period the loan is outstanding. As the company gradually collects on the receivables, it remits these collections to the bank in payment of the loan. This whole procedure is referred to as an *assignment of receivables*. It is important to note that the receivables have not been sold or transferred to the bank; they have merely been pledged as collateral.

EXAMPLE 11

On January 1, 19X1, White Corporation borrows $100,000 from the bank and signs a 12% note promising to pay gradually from the collection of its receivables. These receivables, totaling $125,000, have been pledged as collateral. The bank charges an initial 1% fee for the loan. The entries are:

Cash	99,000	
Finance Charge	1,000	
Notes Payable		100,000
Accounts Receivable Assigned	125,000	
Accounts Receivable		125,000

The latter entry removes the receivables from their regular account and places them into a special account so that it becomes known that they have been pledged.

On February 1, White Company collects $65,000 on its receivables ($70,000 less sales returns of $5,000) and remits this amount, plus 1 month's interest, to the bank. The entries are:

Cash	65,000	
Sales Returns	5,000	
Accounts Receivable Assigned		70,000
Notes Payable	65,000	
Interest Expense	1,000*	
Cash		66,000

$$*\$100,000 \times 12\% \times \tfrac{1}{12}.$$

[The balance now due on the note is $35,000 (100,000 − 65,000).]

On March 1, White Company collects $50,000 of accounts receivable and remits the $35,000 balance on the note, plus interest, to the bank. The entries are:

Cash	50,000	
Accounts Receivable Assigned		50,000

The Accounts Receivable Assigned account now contains $5,000 ($125,000 − $70,000 − $50,000). This is now returned to the Accounts Receivable account via the following entry:

Accounts Receivable	5,000	
Accounts Receivable Assigned		5,000

The entry to pay the bank is:

Notes Payable	35,000	
Interest Expense*	350	
Cash		35,350

*$35,000 × 12% × $\frac{1}{12}$.

7.5 SALE (TRANSFER) OF ACCOUNTS RECEIVABLE

Instead of borrowing money and pledging the receivables as collateral, companies will sometimes sell the receivables outright. This is often referred to as *factoring*. This may be done *without recourse* or *with recourse*. If the seller is responsible to the bank for any receivable that goes bad, it is a ''with recourse'' situation; if not, it is a ''without recourse'' situation. Either way, the seller is responsible for any reduction in the collection of the receivables due to sales returns and discounts.

We shall discuss sales *without recourse* first. The procedure works as follows: The holder of the receivables sells them to a bank or finance company, which charges a fee for the service and also holds back a certain percentage to cover possible future sales returns or discounts. This amount is later returned to the seller, minus any returns and discounts. The receivables are collected directly from the customers by the bank. Should any of the receivables go bad, it is the bank's loss. These transactions are illustrated in the next example.

EXAMPLE 12

Green Corporation transfers receivables of $100,000 *without recourse* to Finance Bank. Finance Bank charges a 2% service fee and withholds an additional 5% to cover sales returns and discounts. The entry for Green is:

Cash	93,000	
Loss on Sale of Receivables	2,000	
Due from Factor	5,000	
Accounts Receivable		100,000

Since Green has sold receivables of $100,000 for only $98,000, there is a $2,000 loss on the sale. If a sales return of $1,200 takes place, the entry is:

Sales Return	1,200	
Due from Factor		1,200

If there are no other returns or discounts, Finance Bank will then return $3,800 ($5,000 − $1,200) to Green. Green's entry is:

Cash   3,800
    Due from Factor   3,800

If the transfer is made *with recourse*, an important question arises. Is this transaction really a sale, thus requiring the treatment just discussed? Or, since the holder (Green) is responsible for bad debts, is this not a sale, but a *borrowing*? Green has in essence *borrowed* money from the bank, is paying the loan via the collection of the receivables by the bank, and the initial charge is *not* a loss on the sale, but a finance charge.

The accounting profession has ruled that if the transfer meets *all* three of the following conditions, it is a sale; if it does not, it should be treated as a borrowing. The conditions are:

1.   The transferor surrenders control of the future economic benefits of the receivables.

2.   The obligation under the recourse provision can be reasonably estimated.

3.   The transferee cannot require the transferor to repurchase the receivables.

EXAMPLE 13

Assume the same information as in Example 12, except that the transfer is made *with recourse*. If the three conditions have been met, the entries are exactly as discussed above. If they have *not* been met, however, the initial entry would instead be:

Cash   93,000
Finance Charge   2,000
Due from Factor   5,000
    Loan Payable to Factor   100,000

Notice that no loss on sale is recognized, since no sale has taken place. Also notice that Accounts Receivable is not credited, since the receivables have not been sold. Instead, Green has *borrowed* money from the bank and thus recognizes a liability.

7.6   NOTES RECEIVABLE WITH REASONABLE INTEREST RATES

Notes receivable are written promises to pay a certain sum of money by a certain date. Interest-bearing notes have an explicitly stated rate of interest, while non-interest-bearing notes have the interest "hidden" in the face amount. We shall discuss interest-bearing notes first.

The rate of interest stated in the note is referred to as the contract rate. If this rate is equal to the market rate of interest, the amount given for the loan will be exactly equal to the face value of the note.

EXAMPLE 14

Lender Co. lends money to Borrower Co. on January 1, 19X1, and receives a $20,000 note receivable in exchange. The contract and market rates are each 10%, and the note is due in 5 years. Since the rates are equal, the amount of the loan will be exactly $20,000 and Lender makes the following entry:

Note Receivable   20,000
    Cash   20,000

Each December 31 Lender receives interest of $2,000 ($20,000 $\times$ 10%). Its entry is:

Cash   2,000
    Interest Revenue   2,000

When the loan is repaid to Lender, its entry is:

Cash	20,000	
Notes Receivable		20,000

If the contract rate is *not* equal to the market rate, the amount of the loan will not be the face value. If it is below the market rate, the loan will be less than the face value (a *discount*); if it is above the market rate, the loan will be more than the face value (a *premium*). In these cases, how do we determine the precise amount of the loan? The answer is as follows:

$$\text{Loan} = \text{present value of principal} + \text{present value of interest payments}$$

The interest payments are an annuity; the principal is not. We must use the interest tables provided in the Appendix to determine these present values, and *the rate to be looked up in the table will always be the market rate*. Let's look at a discount situation.

EXAMPLE 15

Lender Corp. agrees to lend money to Borrower Corp., for which it receives a 5-year, $10,000 note with a contract rate of 10%. Thus this note will pay $1,000 interest annually and $10,000 in 5 years. The market rate, however, is not 10% but 12%. To determine the amount of the loan, we must find the present value of these cash flows at the *market rate* of 12%, as follows:

Present value of $1, five periods, 12% $= 0.567 \times \$10,000 = \$5,670$
Present value annuity of $1, five periods, 12% $= 3.605 \times \$ \ 1,000 = \underline{\ \ 3,605}$
                                                    Loan is $\underline{\underline{\$9,275}}$

Thus the loan will be $9,275, resulting in a discount of $725 ($10,000 − $9,275). At the end of the 5-year period, however, will Lender receive back the $9,275? Or will it receive the full $10,000? The answer is: the full $10,000. Remember the following important rule: *A note always pays exactly what it says*. Since this note says $10,000 and interest of $1,000 (10% × $10,000), that is exactly what it will pay. But *effectively* Lender is earning 12%, since it only lent out $9,275 and receives back the full $10,000. Thus the extra $725 is really *additional interest*.

Let's assume this loan took place on January 1, 19X1. The entry at that time is:

Note Receivable	10,000	
Cash		9,275
Discount on Note Receivable		725

The note receivable account is always debited at the face amount, and the discount acts as a contra to this account. At this point the net receivable is $9,275, and it appears on the balance sheet in the following manner:

Note Receivable	$10,000
Discount on Note	(725)
Net Receivable	$ 9,275 (the present value)

With time, however, the discount account will slowly "vanish" (be amortized to interest revenue); thus the net receivable will get larger until it reaches the full $10,000 by the end of the 5-year period. At all times the net receivable will be equal to the present value of all the future payments. This is an important point.

Each December 31 an entry is made to amortize the discount, as follows:

Discount on Note Receivable	xxx
Interest Revenue	xxx

The discount, as mentioned earlier, represents additional interest. That is why each year we credit interest revenue for a part of the discount. In addition to this, Lender also receives an annual interest check of $1,000 for which it makes the following entry:

Cash   1,000
    Interest Revenue   1,000

Thus Lender's total interest revenue for the year consists of the $1,000 physically received, plus the amortization of the discount.

The amount of the discount to be amortized annually may be determined under two possible methods: the straight-line method and the effective interest method. These are illustrated in the next example.

EXAMPLE 16

Refer to Example 15. Under the straight-line method, Lender would take the $725 discount and divide it by the life of the note (5 years), yielding $145 per year. Under the effective interest method, however, the amortization will differ from year to year and is determined by the use of the following table:

	(1) Contract Rate (10%)	(2) Market Rate (12%)	(3) Amortization of Discount	(4) Discount Balance	(5) Net Receivable
Date of Issue	—	—	—	$725	$9,275
End of Year 1	$1,000	$1,113	$113	612	9,388
End of Year 2	1,000	1,127	127	485	9,515
End of Year 3	1,000	1,142	142	343	9,657
End of Year 4	1,000	1,159	159	184	9,816
End of Year 5	1,000	1,178	178	6	9,994*

*This number should be $10,000, but because we did some rounding in our computations, plus the fact that our interest tables have only three decimal places, we are slightly off the mark.

Here is how this table works. Column 1 is the contract rate of interest multiplied by the face value of $10,000, yielding $1,000 annually. Column 2 is the market rate (12%) multiplied by column 5. The main column is column 3, which gives us what we are looking for: the annual amortization. This is simply the difference between columns 1 and 2. (Thus our annual amortization changes from year to year.) Column 4 shows the discount remaining each year (unamortized), while column 5 shows the net receivable—the $10,000 face value of the note less the discount balance from column 4.

The accounting profession has stated that the effective interest method of amortization should be used, unless the difference between this method and the straight-line method is immaterial.

In Example 16 the market rate was greater than the contract rate. If the market rate is less than the contract rate, however, the note will be issued at a premium—an amount greater than its face value—and the above table would begin with this large amount in column 5 as the net receivable. With time the premium will slowly be amortized *down* to the face value at the end. Thus, while the company lent out an amount *greater* than face value, it will be paid back only the face value. Each annual amortization entry therefore *reduces* interest revenue, as follows:

Interest Revenue   xxx
    Premium on Note Receivable   xxx

Thus the annual interest revenue consists of the physical interest received, *minus* the amortization of the premium.

7.7 NOTES RECEIVABLE WITH NO INTEREST OR UNREASONABLE INTEREST

During the 1960s and 1970s numerous transactions were made involving *in form* either no apparent interest, or unreasonably low interest. However, the accounting profession has always emphasized *substance* over *form* in the recording and reporting of transactions. Thus, for accounting purposes, additional "hidden" interest must be recognized.

We shall first discuss notes received for cash with no stated interest rate.

EXAMPLE 17

On January 1, 19X1, Lender lends Borrower cash of $6,810 for a "non-interest"-bearing 5-year note with a face value of $10,000. (This type of note is often referred to as a *zero coupon note*.) In form the note is non-interest-bearing; in substance, however, there *is* interest at 8% (because according to the interest tables, a present value of $6,810 will grow into $10,000 in 5 years at this rate). The entry at issuance will be:

Notes Receivable	10,000	
Discount on Note Receivable		3,190
Cash		6,810

On December 31, 19X1, Lender amortizes the discount and recognizes interest revenue by the following entry:

Discount on Note Receivable	545 (rounded)	
Interest Revenue		545*

*Using the effective interest method, we multiply $6,810 by 8%, yielding $545.

If a note is received for *goods or services* and the note contains either no stated interest rate, an unreasonable stated interest rate, or the face amount of the note is significantly different from the fair market value of the goods and services, the note should be recorded at the fair market value of the goods and services. Any difference between the fair market value and the face amount of the note is considered "hidden" interest.

EXAMPLE 18

Seller sells Buyer a piece of land for a 10-year, non-interest-bearing note of $20,000. The land originally cost Seller $14,000 and its current fair market value is $17,000. It would be incorrect for Seller to make the following entry:

Notes Receivable	20,000	
Land		14,000
Gain on Sale of Land		6,000

This is wrong because the true selling price is the market value of $17,000; the extra $3,000 is "hidden" interest. Thus the gain is only $3,000 and the entry is:

Notes Receivable	20,000	
Discount on Note Receivable		3,000
Land		14,000
Gain on Sale of Land		3,000*

*Selling price of $17,000 − cost of $14,000.

The $3,000 discount is gradually amortized to interest revenue over the 10-year life of the note.

If the fair market value of the goods or services is not known, we must estimate the interest rate by a process called *imputation*, and the resulting rate is called the imputed rate. According to Accounting Principles Board *Opinion No. 21*, this is the rate the buyer would have to pay to obtain financing of a similar nature from other sources at the date of this transaction. We use this rate to obtain the present value of the note and that is the true selling price.

EXAMPLE 19

Seller sells Buyer a piece of land for a 3-year, non-interest-bearing note with a face value of $20,000. Seller's original cost was $14,000, but the current fair market value of the land is unknown. Buyer would have to pay 10% interest in the marketplace for similar financing. Thus the true selling price is the present value of $20,000 at 10% for 3 periods, which is

$$0.751 \times \$20,000 = \$15,020$$

and the gain on the sale will therefore be $1,020 ($15,020 − $14,000). The entry is:

Notes Receivable	20,000	
Discount on Note Receivable		4,980
Land		14,000
Gain on Sale of Land		1,020

The discount will gradually be amortized to interest revenue over the 3-year life, preferably by the effective interest method.

EXAMPLE 20

Seller performs services for Buyer and receives a 2% interest-bearing note for $10,000 due in 5 years. The market value for these services is unknown; the 2% interest rate is unreasonably low in today's market. We therefore must take the present value of *both* the future principal of $10,000 *and* the present value of the annual annuity of $200 ($10,000 × 2%) to arrive at the true selling price. If the buyer's imputed rate is 10%, the computations are:

Present value of $10,000, 5 periods, 10%   = 0.621 × $10,000 = $6,210
Present value of annuity of $200, 5 periods, 10% = 3.791 × $200 =   758
                                        Selling price is: $6,968   (rounded)

The entry is therefore:

Notes Receivable	10,000	
Discount on Note Receivable		3,032
Service Revenue		6,968

Each period Seller makes two entries regarding the interest. One entry is for the physical receipt of $200, as follows:

Cash	200	
Interest Revenue		200

The other entry is for the amortization of the discount:

Discount on Note Receivable	xxx	
Interest Revenue		xxx

The amount of this entry will depend on the amortization method used.

7.8   DISCOUNTING NOTES RECEIVABLE

When we discussed accounts receivable earlier in this chapter, we mentioned that they are often transferred to other parties for the purpose of quick collection before maturity. This is also true of notes receivable and is referred to as *discounting*. The process is quite simple: The holder of the note gives the note to a bank and in exchange receives the maturity value of the note (principal plus interest), minus a discount. At maturity, the bank collects the maturity value from the maker of the note.

Notes may be discounted with or without recourse. If the discounting is done *without recourse*, an outright sale of the note to the bank has taken place. Notes receivable are thus credited and the difference between the book value of the note and the selling price is either a gain or loss.

If the discounting is done on a *with recourse* basis, then the transaction is considered a sale if the three conditions mentioned earlier (for the transfer of accounts receivable) are met. If not, the transaction is not a sale but a borrowing from the bank, and interest expense or revenue is recognized, instead of a gain or loss.

The following steps are taken to determine the proceeds paid by the bank, the note's book value, and the gain or loss (or interest) on the transaction, for the discounting of a note:

1. Compute the maturity value (principal plus interest at maturity).
2. Compute the discount. This is equal to the maturity value times the bank's discount rate times the time to maturity from the discount date.
3. Compute the proceeds. This is the maturity value minus the discount.
4. Compute the book value of the note. This is the face value of the note plus any interest accrued to the date of the discounting.
5. Compute the gain, loss, or interest. This is the proceeds minus the book value.

EXAMPLE 21

On July 31, White Company discounts at the bank a customer's 3-month, $5,000 note dated May 31 and bearing interest at 12% per annum. The bank accepts the note *with recourse* and discounts it at 15%. The five-step procedure listed above is carried out as follows:

1. Maturity value = principal + interest
$$= \$5,000 + (\$5,000 \times 0.12 \times \tfrac{3}{12})$$
$$= \$5,000 + \$150$$
$$= \$5,150$$

2. Discount = maturity value × discount rate × discount period
$$= \$5,150 \times 0.15 \times \tfrac{1}{12}$$
$$= \$64 \quad \text{(rounded)}$$

3. Proceeds = maturity value − discount
$$= \$5,150 - \$64$$
$$= \$5,086$$

4. Note book value = Face of note + accrued interest
$$= \$5,000 + (\$5,000 \times 0.12 \times \tfrac{2}{12})$$
$$= \$5,000 + (\$100)$$
$$= \$5,100$$

5. Proceeds minus book value = $5,086 − $5,100
$$= \$14$$

If the transaction is treated as a sale, the $14 is a loss on the sale; if it is treated as a borrowing, the $14 is interest expense.

EXAMPLE 22

Let's prepare the journal entries for the previous example.

If treated as a sale
To accrue interest at July 31:

Interest Receivable	100	
Interest Revenue		100*

*$5,000 \times 0.12 \times \frac{2}{12}$

For the discounting:

Cash	5,086	
Loss on Sale of Note	14	
Note Receivable		5,000
Interest Receivable		100

For the collection of the note on August 31:
No entry (the bank collects the money)

If treated as a borrowing
To accrue interest at July 31:

Interest Receivable	100	
Interest Revenue		100

For the discounting:

Cash	5,086	
Interest Expense	14	
Liability to Bank		5,000
Interest Receivable		100

For the collection of the note on August 31:

Liability to Bank	5,000	
Notes Receivable		5,000

If the note was discounted *with recourse*, the bank has a right to go back to the transferor and demand the maturity value plus a clerical fee (''protest fee'') if the maker defaults on the payment. If this happens, the transferor may then go back to the maker and demand to be reimbursed for the payment to the bank.

EXAMPLE 23

If, in Example 22, the maker defaulted on August 31, and the bank charges the transferor the maturity value of $5,150 plus a $25 protest fee, the entries for the transferor under both methods are:

If treated as a sale

Accounts Receivable (Maker)	5,175	
Cash		5,175

If treated as a borrowing

Accounts Receivable (Maker)	5,175	
Cash		5,175
Liability to Bank	5,000	
Notes Receivable		5,000

Summary

1. Receivables may be classified under two broad categories: trade and non-trade. *Trade receivables* are due from customers for goods and services and may be oral or written. Oral ones are accounts receivable; written ones are notes receivable. *Non-trade receivables* arise from other transactions, such as advances to employees and officers, dividends, and interest.

2. Cash discounts are reductions of the selling price for early payment. Under the *gross method*, the sale is recorded at the full selling price. If the customer pays early, the discount is recorded in the sales discount account, which is a contra to the sales account.

3. Under the *net method*, the sale is recorded at the net selling price. If the customer pays *after* the discount period, the extra amount goes to the revenue account, Sales Discounts Forefeited. The accounting profession prefers this method.

4. Because of the matching principle, the accounting for bad debts uses the allowance method. This method requires the recognition of bad debts even before they take place, via an adjusting entry

using estimates. This entry debits bad debts expense and credits Allowance for Doubtful Accounts which acts as a contra to Accounts Receivable.

5.   When we find out for certain that a customer will not pay, we "write off" his or her account by debiting the allowance account and crediting accounts receivable.

6.   The estimate of bad debts expense may be based on either a percentage of the receivables (the aging method) or a percentage of credit sales. There is a critical, subtle difference between the two: The former method takes into account what already is in the allowance account; the latter method does not.

7.   *Assignment of receivables* involves borrowing money from a bank or finance company, pledging the receivables as collateral, and paying an initial finance charge plus interest during the period the loan is outstanding.

8.   *Sales of receivables* involve an outright transfer of the receivables to the finance company. Also known as *factoring*, this transfer may be done with or without recourse. In a *with recourse* situation, the seller is responsible for any bad debts; in a *without recourse* situation, the seller is not. In both cases the seller *is* responsible for sales returns and discounts.

9.   When the transfer is made without recourse, it is treated as a sale for accounting purposes. If the transfer is made with recourse, however, three conditions need to be met to consider it a sale. If they are not met, the transfer, for accounting purposes, is not a sale but a borrowing.

10. *Notes* are written promises to pay a certain sum in the future. Interest-bearing notes have an explicitly stated rate of interest; non-interest-bearing notes have "hidden" interest.

11. If the rate stated in the note (the contract rate) is equal to the market rate, the note will be issued at its face value. If it is below the market rate, it will be issued at a discount; if it is above the market rate, it will be issued at a premium.

12. To determine the amount the note will be issued for, use the following formula:

Loan = present value of principal + present value of interest payments

For these present values, the interest tables should be looked up at the *market rate*, not the contract rate.

13. *Discounts* represent an addition to interest revenue; *premiums* represent a reduction. Both discounts and premiums should be amortized via the effective interest method, unless the straight-line method produces results that are not materially different.

14. If a note is received for goods or services and it contains no stated interest or unreasonably low interest, the note should be recorded at the fair market value of the goods or services. Any difference between this value and the face of the note is considered "hidden" interest. If the fair market value is unknown, we must use an *imputed* rate. This is the rate the buyer would have to pay to obtain financing of a similar nature from other sources.

15. Notes receivable may be transferred to other parties by a process called *discounting*. The holder of the note transfers the note to a bank and in exchange receives the maturity value minus a discount. When the note matures, the banker collects the maturity value from the original maker of the note. Discounting may be done with or without recourse, and our earlier discussion of these matters with regard to accounts receivable applies to notes receivable as well.

Rapid Review

1. Receivables due from customers for goods and services are called _____ receivables.

2. The two methods for recording sales with cash discounts are the _____ method and the _____ method.

3. The direct method of accounting for bad debts is a violation of the _____ principle.

4. The Allowance for Doubtful Accounts acts as a contra to the _____ account.

5. When it becomes clear that a customer will definitely not pay a receivable, we make a _____ entry.

6. Borrowing money from the bank and pledging the receivables as collateral is called _____.

7. If the receivables are sold with _____, the seller is responsible for bad debts. In all cases, the seller is responsible for _____ and _____.

8. If notes do not contain a reasonable interest rate, we assume that there is _____ interest.

9. The rate stated in the note is referred to as the _____ rate.

10. If the stated rate is below the market rate, the note will be issued at a _____; if it is above the market rate, it will be issued at a _____.

11. The loan will be equal to the present value of the _____ plus the present value of the _____.

12. The amortization of a premium _____ the interest revenue, while the amortization of a discount _____ it.

13. For notes with no interest or unreasonably low interest, the estimated rate we use is referred to as the _____ rate.

14. Notes may be transferred to other parties by a process called _____.

Answers: **1.** trade **2.** gross; net **3.** matching **4.** Accounts Receivable **5.** write-off **6.** assignment **7.** recourse; returns; discounts **8.** hidden **9.** contract **10.** discount; premium **11.** principal; interest **12.** decreases; increases **13.** imputed **14.** discounting

Solved Problems

Accounts Receivable: General

7.1   A product has a list price of $200, a trade discount of 25% and terms of 2/10, N/30. If goods worth $30 are returned and payment is made within the discount period, determine the amount paid.

SOLUTION

	$200	
Trade discount	− 50	
	$150	
Return	− 30	
	$120	
Discount	− 2.40	2% of $120
Amount paid	$117.60		[Section 7.2]

7.2   Goods of $500 are sold on terms of 3/10, N/30. Prepare the entries under both the gross and net methods for the sale, for payment within the discount period and payment after the discount period.

SOLUTION

GROSS METHOD

Accounts Receivable	500	
Sales		500

Cash	485	
Sales Discount	15	
Accounts Receivable		500

Cash	500	
Accounts Receivable		500

NET METHOD

Accounts Receivable	485	
Sales		485

Cash	485	
Accounts Receivable		485

Cash	500	
Accounts Receivable		485
Sales Discount Forfeited		15

[Section 7.2]

Accounts Receivable: Bad Debts

7.3   Company A has given you the following information regarding bad debts:

Dec. 31, 19X1   Estimate bad debt expense to be 5% of its net sales of $50,000.
Jan. 15, 19X2   Mr. Poor defaults on his $1,400 balance.
Feb. 2, 19X3   Mr. Poor repays $800 of the $1,400.

Prepare entries for this information.

SOLUTION

Dec. 31, 19X1	Bad Debts Expense	2,500	
	Allowance for Doubtful Accounts		2,500

Jan. 15, 19X2	Allowance for Doubtful Accounts	1,400	
	Accounts Receivable		1,400

Feb. 2, 19X3	Accounts Receivable	800	
	Allowance for Doubtful Accounts		800

| Cash | 800 | |
| Accounts Receivable | | 800 |

[Section 7.3]

7.4 Company B has an allowance account with a *credit* balance of $1,500. Prepare the entry to recognize bad debt expense if:

(*a*) Bad debts are estimated at 3% of credit sales of $40,000.

(*b*) Bad debts are estimated at 6% of accounts receivable whose balance is $30,000.

    In addition, show the allowance account *after* the above entry has been made, for both parts (*a*) and (*b*).

SOLUTION

(*a*)   Bad Debts Expense   1,200

                      Allowance for Doubtful Accounts   1,200

Allowance for Doubtful Accounts	
	1,500
	1,200
	2,700 Bal.

(*b*)   Bad Debts Expense   300

                      Allowance for Doubtful Accounts   300*

                  *($1,500 − [6% × 30,000]).

Allowance for Doubtful Accounts	
	1,500
	300
	1,800 Bal.

[Section 7.3]

7.5 Assume the same information as in Problem 7.4, except that the allowance account has a *debit* balance of $700. Answer parts (*a*) and (*b*) of Problem 7.4.

SOLUTION

(*a*)   Bad Debts Expense   1,200

                      Allowance for Doubtful Accounts   1,200

Allowance for Doubtful Accounts	
700	1,200
	500 Bal.

(*b*)   Bad Debts Expense   2,500

                      Allowance for Doubtful Accounts   2,500

Allowance for Doubtful Accounts	
700	2,500
	1,800 Bal.

[Section 7.3]

7.6   Company C uses the following probabilities to age its receivables:

Age	Balance	Probability of Default
1–60 days	$50,000	1%
61–120 days	40,000	3%
121–180 days	10,000	7%
Over 180 days	2,000	10%

(*a*)   Determine estimated bad debts.

(*b*)   Prepare the necessary adjusting entry. Assume that the allowance account has a *credit* balance of $2,200.

SOLUTION

(*a*)
$$\$50,000 \times 1\% \ = \$ \ \ 500$$
$$40,000 \times 3\% \ = \ 1,200$$
$$10,000 \times 7\% \ = \ \ \ 700$$
$$2,000 \times 10\% = \ \ \ 200$$
$$\$2,600$$

(*b*)

Bad Debt Expense	400*	
Allowance for Doubtful Accounts		400

*$2,600 − $2,200.   [Section 7.3]

7.7   Company D has the following transactions for 19X2 and 19X3.

Feb. 18, 19X2   Make sales on account of $80,000.
June 15, 19X2   Collect $50,000 on account.
Dec. 31, 19X2   Estimate bad debts at 3% of the accounts receivable balance. At this point the allowance account has a credit balance of $800.
Jan. 10, 19X3   Write off Mr. Goodman for $200.
Feb. 22, 19X3   Recover the $200.

SOLUTION

Feb. 18, 19X2	Accounts Receivable	80,000	
	Sales		80,000
June 15, 19X2	Cash	50,000	
	Accounts Receivable		50,000
Dec. 31, 19X2	Bad Debts Expense	100	
	Allowance for Doubtful Accounts		100
	[3% × ($80,000 − $50,000)] − $800.		
Jan. 10, 19X3	Allowance for Doubtful Accounts	200	
	Accounts Receivable		200
Feb. 22, 19X3	Accounts Receivable	200	
	Allowance for Doubtful Accounts		200

Cash		200	
Accounts Receivable			200

[Section 7.3]

Assignment of Accounts Receivable

7.8 Company E engages in the following transactions involving the assignment of its receivables.

Jan. 15   Pledges $80,000 of receivables for a $70,000 loan at 10% annual interest; pays a 1% finance fee.

Feb. 15   Collects $50,000 of the receivables and remits the cash to the bank with interest.

Apr. 15   Collects $28,000 of the remaining $30,000 of the receivables ($2,000 is a sales return). Pays the balance of the bank loan, plus interest.

Prepare entries for these transactions.

SOLUTION

Jan. 15	Accounts Receivable Assigned	80,000	
	Accounts Receivable		80,000
	Cash	69,300	
	Finance Charge	700	
	Note Payable		70,000
Feb. 15	Cash	50,000	
	Accounts Receivable Assigned		50,000
	Note Payable	50,000	
	Interest Expense	583*	
	Cash		50,583

*$70,000 × 10% × 1/12 = $583 (rounded).

Apr. 15	Cash	28,000	
	Sales Returns	2,000	
	Accounts Receivable Assigned		30,000
	Note Payable	20,000	
	Interest Expense	500[†]	
	Cash		20,500

[†]($70,000 − $50,000) × 10% × $\frac{3}{12}$.

[Section 7.4]

Sale (Transfer) of Accounts Receivable

7.9 Company E transfers receivables of $80,000 *without* recourse to Finance Bank. The bank charges a 3% fee and withholds an additional 7% to cover sales returns and discounts. Prepare the entries for:

(*a*)   The transfer

(*b*)   A sales return of $1,000

(*c*)   Collection of the balance due from Finance Bank

SOLUTION

(a)

Cash		72,000	
Loss on Receivable Sale		2,400	
Due from Factor		5,600	
Accounts Receivable			80,000

(b)

Sales Returns		1,000	
Due from Factor			1,000

(c)

Cash		4,600		
Due from Factor			4,600	[Section 7.5]

7.10 What are the three conditions that need to be fulfilled for a transfer with recourse to be considered a sale? Must all three be fulfilled? Or is any one satisfactory?

SOLUTION

All three conditions must be fulfilled, and they are:

1. The transferor surrenders control of the future economic benefits.
2. The obligation under the recourse provision can be reasonably estimated.
3. The transferee cannot require the transferor to repurchase the receivables.   [Section 7.5]

7.11 Company F transfers a receivable of $25,000 with recourse to Finance Factor. The Factor charges a 2% fee and withholds an additional 6% for possible returns and discounts. Prepare the entry for the transfer if:

(a) The three conditions have been met.
(b) The three conditions have not been met.

SOLUTION

(a)

Cash		23,000	
Loss on Sale of Receivables		500	
Due from Factor		1,500	
Accounts Receivable			25,000

(b)

Cash		23,000		
Finance Charge		500		
Due from Factor		1,500		
Loan Payable to Factor			25,000	[Section 7.5]

Notes Receivable with Reasonable Interest Rates

7.12 On January 1, 19X1, Company G lends money to Company H in exchange for a $50,000 note. Both the contract and market rates are 10% annually, and payment is due in 3 years. Determine the amount of the loan and prepare entries for the loan, the receipt of interest on December 31, and the repayment of the loan.

SOLUTION

Since the contract rate and market rate are equal, the loan is equal to the $50,000 face value of the note.

Jan. 1, 19X1	Notes Receivable		50,000	
	Cash			50,000
Dec. 31	Cash		5,000	
	Interest Revenue			5,000
At maturity	Cash		50,000	
	Notes Receivable			50,000	[Section 7.6]

7.13 Assume the same information as in Problem 7.12, except that the market rate is 14%.

(a) Determine the amount of the loan.

(b) Prepare entries for the loan, the receipt of the interest, the amortization of premium or discount, and the repayment at maturity.

Use the straight-line method of amortization.

SOLUTION

(a)   Present value $50,000, 14%, 3 periods $= 0.675 \times \$50,000 = \$33,750$
         Present value $5,000* annuity, 14%, 3 periods $= 2.322 \times \$ 5,000 = \underline{11,610}$
                                                         Loan: $45,360

         ―――――――――
         *50,000 × 10%.

(b)   Jan. 1, 19X1   Notes Receivable   50,000
                              Discount on Note   4,640
                              Cash   45,360

         Dec. 31   Cash   5,000
                              Interest Revenue   5,000
                         Discount on Note   1,547 (rounded)
                              Interest Revenue   1,547
                              ($4,640 ÷ 3).

         At maturity   Cash   50,000
                              Notes Receivable   50,000

                                                              [Section 7.6]

7.14 An 8% note with a face value of $30,000 is received for a loan to yield the market rate of 10%. The note becomes due in 3 years.

(a) Determine the amount of the loan.

(b) Prepare an amortization table.

SOLUTION

(a)   Present value $30,000, 3 years, 10%   = 0.751 × $30,000 = $22,530
       Present value $2,400* annuity, 3 years, 10% = 2.487 × $ 2,400 =   5,969
                                                                   Loan: $28,499   (rounded)

*30,000 × 8%.

(b)

	8%	10%	Amortization	Discount Balance	Net Receivable
Date of Issue	—	—	—	$1,501	$28,499
End of Year 1	$2,400	$2,850	$450	1,051	28,949
End of Year 2	2,400	2,895	495	556	29,444
End of Year 3	2,400	2,944	544	0 (rounded)	30,000

[Section 7.6]

7.15 On January 1, 19X1 Company J lends money to Company K for a $60,000 note due in 3 years. The contract rate is 10%; the market rate is 9%.

(a)   Determine the amount of the loan.

(b)   Prepare entries on the books of Company J for the loan, the receipt of the annual interest, the annual amortization (straight-line method), and the repayment at maturity.

(c)   Determine net interest revenue for the year.

SOLUTION

(a)   Present value of $60,000, 9%, 3 periods   = 0.772 × $60,000 = $46,320
       Present value of $6,000* annuity, 9%, 3 periods = 2.531 × $ 6,000 = 15,186
                                                                   Loan: $61,506   (rounded)

*$60,000 × 10%.

(b)   Jan. 1, 19X1   Notes Receivable   60,000
                                  Premium on Note   1,506
                                       Cash   61,506

                 Dec. 31   Cash   6,000
                                       Interest Revenue   6,000

                                  Interest Revenue   502
                                       Premium on Note   502
                                       ($1,506 ÷ 3).

                 At maturity   Cash   60,000
                                       Notes Receivable   60,000

(c) $5,498 ($6,000 − $502)   [Section 7.6]

7.16 An 8% note with a face value of $70,000 is received for a loan yielding the market rate of 6%. The note is due in 3 years. Determine the amount of the loan and prepare an amortization table.

SOLUTION

Present value of $70,000, 6%, 3 periods $= 0.840 \times \$70,000 = \$58,800$
Present value of annuity of $5,600*, 6%, 3 periods $= 2.673 \times \$ \ 5,600 = \underline{\ \ \ 14,969}$
                                                        Loan: $\overline{\$73,769}$ (rounded)

_____

*8% × $70,000.

	8%	6%	Amortization	Premium Balance	Net Receivable
Date of Issue	—	—	—	$3,769	$73,769
End of Year 1	$5,600	$4,426	$1,174	2,595	72,595
End of Year 2	5,600	4,356	1,244	1,351	71,351
End of Year 3	5,600	4,281	1,319	0 (rounded)	70,000

[Section 7.6]

Notes Receivable with No Interest or Unreasonable Interest

7.17 On January 1, 19X1, Lender lends Borrower cash of $9,968 for a 3-year, $14,000, non-interest-bearing note.

(a) Determine the implicit interest rate.

(b) Prepare the journal entry for the loan.

(c) Prepare an amortization entry on December 31, 19X1, using the effective interest method.

SOLUTION

(a) $14,000 (table value) = $9,968
              Table value = 0.712
     Searching the table for 0.712 at the 3-period row yields a rate of 12%.

(b)   Notes Receivable   14,000
                             Cash   9,968
                             Discount on Note   4,032

(c)   Discount on Note   1,196*
                             Interest Revenue   1,196
                        *$9,968 × 12% = $1,196 (rounded).   [Section 7.7]

7.18 Morty Milner performs legal services for Green Corporation and receives a $10,000, non-interest-bearing note due in 4 years. Prepare the journal entry for Morty Milner if:

(a) The fair market value of these services is $7,000.

(b) The fair market value is unknown; however, Green's imputed interest rate is 10%.

SOLUTION

(a)   Notes Receivable   10,000
                             Discount on Note   3,000
                             Service Revenue   7,000

(b) Present value of $10,000, 4 periods, 10% = 0.683 × $10,000 = $6,830.

Notes Receivable	10,000	
Discount on Note		3,170
Service Revenue		6,830

[Section 7.7]

7.19 Seller sells Buyer a piece of land with original cost of $12,000 for an $18,000, non-interest-bearing note due in 4 years. The fair market value of the land is $16,000. Prepare the entry for the sale and the amortization of the discount (straight-line method).

SOLUTION

Note Receivable	18,000	
Discount on Note		2,000
Land		12,000
Gain on Sale of Land		4,000
Discount on Note	500	
Interest Revenue		500*

*$2,000 ÷ 4.

[Section 7.7]

7.20 Seller performs services for Buyer and receives a 2% interest-bearing note for $25,000 due in 4 years. The market value of these services is unknown; the 2% rate is unreasonably low for the present market, where the rate is 10%.

(a) Determine how much *physical* interest Seller will receive annually.

(b) Determine the true selling price for these services.

(c) Prepare a journal entry for the rendering of the services and the annual physical interest.

(d) Prepare the necessary amortization entry under the straight-line method.

SOLUTION

(a) $25,000 × 2% = $500.

(b)
Present value, $25,000, 10%, 4 periods   = 0.683 × $25,000 = $17,075
Present value, $500 annuity, 10%, 4 periods = 3.170 × $ 500 =   1,585
                                                      True selling price: $18,660

(c)
Notes Receivable	25,000	
Discount on Note		6,340
Service Revenue		18,660
Cash	500	
Interest Revenue		550

(d)
Discount on Note	1,585	
Interest Revenue		1,585

[Section 7.7]

Discounting Notes Receivable

7.21 On July 1, Aron Englard discounts at the bank a customer's 6-month, $14,000 note dated March

1 and bearing interest at 10% per annum. The bank accepts the note with recourse and discounts it at 12%. Determine the note's maturity value, the discount, the proceeds, and the book value of the note.

SOLUTION

$$
\begin{aligned}
\text{Maturity value} &= \$14,000 + (\$14,000 \times 0.10 \times \tfrac{6}{12}) \\
&= \$14,000 + \$700 \\
&= \$14,700 \\
\text{Discount} &= \$14,700 \times 0.12 \times \tfrac{2}{12} \\
&= \$294 \\
\text{Proceeds} &= \$14,700 - \$294 \\
&= \$14,406 \\
\text{Book value} &= \$14,000 + (\$14,000 \times 0.10 \times \tfrac{4}{12}*) \\
&\quad *(\text{Mar. 1 to July 1 is 4 months}) \\
&= \$14,000 + (\$467) \\
&= \$14,467 \qquad\qquad\qquad \text{[Section 7.8]}
\end{aligned}
$$

7.22 For the note in Problem 7.21, prepare journal entries for the accrued interest at July 1, the discounting on that date, and the bank collection on September 1. Assume the following two cases:

Case I: The discounting is to be treated as a sale.

Case II: The discounting is to be treated as a borrowing.

SOLUTION

Case I			Case II		
Interest Receivable	467		Interest Receivable	467	
Interest Revenue		467	Interest Revenue		467
($14,000 \times 0.10 \times \tfrac{4}{12}$).					
Cash	14,406		Cash	14,406	
Loss on Sale of Note	61*		Interest Expense	61	
Note Receivable		14,000	Liability to Bank		14,000
Interest Receivable		467	Interest Receivable		467
*(Book value − proceeds)					
Sept. 1			*Sept. 1*		
No entry			Liability to Bank	14,000	
			Notes Receivable		14,000

[Section 7.8]

7.23 For the note in Problems 7.21 and 7.22, prepare the entries for both cases if on Sept. 1 the maker defaults on payment to the bank.

SOLUTION

	Case I			**Case II**	
Accounts Receivable	14,700		Accounts Receivable	14,700	
Cash		14,700	Cash		14,700
			Liability to Bank	14,000	
			Notes Receivable		14,000

[Section 7.8]

Supplementary Problems

7.24 Goods are sold at $9,000 with terms of 4/10, N/30. If goods costing $2,000 are returned and payment is made within the discount period, determine the amount paid.

7.25 Goods of $800 are sold with a trade discount of 10% and under terms of 2/10, N/30. Prepare the entries under the gross and net methods for the sale, payment within the discount period, and payment after the discount period.

7.26 Prepare entries for the following transactions involving receivables.

Dec. 31, 19X1   Estimate of bad debts is 4% of the accounts receivable balance of $10,000. The allowance account presently has a $350 credit balance.
Feb. 16, 19X2   Mr. Kind defaults on his $225 balance.
Mar. 2, 19X2   Mr. Kind pays $180 of the $225.

7.27 Supercredit Corporation has an allowance account with a debit balance of $2,000. Prepare the entry to recognize bad debt expense if:

(*a*) Bad debts are estimated at 4% of credit sales of $80,000.

(*b*) Bad debts are estimated at 4% of accounts receivable of $90,000.

Show what the allowance account would look like after these entries.

7.28 Brown Company uses the following categories and probabilities to age its receivables:

Age	Balance	Probability of Default
1–120 days	$70,000	2%
Over 120 days	30,000	6%

(*a*) Determine estimated bad debts.

(*b*) Prepare the necessary entry. Assume that the allowance account has a credit balance of $2,600.

7.29 Blue Company engages in the following transactions involving the assignment of its receivables:

Apr. 10   Pledges $50,000 for a $38,000 loan at 10% annual interest. The finance fee is 2% of the loan.
May 10   Collects $30,000 of the receivable and remits it to the bank plus interest.
July 10   Collects the balance of the receivables minus a $1,500 sales return, and pays the balance of the loan, plus interest.

Prepare entries for these transactions.

7.30   Tan Corporation transfers receivables of $60,000, without recourse, to Finance Factor. Finance Factor charges a 2% fee and withholds an additional 4% to cover returns and discounts. Prepare the entries for Tan to record the transfer, a sales discount of $2,300, and collection of the balance due from Finance Factor.

7.31   Assume the same information as in Problem 7.30, except that the transfer is made with recourse. Prepare the entries for the above transactions if:

(a)   The three conditions have not been met.

(b)   The three conditions have been met.

7.32   On January 1, 19X1, Company Y lends money to Company Z in exchange for a $70,000 note due in 4 years. Both the contract rate and market rate are 7%. Determine the amount of the loan and prepare entries on the books of Company Y for the loan, the receipt of interest on December 31, and the repayment of the loan on December 31, 19X4.

7.33   Assume the same information as in Problem 7.32, except that the market rate is 9%.

(a)   Determine the loan amount.

(b)   Prepare entries for the loan, the receipt of interest, the amortization of the discount, and the repayment at maturity. Use the straight-line method of amortization.

7.34   Do Problem 7.33 if the market rate is only 6%.

7.35   If a 5%, $20,000, four-year note is received for a loan, and the market rate is 6%, determine the amount of the loan and prepare an amortization table.

7.36   A 16% note with a face value of $16,000 is received for a loan. The market rate is 14%, and the loan is due in 3 years. Determine the loan amount and prepare an amortization table.

7.37   Stanley Bodner, M.D., performs medical services for Sickman and receives a $4,000, non-interest-bearing note due in 3 years. Prepare the journal entry for Dr. Bodner if:

(a)   The fair market value of these services is $3,200.

(b)   The fair market value is unknown; however, Sickman's imputed interest rate is 12%.

7.38   A sells B a piece of land for $25,000 and receives a 3-year, non-interest-bearing note for this amount. The land's original cost to A was $17,000; its current market value is $22,000. Prepare the entry for the sale and the amortization of any discount or premium (straight-line method).

7.39   A performs services for B and receives a 3% interest-bearing note for $20,000 due in 3 years. The market value of these services is unknown; the market rate of interest is 10%.

(a)   Determine the true selling price of these services.

(b)   Prepare a journal entry for the services and the receipt of the annual interest check.

(c)   Prepare the amortization entry under the straight-line method.

7.40   On August 1, Harry Dym discounts at the bank a client's 8-month, $8,000 note dated May 1 and bearing interest at 10% per annum. The bank accepts the note with recourse and discounts it at 12%. Determine the note's maturity value, the discount, the proceeds and the note's book value.

7.41   For Problem 7.40, prepare journal entries for the accrued interest on August 1, the discounting of the note, and the collection by the bank on November 1. Assume two cases:

Case I: The discounting is treated as a sale.

Case II: The discounting is treated as a borrowing.

7.42   For Problem 7.41, prepare the entries for both cases if on November 1 the maker defaults on payment to the bank.

Chapter 8

Inventories: General Topics

8.1 INTRODUCTION

In a merchandising company, inventories are goods held for sale in the ordinary course of business. Thus, in a grocery store, the inventory is the groceries; in an office supply store, the inventory is the paper, pencils, folders, staplers, and other office supplies being sold. No matter what the nature of the inventory is, it is an asset—usually a major one—and it appears on the balance sheet as such.

In a manufacturing company, inventory consists of the finished goods held for sale and other goods that are at various stages of production. Thus, in this type of company there are three inventories: raw materials, work in process, and the finished goods. We will not discuss manufacturing companies in this chapter, since their accounting is discussed in detail in cost accounting textbooks.

All goods owned by a company on December 31 should appear as the asset, "merchandise inventory," on the balance sheet. What about goods that have been shipped to us but are still in transit on this date? If the goods were sent F.O.B. (free on board) shipping point, title passes to us the moment they are shipped and, therefore, we include them on our balance sheet. If, however, they were sent F.O.B. destination, title does not pass until they reach their destination, and we do *not* include them on the balance sheet. They appear on the seller's balance sheet instead.

Consignment goods are goods sent by a *consignor* to a *consignee*. Title *does not* pass to the consignee, who may return them to the consignor. The consignee is merely an *agent* of the consignor to sell the goods. If they are sold, the consignee receives a commission and reimbursement for expenses incurred; if not, the consignee returns the goods. Accordingly, the consignee does *not* include these goods on his or her balance sheet—they belong to the consignor.

Delivery charges on the purchase of goods are not expensed but are added to the cost of the asset inventory. Thus, if goods costing $500 are purchased and there is a delivery charge of $10, it is considered that the goods really cost $510, and this is the balance sheet amount.

The treatment of interest charges, however, is different. If a company borrows money in order to purchase goods, interest on the loan *is an expense* and is not an addition to the cost of the inventory asset.

8.2 PERIODIC SYSTEM VERSUS PERPETUAL SYSTEM

A company may use one of two systems for the record keeping of inventories: periodic or perpetual. Both systems use an account called Merchandise Inventory; however, the *periodic system* does not use this account during the accounting period. Purchases are not debited to this account—they are debited to the Purchases account. Sales are not credited to Merchandise Inventory—they are credited to the Sales account. There is no account used *during the period* called Cost of Goods Sold, and therefore this important figure must be determined by the following computation:*

Cost of goods sold = beginning merchandise inventory + net purchases − ending merchandise inventory

Thus, under the periodic system, the Merchandise Inventory account, having been quite inactive during the period, is out of date by the end of the period and must be updated via a closing entry.

Under the *perpetual system*, the Merchandise Inventory account is very active during the period. It is debited for purchases and credited for sales (at cost, not selling price). No Purchases account is

---

*There is a Cost of Goods Sold account *created at period-end* for use in the closing process, but it does not exist *during the period*.

necessary, and there is a special Cost of Goods Sold account. Closing entries to update the Merchandise Inventory account at period-end are not necessary, except in special cases to be discussed later.

These procedures are illustrated in the following example.

EXAMPLE 1

Company A has the following information relating to its merchandise for 19X1.

Beginning Inventory	$80,000	Ending Inventory	$60,000*
Purchases (on account)	20,000	Purchases Returns	5,000
Sales on account:			
At Cost	35,000		
At Selling Price	50,000		

*Determined by physical count.

The entries under both systems are as follows:

Periodic System			**Perpetual System**		
For the Purchases:			*For the Purchases:*		
Purchases	20,000		Merchandise Inventory	20,000	
Accounts Payable		20,000	Accounts Payable		20,000
For the Purchases Returns:			*For the Purchases Returns:*		
Accounts Payable	5,000		Accounts Payable	5,000	
Purchases Returns		5,000	Merchandise Inventory		5,000
For the Cost of Goods Sold:			*For the Cost of Goods Sold:*		
No entry			Cost of Goods Sold	35,000	
			Merchandise Inventory		35,000
For the Selling Price:			*For the Selling Price:*		
Accounts Receivable	50,000		Accounts Receivable	50,000	
Sales		50,000	Sales		50,000
Closing Entries (to update merchandise inventory):			*Closing Entries* (to update merchandise inventory):		
Cost of Goods Sold	80,000		None		
Merchandise Inventory (beginning)		80,000			
Merchandise Inventory (end)	60,000				
Cost of Goods Sold		60,000			

(For a review of closing entries, see Chapter 1.)

If we examine the Merchandise Inventory account under the *perpetual system*, we clearly see that it is up to date and thus requires no closing entry, as follows:

Merchandise Inventory			
Beginning Balance	80,000	5,000	Purchases Returns
Purchases	20,000	35,000	Cost of Goods Sold
Ending Balance	20,000		

The $20,000 ending balance agrees perfectly with the physical count.

Under the perpetual system the Merchandise Inventory account may occasionally not agree with the physical count at period-end. This is due to errors or shoplifting. In such a situation, an adjusting entry needs to be made to correct this account.

EXAMPLE 2

At period-end the merchandise inventory account shows a balance of $18,500. However, the physical count shows $18,300. The adjusting entry is:

Inventory Short or Over	200	
Merchandise Inventory		200

The Inventory Short or Over account has a dual nature: It is used as both an expense and a revenue account. In the case of a shortage, it is an expense account.

EXAMPLE 3

If the Merchandise Inventory account has a balance of $14,100 but the physical count shows $14,500, we have an overage situation which is considered to be revenue. The adjusting entry is:

Merchandise Inventory	400	
Inventory Short or Over		400

8.3   GROSS METHOD VERSUS NET METHOD

We mentioned that under the periodic system the account purchases is used to record purchases of merchandise. If the purchase is subject to a cash discount for early payment, two methods may be used to record the purchase and other related entries. The *gross method* requires the purchase to be recorded at the full gross amount. If the discount is later taken, then a contra purchases account—Purchases Discounts—is used to reduce the purchase. The *net method* requires the purchase to be recorded at net purchase price minus the discount. Let's look at an example.

EXAMPLE 4

Company B purchases merchandise of $5,000 with terms of 2/10, N/30. The entries under both methods are:

Gross Method			**Net Method**		
For the Purchase:			*For the Purchase:*		
Purchases	5,000		Purchases	4,900	
Accounts Payable		5,000	Accounts Payable		4,900
For Payment within 10 Days:			*For Payment within 10 Days:*		
Accounts Payable	5,000		Accounts Payable	4,900	
Purchases Discounts		100	Cash		4,900
Cash		4,900			
For Payment after 10 Days:			*For Payment after 10 Days:*		
Accounts Payable	5,000		Accounts Payable	4,900	
Cash		5,000	Purchases Discounts Lost	100	
			Cash		5,000

Under the gross method, if payment is made early, the purchase "shrinks" to $4,900; if not, it stays at $5,000. Under the net method, however, the purchase is $4,900 regardless of the time of payment (because since the buyer has the right to pay early, that is an indication that the true price is really only $4,900). Any extra money paid by the buyer for payment after the discount period (in this case, $100) is considered an expense and is debited to Purchases Discounts Lost—an account similar to Interest Expense.

The accounting profession prefers the net method on the theoretical grounds just discussed. However, since the difference between the two methods is usually small and immaterial, either method may be used in practice.

8.4   INVENTORY ERRORS

We have seen in previous chapters that cost of goods sold—a major expense—can be determined in the following manner:

> Beginning inventory
> \+ Net purchases
> _____
> Goods available for sale
> − Ending Inventory
> _____
> Cost of goods sold

Thus, if an error is made in the valuation of the *ending inventory*, cost of goods sold will be affected, and so will net income. If the ending inventory is understated, cost of goods sold will be overstated and thus net income will be understated (because cost of goods sold is an expense and thus plays a role in determining net income). Conversely, if the ending inventory is overstated, cost of goods sold will be understated and net income will be overstated.

The reverse of the above will occur for errors in *beginning inventory*. If the beginning inventory is understated, cost of goods sold will be understated and net income will be overstated. If the beginning inventory is overstated, cost of goods sold will be overstated and net income understated.

EXAMPLE 5

The numbers for the beginning inventory, ending inventory, and cost of goods sold of Company C are as follows:

	Correct	**Incorrect**	
Beginning Inventory	$20,000	$20,000	
Net Purchases	+ 50,000	+ 50,000	
Goods Available for Sale	$70,000	$70,000	
Ending Inventory	− 40,000	− 45,000	overstatement
Cost of Goods Sold	$30,000	$25,000	

These numbers demonstrate that the overstatement of the ending inventory resulted in an understatement of cost of goods sold by the same amount.

EXAMPLE 6

Company D shows the following correct and incorrect numbers for its calculation of cost of goods sold:

	Correct	Incorrect	
Beginning Inventory	$ 90,000	$100,000	overstatement
Net Purchases	+ 60,000	+ 60,000	
Goods Available for Sale	$150,000	$160,000	
Ending Inventory	− 80,000	− 80,000	
Cost of Goods Sold	$ 70,000	$ 80,000	

These numbers demonstrate that an overstatement of the beginning inventory results in an overstatement of cost of goods sold by the same amount.

If an error is made in purchases and the same error—both in direction and in amount—is made in the ending inventory, cost of goods sold will not be affected. The two errors counterbalance each other, resulting in a *correct* cost of goods sold. For example, suppose we purchase goods with terms of F.O.B. shipping point and the goods were shipped on December 28, but did not arrive until January 2. Legally the goods became ours at time of shipment on December 28 and should have been included both in purchases for the period and as part of our ending inventory. However, our staff people, not having seen the goods by December 31, neither recorded the purchase nor included it in the ending inventory count. While the ending inventory presented on the balance sheet will be understated, cost of goods sold on the income statement will *be correct*.

EXAMPLE 7

Company E failed to both record a purchase of $7,000 and include it in the ending inventory. The correct and incorrect figures follow:

	Correct	Incorrect	
Beginning Inventory	$20,000	$20,000	
Purchases	+ 60,000	+ 53,000	understatement
Goods Available for Sale	$80,000	$73,000	
Ending Inventory	− 70,000	− 63,000	understatement
Cost of Goods Sold	$10,000	$10,000	

As we can see, the cost of goods sold is unaffected. This will be true whether the error is an understatement or an overstatement, provided the error is in *both* purchases and ending inventory and is in the *same direction*.

The topic of inventory errors is discussed in greater detail in *Intermediate Accounting II* of this series.

8.5 INVENTORY COSTING METHODS: PERIODIC SYSTEM

The value of the inventory at period-end is a critical one. It is presented on the balance sheet as an asset and plays a major role in the determination of cost of goods sold (and thus net income) on the income statement. Thus it is important for this number to be accurate and in accordance with generally accepted accounting principles.

If goods are purchased in different batches during the period, and at different prices (which is the usual case), a problem arises as to the valuation of the ending inventory. Does this last, remaining batch consist of goods purchased early in the period? Does it consist of goods purchased late in the period? Or perhaps it is a mixture of both? If companies were able to attach a tag to each item displaying its cost, then this problem would not arise. But this is practical only if the company deals with a small quantity of goods. It would be hard to imagine a department store attaching tags to all its items.

The *FIFO method* (first in, first out) says that the ending inventory consists of the later goods; the

LIFO method (last in, first out) says that it consists of the earlier goods; the *average method* says that it is a mixture of both.

In other words, FIFO says that if you purchase goods on Monday and then make an additional purchase on Tuesday, then on Wednesday you will first sell Monday's goods before Tuesday's goods. LIFO says you will sell Tuesday's goods first, while the average method says you will sell a mixture of both.

Most companies physically sell their earliest goods first (FIFO). However, the accounting profession has stated that the accounting method does *not* have to match the physical flow.

We mentioned earlier the two systems of inventory record keeping: periodic an perpetual. Let's first demonstrate the three inventory costing methods under the *periodic system*.

EXAMPLE 8

Company F engaged in the following merchandise transactions during 19X1:

Jan. 1	Beginning Balance	100 units @ $5.00
Apr. 1	Purchase	200 units @ $6.00
May 1	Sale	125 units
July 15	Purchase	250 units @ $7.00
Sept. 9	Sale	140 units
Oct. 8	Purchase	70 units @ $8.00
Nov. 28	Sale	200 units

We need to determine the cost of goods sold and the ending inventory balance. For the *periodic system*, all computations are done at the end of the period, and we therefore arrange the above information in the following manner:

Jan. 1	Beginning Balance	100 units @ $5.00
Apr. 1	Purchase	200 units @ $6.00
July 15	Purchase	250 units @ $7.00
Oct. 8	Purchase	70 units @ $8.00
	Goods Available for Sale	620 units
	Sold	− 465
	Ending Inventory	155 units

Under FIFO we sell the *earliest* batches first. Thus the 465 units sold (cost of goods sold) consists of the 100 units at $5.00, the 200 units at $6.00, and another 165 units at $7.00, for a total of $2,855. The units remaining in ending inventory consist, therefore, of 85 units (250−165 sold) at $7.00 and 70 units at $8.00, totaling $1,155.

Under LIFO we sell the *latest* batches first. Therefore, units sold (cost of goods sold) consists of the following:

$$
\begin{aligned}
70 @ \$8.00 &= \$\ \ 560 \\
250 @ \ \ 7.00 &= \ \ 1,750 \\
145 @ \ \ 6.00 &= \ \ \ \ 870 \\
&\ \ \ \$3,180
\end{aligned}
$$

The ending inventory thus consists of:

$$
\begin{aligned}
55 \ (200 - 145 \text{ sold}) @ \$6.00 &= \$330 \\
100 \qquad\qquad @ \ \ 5.00 &= \ \ 500 \\
&\ \ \$830
\end{aligned}
$$

The *average method*, which under the periodic system is referred to as *weighted average*, calculates an average price by multiplying each batch by its unit price and then dividing the total cost by the total units available, as follows:

$$
\begin{array}{llrl}
\text{Jan. 1} & 100 \times \$5.00 = & \$ & 500 \\
\text{Apr. 1} & 200 \times \ 6.00 = & & 1,200 \\
\text{July 15} & 250 \times \ 7.00 = & & 1,750 \\
\text{Oct. 8} & 70 \times \ 8.00 = & & \underline{560} \\
\text{Total cost} & & & \$4,010 \\
& \div & & \underline{620}\ \text{units available} \\
\text{(rounded)} & & \$\ & 6.47\ \text{average cost per unit}
\end{array}
$$

Thus, cost of goods sold is 465 units $\times$ $6.47 = $3,009 (rounded) and the ending inventory is 155 units $\times$ 6.47 = $1,003 (rounded). Notice that these numbers are somewhere in between the numbers of FIFO and LIFO.

8.6   INVENTORY COSTING METHODS: PERPETUAL SYSTEM

Let's use the information of the previous example to demonstrate FIFO, LIFO, and average under the *perpetual system.*

EXAMPLE 9

Jan. 1	Beginning Balance	100 units @ $5.00
Apr. 1	Purchase	200 units @ $6.00
May 1	Sale	125 units
July 15	Purchase	250 units @ $7.00
Sept. 9	Sale	140 units
Oct. 8	Purchase	70 units @ $8.00
Nov. 28	Sale	200 units

For *perpetual systems* we do *not* rearrange the information the way we did for periodic systems: We leave it as is. Under FIFO, we always sell the earlier batches before the later batches. Therefore, the sale of May 1 consists of the 100 units at $5.00 plus 25 units at $6.00.

Let's now take a "snapshot" of the situation:

Apr. 1	175 units (200 − 25) @	$6.00
July 15	250 units	@ 7.00
Sept. 9	140 units (sale)	
Oct. 8	70 units	@ 8.00
Nov. 28	200 units (sale)	

Cost of Goods Sold

$$
\begin{array}{rll}
100 & @ & \$5.00 \\
25 & @ & 6.00
\end{array}
$$

We now go to the sale of September 9. These 140 units come from the April 1 batch of 175 units at $6.00. The snapshot now appears as follows:

Apr. 1	35 units (175 − 140) @	$6.00
July 15	250 units	@ 7.00
Oct. 8	70 units	@ 8.00
Nov. 28	200 units (sale)	

Cost of Goods Sold

100	@	$5.00
25	@	6.00
140	@	6.00

We now go to the sale on November 28 of 200 units. Thirty-five of these came from the April 1 batch, while the remaining 165 came from the July 15 batch. Thus the final snapshot appears as follows:

July 15	85 units (250 − 165)	@ $7.00 =	$ 595
Oct. 8	70 units	@ $8.00 =	560
Total Ending Inventory on Dec. 31			$1,155

Cost of Goods Sold

100 @ $5.00 =	$ 500
25 @ 6.00 =	150
140 @ 6.00 =	840
35 @ 6.00 =	210
165 @ 7.00 =	1,155
Total	$2,855

If you compare these results to the results achieved under FIFO for the periodic system, you will notice they are the same. This will always be true: *FIFO under both systems will yield the same results.*

EXAMPLE 10

Let's repeat the given of the previous example and see how LIFO would be done:

Jan. 1	Beginning Balance	100 units @ $5.00
Apr. 1	Purchase	200 units @ $6.00
May 1	Sale	125 units
July 15	Purchase	250 units @ $7.00
Sept. 9	Sale	140 units
Oct. 8	Purchase	70 units @ $8.00
Nov. 28	Sale	200 units

Under LIFO we always sell from the *later* batches first. Therefore the sale of May 1 will come from the April 1 batch at $6.00. Our snapshot will now be:

Jan. 1	100		@ $5.00
Apr. 1	75 (200 − 125)	@	6.00
July 15	250		@ 7.00
Sept. 9	140 (sale)		
Oct. 8	70		@ 8.00
Nov. 28	200 (sale)		

Cost of Goods Sold

125	@	$6.00

We now go to the sale of September 9, which will come out of the July 15 batch. Our snapshot will now be:

Jan. 1	100	@ $5.00
Apr. 1	75	@ 6.00
July 15	110 (250 − 140)	@ 7.00
Oct. 8	70	@ 8.00
Nov. 28	200 (sale)	

Cost of Goods Sold

| 125 | @ | $6.00 |
| 140 | | 7.00 |

Finally we arrive at the November 28 sale, which will come out of the October 8, July 15, and April 1 batches. Thus our final snapshot will look like this:

Jan. 1	100	@ $5.00 = $500
Apr. 1	55 (75 − 20)	@ 6.00 = 330
Total Ending Inventory		$830

Cost of Goods Sold

125 @ $6.00 =	$ 750
140 @ 7.00 =	980
70 @ 8.00 =	560
110 @ 7.00 =	770
20 @ 6.00 =	120
Total cost of goods sold	$3,180

EXAMPLE 11

Let's once again repeat the same given information in order to demonstrate the *average method* (referred to as *moving average*) for the perpetual system:

Jan. 1	Beginning Balance	100 @ $5.00
Apr. 1	Purchase	200 @ $6.00
May 1	Sale	125
July 15	Purchase	250 @ $7.00
Sept. 9	Sale	140
Oct. 8	Purchase	70 @ $8.00
Nov. 28	Sale	200

Under the perpetual system, we must recalculate the average cost per unit after each new purchase. Thus on April 1 our average cost is calculated as follows:

100 units @ $5.00 =	$ 500
200 units @ 6.00 =	1,200
300 units	$1,700

$1,700 divided by 300 units yields an average cost of $5.67 (rounded). On May 1 we sell 125 units at this cost. Our cost of goods sold snapshot thus appears as follows:

$$125 \text{ units @ } \$5.67 = \$708.75$$

We now have 175 units remaining (300 − 125) at $5.67, totaling $992.25. On July 15 we purchase 250 units at $7.00, requiring the recalculation of the average cost, as follows:

$$175 @ \$5.67 = \$ \ \ 992.25$$
$$\underline{250} @ \ \ 7.00 = \ \underline{1,750.00}$$
$$425 \text{ units} \qquad \$2,742.25$$

The new average is $\$2,742.25 \div 425 = \$6.45$ (rounded). Thus on September 9 we sell 140 units at this cost, yielding the following cumulative cost of goods sold:

$$125 @ \$5.67 = \$ \ \ 708.75$$
$$140 @ \ \ 6.45 = \ \underline{\ \ 903.00}$$
$$\$1,611.75$$

We now have 285 units $(425 - 140)$ on hand at $\$6.45$. On October 8, when we purchase 70 units at $\$8.00$, we recalculate the average as follows:

$$285 \text{ units} @ \$6.45 = \$1,838.25$$
$$\underline{\ \ 70} \text{ units} @ \ \ 8.00 = \ \underline{\ \ 560.00}$$
$$355 \text{ units} \qquad \ \ \$2,398.25$$

Dividing $\$2,398.25$ by 355 units results in a new unit price of $\$6.76$ (rounded). When, on November 28, we sell 200 units, we remain with an ending inventory of 155 units at $\$6.76$, totaling $\$1,047.80$, and our cumulative cost of goods sold is thus:

$$125 @ \$5.67 = \$ \ \ 708.75$$
$$140 @ \ \ 6.45 = \ \ \ \ 903.00$$
$$200 @ \ \ 6.76 = \ \underline{1,352.00}$$
$$\$2,963.75$$

8.7   ADVANTAGES AND DISADVANTAGES OF FIFO AND LIFO

One advantage of FIFO is that it often resembles the physical flow of the goods, since most companies will actually sell their first purchases first.

Another advantage is that the ending inventory will be valued at an amount close to current cost—the cost of replacing these goods—on the balance sheet date. This is because since under FIFO the earliest goods in are the earliest out, the remaining goods in inventory will be composed of the most recent, current purchases.

A disadvantage of FIFO is that since cost of goods sold consists of the older (usually lower-priced) units, and these costs are charged against current (usually higher-priced) revenues, distortions in gross profit will result, with an accompanying distortion of the net income. LIFO, on the other hand, does not have this disadvantage, since it matches the latest, current costs against revenue.

An advantage of LIFO is its tax benefit. In times of inflation, cost of goods sold will be higher (because the most recent, higher-priced goods are the ones sold). If cost of goods sold is higher, gross profit and net income will be lower, thus resulting in lower income taxes. But a related disadvantage of this is that the income statement will show a lower net income, thus presenting a less rosy picture of the company's operations for the year. In recent years, however, the IRS has allowed companies to use LIFO for the tax return and FIFO for the income statement. Thus this advantage has been nullified.

Another disadvantage of LIFO is that the ending inventory is valued at the older, usually outdated, cost figures. This understates the inventory and presents a weaker working capital position.

8.8   DOLLAR-VALUE LIFO

The *dollar-value LIFO method* is a form of LIFO that measures the ending inventory in terms of dollar values rather than in terms of physical units. It uses a price index—usually the Consumer Price

Index for Urban Consumers (CPI-U)—in its calculations. According to a survey published in the June 1987 issue of *Accounting Horizons*, most companies that use LIFO use the dollar-value version.

Under this method, one year is chosen as the "base year" and the prices of all subsequent years are expressed in terms of the base year's price. This base year is assigned an index of 100, while the subsequent years are assigned their own respective consumer price index.* Each year's ending inventory is *initially* valued at its December 31 current replacement price, but this value is then modified according to the following steps:

Step 1. Divide the December 31 current replacement price by the price index for the year.

Step 2. Compare the result of step 1 to the previous year's inventory at base-year prices. If the result is *greater* than the previous year, multiply the increment by this year's price index and then "pile it" on top of last year's ending inventory as an additional inventory "layer."

Step 3. If the result is *less* than the previous year's, then reduce the inventory by removing the most recently added layer (last in, first out).

These steps will become more clear from the following example.

EXAMPLE 12

Company M has the following information regarding its ending inventories for the years 19X1, 19X2, 19X3, and 19X4.

	Dec. 31	Current Year-End Prices	÷	Price Index	=	Inventory at Base-Year Prices	Dollar-Value LIFO
(Base)	19X1	$10,000	÷	100	=	$10,000	$10,000
	19X2	17,000	÷	110	=	15,455	Goal
	19X3	22,000	÷	120	=	18,333	Goal
	19X4	20,000	÷	125	=	16,000	Goal

The chart thus far is an illustration of step 1—that of dividing each year's ending inventory (at current prices) by that year's price index. Since the base-year index is always 100 (1.00), all the columns for the base year across the board will show the same amount (in this case, $10,000).

We now go to 19X2. Following step 1, we divide $17,000 by 1.10, yielding $15,455 (rounded). We then execute step 2 by comparing this number to last year (at base-year prices) and see that the inventory has increased by $5,455 ($15,455 − $10,000). We therefore continue with step 2 by multiplying the $5,455 by *this year's* index of 110, yielding a new layer of $6,000, which is then piled on the old base layer of $10,000 for a total of $16,000. Thus the dollar-value LIFO column (the "goal") for 19X2 consists of two layers, as follows:

Base Layer	$10,000
19X2 Layer ($5,455 × 1.10)	6,000
	$16,000

We now proceed to 19X3. Once again, in accordance with step 1, we divide the current price of $22,000 by the current index of 120, yielding $18,333. Once again, under step 2 we notice that the inventory has increased by $2,878 over and above the 19X2 amount at base-year prices ($18,333 − $15,455). Once again, therefore, we pile this on as an additional layer of inventory, resulting in the following dollar-value LIFO (the "goal") amount for 19X3:

Base Layer	$10,000
19X2 Layer ($5,455 × 1.10)	6,000
19X3 Layer ($2,878 × 1.20)	3,454
	$19,454

---

*For example, if 1992 is assigned a base index of 100 and the 1993 index is 110, this means that prices in 1993 were 10% higher than 1992. The number of 110 is understood to mean 1.10, even though the custom is to omit the decimal.

Thus far the inventory has increased from year to year and step 3 has not been implemented. But now let's see what happens in 19X4. Under step 1 we attain a $16,000 value at base-year prices for 19X4. However, when we now compare this to 19X3 (at base-year prices), we find a *decrease* of $2,333 ($16,000 − $18,333). Thus step 3 must be implemented, which requires that we remove (or "peel off") some inventory from the *most recently added layers*. We therefore go to the latest layer—19X3 consisting of $2,878 × 1.20—and reduce it by $2,333, yielding $545 × 1.20. Thus the dollar-value LIFO column (the "goal") for 19X4 consists of the following layers:

Base Layer	$10,000
19X2 Layer ($5,455 × 1.10)	6,000
19X3 Layer ($545 × 1.20)	654
	$16,654

Sometimes, in implementing step 3, we need to reduce several previous layers, as the next example illustrates.

EXAMPLE 13

Company N has the following information regarding its ending inventories for 19X1, 19X2, 19X3 and 19X4.

	Dec. 31	Current Year-End Prices	÷	Price Index	=	Inventory at Base-Year Prices	Dollar-Value LIFO
(Base)	19X1	$30,00	÷	100	=	$30,000	$30,000
	19X2	40,000	÷	110	=	36,364	Goal
	19X3	50,000	÷	120	=	41,667	Goal
	19X4	42,000	÷	130	=	32,308	Goal

We start with 19X1. Since 19X1 is the base year, we carry its $30,000 amount across the board, and then proceed to 19X2. We divide the $40,000 year-end price by the index of 110, yielding $36,364. Since this is greater than last year by $6,364, we implement step 2 and pile it on as a new layer. Thus the dollar-value LIFO for 19X2 consists of the following layers:

Base Layer	$30,000
19X2 Layer ($6,364 × 1.10)	7,000
	$37,000

We now proceed to 19X3, divide $50,000 by 120 to yield $41,667, representing an increase of $5,303 over last year ($41,667 − $36,364), and determine the dollar-value LIFO as follows:

Base Layer	$30,000
19X2 Layer ($6,364 × 1.10)	7,000
19X3 Layer ($5,303 × 1.20)	6,364
	$43,364

We now proceed to 19X4 and find that the inventory has decreased by $9,359 ($41,667 − $32,308). The removal of the 19X3 layer of $5,303 × 1.20 is not enough; we must remove another $4,056 ($9,359 − $5,303). So we go back up to the most *recent* layer (19X2) and reduce it by $4,056. Thus that layer has now become $2,308 × 1.10. The dollar-value LIFO now consists of the following:

Base Layer	$30,000
19X2 Layer ($2,308 × 1.10)	2,539
(19X3 Layer Gone)	$32,539

Summary

1. A company's merchandise inventory consists of the goods it owns which are held for sale in the ordinary course of business. If goods have been shipped to the company F.O.B. shipping point, they should be included in the ending inventory count regardless of whether or not they have been received. If they have been shipped F.O.B. destination, they should not be included until they are actually received.

2. Since a consignee is merely an agent of the consignor and no sale has actually taken place, consigned goods should be included in the inventory of the consignor rather than of the consignee.

3. Delivery charges on the purchase of goods are not expensed but are added to the cost of the merchandise. Interest charges on loans to purchase goods, however, are treated as expenses.

4. Companies may use either the *periodic system* or the *perpetual system* for recording inventory. Both systems have an account called Merchandise Inventory; however, the periodic system does not use this account during the accounting period. It uses Purchases, Purchases Returns, and Purchases Discounts instead. Thus the Merchandise Inventory account, having not been used during the entire period, is out of date and must be updated via a closing entry.

5. Under the perpetual system, the Merchandise Inventory account is active during the period. There are no special accounts for purchases, returns, and discounts. Accordingly, no closing entry is needed at year-end to update the merchandise account, unless the year-end physical count disagrees with the balance of this account. If there is a disparity, an adjustment is made via the Inventory Short or Over account.

6. The *gross method* requires purchases to be recorded at their full, gross amount. If a discount is later taken, the account Purchases Discounts is used to record the price reduction. The *net method*, on the other hand, records the original purchase at net purchase price minus the discount. Any failure to pay within the discount period is treated as an expense and debited to Purchases Discounts Lost—an account similar to Interest Expense.

7. The *cost of goods sold*—a major expense on the income statement—can be determined in the following manner:

    Beginning inventory + net purchases − ending inventory

8. An overstatement of the *ending inventory* will result in an understatement of the cost of goods sold, and vice versa. An overstatement of the *beginning inventory* will result in an overstatement of the cost of goods sold, and vice versa.

9. If an error is made in purchases and the same error—both in direction and in amount—is made in the ending inventory, cost of goods sold will not be affected. The two errors will counterbalance each other.

10. If goods are purchased in different batches during the period and at different prices, a problem arises as to the valuation of the ending inventory and the cost of goods sold. *FIFO* says first in, first out and the ending inventory consists of the later batches. *LIFO* says last in, first out and the ending inventory consists of the earlier batches. The *average method* says that a mixture of both early and late batches was sold and also remains in ending inventory.

11. The FIFO method yields the same results under both the periodic and perpetual systems; the LIFO and average methods do not.

12. Advantages and disadvantages of FIFO are

   (*a*) It often resembles the physical flow of the goods.

   (*b*) The ending inventory is valued at an amount close to current cost.

   (*c*) Improper matching of old costs against current revenues results in distorted gross profits.

13. Advantages and disadvantages of LIFO include:

   (*a*) Lower taxes during inflationary periods.

   (*b*) Lower reported net income on the income statement.

   (*c*) Valuation of ending inventory at older, outdated costs, thus understating the inventory and presenting a weaker working capital position.

14. The dollar-value LIFO method measures the ending inventory in terms of dollar values rather than physical units. The calculation is done via the following steps.

   Step 1. Divide the December 31 current replacement price by the price index for the year.

   Step 2. Compare the result of step 1 to the previous year's inventory at base-year prices. If the result is *greater* than the previous year, multiply the increment by this year's price index and then "pile" it on top of last year's ending inventory as an additional inventory "layer."

   Step 3. If the result is *less* than the previous year's, then reduce the inventory by removing the most recently added layer (last in, first out).

Rapid Review

1. If goods have been shipped to the buyer on terms of F.O.B. _____, they *should* be included in the buyer's ending inventory.

2. A consignee is considered an _____ of the consignor, and, therefore, consigned goods are part of the inventory of the _____.

3. Interest charges are not considered part of the cost of merchandise, but are treated as _____.

4. The two systems of accounting for merchandise are the _____ system and the _____ system.

5. Under the _____ system, entries to adjust for a disparity between the merchandise account and the physical count are made via the _____ account.

6. Under the net method, the account _____ is used to record additional payments required due to a failure to pay within the discount period.

7. An understatement of the ending inventory will result in an _____ of cost of goods sold.

8. If equal errors are made in both Purchases and Ending Inventory, these errors will _____.

9. The _____ method yields the same results under both the periodic and perpetual systems.

10. The inventory method that measures ending inventory in terms of dollar values rather than physical units is the _____ method.

Answers: **1.** shipping point **2.** agent; consignor **3.** expenses **4.** periodic; perpetual **5.** perpetual; Inventory Short or Over **6.** Purchases Discounts Lost **7.** overstatement **8.** counterbalance **9.** FIFO **10.** dollar-value LIFO

Solved Problems

Introduction

8.1   Determine the proper accounting treatment for each of the following.

(a)   Goods shipped from Company A to Company B on terms of F.O.B. shipping point are still in transit on December 31.

(b)   Same information as part (a), except that the goods were shipped F.O.B. destination.

(c)   Goods in the hands of consignees.

(d)   Freight charges on merchandise purchases.

(e)   Interest charges on loans to purchase merchandise.

SOLUTION

(a)   Count as part of the inventory of Company B.

(b)   Count as part of the inventory of Company A.

(c)   Count as part of the inventory of the consignor.

(d)   Consider as an additional cost of the purchase.

(e)   Consider as an expense.   [Section 8.1]

Periodic System versus Perpetual System

8.2   From the following information, determine cost of goods sold.

Purchases	$40,000
Inventory (Jan. 1)	70,000
Freight In	2,000
Purchases Returns	4,000
Purchases Discounts	1,000
Inventory (Dec. 31)	48,000

SOLUTION

Beginning Inventory		$ 70,000
Purchases	$40,000	
Freight In	2,000	
Purchases Returns	(4,000)	
Purchases Discounts	(1,000)	
Net Purchases		37,000
Merchandise Available for Sale		$107,000
Ending Inventory		48,000
Cost of Goods Sold		$ 59,000 [Section 8.2]

8.3 Company A has the following information relating to its merchandise for 19X1:

Beginning Inventory	$120,000	Ending Inventory*	$147,000
Purchases (on account)	90,000	Purchases Discounts	3,000
Sales on Account			
At Cost	60,000		
At Selling Price	95,000		

*Determined by physical count.

Prepare the necessary journal entries under the periodic system.

SOLUTION

Purchases	90,000		Accounts Receivable	95,000	
Accounts Payable		90,000	Sales		95,000
Accounts Payable	3,000				
Purchases Discounts		3,000			
Closing Entry:			*Closing Entry:*		
Cost of Goods Sold	120,000		Merchandise Inventory	147,000	
Merchandise Inventory		120,000	Cost of Goods Sold		147,000
					[Section 8.2]

8.4 Prepare the journal entries for Problem 8.3 under the perpetual system.

SOLUTION

Merchandise Inventory	90,000		Accounts Receivable	95,000	
Accounts Payable		90,000	Sales		95,000
Accounts Payable	3,000		Cost of Goods Sold	60,000	
Merchandise Inventory		3,000	Merchandise Inventory		60,000
					[Section 8.2]

8.5 The merchandise inventory account of Company B shows a $7,000 balance on December 31. However, the physical count yields a balance of $6,000. Prepare the necessary correction entry.

SOLUTION

Inventory Short or Over	1,000	
Merchandise Inventory		1,000 [Section 8.2]

Gross Method versus Net Method

8.6   Company C purchases goods of $10,000 under terms of 2/10, N/30. Prepare entries under the gross method for payment within 10 days and, also, for payment made after 10 days. Is this the preferred method?

SOLUTION

Purchases	10,000	
Accounts Payable		10,000

For Payment within 10 Days:

Accounts Payable	10,000	
Purchases Discounts		200
Cash		9,800

For Payment after 10 Days:

Accounts Payable	10,000	
Cash		10,000

The preferred method is the net method.   [Section 8.3]

8.7   Prepare entries for Problem 8.6 under the net method.

SOLUTION

Purchases	9,800	
Accounts Payable		9,800

For Payment within 10 Days:

Accounts Payable	9,800	
Cash		9,800

For Payment after 10 Days:

Accounts Payable	9,800	
Purchases Discounts Lost	200	
Cash		10,000

[Section 8.3]

Inventory Errors

8.8   Indicate what effect each of the following errors will have on cost of goods sold.

   (*a*)   Overstatement of ending inventory

   (*b*)   Overstatement of beginning inventory

   (*c*)   Understatement of ending inventory

   (*d*)   Understatement of beginning inventory

   (*e*)   Understatement of purchases

   (*f*)   Overstatement of purchases and ending inventory

SOLUTION

(*a*)	Understate	(*d*)	Understate
(*b*)	Overstate	(*e*)	Understate
(*c*)	Overstate	(*f*)	No effect—they counterbalance [Section 8.4]

Inventory Costing Methods: Periodic and Perpetual Systems

8.9 (*Note:* All inventory computations are rounded to the nearest dollar.) Company D has the following information regarding its merchandise for 19X4.

Jan. 1	Balance	400 units @ $3
May 1	Purchase	200 units @ $4
July 15	Sale	300 units
Oct. 10	Purchase	250 units @ $5
Nov. 14	Sale	400 units
Dec. 9	Purchase	100 units @ $8
Dec. 18	Sale	125 units

Using the periodic system, determine cost of goods sold and the ending Merchandise Inventory balance under FIFO, LIFO, and weighted average.

SOLUTION

For the periodic system, it is helpful to arrange the given information in the following manner:

Beginning Balance	400 units @ $3
Purchase	200 units @ $4
Purchase	250 units @ $5
Purchase	100 units @ $8
Available	950 units
Sold	− 825
Ending Balance	125 units

Under FIFO we always sell the earliest goods first. Therefore, cost of goods sold consist of 400 units at $3, 200 units at $4, and 225 units at $5, for a total of $3,125. Thus the ending balance consists of 25 units at $5 and 100 units at $8, for a total of $925.

Under LIFO, cost of goods sold consists of 100 units at $8, 250 units at $5, 200 units at $4, and 275 units at $3, for a total of $3,675. The ending balance therefore consists of 125 units at $3, for a total of $375.

Under the weighted average method we calculate the average as follows:

$$
\begin{array}{ll}
400 \text{ units @ } \$3 = & \$1,200 \\
200 \text{ units @ } \$4 = & 800 \\
250 \text{ units @ } \$5 = & 1,250 \\
100 \text{ units @ } \$8 = & \underline{\quad 800} \\
950 \text{ units} & \$4,050
\end{array}
$$

$$\text{Average} = \frac{\$4,050}{950} = \$4.26 \text{ per unit} \quad \text{(rounded)}$$

Thus cost of goods sold is 825 at $4.26 = $3,515, and the ending inventory balance is 125 at $4.26 = $533 (rounded).   [Section 8.5]

8.10 For Problem 8.9, determine FIFO, LIFO, and moving average under the *perpetual system*.

SOLUTION

For the perpetual system, we leave the given information in its original form, and calculate cost of goods sold each time a sale is made instead of waiting until period-end. Thus, cost of goods sold under FIFO consists of the following:

$$
\begin{array}{rl}
300 @ \$3 = \$ & 900 \\
100 @ \$3 = & 300 \\
200 @ \$4 = & 800 \\
100 @ \$5 = & 500 \\
125 @ \$5 = & \underline{625} \\
& \$3,125
\end{array}
$$

The ending balance consists of:

$$
\begin{array}{rl}
25 @ \$5 = & \$125 \\
100 @ \$8 = & \underline{800} \\
& \$925
\end{array}
$$

Under LIFO, cost of goods sold consists of the following:

$$
\begin{array}{rl}
200 @ \$4 = \$ & 800 \\
100 @ \$3 = & 300 \\
250 @ \$5 = & 1,250 \\
150 @ \$3 = & 450 \\
100 @ \$8 = & 800 \\
25 @ \$3 = & \underline{75} \\
& \$3,675
\end{array}
$$

The ending balance consists of 125 units @ $3 = $375.

Under the moving average method we have the following calculations:

Beginning Balance	400	@ $3	= $1,200
Purchase	$\underline{200}$	@ $4	= $\underline{800}$
	600 units		$2,000

$$(average = \frac{\$2,000}{600} = \$3.33 \text{ rounded})$$

Sold	(300)	@ $3.33	
Balance	300 units	@ $3.33	= $ 999
Purchase	$\underline{250}$	@ $5.00	= $\underline{1,250}$
	550		$2,249

$$(average = \frac{\$2,249}{550} = \$4.09)$$

Sold	(400)	@ $4.09	
Balance	150 units	@ $4.09	= $ 614
Purchase	$\underline{100}$	@ $8.00	= $\underline{800}$
	250 units		$1,414

$$(average = \frac{\$1,414}{250} = \$5.66)$$

Sold	(125)	@ $5.66	
Ending Balance	125	@ $5.66	= $\underline{\$ 708}$

Cost of Goods Sold Consists of:

$$
\begin{array}{rl}
300 @ \$3.33 = \$ & 999 \\
400 @ \ \ 4.09 = & 1,636 \\
125 @ \ \ 5.66 = & \underline{708} \\
& \$3,343
\end{array}
$$

[Section 8.6]

8.11   Company E has the following information regarding its merchandise transactions for 19X5.

Jan. 1	Balance		100 units @ $50
Mar. 30	Purchase		200 units @ $55
Apr. 15	Sale	125 units	
June 2	Purchase		300 units @ $49
Aug. 5	Sale	250 units	
Oct. 8	Purchase		275 units @ $63
Dec. 10	Sale	350 units	

Determine the cost of goods sold and ending inventory balance under FIFO, LIFO, and weighted average, under the *periodic system*.

SOLUTION

For the periodic system, it is helpful to rearrange the given information into the following format:

Jan. 1	Balance	100 units @ $50 = $ 5,000
Mar. 30	Purchase	200 units @ $55 = 11,000
June 2	Purchase	300 units @ $49 = 14,700
Oct. 8	Purchase	275 units @ $63 = 17,325
		$48,025

Available	875 units
Sold	− 725
Ending Balance	150 units

Note: All computations are rounded to the nearest dollar.

Under FIFO, we sell the earliest goods first. Therefore, cost of goods sold consists of: 100 units at $50, 200 units at $55, 300 units at $49, and 125 units at $63, for a total of $38,575. The ending balance therefore consists of 150 units at $63 = $9,450.

Under LIFO, we sell the latest goods first. Therefore cost of goods sold is comprised of: 275 units at $63, 300 units at $49, and 150 units at $55, for a total of $40,275. The ending inventory balance, therefore, is comprised of 50 units at $55 and 100 units at $50, for a total of $7,750.

Under the weighted average system, we divide the total *dollar value* of all the units available ($48,025) by the total *units* available (875) to arrive at a weighted-average unit price of $54.89 (rounded). Thus cost of goods sold is $725 \times \$54.89 = \$39,795$, and the ending inventory is $150 \times \$54.89 = \$8,234$.

[Section 8.5]

8.12   Determine FIFO, LIFO, and moving average for Problem 8.11 under the *perpetual system*.

SOLUTION

Let's repeat the original given information:

Balance		100 units @ $50
Purchase		200 units @ $55
Sale	125 units	
Purchase		300 units @ $49
Sale	250 units	
Purchase		275 units @ $63
Sale	350 units	

Under FIFO, cost of goods sold consists of:

$$
\begin{array}{rll}
100 \text{ units @ } \$50 = & \$ & 5,000 \\
25 \text{ units @ } \$55 = & & 1,375 \\
175 \text{ units @ } \$55 = & & 9,625 \\
75 \text{ units @ } \$49 = & & 3,675 \\
225 \text{ units @ } \$49 = & & 11,025 \\
125 \text{ units @ } \$63 = & & 7,875 \\
\hline
& \$ & 38,575 \\
\end{array}
$$

The ending inventory, therefore, consists of 150 units at $63 = \$9,450$.
Under LIFO, cost of goods sold consists of the following:

$$
\begin{array}{rll}
125 \text{ units @ } \$55 = & \$ & 6,875 \\
250 \text{ units @ } \$49 = & & 12,250 \\
275 \text{ units @ } \$63 = & & 17,325 \\
50 \text{ units @ } \$49 = & & 2,450 \\
25 \text{ units @ } \$55 = & & 1,375 \\
\hline
& \$ & 40,275 \\
\end{array}
$$

The ending inventory, therefore, consists of 100 units at $50 and 50 units at $55, for a total of $7,750.
Under the moving average method, we have the following computations:

Balance	100 units @ $50	=	$ 5,000
Purchase	200 @ $55	=	11,000
Average: $16,000 ÷ 300 = $53.33 (rounded)	300 @ $53.33	=	$ 16,000
Sale	(125) @ $53.33	=	(6,666)
Balance	175 @ $53.33	=	9,334
Purchase	300 @ $49	=	14,700
Average: $24,034 ÷ 475 = $50.60 (rounded)	475 @ $50.60	=	$ 24,034
Sale	(250) @ $50.60	=	(12,650)
Balance	225 @ $50.60	=	$ 11,384
Purchase	275 @ $63	=	17,325
Average: $28,709 ÷ 500 = $57.42 (rounded)	500 @ $57.42	=	$ 28,709
Sale	(350) @ $57.42	=	(20,097)
Ending Balance	150 @ $57.42	=	$ 8,612

The ending inventory balance is $8,612 and cost of goods sold consists of the following:

$$
\begin{array}{rll}
125 \text{ units @ } \$53.33 = & \$ & 6,666 \\
250 \text{ @ } \$50.60 = & & 12,650 \\
350 \text{ @ } \$57.42 = & & 20,097 \\
\hline
& \$ & 39,413 \\
\end{array}
$$

[Section 8.6]

Dollar-Value LIFO

8.13 Company F has the following information regarding its ending inventories for the years 19X1–19X4.

	Dec. 31	Current Year-End Prices	Price Index	Inventory at Base-Year Prices	Dollar-Value LIFO
(Base)	19X1	$ 7,000	100	?	?
	19X2	12,000	115	?	?
	19X3	20,000	120	?	?
	19X4	18,000	130	?	?

Fill in the missing numbers in the table using the dollar-value LIFO method.

SOLUTION

	Inventory at Base-Year Prices*	Dollar-Value LIFO
19X1	$ 7,000	$ 7,000
19X2	10,435	10,950 (1)
19X3	16,667	18,428 (2)
19X4	13,846	15,043 (3)

*We arrive at this column by dividing the current year-end price by the price index.

(1) Base Layer $7,000   × 1.00 = $ 7,000
     19X2 Layer   3,435   × 1.15 =   3,950
                                           $10,950

(2) Base Layer $7,000   × 1.00 = $ 7,000
     19X2 Layer   3,435   × 1.15 =   3,950
     19X3 Layer   6,232   × 1.20 =   7,478
                                           $18,428

(3) Base Layer $7,000   × 1.00 = $ 7,000
     19X2 Layer   3,435   × 1.15 =   3,950
     19X3 Layer   ($6,232 − $2,821)   × 1.20 =   4,093
                                                     $15,043   [Section 8.8]

8.14 Company G has the following information regarding its ending inventories for the years 19X1–19X5.

	Dec. 31	Current Year-End Prices	Price Index	Inventory at Base-Year Prices	Dollar-Value LIFO
(Base)	19X1	$30,000	100	?	?
	19X2	40,000	105	?	?
	19X3	39,000	112	?	?
	19X4	45,000	118	?	?
	19X5	39,000	125	?	?

Fill in the missing amounts in the table.

SOLUTION

	Inventory at Base-Year Prices	Dollar-Value LIFO
19X1	$30,000	$30,000
19X2	38,095	38,500*
19X3	34,821	35,062†
19X4	38,136	38,974‡
19X5	31,200	31,260§

*Base Layer	
*Base Layer	$30,000 × 1.00 = $30,000
19X2 Layer	8,095 × 1.05 = 8,500
	$38,500

†Base Layer	$30,000 × 1.00 = $30,000
19X2 Layer ($8,095 − $3,274) =	4,821 × 1.05 = 5,062
	$35,062

‡Base Layer	$30,000 × 1.00 = $30,000
19X2 Layer ($8,095 − $3,274) =	4,821 × 1.05 = 5,062
19X4 Layer	3,315 × 1.18 = 3,912
	$38,974

§The decrease of $6,936 ($38,136 − $31,200) completely erodes the 19X4 layer and reduces the 19X2 layer by $3,621 × 1.05.

Base Layer	$30,000 × 1.00 = $30,000
19X2 Layer	1,200 × 1.05 = 1,260
	$31,260

[Section 8.8]

Supplementary Problems

8.15   Use the following information to determine the ending inventory:

Purchases	$50,000
Inventory (Jan. 1)	80,000
Freight In	2,000
Purchases Returns	1,000
Purchases Discounts	4,000
Sales Returns	9,000
Cost of Goods Sold	75,000

8.16   Use the following information to prepare the required entries under the periodic system.

Purchases (on account)	$ 80,000	
Beginning Inventory	110,000	
Sales on Account:		
At Cost	90,000	
At Selling Price	140,000	
Ending Inventory	93,000	(by physical count)
Purchases Returns	6,000	

8.17   Prepare entries for Problem 8.16 under the perpetual system.

8.18   The merchandise account shows a balance of $25,000 on December 31, but the physical count shows $29,000. Prepare the required correction entry.

8.19   Company H purchases goods of $86,000 with terms of 3/10, N/30. Prepare all entries under the *gross* method if:

(a)   Payment is made within the discount period.

(b)   Payment is made after the discount period.

8.20   Prepare the entries for Problem 8.19 under the *net* method.

8.21   What effect will each of the following errors have on cost of goods sold and gross profit?

(a)   Overstatement of beginning inventory

(b)   Overstatement of ending inventory

(c)   Overstatement of beginning inventory and ending inventory

(d)   Understatement of ending inventory

(e)   Understatement of beginning inventory and overstatement of ending inventory

(f)   Understatement of purchases and ending inventory

8.22   Company I has the following information regarding its merchandise for 19X3.

Jan. 1	Balance	50 units @ $30
Apr. 10	Purchase	100 units @ $35
June 22	Sale	75 units
July 31	Purchase	125 units @ $40
Aug. 19	Sale	140 units
Oct. 29	Purchase	80 units @ $38
Dec. 14	Sale	90 units

Determine cost of goods sold and the ending inventory balance for FIFO, LIFO, and weighted average under the periodic system.

8.23   For Problem 8.22, determine the cost of goods sold and ending inventory for FIFO, LIFO, and moving average under the perpetual system.

8.24   Company J has the following information regarding its ending inventories for the years 19X1–19X5.

	Dec. 31	Current Year-End Prices	Price Index	Inventory at Base-Year Prices	Dollar-Value LIFO
(Base)	19X1	$17,000	100	?	?
	19X2	25,000	110	?	?
	19X3	35,000	120	?	?
	19X4	33,000	130	?	?
	19X5	38,000	140	?	?

Fill in the missing numbers on the chart.

8.25   Company K has the following information regarding its inventories for 19X1–19X5.

Dec. 31	Current Year-End Prices	Price Index	Inventory at Base-Year Prices	Dollar-Value LIFO
(Base) 19X1	$5,000	100	?	?
19X2	6,000	105	?	?
19X3	6,100	110	?	?
19X4	8,000	115	?	?
19X5	7,500	120	?	?

Complete the chart.

Chapter 9

Inventories: Additional Issues and Methods

9.1 LOWER OF COST OR MARKET (LCM)

This chapter deals with several important issues and methods relating to merchandise inventory that were not discussed in the previous chapter. These include lower of cost or market, valuation at net realizable value, the relative sales value method, purchase commitments, and the gross profit and retail methods of inventory valuation. We shall discuss lower of cost or market first.

The cost principle discussed in Chapter 4 mandates that inventories, as well as other assets, be recorded at cost—what was paid to acquire them. However, this principle is abandoned if the market value of the inventory—its revenue-producing ability—drops below the cost. In this case, we must reduce the inventory to the lower market value and present it on the balance sheet as such.

EXAMPLE 1

If the cost of inventory is $500 and its market value falls to $475, we reduce its value on the books to $475 and report it as $475 on the balance sheet. If, however, the market value is above cost, we do nothing.

The question is: What does "market value" mean? The answer is it means replacement cost—what we would presently have to pay to our suppliers to replace this item. However, this value cannot exceed a certain "ceiling" nor be below a certain "floor." The ceiling is called net realizable value; the floor is net realizable value minus the normal profit margin. *Net realizable value* is the item's selling price less disposal costs and completion costs (if the item still needs additional processing). If we thus line up the replacement cost, ceiling, and floor in ascending or descending order, we choose the middle of the three and refer to it as "designated" market. We then compare this number to the original cost and choose the lower one.

EXAMPLE 2

An item's original cost was $25. Its replacement cost is $18, while its net realizable value (NRV) and NRV minus profit are $22 and $21, respectively. Thus the designated market is the middle value of $18, $22, and $21, which is $21, and this is then compared to the original cost of $25. Since $21 is lower than $25, the inventory item is valued at $21.

EXAMPLE 3

If in Example 2 the original cost was $20, we would leave the item at this value, since $20 is less than $21. Remember: We compare the original cost to the designated market and choose the *lower* value.

EXAMPLE 4

An item's original cost was $35, and its current replacement cost is $32. It can presently be sold for $37, but this will entail disposal costs of $1. The normal profit per unit is $5. We thus have the following:

Replacement Cost	$32	Designated market
NRV	36	
NRV − Profit:	31	

We now compare the designated market of $32 to the cost of $35 and choose $32.

The LCM procedure may be applied on an item-by-item basis, on a category-by-category basis, or on the inventory as a whole. The most commonly used approach is item by item, although any approach is acceptable provided it is used consistently from year to year.

EXAMPLE 5

Merchandise Whiz has the following items in its December 31 inventory, which is divided into two categories: raw and cooked.

| | Cost | Designated Market | Lower of Cost or Market By: | | |
			Individual Items	Categories	Total Inventory
Raw:					
Item A	$ 80	$104	$ 80		
Item B	100	90	90		
Item C	50	40	40		
Total Raw	230	234		$230	
Cooked:					
Item D	90	47	47		
Item E	95	92	92		
Total Cooked	185	139		139	
Total Inventory	$415	$373	$349	$369	$373

We thus see different results under each approach.

9.2   RECORDING LCM

As we just mentioned, if on December 31 the market price of the inventory is below the cost, the inventory must be recorded on the books at market. This can be done via one of two methods: the direct method or the indirect method.

Let's first assume the use of the periodic inventory system. Under this system, as you recall from Chapter 1, the inventory account is not touched all period long and the new, end-of-period balance is inserted into the inventory account via the following closing entry:*

Inventory	xxx	
Cost of Goods Sold		xxx

If we use the direct method of recording LCM, this entry is made at the lower (market) value. Thus no specific loss account is debited for the decline in value; the loss is buried in cost of goods sold (because cost of goods sold = merchandise available – ending inventory, a smaller ending inventory automatically produces a larger cost of goods sold). If, however, we use the indirect method of recording LCM, the loss is recognized explicitly via a debit to a loss account. These methods are illustrated in the next example.

EXAMPLE 6

Company Q has an ending inventory of $10,000 at cost and $8,000 at market. Under the direct method the end-of-period closing entry is:

---

* We are being consistent with our discussion of Chapter 1, where we stated that Cost of Goods Sold is used for the updating of the inventory. However, many accountants use Income Summary instead.

Inventory	8,000	
Cost of Goods Sold		8,000

Under the indirect method, there are two closing entries, as follows:

Inventory	10,000	
Cost of Goods Sold		10,000
Loss Due to Market Decline of Inventory	2,000	
Allowance to Reduce Inventory to Market		2,000

The loss account is an expense account and appears on the income statement as such; the allowance account is a contra asset to Inventory and appears on the balance sheet.

Under the indirect method, if the market value rises during the next period, it is permissible to recognize a recovery of the previous loss. However, gains above the original cost are not recognized.

EXAMPLE 7

If, in Example 6, the market value rises to $11,000 by the end of the next period, we recognize a recovery of the $2,000 loss, but no gain of $1,000 (from $10,000 to $11,000). The entry is:

Allowance to Reduce Inventory to Market	2,000	
Recovery of Loss Due to Market Decline of Inventory		2,000

The recovery account is a revenue type of account.

Under the perpetual inventory system, no closing entries are generally needed at period-end to update inventory, since this account is already up to date. For LCM purposes, however, we do need a special entry. Under the indirect method, the loss is recognized explicitly with the same entry mentioned above; under the direct method, the loss is buried in cost of goods sold via the following entry:

Cost of Goods Sold	xxx	
Inventory		xxx

EXAMPLE 8

Company M uses the perpetual system and has an ending, up-to-date inventory of $5,000 at cost and $4,000 at market. Under the direct method, the entry is:

Cost of Goods Sold	1,000	
Inventory		1,000

Under the indirect method, the entry is:

Loss Due to Market Decline of Inventory	1,000	
Allowance to Reduce Inventory to Market		1,000

9.3 VALUATION AT NET REALIZABLE VALUE

We have seen that inventory is recorded and reported at the *lower* of cost or market. In certain special cases, however, the inventory may be recorded at net realizable value (selling price less disposal and completion costs), even if this is above cost. This is permitted where there is a controlled market with a quoted price applicable to all quantities and no *significant* disposal costs are expected. This is often the case with precious metals and certain agricultural products.

EXAMPLE 9

Precious Metals Corporation owns 5 ounces of gold which it purchased at $350 per ounce. The market price has now risen to $360 per ounce. Precious raises the inventory value by $10 and recognizes a gain, as follows:

Gold Inventory	10	
Gain Due to Rise in Market Value of Inventory		10

9.4 VALUATION AT RELATIVE SALES VALUE

If a group of different types of units is purchased for a single lump-sum amount (a "basket" purchase), this amount should be allocated to the units in the *ratio* of their respective sales values.

EXAMPLE 10

Diversified Buyers purchases 100 widgets for a lump-sum price of $1,000. Fifty of these widgets are considered grade A and have a selling price of $50 each; 30 are considered grade B and sell at $40 each; 20 are grade C and sell at $35 each. It would be inappropriate simply to divide the $1,000 cost by 100 units to arrive at a uniform cost per unit of $10, since the units are of different grades. It would also be inappropriate to value the units at their *actual* selling prices, since this is permitted only in special cases. The correct approach is to use the selling prices to establish ratios, and then apply these ratios to apportion the cost, as follows:

Grade	Quantity	Selling Price per Unit	Total Sales Value	Ratio
A	50 units	$50	$2,500	2,500/4,400
B	30 units	40	1,200	1,200/4,400
C	20 units	35	700	700/4,400
			$4,400	

The allocation is:

$$\text{Grade A:} \quad \frac{\$2,500}{\$4,400} = 0.568 \text{ (rounded)} \times \$1,000 = \$568$$
$$\text{Per unit:} \quad \$568 \div 50 = \quad \$11.36$$

$$\text{Grade B:} \quad \frac{\$1,200}{\$4,400} = 0.273 \text{ (rounded)} \times \$1,000 = \$273$$
$$\text{Per unit:} \quad \$273 \div 30 = \quad \$ 9.10$$

$$\text{Grade C:} \quad \frac{\$700}{\$4,400} = 0.159 \text{ (rounded)} \times \$1,000 = \$159$$
$$\text{Per unit:} \quad \$159 \div 20 = \quad \$ 7.95$$

9.5 PURCHASE COMMITMENTS

We have seen in previous chapters that when goods are purchased and title has passed to the buyer, an entry is made by the buyer debiting Purchases (or Merchandise Inventory) and crediting Accounts Payable. When title has not yet passed, however, no entry is made. For example, if the buyer has merely committed himself to a purchase by signing a contract but the goods have not yet been shipped, an entry is not made and the commitment does *not* appear in the financial statements (except in the footnotes, if the amount is significant). This is true even if the contract is noncancelable.

If goods are purchased at a price that is *significantly* above their true market value, they should not be recorded at cost, but at market value, and a loss should be recognized for the difference. This is not a violation of the cost principle, for this principle is tempered by the concept of *prudent cost*—costs should not be recognized in an amount significantly above what a prudent person would pay for similar goods.

EXAMPLE 11

Buyer pays $100 for goods that have a fair market value of $50. Buyer should *not* make the following entry:

Purchases	100	
Accounts Payable		100

The correct entry is:

Purchases	50	
Loss on Purchases	50	
Accounts Payable		100

If a buyer makes a purchase commitment to buy goods at a given price, and before the delivery the market value of the goods drops significantly, a loss should *immediately* be recognized on the purchase. It is not permitted to defer this loss to the date of delivery.

EXAMPLE 12

Buyer commits himself to purchase goods under a noncancelable contract for $5,000. As mentioned earlier, no entry is made at this time. Before delivery takes place, the market value of these goods drops to $3,000. Buyer should immediately recognize a loss of $2,000 with the following entry:

Loss on Purchase Commitment	2,000	
Estimated Liability on Purchase Commitment		2,000

At the time delivery takes place, Buyer's entry is:

Purchases	3,000	
Estimated Liability on Purchase Commitment	2,000	
Accounts Payable		5,000

If, by the time delivery takes place, the market value has risen, it is permissible to recover the previously recognized loss. But gains over and above the original cost may not be recognized.

EXAMPLE 13

Let's return to the previous example. If by delivery time the market value has risen to $3,800, the entry for the purchase is:

Purchases	3,800	
Estimated Liability on Purchase Commitment	2,000	
Accounts Payable		5,000
Recovery of Loss on Purchase Commitment		800

The loss is an expense item; the recovery is a revenue item.

9.6 THE GROSS PROFIT PERCENTAGE METHOD

We have discussed several methods so far for determining the cost of the ending inventory: FIFO, LIFO, average, and others. Another commonly used method is the *gross profit percentage method*. This method may be used for interim reporting or for situations in which a physical count cannot be taken (such as when the ending inventory has been destroyed by fire). Otherwise, it is not acceptable for financial accounting purposes.

This method relies on a key percentage—the gross profit percentage—which may be calculated in two ways: gross profit percentage on *selling price* and gross profit percentage on *cost*. The percentage on selling price is computed by dividing the gross profit by the selling price; the percentage on cost is computed by dividing the gross profit by the cost.

EXAMPLE 14

An item that cost $80 is sold for $100, thus yielding a gross profit of $20. The gross profit percentage on selling price is

$$\frac{20}{100} = 20\%$$

The gross profit percentage on cost, however, is:

$$\frac{20}{80} = 25\%$$

Which of these percentages should be used for the gross profit percentage inventory method? The answer is that while either one may be used, it is easier to use the percentage on selling price. But suppose you are given the percentage on cost? No problem! There is a conversion formula that will convert that percentage into the percentage on selling price, as follows:

$$\text{Percentage on selling price} = \frac{\text{percentage on cost}}{1 + \text{percentage on cost}}$$

Conversely, if you are given the percentage on selling price and wish to convert it to percentage on cost, the formula is:

$$\text{Percentage on cost} = \frac{\text{percentage on selling price}}{1 - \text{percentage on selling price}}$$

EXAMPLE 15

If the percentage on cost is given as 25%, the percentage on selling price is:

$$\frac{0.25}{1 + 0.25} = 0.20 = 20\%$$

Conversely, if the percentage on selling price is given as 20%, you would get the percentage on cost of 25% by the following:

$$\frac{0.20}{1 - 0.20} = 0.25 = 25\%$$

Now that we have learned how to determine the profit percentage on selling price, let's see how the gross profit percentage inventory method works by reviewing the portion of the income statement dealing with the computation of gross profit. Here it is:

Sales		xxx
Beginning Inventory	xxx	
+ Net Purchases	xxx	
= Merchandise Available	xxx	
− Ending Inventory	(xxx)	
Cost of Goods Sold		(xxx)
Gross Profit		xxx

We will use this structure to determine the ending inventory under the gross profit method, as illustrated in the next example.

EXAMPLE 16

Company M had a beginning inventory of $20,000, net purchases of $90,000, and sales of $120,000. Its profit percentage on *selling price* is 20%, and we wish to determine the ending inventory. Let's set up the structure:

Sales		$120,000
Beginning Inventory	$ 20,000	
+ Net Purchases	90,000	
= Merchandise Available	110,000	
− Ending Inventory	? (3)	
Cost of Goods Sold		? (2)
Gross Profit		? (1)

Since the profit percentage is 20% of selling price, gross profit (item 1) is $24,000 (20% of $120,000). Therefore, by subtraction, cost of goods sold (item 2) is $96,000 ($120,000 − $24,000). Finally, by subtraction, ending inventory (item 3) is $14,000 ($110,000 − $96,000).

EXAMPLE 17

If, in Example 16, the profit percentage was given as 20% on *cost*, then the profit percentage on selling price would be:

$$\frac{0.20}{1 + 0.20} = 16.67\% \quad \text{(rounded)}$$

Therefore, gross profit (item 1) is $20,004 (16.67% of $120,000), cost of goods sold (item 2) is $99,996 by subtraction, and ending inventory (item 3), also by subtraction, is $10,004 ($110,000 − $99,996).

9.7   THE RETAIL METHOD OF INVENTORY (AVERAGE COST VERSION)

The retail method of inventory, *which is acceptable* for financial statement purposes and does not require a physical count, establishes a percentage relationship between the *cost* of goods available and their *retail* selling price. It then uses this percentage to determine the ending inventory value. Let's look at an example.

EXAMPLE 18

Merchandise Whiz has the following cost and retail figures for its goods during 19X1.

	Cost	Retail
Beginning Inventory	$40,000	$60,000
Net Purchases	20,000	35,000
Merchandise Available for Sale	$60,000	$95,000
Sales	?	49,000
Ending Inventory	Goal	$46,000

Merchandise available for sale at cost and retail price is $60,000 and $95,000, respectively. Thus cost is 63.16% of retail ($60,000 ÷ $95,000, rounded). We now take this percentage and multiply it by the ending inventory at *retail* of $46,000 to arrive at the *cost* figure (our goal) of $29,054. This is the essence of the retail method.

9.8   MARKUPS, MARKDOWNS; THE CONVENTIONAL (LCM) RETAIL METHOD

Retail prices are often marked up or down depending on how well the goods are selling. *Markups* are additions to the original selling price; *markup cancellations* cancel these markups (but do not reduce the item below the original selling price). *Markdowns* are reductions from the original selling price; *markdown cancellations* cancel these markdowns (but do not raise the price above the original selling price). Markups less markup cancellations are referred to as *net markups*; markdowns less markdown cancellations are referred to as *net markdowns*.

EXAMPLE 19

An item, originally marked to sell at $20, is selling briskly. The owner therefore raises its price to $25. We thus have a markup of $5. A week later, after seeing sales slow down, she reduces the price to $23. This represents a markup cancellation of $2, so net markups are therefore $3.

EXAMPLE 20

An item, originally marked to sell at $38, is not selling well. The owner therefore reduces the price to $27. We thus have a markdown of $11. Two weeks later, after seeing the sales improve, she raises the price to $32. This represents a markdown cancellation of $5, so net markdowns are therefore $6.

EXAMPLE 21

Item Q was placed on the shelves 2 weeks ago and marked to sell at $50. Since then, its price has undergone the following changes:

Oct.   1   Price increase to $58.
     8   Price decrease to $53.
   15   Price decrease to $47.
   20   Price increase to $48.
   23   Price increase to $52.

The October 1 increase of $8 represents a markup, while the October 8 decrease of $5 represents a markup cancellation. Thus far net markups are $3.

Let's go now to October 15. The decrease of $6 represents another markup cancellation of $3 and a markdown (below the original price of $50) of $3. The October 20 increase to $48 represents a markdown cancellation of $1; and finally, the increase to $52 of October 23 represents an additional markdown cancellation of $2, and a markup of $2 (to $52).

Let's now see what role markups and markdowns play in the retail inventory method. Markups increase the retail column; markup cancellations decrease it. Markdowns decrease the retail column; markdown cancellations increase it. The cost column, however, is not affected by any of these, since the cost remains the same regardless of how the goods are marked to sell on the shelves.

Under the average cost version of the retail method discussed previously, markups, markdowns, and their related cancellations enter into the determination of the cost to retail percentage. However, under the LCM version of the retail method (also referred to as the *conventional retail method*), markdowns and markdown cancellations do *not* enter into the percentage. This yields a smaller percentage, resulting in a lower valuation for the ending inventory—a valuation that should approximate the low amount attained under the lower-of-cost-or-market calculation. Let's look at an example.

EXAMPLE 22

Company A has the following cost and retail data regarding its merchandise for 19X1.

	Cost	Retail
Beginning Inventory	$10,000	$15,000
Net Purchases	30,000	60,000
Merchandise Available	$40,000	$75,000
Markups	—	12,000
Markup Cancellations	—	(3,000)
	$40,000	$84,000

Cost-to-Retail Ratio (LCM):
$$\frac{\$40,000}{\$84,000} = 47.62\%$$

	Cost	Retail
Markdowns	—	(5,000)
Markdown Cancellations	—	1,000
Goods Available for Sale	$40,000	$80,000

Cost-to-Retail Ratio (non-LCM):
$$\frac{\$40,000}{\$80,000} = 50\%$$

	Cost	Retail
Sales	?	60,000
Ending Inventory	Goal	$20,000

Under the LCM version, markdowns and markdown cancellations do not enter into the cost-to-retail ratio. Thus the ratio is 47.62% (rounded), and multiplying this by the ending inventory of $20,000 at retail yields a cost of $9,524. Under the average version, however, markdowns and markdown cancellations *are* included in the ratio, thus yielding a higher ratio of 50%. When we multiply this against the ending inventory of $20,000, we get $10,000 at cost.

9.9 THE LIFO RETAIL METHOD

The LIFO retail method usually results in a lower ending inventory, a higher cost of goods sold, a lower gross profit, and thus lower income taxes. For this reason, and for the reason that it also provides a better matching of current costs against current revenues, it has been adopted by many retail companies.

This method is applied in different ways depending on whether there are stable prices during the period, or fluctuating prices. Either way, since this method is a cost method and does not try to approximate lower of cost or market, net markdowns *are* included in the cost-to-retail percentage.

In a stable price situation, two percentages are calculated: one for the beginning inventory, the other for the purchases and related markups and markdowns. A major assumption of this method is that the markups and markdowns apply only to the purchases and not to the beginning inventory. Let's look at an example.

EXAMPLE 23

Sharf Corporation has the following cost and retail data for its merchandise transactions during 19X1.

	Cost	Retail
Beginning Inventory	$ 50,000	$ 75,000
Net Purchases	100,000	125,000
Net Markups	—	4,000
Net Markdowns	—	(1,000)
Goods Available	$150,000	$203,000
Net Sales	?	(120,000)
Ending Inventory	Goal	$ 83,000

Let's first assume that prices have remained stable from the beginning of 19X1 to the end. Therefore, the increase in the retail value of the inventory from beginning to end of $8,000 ($83,000 − $75,000) represents a *physical* increase in the units on hand. We now compute two percentages—one for the beginning inventory, the other for the new goods (purchases, markups, and markdowns), as follows:

$$\text{Beginning Inventory Percentage} = \frac{\$50,000}{\$75,000} = 67\% \quad \text{(rounded)}$$

$$\text{New Goods Percentage} = \frac{\$100,000}{\$128,000} = 78\% \quad \text{(rounded)}$$

Since under LIFO we assume that the goods that came in last go out first, the ending inventory of $83,000 consists of two batches: the old beginning inventory batch of $75,000 and another batch of $8,000 of new goods. These batches are now multiplied by their respective percentages as follows:

$$
\begin{array}{lr}
\$75,000 \times 0.67 = & \$50,250 \\
\$8,000 \times 0.78 = & \underline{6,240} \\
\text{Ending inventory at cost} & \$56,490 \quad \text{(Goal)}
\end{array}
$$

As we have just seen, the ending inventory for 19X1 consists of two batches, and 19X2 will begin with these batches. If during 19X2 the inventory increases once again from beginning to end, a new, third batch will be recognized.

If, however, the inventory level decreases during 19X2, we will have to reduce one of these batches. Since LIFO assumes that what comes in last leaves first, we must reduce the second batch.

EXAMPLE 24

Again, refer to Example 23, where the ending inventory for 19X1 consists of two batches:

Retail	Cost Percentage	Cost
$75,000	67%	$50,250
8,000	78%	6,240
$83,000		$56,490

If, at the end of 19X2, the inventory at *retail* drops by $7,000 to $76,000, we *reduce* the second batch, as follows:

Retail	Cost Percentage	Cost
$75,000	67%	$50,250
1,000*	78%	780
$76,000		$51,030 (Goal)

*$8,000 − $7,000.

Until now we assumed that prices have remained stable. If they have fluctuated, however, our computations will change. We will need to use price indexes and employ an approach similar to the dollar-value LIFO method discussed in Chapter 8 (you should briefly review that material at this time).

Under that method we set up the following chart:

Date	Current Year-End Prices	÷ Price Index	= Inventory at Base-Year Prices	Dollar-Value LIFO
xxx	xxx	xxx	xxx	xxx

To arrive at the last column, we took the inventory at base-year prices, broke it down into layers, and multiplied each layer by the index in effect when that layer was created. We will now do the same under the LIFO retail method with one additional multiplication: Each layer will also have to be multiplied by the cost-to-retail percentage in effect when the layer was created (in order to reduce it from retail down to cost). Let's look at an example.

EXAMPLE 25

Let's use the same information as in Example 23 in order to contrast the fluctuating price situation with the stable price situation.

	Cost (19X1)	Retail
Beginning Inventory	$ 50,000	$ 75,000
Net Purchases	100,000	125,000
Net Markups	—	4,000
Net Markdowns	—	(1,000)
Goods Available	$150,000	$203,000
Net Sales	?	(120,000)
Ending Inventory	Goal	$ 83,000

Let's assume that the price index before 19X1 was 100; the price index for 19X1 itself was 105. The cost-to-retail percentage at the beginning of 19X1 is approximately 67% ($50,000 ÷ $75,000), and the percentage during 19X1 is approximately 78% ($100,000 ÷ $128,000). We now set up our chart as follows:

Date	Retail Price	÷	Price Index	=	Inventory at Base-Year Prices	LIFO Retail
Jan. 1, 19X1	$75,000	÷	1.00	=	$75,000	$50,250*
Dec. 31, 19X1	83,000	÷	1.05	=	79,048	53,565

*$75,000 × 0.67 = $50,250.

On December 31, we divide the ending inventory of $83,000 by the current index of 1.05 to yield $79,048. When we compare this to last year's number of $75,000, we notice an increment of $4,048. This is then multiplied by the current index of 1.05 (as we did in Chapter 8) *and* by the 19X1 cost-to-retail percentage of 78%. Thus the ending inventory is comprised of two layers:

$$\begin{aligned}
\text{Base Layer:} \quad & \$75,000 \times 1.00 \times 0.67 = \$50,250 \\
\text{19X1 Layer:} \quad & \$\ 4,048 \times 1.05 \times 0.78 = \underline{\quad 3,315} \\
& \hphantom{\$\ 4,048 \times 1.05 \times 0.78 = } \$53,565
\end{aligned}$$

If in subsequent years the ending inventory rises, we add on new layers; if it falls, we reduce the most recent layer since we are using LIFO.

EXAMPLE 26

Let's continue with the problem presented in the previous example. Assume that the ending inventory at retail for 19X2 is $95,000, the 19X2 index is 108, and the cost-to-retail percentage for 19X2 is 80%.
The chart is as follows:

Date	Retail Price	÷	Price Index	=	Inventory at Base-Year Prices	LIFO Retail
Jan. 1, 19X1	$75,000	÷	100	=	$75,000	$50,250
Dec. 31, 19X1	83,000	÷	105	=	79,048	53,565
Dec. 31, 19X2	95,000	÷	108	=	87,963	61,268

When we compare December 31, 19X2, to December 31, 19X1, we find an increment of $8,915 ($87,963 − $79,048). Thus at the end of 19X2, the inventory consists of three layers:

$$
\begin{aligned}
\text{Base Layer:} \quad & \$75,000 \times 1.00 \times 0.67 = \$50,250 \\
\text{19X1 Layer:} \quad & \$4,048 \times 1.05 \times 0.78 = 3,315 \\
\text{19X2 Layer:} \quad & \$8,915 \times 1.08 \times 0.80 = 7,703 \\
\hline
& \$61,268
\end{aligned}
$$

To sum matters up, the LIFO retail method for a fluctuating price situation is the same as the dollar-value LIFO method discussed in the previous chapter, with one additional step: Each year's layer must be multiplied by its respective cost-to-retail percentage to reduce the retail value down to cost.

9.10 SPECIAL ITEMS RELATING TO THE RETAIL METHOD

Certain special items must be taken into account in the computations for the retail method. Some affect both columns, others affect just the cost column, and yet others affect only the retail column.

Freight costs add to the cost column; purchases returns reduce both the cost and retail columns. Purchases discounts reduce the cost column but not the retail column, since the selling price is usually not reduced to reflect a purchase discount. Sales returns reduce sales in the retail column; sales discounts do not.

Goods transferred in from another department are treated just like purchases: They increase both columns. Normal shortages (from theft, breakage, and shrinkage) reduce the *retail* column *below* the goods available for sale line (just like sales do), and thus *do not* affect the cost-to-retail percentage. Abnormal shortages, however, reduce *both* the cost and retail columns *above* the goods available for sale line and thus *do* affect the percentage. Employee discounts are treated just like sales: They are subtracted from the goods available to arrive at the ending inventory.

These points are illustrated in the next example.

EXAMPLE 27

Merchandise Corp. uses the average-cost retail method, and it has most of the special items just discussed: purchases returns, purchases discounts, normal and abnormal shortages, sales returns and discounts, and employee discounts. The actual numbers are as follows:

	Cost	Retail
Beginning Inventory	$25,000	$ 40,000
Purchases	50,000	100,000
Purchases Returns	(1,000)	(2,000)
Purchases Discounts	(3,000)	—
Abnormal Shortage	(3,000)	(6,000)
Net Markups	—	4,000
Net Markdowns	—	(3,000)
Goods Available for Sale	$68,000	133,000
Cost-to-Retail Percentage: $68,000 ÷ $133,000 = 51.13% (rounded)		
Sales (net of returns, but not discounts)	—	(85,000)
Employee Discounts	—	(4,000)
Normal Shortages	—	(3,000)
Ending Inventory	Goal	$ 41,000

The cost is $41,000 × 51.13%, which equals $20,963. Notice that while purchases returns were deducted in both columns, purchases discounts were deducted only in the cost column. Also notice that abnormal shortages entered into the cost-to-retail percentage; normal shortages did not.

Summary

1. If on December 31 the market value of the inventory is below its cost, we must make an entry to reduce the inventory to the market value. If however, the market value has risen above cost, no entry is made. This is referred to as lower of cost or market (LCM).

2. *Market* is defined as the replacement cost of the item. However, this cannot exceed the ceiling—net realizable value—nor be below the floor—net realizable value minus normal profit. We thus place these three values in either ascending order or descending order and choose the middle number. This is referred to as *designated market* and is then compared to cost for LCM purposes.

3. The LCM procedure may be applied on an item-by-item basis, a category-by-category basis, or to the inventory as a whole. The most commonly used approach is the item-by-item basis.

4. Under the direct method of recording LCM, no specific loss account is debited for the decline in value (it is buried in cost of goods sold). Under the indirect method, however, we debit a specific loss account called Loss Due to Market Decline of Inventory.

5. In certain special cases inventory may be recorded at net realizable value even if this is above cost. This is permitted if there is a controlled market for this item *and* no significant disposal costs are expected. This is often the case with precious metals and certain agricultural products.

6. For basket purchases—different types of units purchased at a single lump-sum amount—the cost should be allocated to the units in the ratio of their respective sales values.

7. If a commitment is made to purchase goods at a given price and before delivery the market value drops significantly, a loss should immediately be recognized on the purchase. The entry is:

Loss on Purchase Commitment	xxx	
Estimated Liability on Purchase Commitment		xxx

At the time of delivery the purchase should be recorded at market value, not at the inflated contract price. To do so would violate the principle of prudent cost.

8. The gross profit percentage may be calculated in two ways:

$$1. \quad \frac{\text{Gross profit}}{\text{Selling price}}$$

$$2. \quad \frac{\text{Gross profit}}{\text{Cost}}$$

9. Either one of these may be converted to the other via the following formulas:

$$\text{Gross profit percentage on selling price} = \frac{\text{gross profit percentage on cost}}{1 + \text{gross profit percentage on cost}}$$

$$\text{Gross profit percentage on cost} = \frac{\text{gross profit percentage on selling price}}{1 - \text{gross profit percentage on selling price}}$$

10. The retail inventory method establishes a relationship between the cost of the goods and their retail price. It then multiplies this percentage by the ending inventory at retail to determine cost. No physical count is required under this method.

11. *Markups* are additions to the original selling price; *markdowns* are reductions from the original selling price. *Markup cancellations* negate markups; *markdown cancellations* negate markdowns.

12. Under the *average* version of the retail method, markdowns and their cancellations (net markdowns) are included in the computation of the cost to retail percentage; under the *LCM* version (the *conventional retail method*) they are not. Under all methods, however, they appear on the chart affecting the goods available for sale line.

13. The LIFO retail method will usually provide a lower gross profit figure and thus lower taxes. This, plus the fact that it provides a better matching of current costs against current revenues, has made it widely accepted.

14. During a period of stable prices, this method does not use price indexes; during a period of fluctuating prices, it does. In that case, it will resemble the dollar-value LIFO method discussed in Chapter 8.

15. Freight costs are additions to the cost column; purchases returns are subtractions from both the cost and retail columns; purchases discounts reduce only the cost column. Sales returns reduce sales in the retail column; sales discounts do not.

16. Transfers in from other departments increase both the cost and retail columns. Normal shortages reduce the retail column *below* the goods available for sale line and thus do *not* affect the cost-to-retail percentage. Abnormal shortages reduce both the cost and retail columns and do so *above* the goods available for sale line, thereby affecting the percentage. Employee discounts are treated just like sales.

Rapid Review

1. If the cost of inventory is lower than the market value, we choose the _____.

2. The ceiling above which replacement cost cannot go is _____.

3. Selling price minus disposal and completion costs is called _____.

4. The number between the ceiling and the floor is called _____.

5. Under the direct method of recording LCM, the loss due to a decline in market value is buried in _____.

6. The Allowance to Reduce Inventory to Market account is a _____ account.

7. A group of different units purchased at a lump-sum price is called a _____.

8. For the statement above, the units should be recorded in the ratio of their respective _____.

9. To record a purchase at a contract price significantly higher than market value would violate the principle of _____.

10. To convert the profit percentage on cost to a percentage on selling price, you would divide the _____ by _____.

11. Reductions to retail price below the original selling price are called _____.

12. Under the _____ version of the retail method, net markdowns are not included in the cost-to-retail percentage.

13. Purchase discounts reduce the _____ column, but not the _____ column.

14. Freight costs are added to the _____ column, but not the _____ column.

15. Sales _____ reduce sales, but sales _____ do not.

16. Normal shortages reduce the _____ column.

17. Employee discounts reduce the _____ column.

Answers: **1.** cost **2.** net realizable value **3.** net realizable value **4.** designated market **5.** cost of goods sold **6.** contra asset **7.** basket purchase **8.** sales values **9.** prudent cost **10.** percentage on cost; 1 + percentage on cost **11.** markdowns **12.** LCM **13.** cost; retail **14.** cost; retail **15.** returns; discounts **16.** retail **17.** retail

Solved Problems

Lower of Cost or Market

9.1 Determine the value to be reported for the inventory in the following cases:

(*a*) Cost, $2,000; market, $1,800

(*b*) Cost, $1,300; market, $1,900

SOLUTION

(*a*) $1,800

(*b*) $1,300   [Section 9.1]

9.2 An item's cost is $40 and its current replacement cost is $46. Its net realizable value (NRV) and NRV minus profit are $38 and $35, respectively.

(*a*) Determine the designated market value.

(*b*) Determine the value to be assigned to the item.

SOLUTION

(*a*) $38

(*b*) $38   [Section 9.1]

9.3 If the cost in Problem 9.2 was $34, what value should we assign to the item?

SOLUTION

$34 [Section 9.1]

9.4 An item originally cost $100. Today it can be purchased at $69 and sold at $75. Disposal costs are $3, and normal profit is $6 per unit. Determine:

(a) Replacement cost

(b) Net realizable value (NRV)

(c) NRV − profit

(d) Designated market

(e) Value to be assigned to the item

SOLUTION

(a) $69

(b) $72 ($75 − $3)

(c) $66 ($72 − $6)

(d) $69

(e) $69 [Section 9.1]

9.5 Company A has two categories of goods: hot and cold. Within the hot category there are three items, A, B, and C, with costs of $60, $80, and $30, respectively, and market values of $89, $75, and $25, respectively.

Within the cold category there are two items, D and E, with costs of $70 and $75, respectively, and market values of $27 and $72, respectively.

Determine LCM in three possible ways.

SOLUTION

	Cost	Designated Market	Lower of Cost or Market By: Individual Items	Categories	Total Inventory
Hot:					
A	$ 60	$ 89	$ 60		
B	80	75	75		
C	30	25	25		
Total Hot	$170	$189		$170	
Cold:					
D	$ 70	$ 27	27		
E	75	72	72		
Total Cold	$145	$ 99	___	99	
Total Inventory	$315	$288	$259	$269	$288

[Section 9.1]

Recording LCM

9.6 Company B uses the periodic inventory system. Its ending inventory at cost and market value is $40,000 and $35,000, respectively. Prepare the required entries under both the direct and indirect methods.

SOLUTION

Direct Method:

Inventory	35,000	
Cost of Goods Sold		35,000

Indirect Method:

Inventory	40,000	
Cost of Goods Sold		40,000
Loss Due to Market Decline of Inventory	5,000	
Allowance to Reduce Inventory to Market		5,000

[Section 9.2]

9.7 If, in Problem 9.6 (under the indirect method), the market value rises during the next period to $39,000 and the cost is still $40,000, prepare the appropriate entry.

SOLUTION

Allowance to Reduce Inventory to Market	4,000	
Recovery of Loss Due to Market Decline of Inventory		4,000

[Section 9.2]

9.8 If the market value of the inventory in Problems 9.6 and 9.7 later rises to $42,000 and the cost remains the same, what entry should be made?

SOLUTION

We should make another recovery entry to recover $1,000 (from $39,000 to $40,000). The extra $2,000 (from $40,000 to $42,000) is a gain that may not be recognized.   [Section 9.2]

9.9 Company C uses the perpetual inventory system. On December 31 its inventory account shows $60,000, but the market value is only $55,000. Prepare the necessary entries under both the direct and indirect methods.

SOLUTION

Direct Method:

Cost of Goods Sold	5,000	
Merchandise Inventory		5,000

Indirect Method:

Loss Due to Market Decline of Inventory	5,000	
Allowance to Reduce Inventory to Market		5,000 [Section 9.2]

Valuation at Relative Sales Value

9.10 Company D purchases 60 parcels of land at a lump-sum price of $100,000. Twenty of these are considered grade A quality and sell at $7,000 each; 30 are considered grade B quality and sell at $5,000 each, and the remaining 10 are considered grade C quality and sell at $4,000 each. Allocate the $100,000 cost to each grade and to each parcel.

SOLUTION

Grade	Parcels	Selling Price per Parcel	Total Sales Value	Ratio	Allocation
A	20	$7,000	$140,000	$140/330 \times \$100,000 = \$42,424$	
B	30	5,000	150,000	$150/330 \times 100,000 = 45,455$	
C	10	4,000	40,000	$40/330 \times 100,000 = 12,121$	
			$330,000		

(*Note:* The ratio was *not* rounded in the above allocation.)
The cost per parcel is:

Grade A: $42,424 ÷ 20 parcels = $2,121   (rounded to nearest dollar)
Grade B: $45,455 ÷ 30 parcels = 1,515
Grade C: $12,121 ÷ 10 parcels = 1,212   [Section 9.4]

Purchase Commitments

9.11 Goods with a market value of $800 are purchased for $1,600. Prepare the entry for the purchase.

SOLUTION

Purchase	800	
Loss on Purchases	800	
Accounts Payable		1,600 [Section 9.5]

9.12 On November 15, 19X1, Company E commits itself to a noncancelable contract to purchase goods in 19X2 for $20,000. On December 31, 19X1, the market value of these goods falls to $12,000. Prepare the entry on December 31, 19X1, and on the date of delivery in 19X2.

SOLUTION

Dec. 31, 19X1	Loss of Purchase Commitment	8,000	
	Estimated Liability on Purchase Commitment		8,000
Date of Delivery	Purchases	12,000	
	Estimated Liability on Purchase Commitment	8,000	
	Accounts Payable		20,000

[Section 9.5]

The Gross Profit Percentage Method

9.13 Complete the following table.

	Profit % on Cost	Profit % on Selling Price
(a)	20%	?
(b)	?	20%
(c)	15%	?
(d)	?	40%
(e)	30%	?

SOLUTION

(a) 16.66%

(b) 25%

(c) 13.04%

(d) 66.67%

(e) 23.08%   [Section 9.6]

9.14 In 19X1, Company F had sales of $300,000, a beginning inventory of $40,000, and net purchases of $200,000. If its gross profit percentage is 30% on selling price, find the ending inventory.

SOLUTION

Sales		$300,000
Beginning Inventory	$ 40,000	
Net Purchases	200,000	
Merchandise Available	240,000	
Ending Inventory	?	
Cost of Goods Sold		?
Gross Profit		?

$$\begin{aligned} \text{Gross Profit} &= 0.30 \times \$300,000 \\ &= \$90,000 \end{aligned}$$

$$\begin{aligned} \text{Cost of Goods Sold} &= \$300,000 - \$90,000 \\ &= \$210,000 \end{aligned}$$

$$\begin{aligned} \text{Ending Inventory} &= \$240,000 - \$210,000 \\ &= \$30,000 \end{aligned}$$ [Section 9.6]

9.15 Company G had sales during 19X1 of $160,000, a beginning inventory of $70,000, and net purchases of $90,000. If its gross profit percentage on cost is 25%, find the ending inventory.

SOLUTION

Sales		$160,000
Beginning Inventory	$ 70,000	
Net Purchases	90,000	
Merchandise Available	160,000	
Ending Inventory	?	
Cost of Goods Sold		?
Gross Profit		?

$$\text{Profit Percentage on Selling Price} = \frac{0.25}{1.25} = 0.20$$

Gross Profit	$= 0.20 \times \$160,000$
	$= \$32,000$
Cost of Goods Sold	$= \$160,000 - \$32,000$
	$= \$128,000$
Ending Inventory	$= \$160,000 - \$128,000$
	$= \$32,000$ [Section 9.6]

The Retail Method of Inventory (Average and LCM Versions)

9.16 Company H has the following data regarding its merchandise for 19X1:

Purchases: cost, $10,000; retail, $25,000

Purchases returns: cost, $1,000; retail, $2,500

Beginning inventory: cost, $50,000; retail, $110,000

Purchases discounts: cost, $2,000

Markdowns: $2,000

Markdown cancellations: $1,200

Normal shortages, retail: $1,500

Employee discounts: $4,000

Freight in: $800

Markups: $3,000

Markup cancellations: $1,000

Sales: $82,000

Sales returns: $2,000

Sales discounts: $2,200

Determine the cost of the ending inventory using the retail method—average version.

SOLUTION

	Cost	Retail
Beginning Inventory	$50,000	$110,000
Purchases	10,000	25,000
Purchases Returns	(1,000)	(2,500)
Purchases Discounts	2,000	—*
Freight In	800	—
Markups	—	3,000
Markup Cancellations	—	(1,000)
Markdowns	—	(2,000)
Markdown Cancellations	—	1,200
Goods Available	$61,800	133,700
Normal Shortages	—	(1,500)
Employee Discounts	—	(4,000)
Sales (less sales returns)[†]	?	(80,000)
Ending Inventory	Goal	$ 48,200

$$\text{The cost-to-retail ratio is } \frac{\$61,800}{\$133,700} = 46\% \quad \text{(rounded)}$$

$$\text{Ending inventory} = \$48,200 \times 0.46$$
$$= \$22,172$$

---

*Purchases discounts are not subtracted from the retail column.
†Sales discounts are ignored.   [Sections 9.7, 9.10]

9.17 For Problem 9.16, determine the ending inventory under the LCM version of the retail method.

SOLUTION

For the LCM version, markdowns and markdown cancellations do not enter into the ratio (although they appear on the chart). Thus the numerator will remain $63,800; the denominator, however, ignores the net markdowns of −$800 ($2,000 − $1,200) and therefore will be $139,500 ($138,700 + $800). The ratio now is:

$$\frac{63,800}{139,500} = 45.73\%$$

$$\text{Ending inventory} = 53,200 \times 45.73\% \quad \text{(rounded)}$$
$$= \$24,328 \qquad \text{[Sections 9.8, 9.10]}$$

9.18 Company J has provided the following data regarding its merchandise for 19X3.

Purchases: cost, $17,000; retail, $30,000

Purchases returns: cost, $1,500; retail, $2,650

Transfers in: cost, $14,000; retail, $24,000

Beginning inventory: cost, $70,000; retail, $150,000

Abnormal shortages: cost, $10,000; retail, $17,600

Normal shortages, retail: $8,000

Net markups: $4,000

Net markdowns: $2,000

Freight in: $500

Employee discounts: $3,000

Sales: $90,000

Sales returns: $5,000

Determine the ending inventory under the retail method (average version).

SOLUTION

	Cost	Retail
Beginning Inventory	$ 70,000	$150,000
Transfers In	14,000	24,000
Purchases	17,000	30,000
Purchases Returns	(1,500)	(2,650)
Freight In	500	—
Abnormal Shortages	(10,000)	(17,600)
Net Markups	—	4,000

Net Markdowns	—	(2,000)
Goods Available	$ 90,000	$185,750
Sales (less sales returns)	?	(85,000)
Normal Shortages	—	(8,000)
Employee Discounts	—	(3,000)
Ending Inventory	Goal	$ 89,750

$$\text{Cost-to-retail ratio} = \frac{\$\ 90,000}{\$185,750} = 48.45\% \quad \text{(rounded)}$$

$$\text{Ending inventory} = \$89,750 \times 48.45\% = \$43,484 \qquad \text{[Sections 9.7, 9.10]}$$

9.19   For Problem 9.18, determine the ending inventory under the LCM version.

SOLUTION

For the LCM version the net markdowns do not enter into the cost to retail ratio. Therefore:

$$\text{Cost-to-retail ratio} = \frac{\$\ 90,000}{\$187,750} = 47.94\%$$

$$\text{Ending inventory} = \$\ 89,750 \times 47.94\% = \$43,026 \qquad \text{[Sections 9.8, 9.10]}$$

The LIFO Retail Method

9.20   Company J has the following inventory data for 19X1:

	Cost	Retail
Beginning Inventory	$20,000	$ 60,000
Net Purchases	50,000	100,000
Net Markups	—	5,000
Net Markdowns	—	(2,000)
Goods Available	$70,000	$163,000
Net Sales	?	80,000
Ending Inventory	Goal	$ 83,000

Assume that prices have remained stable during 19X1. Determine the ending inventory at cost under the LIFO retail method.

SOLUTION

$$\text{Beginning inventory percentage} = \frac{\$20,000}{\$60,000} = 0.33 \quad \text{(rounded)}$$

$$\text{New goods percentage} = \frac{\$50,000}{\$103,000} = 0.49 \quad \text{(rounded)}$$

Ending inventory:

	Retail	Cost Percentage	Cost	
Beginning Batch	$60,000	0.33	$19,800	
New Batch	23,000	0.49	11,270	
	$83,000		$31,070	(goal)

[Section 9.9]

9.21   Assume the same data as in Problem 9.20 and that, for 19X2, the ending inventory at retail has
fallen to $73,000. Determine the ending inventory at cost for 19X2. Assume stable prices.

SOLUTION

	Retail	Cost Percentage	Cost
Oldest Batch	$60,000	0.33	$19,800
Next Batch	13,000*	0.49	6,370
	$73,000		$26,170 (goal)

*$23,000 − $10,000.

[Section 9.9]

9.22   Company K has the following inventory data for 19X1:

	Cost	Retail
Beginning Inventory	$ 69,000	$100,000
Net Purchases	40,000	75,000
Net Markups	—	6,000
Net Markdowns	—	(2,000)
Goods Available	$109,000	$179,000
Net Sales	—	(64,000)
Ending Inventory	Goal	$115,000

Assume that prices have remained stable during 19X1. Determine the ending inventory
under the LIFO retail method.

SOLUTION

$$\text{Beginning inventory percentage} = \frac{\$69,000}{\$100,000} = 69\%$$

$$\text{New goods percentage} = \frac{\$40,000}{\$79,000} = 51\% \quad \text{(rounded)}$$

Ending inventory:

	Retail	Cost Percentage	Cost
Beginning Batch	$100,000	69%	$69,000
New Batch	15,000	51%	7,650
	$115,000		$76,650 [Section 9.9]

9.23   Use the same data as in Problem 9.22 and go to 19X2. During this year there were no markups or
markdowns, purchases were $50,000 and $62,500 at cost and retail, respectively, and the ending
inventory at retail is $125,000. Determine the ending inventory at cost. Assume stable prices.

SOLUTION

We now have a new, third layer at 80% ($50,000 ÷ $62,500).

	Retail	Cost Percentage	Cost
Oldest Batch (19X1)	$100,000	69%	$69,000
Next Batch (19X1)	15,000	51%	7,650
19X2 Batch	10,000	80%	8,000
	$125,000		$84,650 [Section 9.9]

9.24 Company L has the following information regarding its merchandise for 19X2:

	Cost	Retail
Beginning Inventory (Jan. 1, 19X2)	$10,000	$ 40,000
Net Purchases	20,000	60,000
Net Markups	—	12,000
Net Markdowns	—	(6,000)
Goods Available	$30,000	$106,000
Net Sales	?	(50,000)
Ending Inventory	Goal	$ 56,000

Assume that the price indexes for 19X1 and 19X2 are 100 and 110, respectively. Determine the cost of the ending inventory under the LIFO retail method.

SOLUTION

$$\text{Cost percentage for beginning inventory} = \frac{\$10,000}{\$40,000} = 25\%$$

$$\text{Cost percentage for new goods} = \frac{\$20,000}{\$66,000} = 30\% \quad \text{(rounded)}$$

To deflate the ending inventory and determine the inventory layers:

Date	Retail Price	÷ Price Index	=	Inventory at Base-Year Prices	LIFO Retail
Jan. 1, 19X2	$40,000	÷ 100	=	$40,000 × 0.25	$10,000
Dec. 31, 19X2	56,000	÷ 110	=	50,909	13,600*
				(Increase of $10,909)	

*Base Layer: $40,000 × 1.00 × 0.25 = $10,000
19X2 Layer: $10,909 × 1.10 × 0.30 =   3,600
                                    $13,600   [Section 9.9]

9.25 Use the information from Problem 9.24 and go to 19X3, whose merchandise information is as follows:

	Cost	Retail
Beginning Inventory	$13,600	$56,000
Net Purchases	10,000	20,000
Net Markups	—	5,000
Net Markdowns	—	(2,000)
Goods Available	$23,600	$79,000
Net Sales	?	(10,000)
Ending Inventory	Goal	$69,000

Assume that the price index for 19X3 is 113. Determine the cost of the ending inventory using the LIFO retail method.

SOLUTION

$$\text{Cost percentage for new goods} = \frac{\$10,000}{\$23,000} = 43\% \quad \text{(rounded)}$$

To deflate the ending inventory and determine the inventory layers:

Date	Retail Price	÷	Price Index	=	Inventory at Base-Year Prices	LIFO Retail
Dec. 31, 19X2	$56,000	÷	110	=	$50,909	$13,600
Dec. 31, 19X3	69,000	÷	113	=	61,062	18,533*
					(Increase of $10,153)	

*Base Layer: $40,000 × 1.00 × 0.25 = $10,000
19X2 Layer: $10,909 × 1.10 × 0.30 =   3,600
19X3 Layer: $10,153 × 1.13 × 0.43 =   4,933
                                     $18,533

[Section 9.9]

9.26 Company M has the following information for 19X2:

	Cost	Retail
Beginning Inventory	$ 5,000	$20,000
Purchases	30,000	60,000
Goods Available	$35,000	$80,000
Sales	?	(40,000)
Ending Inventory	Goal	$40,000

The 19X1 price index is 100; the 19X2 index is 130. Determine the ending inventory.

SOLUTION

$40,000 ÷ 1.30 = $30,769
Base Layer   = 20,000
Increment   = 10,769

$$\text{Beginning Inventory Cost Percentage} = \frac{\$5,000}{\$20,000} = 25\%$$

$$\text{New goods cost percentage} = \frac{\$30,000}{\$60,000} = 50\%$$

Ending inventory:

$$Base\ Layer: \quad \$20{,}000 \times 1.00 \times 0.25 = \$\ 5{,}000$$
$$New\ Layer: \quad \$10{,}769 \times 1.30 \times 0.50 = \underline{\quad 7{,}000}$$
$$\underline{\$12{,}000}$$

[Section 9.9]

Special Items Relating to the Retail Method

9.27 Complete the following table. The first item is given as an example.

	Item	Add/Subtract	Cost Column	Retail Column	Affects Cost Percentage?
(a)	Purchases	+	Yes	Yes	Yes
(b)	Markups				
(c)	Transfers In				
(d)	Sales				
(e)	Purchases Returns				
(f)	Purchases Discounts				
(g)	Normal Shortages				
(h)	Abnormal Shortages				
(i)	Employee Discounts				
(j)	Markdowns				

SOLUTION

	Item	Add/Subtract	Cost Column	Retail Column	Affects Cost Percentage?
(a)	Purchases	+	Yes	Yes	Yes
(b)	Markups	+	No	Yes	Yes
(c)	Transfers In	+	Yes	Yes	Yes
(d)	Sales	−	No	Yes	No
(e)	Purchases Returns	−	Yes	Yes	Yes
(f)	Purchases Discounts	−	Yes	No	Yes
(g)	Normal Shortages	−	No	Yes	No
(h)	Abnormal Shortages	−	Yes	Yes	Yes
(i)	Employee Discounts	−	No	Yes	No
(j)	Markdowns	−	No	Yes	Yes (average version only)

[Section 9.10]

Supplementary Problems

9.28 An item originally cost $20 and its current replacement cost is $13. Its NRV is $18 and the normal profit per unit is $3.

(a) Determine designated market value.

(b) Determine the value to be assigned to the item.

(c) Assume the same information as above except that original cost was $14. Determine the value to be assigned to the item.

9.29 An item originally cost $80. Today it can be purchased at $76 and sold at $88. Disposal cost per unit is $3; profit per unit is $6. Determine:

(a) Replacement cost

(b) NRV

(c) NRV − profit

(d) Designated market

(e) Value to be assigned to the item

9.30 Company K has two categories of goods: wet and dry. The wet category consists of three items, A, B, and C, with costs of $120, $160, and $60, respectively, and market values of $180, $150, and $50, respectively.

The dry category is comprised of two items, X and Y, with costs of $140 and $150, respectively, and market values of $55 and $145, respectively.

Determine LCM by individual units, by categories, and by the inventory as a whole.

9.31 Company L uses the periodic inventory system. Its ending inventory at cost and market value is $22,000 and $14,000, respectively. Prepare the required entries under both the direct and indirect methods.

9.32 Assume the same information as in Problem 9.31, and that during the next period the market value rises to $17,000, while the cost stays the same. Prepare the appropriate entry under the indirect method.

9.33 If, in Problem 9.32, the market value rose to $23,000 instead of $17,000, prepare the appropriate entry.

9.34 Company M uses the perpetual inventory system. On December 31, 19X1, its inventory account shows $94,000 but the market value is $87,000. Prepare the necessary entries under both the direct and indirect methods.

9.35 Company N purchases 80 parcels of land at a lump-sum price of $80,000. Fifty parcels are considered high quality and sell at $8,000 each, 20 are considered medium quality and sell at $5,000 each, while the remaining 10 are low quality and sell at $2,000 each. Allocate the $80,000 cost to each grade and each parcel, under the relative sales value method.

9.36 Goods having a market value of $2,500 are purchased at $4,500. Prepare the entry for the purchase.

9.37 On December 23, 19X1, Company O commits itself to purchase goods for $35,000 under a noncancelable contract. By December 31 the market value of these goods has fallen to $29,000. Prepare the required entry on December 31, 19X1, and on January 5, 19X2, the date of delivery.

9.38 Complete the following table:

	Profit % on Cost	Profit % on Selling Price
(a)	18%	?
(b)	?	50%
(c)	28%	?
(d)	?	25%
(e)	35%	?

9.39 During 19X3, Company P had sales of $90,000, a beginning inventory of $40,000, and net purchases of $60,000. If the gross profit percentage on selling price is 25%, find the ending inventory.

9.40 If, in Problem 9.39, the gross profit percentage is 25% on cost, find the ending inventory.

9.41 Company Q has the following information regarding its merchandise for 19X3:

> Purchases: cost, $18,000; retail, $27,000
>
> Purchases returns: cost, $1,000; retail, $1,500
>
> Beginning inventory: cost, $70,000; retail, $150,000
>
> Purchases discounts: cost, $1,200
>
> Net markdowns: $4,000
>
> Normal shortages, retail: $2,000
>
> Transfers in: cost, $5,000; retail, $9,000
>
> Abnormal shortages: cost, $5,000; retail, $7,500
>
> Employee discounts: $6,000
>
> Freight in: $1,800
>
> Markups: $8,000
>
> Markup cancellations: $5,000
>
> Sales: $135,000
>
> Sales returns: $7,000
>
> Sales discounts: $4,000

Determine the cost to be assigned to the ending inventory under the average version of the retail method.

9.42 For Problem 9.41, determine the ending inventory under the LCM version of the retail method.

9.43 Complete the following table. The first item is given as an example.

	Item	Add/Subtract	Cost Column	Retail Column	Affects Cost Percentage?
(a)	Beginning Inventory	+	Yes	Yes	Yes
(b)	Markups				
(c)	Markup Cancellations				
(d)	Markdown Cancellations				
(e)	Sales Returns				
(f)	Freight In				
(g)	Sales Discounts				
(h)	Transfers In				

9.44 Company R has the following inventory data for 19X1:

	Cost	Retail
Beginning Inventory	$ 60,000	$ 80,000
Net Purchases	50,000	75,000
Net Markups	—	4,000
Net Markdowns	—	(2,000)
Goods Available	$110,000	$157,000
Net Sales	?	57,000
Ending Inventory	Goal	$100,000

Assume that prices have remained stable during 19X1. Determine the ending inventory at cost under the LIFO retail method.

9.45 Assume the same information for 19X1 as in Problem 9.44. During 19X2, the ending inventory at retail has fallen by $15,000, to $85,000. Determine the ending inventory at cost. Once again, assume stable prices.

9.46 Company S has provided you with the following information regarding its merchandise for 19X6:

	Cost	Retail
Beginning Inventory	$50,000	$80,000
Net Purchases	20,000	40,000
Net Markups	—	6,000

The price indexes for 19X5 and 19X6 are 100 and 110, respectively. If the ending inventory at retail for 19X6 is $100,000, determine the ending inventory at cost under the LIFO retail method.

9.47 Refer to Problem 9.45. If the ending inventory at retail for 19X7 is $150,000, the 19X7 index is 115, and the cost-to-retail percentage for 19X7 is 40%, determine the ending inventory at cost.

Examination III

Chapters 7, 8, 9

A. True–False Questions. Place the letter T or F next to the question.

1. _____ If the market value of inventory has risen above cost, an entry should be made to reflect the increment.

2. _____ The indirect method uses a specific loss account to recognize LCM.

3. _____ Losses on purchase commitments should be recognized in the period of payment.

4. _____ Under the conventional retail method, net markdowns are not included in the cost-to-retail percentage.

5. _____ Markup cancellations increase the retail selling price.

6. _____ Purchase discounts reduce both the cost and retail columns.

7. _____ Normal shortages reduce the retail column only.

8. _____ If goods are sent F.O.B. shipping point, they should be counted as part of the buyer's ending inventory.

9. _____ Delivery charges paid by the buyer on the purchase of goods should be treated as an expense.

10. _____ The perpetual inventory system uses an account called Purchases Returns.

11. _____ If the ending inventory is understated, cost of goods sold will be overstated.

12. _____ If the beginning inventory is overstated, cost of goods sold will be understated.

13. _____ LIFO yields the same results under both the periodic and perpetual systems.

14. _____ The base year (under the dollar-value LIFO method) always uses an index of 200.

15. _____ Trade receivables may be oral or written.

16. _____ The account Sales Discounts Forfeited is an expense account.

17. _____ Under the allowance method, Bad Debts Expense is debited when it becomes clear that a customer will not pay.

18. _____ Pledging receivables as collateral is referred to as assignment.

19. _____ If a sale of receivables is made without recourse, the seller is responsible for bad debts.

20. _____ If the contract rate is below the market rate, the note will be issued at a discount.

B. Completion Questions. Fill in the blanks.

21. The middle value of an item's replacement cost, net realizable value, and net realizable value minus profit is called _____.

22. The method which uses no specific loss account to record LCM is known as the _____ method.

23. Inventories of precious metals may be recorded at _____.

24. Basket purchases should have their costs allocated in the ratio of respective _____.

25. Losses on purchase commitments should be recognized via a debit to a loss account and a credit to a _____ account.

26. If you divide the gross profit percentage on cost by _____ you will then arrive at the gross profit percentage on selling price.

27. The retail method establishes a relationship between cost and _____.

28. During a period of fluctuating prices, the LIFO retail method uses _____.

29. Freight costs are added only to the _____ column.

30. One company holding another company's goods for sale in the capacity of an agent is referred to as a _____.

31. Interest charges incurred to purchase goods should be treated as an _____.

32. Under the _____ system, the merchandise inventory account is constantly up to date during the period.

33. Under the net method, a failure to pay within the discount period requires a debit to _____.

34. An understatement of the ending inventory will result in an _____ of the net income.

35. The two broad categories of receivables are _____ and _____.

36. Bad debts expenses are recognized in the period of the sale, rather than at the actual time of default because of the _____ principle.

37. An outright transfer of receivables may be done with _____ or without _____.

38. If a note's contract rate is above the market rate, the note will be issued at a _____.

39. Discounts on notes are really additional _____.

40. The rate the buyer would have to pay to obtain similar financing from other sources is referred to as the _____ rate.

41. Transferring a note to other parties for the maturity value minus a small percentage is called _____.

C. Problems

42. Item Q originally cost $18. Its current replacement cost is $13, it could be sold for $20, and disposal costs would be $4. The normal profit per unit is $2. Find the LCM valuation to be assigned to Item Q.

43. The ending inventory of Merchandise Corporation is $29,000 at cost and $26,000 at market. Prepare the appropriate journal entries under both the direct and indirect methods.

44. Complete the following table:

	Profit % on Cost	Profit % on Selling Price
(a)	20%	?
(b)	?	30%
(c)	25%	?
(d)	?	50%

45. Determine the cost of the ending inventory for Good Corporation under both the average and LCM versions of the retail method:

	Cost	Retail
Beginning Inventory	$14,000	$ 28,000
Purchases	50,000	75,000
Net Markups	—	5,000
Net Markdowns	—	(2,000)
Goods Available	$64,000	$106,000
Sales	—	50,000
Ending Inventory	?	$ 56,000

46. Use the following information to determine the ending inventory for Corporation Q under the LIFO retail method. Assume stable prices.

	Cost	Retail
Beginning Inventory	$ 8,000	$12,000
Purchases	20,000	28,000
Net Markdowns	—	(4,000)
Goods Available	28,000	$36,000
Sales	—	18,000
Ending Inventory	?	$18,000

47. Given the following information, determine the ending inventory under FIFO, LIFO, and weighted average. Use the periodic system.

Beginning Inventory	200 units @ $20
Purchase	100 units @ $22
Purchase	80 units @ $23
Purchase	50 units @ $27

Assume that 225 units were sold during the period.

48. Company M, which had a beginning inventory of $15,000, engaged in the following transactions during 19X3:

1. Purchased goods of $3,000.
2. Returned goods of $400.
3. Sold goods of $1,000 for $1,600.
4. Determined the ending inventory via physical count to be $16,300.

Prepare entries for these transactions under both the periodic and perpetual systems.

49. Use the dollar-value LIFO method to complete the following table:

Dec. 31	Current Year-End Prices	Index	Inventory at Base Prices	Dollar-Value LIFO
(Base) 19X1	$ 5,000	100	?	?
19X2	8,000	110	?	?
19X3	14,000	115	?	?
19X4	19,000	120	?	?

50. Company A makes a sale of $500 with terms of 2/10, N/30. Prepare entries under both the gross method and the net method for the sale, for payment within 10 days and payment after 10 days.

51. The allowance for doubtful accounts before adjustment shows a balance of $700. The aging method for estimating bad debts predicts that $1,000 of receivables will go bad; the percentage-of-sales method predicts $1,200. Prepare entries under both methods.

52. Blue Company transfers receivables of $5,000 to Finance Bank. Finance Bank charges a 2% service fee and withholds an additional 5% to cover sales returns and discounts. Prepare the entry for the transfer if:

(a) The transfer is done without recourse.
(b) The transfer is done with recourse and the three conditions have not been fulfilled.

Answers to Examination III

1. True–False Questions

1. F 2. T 3. F 4. T 5. F 6. F 7. T 8. T 9. F 10. F 11. T 12. F 13. F 14. F 15. T 16. F 17. F 18. T 19. F 20. T

B. Completion Questions

21. designated market 22. direct 23. selling prices 24. sales prices 25. liability 26. 1 − itself 27. retail 28. price indexes 29. cost 30. consignee 31. expense 32. perpetual 33. Purchases Discounts Lost 34. understatement 35. trade; nontrade 36. matching 37. recourse; recourse 38. premium 39. interest 40. imputed 41. discounting

C. Problems

42. $13 [replacement cost]
$14 [net realizable value ($20 − $4), "designated market"]
$16 [net realizable value minus profit]
LCM = $14

43.   *Direct Method:*

Merchandise Inventory	26,000	
Cost of Goods Sold		26,000

      Indirect Method:

Merchandise Inventory	29,000	
Cost of Goods Sold		29,000

Loss Due to Market Decline	3,000	
Allowance to Reduce Cost to Market		3,000

44. (*a*) 25%   (*b*) 23.08%   (*c*) 33.33%   (*d*) 33.33%

45. Average version: $\dfrac{\$64,000}{\$106,000}$ = 60.38%   (rounded)

               60.38% × \$56,000 = \$33,813   (rounded)

      LCM version: $\dfrac{\$64,000}{\$108,000}$ = 59.26%   (rounded)

               59.28% × \$56,000 = \$33,186   (rounded)

46. Beginning inventory percentage: $\dfrac{\$8,000}{\$12,000}$ = 0.67   (rounded)

      New goods percentage: $\dfrac{\$20,000}{\$24,000}$ = 0.83   (rounded)

      Ending inventory:

$$\$12,000 \times 0.67 = \$\ 8,040$$
$$6,000* \times 0.83 = \underline{\ \ 4,980}$$
$$\$13,020$$

*18,000 − 12,000

47.
Goods Available for Sale:	430 units	
Sold:	225 units	
Ending Inventory:	205 units	

FIFO Ending Inventory: (75 units @ \$22) + (80 units @ \$23) + (50 units @ \$27) = \$4,840
LIFO Ending Inventory: (5 units @ \$22) + (200 units @ \$20) = \$4,110
Weighted Average Computation:

	200 × \$20 =	\$4,000
	100 × \$22 =	2,200
	80 × \$23 =	1,840
	50 × \$27 =	1,350
Available	430 units	\$9,390

Cost per Unit: $\dfrac{\$9,390}{430}$ = \$21.83   (rounded)

Ending Inventory: 205 units @ \$21.83 = \$4,475

48. *Periodic System:*

Purchases	3,000	
Accounts Payable		3,000

Accounts Payable	400	
Purchases Returns		400

Accounts Receivable	1,600	
Sales		1,600

Merchandise Inventory	16,300	
Cost of Goods Sold		16,300

Cost of Goods Sold	15,000	
Merchandise Inventory		15,000

Perpetual System:

Merchandise Inventory	3,000	
Accounts Payable		3,000

Accounts Payable	400	
Merchandise Inventory		400

Accounts Receivable	1,600	
Sales		1,600

Cost of Goods Sold	1,000	
Merchandise Inventory		1,000

Inventory Short or Over	300	
Merchandise Inventory		300*

*(15,000 + 3,000 − 400 − 1,000) − 16,300

49.

Dec. 31	Inventory at Base Price	Dollar-Value LIFO
19X1	$ 5,000	$ 5,000
19X2	7,273	7,500
19X3	12,174	13,136
19X4	15,833	17,527

50. *Gross Method:*

Accounts Receivable	500	
Sales		500

Cash	490	
Sales Discounts	10	
Accounts receivable		500

Cash	500	
Accounts Receivable		500

Net Method:

Accounts Receivable	490	
Sales		490

Cash	490	
Accounts Receivable		490

Cash	500	
Sales Discounts Forfeited		10
Accounts Receivable		490

51.

Aging Method:

Bad Debts Expense	300	
Allowance for Doubtful Accounts		300

Percentage of Sales Method:
Same entry, but for $1,200

52. (*a*)

Cash	4,650	
Loss on Sale of Receivables	100	
Due from Factor	250	
Accounts Receivable		5,000

(*b*)

Cash	4,650	
Finance Charge	100	
Due from Factor	250	
Loan Payable to Factor		5,000

Chapter 10

Property, Plant, and Equipment

10.1 GENERAL

Property, plant, and equipment, also known as *fixed assets* or *plant assets*, includes the various assets used by a company to carry out its operations. Typical examples of such assets are land, buildings, equipment, machinery, and furniture. These assets are not held for resale—such assets would be classified as inventory—but are intended for long-term use.

Plant assets are recorded at cost plus any other charges incurred to acquire them and make them ready for use. Thus delivery charges, installation charges, testing costs, sales taxes, and insurance while the asset is in transit would all be debited to the asset. These items "fatten up" the asset and should *not* be expensed.

EXAMPLE 1

Company A purchases a machine for $10,000 and pays delivery charges, installation charges, and sales tax in the amounts of $100, $250, and $800, respectively. The journal entry is:

Machine	11,150	
Cash		11,150

If the market value of a plant asset increases, the asset may *not* be written up to reflect this increase. To do so would be a flagrant violation of the cost principle.

EXAMPLE 2

Company B purchased land for $50,000. After 2 years, an independent appraisal determines the land value to be $70,000. Company B should *not* make the following entry:

Land	20,000	
Gain on Market Appreciation		20,000

10.2 LAND

Land which is purchased for use in carrying out the company's operations is classified as a plant asset. If, however, it is purchased by developers for development and resale, it would be classified as inventory.

The cost of land includes the purchase price and all other costs necessary to take title to the land and make it ready for use. Therefore, all the following would be debited to the land account: closing costs (title fees, attorney fees, recording fees), draining costs, filling costs, and general costs. These items should *not* be expensed.

If the buyer agrees to assume an existing mortgage on the land or to pay any back taxes due, these would also increase the land cost.

EXAMPLE 3

Company C purchases land for a $50,000 cash payment and also agrees to assume an existing mortgage on the land of $20,000. Closing costs are $3,000 and another $1,000 is spent to drain the land, which is located in a swamp. The entry is:

Land	74,000	
Mortgage Payable		20,000
Cash		54,000

Because land differs from other plant assets in that it has an unlimited life, no depreciation is recorded. Thus, if improvements are made to the land and their life is unlimited, their cost is debited to the land account, and once again, no depreciation is recorded. If, however, the improvements have a limited life (such as driveways, walks, fences, and parking lots), they should be debited to Land Improvements and depreciated over their useful lives.

EXAMPLE 4

Company D spends $5,000 on an improvement with an unlimited life, and another $3,000 on parking lots whose life is estimated to be 10 years. The entries are:

Land	5,000	
Cash		5,000

Land Improvements	3,000	
Cash		3,000

The $3,000 parking lot would be depreciated at the rate of $300 per year ($3,000 ÷ 10).

If land is purchased with the intention of constructing a building on the land, all costs incurred from the time of purchase up to the excavation of the building are considered to be costs of the *land* and thus not subject to depreciation. Costs incurred from the excavation point through the completion of construction are considered to be costs of the building, and subject to depreciation.

Assume that land is purchased with the intention of constructing a building, but there already exists an old building on the land which must be demolished. Should the cost of demolishing the building be considered part of the cost of the new building, or part of the cost of the land? Since the land was purchased for the purpose of constructing a building, and the demolition of the old building makes the land suitable for its intended purpose, it is considered a cost of the *land*.

EXAMPLE 5

Company E purchases land for $60,000 for the purpose of constructing a building and pays $2,000 to demolish an old building existing on the land. The entire $62,000 is a cost of the land, and the entry is:

Land	62,000	
Cash		62,000

Any money received for the salvage value of the old building reduces the cost of the demolition, and thus the cost of the land. Thus, in Example 5, if Company E received $300 for the salvage value, the demolition cost is considered to be just $1,700 ($2,000 − $300) and the entry is:

Land	61,700	
Cash		61,700

If a company needs to borrow money in order to finance the purchase of land, the interest incurred is *not* considered a cost of the land, but is debited to Interest Expense.

EXAMPLE 6

Company F purchases land on January 1, 19X1, for $100,000, for which it takes out a mortgage at 10%. At the end of 19X1, it pays interest of $10,000. The entries are:

Jan. 1, 19X1	Land	100,000	
	Mortgage		100,000
Dec. 31, 19X1	Interest Expense	10,000	
	Cash		10,000

10.3   BUILDINGS

The cost of a building includes the purchase price, closing costs, and all other costs necessary to make the building ready for use. All these costs are debited to the Building account ("capitalized"); none are expensed.

If a company constructs its own building, all costs from excavation to completion should be debited to Building. These include direct materials, direct labor, and factory overhead—both variable and fixed. However, the total debit to building should not exceed what the building would have cost had it been constructed by an outside construction company. Any excess should be debited to an expense account.

EXAMPLE 7

Company G constructs a building for its own use and incurs the following costs:

Direct Materials	$ 80,000
Direct Labor	90,000
Variable Overhead	10,000
Fixed Overhead	14,000
Total	$194,000

If this building had been constructed by an outsider, the cost would have been $180,000. The journal entries are:

Building	180,000	
Miscellaneous*		180,000
Construction Expense	14,000	
Miscellaneous		14,000

*This includes several manufacturing-type accounts, such as Materials, Factory Overhead, Wages Payable, and Cash.

If interest is incurred to finance a loan for the construction, a question arises as to whether or not the interest should be capitalized in the building account or expensed. This is discussed in Appendix 10A at the end of this chapter.

Idle buildings—those not being used to carry out company operations—should not be classified as property, plant, and equipment, but, rather, as investments.

10.4   EQUIPMENT

The cost of equipment includes the purchase price, delivery charges, insurance while in transit, installation charges, costs of special foundations, and costs incurred to test the equipment before it is put to use. All these costs are debited ("capitalized") to the Equipment account.

Interest incurred to finance the *purchase* of equipment is debited to Interest Expense. Interest incurred to finance the *construction* of equipment is discussed in Appendix 10A at the end of this chapter.

EXAMPLE 8

Company H purchases a piece of equipment on January 1, 19X1, and incurs the following costs:

Purchase Price	$7,000	Testing Charge	$ 80
Delivery Charge	300	Interest on Loan (1 Year)	700
Installation Charge	250	Cost of Special Foundation	200

The entries are:

Equipment	7,830	
Cash		7,830

Interest Expense	700	
Cash		700

10.5   LUMP-SUM PURCHASES; ISSUANCE OF STOCK FOR PLANT ASSETS

Occasionally, land, buildings, and equipment are purchased together for a lump-sum payment. This is referred to as a *basket purchase*. It is important to know how much of the cost belongs to the land, since this portion, unlike the remainder, will not depreciate. We use the fair market values of the individual items to help us allocate the cost, as shown in the following example.

EXAMPLE 9

Company I purchases land, building, and equipment for a lump sum of $90,000. The fair market values (FMVs) of these items, as determined by appraisal or reference to state property tax assessments, are $40,000, $50,000, and $10,000, respectively. It would be inappropriate to debit the assets for these amounts, since their total is $100,000 while the cost principle requires us to use only $90,000. What we do instead is use the fair market values to set up ratios, and then multiply the ratios by the $90,000 cost, as follows:

	Fair Market Value		
Land	$ 40,000	$= 40/100 \times \$90,000 =$	$36,000
Building	50,000	$= 50/100 \times \$90,000 =$	45,000
Equipment	10,000	$= 10/100 \times \$90,000 =$	9,000
	$100,000 $=		$90,000

The journal entry is:

Land	36,000	
Building	45,000	
Equipment	9,000	
Cash		90,000

If stock is issued for a plant asset, we debit the asset for either its own fair market value, or the fair market value of the stock, whichever is more clear. If both are clear, we use the FMV of the asset.

EXAMPLE 10

Company J issues 100 shares of its $100-par common stock for equipment. The FMV of the equipment is $12,000; the FMV of the stock, which is not traded on a national exchange, is unclear. The entry is:

Equipment	12,000	
Common Stock		10,000 (par)
Paid-in Capital in Excess of Par		2,000

EXAMPLE 11

Assume the same information as in Example 10, except that the FMV of the equipment is unclear, while the FMV of the stock is $14,000. The entry is:

Equipment	14,000	
Common Stock		10,000 (par)
Paid-in Capital in Excess of Par		4,000

10.6 DEFERRED PAYMENT CONTRACTS

Plant assets are often purchased under *deferred payment contracts*. This means that, rather than paying the total price at the time of purchase, the purchaser issues a note payable for the amount due and pays it in several installments. If the note bears a reasonable interest rate, no special accounting problems arise, as shown in the following example.

EXAMPLE 12

Company K purchases a machine for $30,000 on January 1, 19X1, and agrees to pay the entire amount in five installments of $6,000 each beginning December 31, 19X1, plus annual interest of 10% on the balance. The entries for the first 2 years are:

Jan. 1, 19X1	Machine	30,000	
	Notes Payable		30,000
Dec. 31, 19X1	Notes Payable	6,000	
	Cash		6,000
	Interest Expense	3,000*	
	Cash		3,000*
	*($30,000 × 10%)		
Dec. 31, 19X2	Notes Payable	6,000	
	Cash		6,000
	Interest Expense	2,400*	
	Cash		2,400*
	*[($30,000 − $6,000) × 10%]		

The entries for 19X3, 19X4, and 19X5 will be similar; only the interest amounts will change.

A special problem arises if the note is non-interest-bearing. Does this mean that the seller is being a "nice guy" and not charging the buyer any interest? The accounting profession says no; there really is interest, but it is "hidden" in the purchase price.

How do we determine how much the "hidden" interest is and what the real purchase price is? If the fair market value of the asset is known, then *that* is the real purchase price and the excess of the face value of the note over and above the FMV is the hidden interest. If the FMV is not known, however, then we must find the present value of the note, and the excess of the note's face value over and above its present value is the hidden interest.

The interest rate to be used in the computation is called the *imputed rate*—it is the rate the purchaser would normally have to pay in the market for a similar transaction.

EXAMPLE 13

Company L purchases a machine on January 1, 19X1, for a $10,000, five-year, non-interest-bearing note. The note is to be paid in five annual installments of $2,000 beginning December 31, 19X1. Assume that the fair market value of the machine is unknown and the imputed rate is 10%. According to the tables in the Appendix to this book, the present value of an annuity of $1 for 5 periods at 10% is 3.791. Thus the machine is debited for $7,582, and the entry on January 1, 19X1, is:

Machine	7,582		(2,000 × 3.791)
Discount on Note Payable	2,418		
Note Payable		10,000	

The discount account is a contra to the Notes Payable account, because at this point no interest has been incurred and thus the amount owed is only $7,582 ($10,000–$2,418). With time, however, interest will start to accumulate and the amount owed will increase. The interest for 19X1 is $758 (10% × $7,582, rounded) and the entries on December 31, 19X1, are:

Interest Expense	758	
Discount on Note Payable		758

By reducing the contra account, we automatically increase the amount due. This entry is referred to as the discount *amortization*.

Notes Payable	2,000	
Cash		2,000

The entries for 19X1 are:

Interest Expense	634*	
Discount on Notes Payable		634*
*($7,582 − $2,000 + $758)		
Notes Payable	2,000	
Cash		2,000

Similar entries are made for 19X3, 19X4, and 19X5—only the amount of the amortization changes.

The amortization method we have been using is called the *effective interest method* of amortization. Alternatively, the straight-line method may be used, in which case the discount is simply divided by the life of the note to arrive at the annual amortization. Under this approach, each year's amortization would be $484 ($2,418 ÷ 5).

The accounting profession has ruled that the straight-line method should *not* be used unless its results are not significantly different from those obtained under the effective interest method.

10.7   DONATIONS

Companies sometimes receive donations of land or buildings from states and cities as an incentive to set up operations in their locales. These are referred to as *nonreciprocal transfers* and are debited at their fair market value plus any incidental costs incurred. At one time the credit went to the account Donated Capital; recently, however, the FASB has ruled that it should go to a revenue account instead.

EXAMPLE 14

Company M receives land as a donation from Sunshine City with a FMV of $50,000, and incurs costs of $2,000 to take title. The entry is:

Land	52,000	
Cash		2,000
Donation Revenue		50,000

If a company donates assets to others, it first recognizes a gain or loss equal to the difference between the assets' book value and FMV (if the FMV is greater, it's a gain; otherwise, it's a loss). It will then recognize an expense (donation expense) for the FMV.

EXAMPLE 15

Company N decides to donate a piece of land to the Red Cross. The book value of the land is $30,000; the FMV is $40,000. It thus recognizes a $10,000 gain, and the entries are:

Land	10,000	
Gain on Revaluation		10,000
Donation Expense	40,000	
Land		40,000

Alternatively, these two entries can be combined into one entry, as follows:

Donation Expense	40,000	
Land		30,000
Gain on Revaluation		10,000

10.8   EXCHANGES OF PLANT ASSETS

Companies sometimes trade or exchange one asset for another. For example, a company may trade in an old car for a new one and pay cash for the difference in value.

When an exchange takes place, there will often be a gain or loss equal to the difference between the FMV and book value of the asset given. If the FMV is greater, we have a gain; if the book value is greater we have a loss.

EXAMPLE 16

Company O trades in an old car with cost, accumulated depreciation, and FMV of $10,000, $3,000, and $6,000, respectively. Since the book value is $7,000 ($10,000 − $3,000) and the FMV is $6,000, there is a loss of $1,000.

If the FMV had been more than $7,000, there would be a gain.

Now that we've defined gains and losses, the question is: Should we recognize them? The answer is that losses are *always* recognized; gains are *sometimes* recognized, depending on whether the assets exchanged are similar (e.g., a car for a car) or dissimilar (e.g., a car for a computer). We shall discuss dissimilar assets first. For dissimilar assets, both losses *and* gains are recognized. The asset acquired (the "new asset") is debited at the FMV of the asset given up (the "old asset"), plus any cash given, minus any cash received. Cash given or received is referred to as *boot*.

EXAMPLE 17

Company P exchanges an old asset with cost and accumulated depreciation of $5,000 and $2,000, respectively, for a new, *dissimilar* asset, and *pays* $1,000 boot. Assume that the FMV of the old asset is $2,500.

In this case, Company P has a loss of $500 because the FMV of $2,500 is less than the book value of $3,000 ($5,000 − $2,000). Company P debits the new asset at the FMV of the old one, plus the boot given ($2,500 + $1,000), and the entry is:

New Asset	3,500	
Accumulated Depreciation	2,000	
Loss on Exchange	500	
Old Asset		5,000
Cash		1,000

EXAMPLE 18

Assume the same information as in Example 17, except that Company P *receives* the boot of $1,000. In this case, Company P debits the new asset at $1,500 ($2,500 − $1,000), and the entry is:

New Asset	1,500	
Accumulated Depreciation	2,000	
Loss on Exchange	500	
Cash	1,000	
Old Asset		5,000

The $1,500 debit to the new asset is the FMV of the old asset *minus* the boot received.

EXAMPLE 19

Assume the same information as above, except that P *pays* the $1,000 boot, and the FMV of the old asset is $3,700 rather than $2,500. In this case, Company P has a gain of $700 because the FMV is $700 more than the $3,000 book value. The new asset is debited at $4,700 ($3,700 + $1,000), a gain is recognized, and the entry is:

New Asset	4,700	
Accumulated Depreciation	2,000	
Old Asset		5,000
Cash		1,000
Gain on Exchange		700

In some cases, the FMV of the *old* asset may not be clearly given, but it can be logically determined from the FMV of the *new* asset, as the next example demonstrates.

EXAMPLE 20

Company Q trades an old asset for a new one and pays $2,000 in cash. The FMV of the new asset is $5,000; the FMV of the old asset is not given. Since the FMV of the new asset is $5,000 and Q is given an old asset plus cash ($2,000), the old asset must be worth $3,000.

The FMV of an asset is not the same as its list price. List price is often a "puffed-up" number intended to trap the unwary. The true FMV is usually significantly lower than the list price, and that value, rather than the list price, should be used for accounting purposes.

EXAMPLE 21

Company R trades an old asset plus $5,000 cash for a new one with a list price of $12,000 and an FMV of $11,000. The FMV of the old asset is $6,000 ($11,000 − $5,000), not $7,000 ($12,000 − $5,000).

To summarize, for dissimilar assets, *both* gains and losses are recognized, and the new asset is debited for the FMV of the old one, plus any boot given, minus any boot received.

We shall now discuss similar assets. For loss purposes, similar assets are treated the same way as dissimilar ones. The loss is recognized and the new asset is debited at the FMV of the old one, plus any boot given, minus any boot received.

EXAMPLE 22

Company S trades an old asset with cost and accumulated depreciation of $8,000 and $3,000, respectively, for a similar asset, and also pays $2,000 in cash. If the FMV of the old asset is $4,000, Company S has incurred a $1,000 loss (book value of 5,000 versus FMV of $4,000), and the new asset is debited at $6,000 ($4,000 + $2,000).

EXAMPLE 23

Assume the same information as in Example 22, except that Company S *receives* $2,000 cash. The loss is still $1,000; the new asset is debited for $2,000 ($4,000 − $2,000), and the entry is:

New Asset	2,000	
Accumulated Depreciation	3,000	
Loss on Exchange	1,000	
Cash	2,000	
Old Asset		8,000

For gain purposes (where the FMV of the old asset is greater than its book value), no gains are recognized for similar assets when cash is *paid*. In such cases, the new asset is debited at the *book value* of the old one, plus the cash given. However, when cash is *received*, a portion of the gain *is recognized* according to the following formula:

$$\text{Recognized gain} = \frac{\text{cash}}{\text{cash} + \text{FMV of new asset}} \times \text{gain}$$

In such cases, the new asset is debited at the *book value* of the old one, plus the recognized gain, minus the cash received.

EXAMPLE 24

Company T exchanges an asset with cost of $10,000 accumulated depreciation of $4,000 (book value of $6,000) and FMV of $8,000, for another, similar asset, and *pays* $3,000 in cash. The gain of $2,000 ($8,000 − $6,000) is *not* recognized; the new asset is debited at the *book value* of the old one ($6,000), plus the cash given ($3,000).

The journal entry is:

New Asset	9,000	
Accumulated Depreciation	4,000	
Cash		3,000
Old Asset		10,000

EXAMPLE 25

Assume the same information as in Example 24, except that Company T *receives* the $3,000 cash. Also assume that the FMV of the new asset is $5,000. In this case, a gain is recognized, as follows:

$$\frac{\$3,000}{\$3,000 + \$5,000} \times \$2,000 = \$750$$

The new asset is debited at $3,750 ($6,000 + $750 − $3,000), and the entry is:

New Asset	3,750	
Accumulated Depreciation	4,000	
Cash	3,000	
Old Asset		10,000
Gain on Exchange		750

The following is a summary of the rules relating to the exchanges of similar assets.

1. A gain or loss on an exchange is defined as the difference between the old asset's book value and its fair market value. If the FMV is greater, there is a gain; if the book value is greater, there is a loss.

2. Whether or not gains and losses are recognized depends on the nature of the assets exchanged— similar or dissimilar.

3. For *dissimilar* assets, both gains and losses are recognized. The new asset is debited at the FMV of the old one, plus any cash (boot) given, minus any cash received.

4. For *similar* assets, losses are always recognized and the same rule applies: The new asset is debited at the FMV of the old one, plus any cash given, minus any cash received.

5. For *similar* assets in a gain situation, the gain is not recognized if no cash is received. The new asset is debited at the *book value* of the old one, plus any cash given. If cash *is* received, however, a portion of the gain is recognized, according to the following formula:

$$\text{Recognized gain} = \frac{\text{cash}}{\text{cash} + \text{FMV of new asset}} \times \text{gain}$$

In this case, the new asset is debited at the book value of the old asset, plus the gain recognized, minus the cash received. It should be noted that the above rule regarding losses on similar assets applies *only* to accounting for financial statement purposes. For tax purposes, losses are *not* recognized.

10.9 COSTS INCURRED SUBSEQUENT TO ACQUISITION

We stated earlier that all costs incurred to acquire a plant asset and prepare it for use are capitalized. But what about additional costs incurred later, such as repairs, maintenance costs, and part replacements? Are these also capitalized? Or are they expensed? The answer depends on the nature of the expenditure.

If the expenditure lengthens the life of the asset, increases the production capacity of the asset, or improves the quality of the asset, it should be capitalized because it provides future economic benefits. Examples of such expenditures are adding a major part to a machine to increase efficiency; adding a room to a building; adding air conditioning or replacing an old car engine with a new one. These are referred to as *capital expenditures*.

If, however, the expenditure does none of the above, but merely maintains the asset in its present condition, it should be debited to an expense account (Repair and Maintenance Expense). This type of cost is referred to as a *revenue expenditure*. Examples include replacement of small parts, repainting, lubrications and oil changes (oil changes do not lengthen a car's life; they merely prevent the car from "dying early").

For items that require capitalization, there is a slight difference in accounting treatment depending on the nature of the expenditure. If the expenditure improves the production capacity of the asset, or improves its quality, the cost should be debited to the asset itself; if it lengthens the asset's life, it should be debited to Accumulated Depreciation. The reason for this is that lengthening of life is the opposite of depreciation. Since depreciation is recorded via a *credit* to Accumulated Depreciation, the lengthening of life should be recorded via a *debit*. The lengthening of the life can be viewed as a rejuvenation of the previous decline and depreciation.

EXAMPLE 26

Company U incurs the following costs relating to its plant assets:

(*a*) It purchases a new machine part for $3,000 that will enable the machine to produce in significantly less time.

(*b*) It adds a cassette tape recorder to the company truck at a cost of $200.

(*c*) It completely overhauls the truck's engine, which will lengthen the truck's life by 3 years. The cost is $1,500.

(*d*) It oils all the company machinery at a cost of $400.

The entries are:

(*a*)	Machine	3,000	
	Cash		3,000
(*b*)	Truck	200	
	Cash		200
(*c*)	Accumulated Depreciation	1,500	
	Cash		1,500
(*d*)	Repair and Maintenance Expense	400	
	Cash		400

10.10 SALES OF PLANT ASSETS

When a plant asset is sold, it should be depreciated to the date of sale, and a gain or loss, if any, should be recognized. If the selling price is greater than the asset's book value, there is a gain; if it is less, there is a loss. Neither the gain nor the loss is considered extraordinary.

EXAMPLE 27

Company V purchased a machine for $10,000 with a 10-year life and no salvage value. After $3\frac{1}{2}$ years, it sells the machine for $6,500. The T-accounts appear as follows:

Machine	Accumulated Depreciation
10,000	1,000
	1,000
	1,000
	500
	3,500

Since the book value is $6,500 ($10,000 − $3,500) and the selling price is the same, there is neither gain nor loss. The entry is:

Cash	6,500	
Accumulated Depreciation	3,500	
Machine		10,000

This entry removes the machine and accumulated depreciation accounts since they are no longer needed, and recognizes the receipt of the cash.

EXAMPLE 28

Assume the same information as in Example 27, except that the selling price is $7,500. We thus have a gain of $1,000 ($7,500 − $6,500). The entry is:

Cash	7,500	
Accumulated Depreciation	3,500	
Machine		10,000
Gain on Sale		1,000

If the machine had been sold for $5,500, there would be a $1,000 loss, and the entry would be:

Cash	5,500	
Accumulated Depreciation	3,500	
Loss on Sale	1,000	
Machine		10,000

EXAMPLE 29

Assume the same information as in the previous examples, except that no buyer can be found and the machine is simply abandoned. In this case, there is a loss equal to the entire book value of $6,500, and the entry is:

Loss on Abandonment	6,500	
Accumulated Depreciation	3,500	
Machine		10,000

If the disposal of a machine is part of the disposal of a business segment, the loss or gain is included as part of the overall loss or gain attributable to the segment, and is presented on the income statement as such. Disposal of a business segment was discussed in Chapter 2.

10.11   INVOLUNTARY CONVERSIONS

Assets destroyed or terminated through fire, theft, or government appropriation are referred to as *involuntary conversions*. A gain or loss is recognized equal to the proceeds received upon the conversion minus the book value. Such gain or loss *is* considered extraordinary, and must be reported as such.

EXAMPLE 30

Company W has a machine with cost and accumulated depreciation of $20,000 and $12,000, respectively. The machine is totally destroyed in a fire, and $7,000 is received from the insurance company. There is thus a loss of $1,000 ($8,000 book value − $7,000 proceeds), which results in the following entry:

Cash	7,000	
Accumulated Depreciation	12,000	
Loss on Fire (extraordinary)	1,000	
Machine		20,000

Summary

1. *Property, plant, and equipment*, also known as *fixed assets* or *plant assets*, includes land, buildings, equipment, machinery, and furniture. These assets are not held for resale, but for use in the operations of the business.

2. These assets are recorded at their purchase price plus any other costs incurred to acquire them and make them ready for use. Examples of such costs are delivery charges, installation charges, testing costs, and sales taxes. These items are *not* expensed.

3. Plant assets may *not* be written up to reflect increases in their market values. To do so would violate the cost principle.

4. The cost of land includes the purchase price, closing costs, draining costs, clearing costs, and filling costs. If the buyer agrees to assume an existing mortgage on the land, or to pay back taxes due, these would also increase the land cost.

5. If improvements with an unlimited life are made to the land, they are debited to the land account and *not* depreciated—just like the land itself. If the improvements have a limited life, however, they are debited to Land Improvements and depreciated over their useful lives.

6. If land is purchased with the intention of constructing a building on the land, all costs incurred from the time of purchase up to the excavation of the building are considered to be costs of the *land* and thus not subject to depreciation. Costs incurred from excavation through completion of construction are costs of the *building* and are subject to depreciation.

7. If land is purchased with the intention of putting up a new building, the cost of razing an old building (to make way for the new one) is a cost of the *land*. Any money received from the salvage of the old building reduces the demolition cost, and thus, the land cost.

8. Interest incurred on money borrowed to finance the purchase of plant assets is not considered a cost of the asset, but is debited, instead, to interest expense.

9. The cost of a building includes the purchase price, closing costs, and all other costs necessary to make the building ready for use. All these costs are capitalized in the Building account; none are expensed.

10. If a company constructs its own building, all costs from excavation to completion should be debited to Building. This includes direct materials, direct labor, and both variable and fixed overhead. However, the total debit to Building should not exceed what the building would have cost had it been constructed by an outsider. Any excess is debited to an expense account.

11. Interest incurred to finance a loan for the *construction* of a building may be capitalized instead of expensed. This is discussed in Appendix 10A at the end of this chapter.

12. If land, buildings, and equipment are purchased together as part of a package, the cost assigned to each should be based on the ratio of their respective fair market values.

13. If stock is issued for a plant asset, the asset should be debited at its own fair market value or the FMV of the stock, whichever is more clear.

14. If a note is issued for a plant asset, and the note is either non-interest-bearing or bears a low interest rate relative to the market, the asset should *not* be debited at the note's face value. Rather, the asset should be debited at its FMV, with the remainder considered "hidden interest."

15. If the FMV of the asset is unclear, the debit should be for the present value of the principal plus the present value of the interest payments, if any. The rate to be used, known as the *imputed rate*, is the rate the buyer would have to pay in the market for a similar purchase.

16. In the above situation, the "hidden interest" is placed into an account called Discount on Note and gradually amortized to interest expense. The preferred method of amortization is the effective interest method; the straight-line method may be used if the results achieved are not significantly different.

17. Donations received should be debited at their FMV plus any incidental costs incurred. The credit goes to a revenue account.

18. If a company donates assets to others, it first recognizes a gain or loss equal to the difference between the assets' book value and FMV. It then makes a second entry to recognize an expense (donation expense) for the assets' FMV.

19. When one asset is exchanged for another, there is often a gain or loss equal to the difference between the book value and the FMV of the asset given. If the FMV is greater, there is a gain; if it is less, there is a loss. Two questions arise: Should the gain or loss be *recognized*? What value should be assigned to the asset received? The answers are summarized in the following rules:

    (a) A gain or loss on an exchange is defined as the difference between the old asset's book value and its FMV. If the FMV is greater, there is a gain; if the book value is greater, there is a loss.

    (b) Whether or not gains and losses are recognized depends on the nature of the assets exchanged—similar or dissimilar.

    (c) For *dissimilar* assets, both gains and losses are recognized. The new asset is debited at the FMV of the old one, plus any cash (boot) given, minus any cash received.

    (d) For *similar* assets, losses are always recognized and the same rule applies: The new asset is debited at the FMV of the old one, plus any cash given, minus any cash received.

    (e) For *similar* assets in a gain situation, the gain is not recognized if no cash is received. The new asset is debited at the *book value* of the old one, plus any cash given. If cash *is* received, however, a portion of the gain is recognized, according to the following formula:

$$\text{Recognized gain} = \frac{\text{cash}}{\text{cash} + \text{FMV of new asset}} \times \text{gain}$$

In this case, the new asset is debited at the book value of the old asset, plus the gain recognized, minus the cash received. It should be noted that the above rule regarding losses on similar assets applies *only* to accounting for financial statement purposes. For tax purposes, losses are *not* recognized.

20. For costs incurred subsequent to the acquisition of a plant asset, the accounting treatment depends on the nature of the expenditure. If the expenditure lengthens the life of the asset, increases its production capacity, or improves its quality, then the expenditure should be capitalized. If it does none of the above but merely maintains the asset in its present condition, it should be expensed. The latter type of expenditure is referred to as a *revenue expenditure*; the former, as a *capital expenditure*.

21. When a plant asset is sold, it should be depreciated up to the point of sale and a gain or loss, if any, should be recognized. If the selling price is greater than the book value, there is a gain; if it is less, there is a loss. Neither the gain nor the loss is considered extraordinary.

22. Assets destroyed or terminated through fire, theft, or government appropriation are referred to as *involuntary conversions*. Any gains or losses on such conversions are considered extraordinary.

Rapid Review

1. Other names for plant assets are _____ and _____.

2. Land differs from other plant assets in that it does not _____.

3. If land is purchased with the intention of constructing a building, the cost of razing an old building on the land is a cost of the _____.

4. Costs debited to building include all costs from excavation to _____.

5. For package purchases, the cost should be allocated to each item in the package based on relative _____.

6. Assets acquired for either non-interest-bearing notes or low-interest-bearing notes should be debited at either _____ or _____.

7. In the above situation, the interest rate used is referred to as the _____ rate.

8. Donations received should be debited at their _____, and the credit should go to a _____ account.

9. For exchanges of assets, if the FMV of the asset given is greater than its book value, there is a _____.

10. For similar assets, _____ are always recognized, but _____ are recognized in only some situations.

11. For similar and dissimilar exchanges in loss situations, the new asset is debited at the _____ of the old asset given, plus any _____, minus any _____.

12. Costs incurred subsequent to acquisition that improve the asset's life are _____; costs that merely maintain the asset are _____.

13. The destruction or theft of assets is referred to as an _____. The loss or gain involved is considered _____.

Answers: **1.** property, plant, and equipment; fixed assets **2.** depreciate **3.** land **4.** completion **5.** fair market values **6.** fair market value; present value of note **7.** imputed **8.** fair market value; revenue **9.** gain **10.** losses; gains **11.** fair market value; cash given; cash received **12.** capitalized; expensed **13.** involuntary conversion; extraordinary

Solved Problems

General

10.1   Company A purchases a machine for $5,000 and incurs the following additional costs:

Installation Charges	$200
Delivery Charges	50
Interest on Loan	250
Testing	35
Sales Tax	400

Prepare an entry to record the purchase.

SOLUTION

Machine	5,685	
Cash		5,685

The interest is not capitalized.   [Section 10.1]

10.2   A desk purchased 10 years ago by Company B for $1,200 has now become a collector's item that can be sold for $5,000. Prepare an entry, if required, to recognize the increase in value.

SOLUTION

An entry is neither required nor permitted under GAAP. Gains may be recognized only upon sale or exchange.   [Section 10.1]

Land

10.3   Company C purchases land for $70,000 and incurs the following additional costs at the time of purchase:

Draining Costs	$5,000
Clearing Costs	3,000
Attorney's Fees	1,000
Assumption of Seller's Mortgage	7,000
Title Fees	1,200
Recording Fees	700
Construction of Fence	800
Payment of Seller's Back Taxes	500

Prepare the necessary entries.

SOLUTION

Land	88,400	
Cash		88,400

Land Improvements	800		
Cash		800	[Section 10.2]

10.4 Company D purchases land for $50,000 and spends $1,000 and $4,000 on building a fence and a parking lot, respectively. These improvements each have a 5-year life.

(*a*) Prepare an entry for all the costs incurred.

(*b*) Prepare the annual depreciation entry, if required.

SOLUTION

(*a*)

Land	50,000	
Cash		50,000

Land Improvements	5,000	
Cash		5,000

(*b*)

Depreciation Expense	1,000		
Accumulated Depreciation		1,000	[Section 10.2]

Buildings

10.5 Company E constructs its own building and incurs the following costs:

Direct Material	$50,000
Direct Labor	80,000
Variable Factory Overhead	20,000
Fixed Factory Overhead	10,000

(*a*) Determine the cost of this building.

(*b*) If an outside construction company had constructed this building, the price would have been $145,000. Would your answer to part (*a*) now change? If yes, what would your new answer be?

SOLUTION

(*a*) $160,000

(*b*) Yes, only $145,000   [Section 10.3]

Lump-Sum Purchases; Issuance of Stock for Plant Assets

10.6 A package of land, building, and equipment is bought at a lump-sum price of $110,000. By appraisal, the FMV of these items is determined to be $50,000, $30,000, and $20,000, respectively. Allocate the $110,000 cost to each item and prepare a journal entry.

SOLUTION

	FMV	Fraction	Total Cost	Allocation
Land	$ 50,000	50/100 ×	$110,000	$55,000
Building	30,000	30/100 ×	110,000	33,000
Equipment	20,000	20/100 ×	110,000	22,000
	$100,000			

The journal entry is:

Land	55,000	
Building	33,000	
Equipment	22,000	
Cash		110,000

[Section 10.5]

10.7 Company F issues 50 shares of its $50-par common stock for equipment. Prepare the journal entry for the following two cases.

(a) The FMV of the equipment is $2,800; the FMV of the stock is unclear.

(b) The FMV of the equipment is unclear; the FMV of the stock is $2,700.

SOLUTION

(a)

Equipment	2,800	
Common Stock		2,500 (par)
Paid in Capital, etc.		300

(b)

Equipment	2,700	
Common Stock		2,500 (par)
Paid-in-Capital, etc.		200

[Section 10.5]

Deferred Payment Contracts

10.8 Company G purchases a machine for $50,000 on January 1, 19X1, and agrees to pay via five equal annual installments of $10,000 beginning December 31, 19X1, plus annual interest at 10%. This rate is in line with the market rate for this type of transaction. Prepare the journal entries for 19X1 and 19X2.

SOLUTION

Jan. 1, 19X1	Machine	50,000	
	Notes Payable		50,000
Dec. 31, 19X1	Notes Payable	10,000	
	Cash		10,000
	Interest Expense	5,000*	
	Cash		5,000*
	*($50,000 × 10%)		

| Dec. 31, 19X2 | Notes Payable | 10,000 | |
| | Cash | | 10,000 |

| | Interest Expense | 4,000* | |
| | Cash | | 4,000* |

*[($50,000 − $10,000 paid in 19X1) × 10%]   [Section 10.6]

10.9 On January 1, 19X1, Company H purchases a machine for a $15,000, three-year, non-interest-bearing note. The note is to be paid in three equal annual installments of $5,000 each, beginning on December 31, 19X1. Assume that the fair market value of the machine is only $12,000.

(a) Prepare the journal entry for the purchase of the machine.

(b) Prepare the amortization entry for each year. Use the straight-line method.

(c) Prepare the annual entry for each installment.

SOLUTION

(a)

Machine	12,000	
Discount on Notes Payable	3,000	
Notes Payable		15,000

(b) The amortization entry would be the same for all three years:

| Dec. 31 | Interest Expense | 1,000* | |
| | Discount on Notes Payable | | 1,000* |

*($3,000 ÷ 3)

(c) The entry for each installment payment is:

| Notes Payable | 5,000 | | |
| Cash | | 5,000 | [Section 10.6] |

10.10 Assume the same information as in Problem 10.9, except that the FMV of the machine is unknown, and the imputed rate is 10%.

(a) Prepare the entry for the purchase.

(b) Determine the annual amortization amount (use the effective interest method of amortization).

SOLUTION

(a)

Machine	11,265*	
Discount on Notes Payable	3,735	
Notes Payable		15,000

---

*Present value of $15,000, 3 periods,
10% is 0.751 × $15,000 = $11,265.

(b) The annual amortization is:

$$19X1: \quad \$11,265 \times 0.10 = \$1,126.50$$

$$19X2: \quad (\$11,265 + \$1,126.50) \times 0.10 = \$1,239.15$$

$$19X3: \quad (\$11,265 + \$1,126.50 + \$1,239.15) \times 0.10 = \$1,363.07$$

Note: The total amortization for the three years combined should equal $3,735; however, due to rounding, the total is only $3,728.72. [Section 10.6]

Donations

10.11 Company I receives land as a donation from Sweet City with a FMV of $107,000. In order to take title to the land, Company I pays $4,000 in various state and local fees. Prepare the necessary entry.

SOLUTION

Land	111,000	
Donation Revenue		107,000
Cash		4,000

[Section 10.7]

10.12 Company J donates a building to the Sunshine Fund. The building has a book value and a FMV of $20,000 and $25,000, respectively. Prepare the required entries.

SOLUTION

Building	5,000	
Gain on Revaluation		5,000
Donation Expense	25,000	
Building		25,000

[Section 10.7]

10.13 For the situation in Problem 10.12, what would the entries be if the FMV was $18,000 instead of $25,000?

SOLUTION

Loss on Revaluation	2,000	
Building		2,000
Donation Expense	18,000	
Building		18,000

[Section 10.7]

Exchanges of Plant Assets

10.14 Company K exchanges land with book value and FMV of $1,000 and $1,200, respectively, for a dissimilar asset. It also pays $3,000 cash.

(a) Is there a gain or loss recognized on this transaction for Company K? If yes, how much?

(b) At what amount should Company K record the new asset?

(c) Prepare a journal entry for the exchange.

SOLUTION

(a) There is a gain of $200 ($1,200 − $1,000).

(b) $4,200 (FMV of $1,200 + $3,000 cash)

(c)

New Asset	4,200	
Land		1,000
Cash		3,000
Gain on Exchange		200

Note: This entry contains no debit to accumulated depreciation, since land does *not* depreciate.

[Section 10.8]

10.15 How would your answers to Problem 10.14 change if the assets were similar?

SOLUTION

(a) The gain would *not* be recognized.

(b) $4,000 (book value of $1,000 + $3,000 cash)

(c)

New Asset	4,000		
Land		1,000	
Cash		3,000	[Section 10.8]

10.16 Company L trades in an old asset with cost and accumulated depreciation of $30,000 and $18,000, respectively, for a new asset and pays $5,000 in cash. Assume that the assets are dissimilar.

(a) Prepare an entry for the exchange. Assume that the FMV of the old asset is $10,000.

(b) Prepare an entry if the FMV is $15,000.

SOLUTION

(a) Since the book value is $12,000 and the FMV is $10,000, there is a loss of 2,000.

New Asset	15,000*	
Accumulated Depreciation	18,000	
Loss on Exchange	2,000	
Old Asset		30,000
Cash		5,000
*($10,000 + $5,000)		

(b) In this case there is a gain of $3,000 ($15,000 − $12,000)

New Asset	20,000*	
Accumulated Depreciation	18,000	
Old Asset		30,000
Gain on Exchange		3,000
Cash		5,000
*($15,000 + $5,000)		[Section 10.8]

10.17 Assume the same information as in Problem 10.16, except that the assets are similar. Prepare the necessary journal entry for each case.

SOLUTION

(a) The entry would be exactly the same as in Problem 10.16.

(b) Since the assets are *similar*, the gain is *not* recognized. The entry would be:

New Asset	17,000*	
Accumulated Depreciation	18,000	
Old Asset		30,000
Cash		5,000
*(Book value plus cash)		[Section 10.8]

10.18 Company M trades an old machine (cost, $27,000; accumulated depreciation, $7,000) for a new one, and *receives* $5,000 in cash. Assume that the machines are *dissimilar* and the FMV of the old machine is $24,000. Prepare the journal entry.

SOLUTION

There is a gain of $4,000 (book value of $20,000 versus FMV of $24,000). The entry is:

New Machine	19,000*	
Accumulated Depreciated	7,000	
Cash	5,000	
Old Machine		27,000
Gain on Exchange		4,000
*(FMV − cash received)		[Section 10.8]

10.19 Assume the same information as in Problem 10.18, except that the assets are *similar*, and the FMV of the new asset is $19,000.

(a) Would the gain be recognized? If yes, how much?

(b) Prepare the journal entry.

SOLUTION

(a) The gain is partially recognized, as follows:

$$\text{Gain recognized} = \frac{\text{cash}}{\text{cash} + \text{FMV of new asset}} \times \text{gain realized}$$

$$= 5{,}000 + \frac{\$5{,}000}{\$19{,}000} \times \$4000 = \$80 \qquad \text{(rounded)}$$

(b)

New Machine	15,840*	
Accumulated Depreciation	7,000	
Cash	5,000	
Old Machine		27,000
Gain on Exchange		840
*(Book value of old machine − cash received		
plus gain recognized)		[Section 10.8]

10.20 Company N trades in an old machine (FMV, $22,000; cost, $18,000; accumulated depreciation, $5,000) for a new machine with a FMV of $17,000 plus $5,000 cash.

(a) What is the book value of the old machine?

(b) How much gain was *realized* on the exchange?

(c) If the assets are dissimilar, how much gain is *recognized*?

(d) If the assets are similar, how much gain is *recognized*?

SOLUTION

(a) $13,000 ($18,000 − $5,000)

(b) $9,000 ($22,000 − $13,000)

(c) $9,000

(d) $2,070

$$\frac{\$5,000}{\$5,000 + \$17,000} \times \$9,000 = \$2,070 \quad \text{(rounded)} \qquad \text{[Section 10.8]}$$

10.21 For Problem 10.20, prepare the journal entry if the assets are similar.

SOLUTION

New Machine	10,070*	
Accumulated Depreciation	5,000	
Cash	5,000	
Old Machine		18,000
Gain on Exchange		2,070

*($13,000 − $5,000 + $2,070)   [Section 10.8]

10.22 Company O trades in an old asset with a book value of $10,000 for a new one with a FMV of $14,000. It also pays $5,000 in cash. Assume that the assets are dissimilar.

(a) What is the FMV of the old asset?

(b) How much gain or loss should be recognized on this exchange?

(c) If the assets are similar, how much gain or loss should be recognized?

SOLUTION

(a) The FMV is $9,000 ($14,000 − $5,000).

(b) There is a $1,000 loss ($10,000 − $9,000).

(c) Once again, there is a $1,000 loss.   [Section 10.8]

10.23 Company P trades in an old asset (cost, $35,000; accumulated depreciation, $17,000) for a new one worth $12,000. It also receives $5,000 in cash. Assume that the assets are dissimilar.

(a) What is the FMV of the old asset?

(b) How much gain or loss is recognized?

SOLUTION

(a) $17,000 ($12,000 + 5,000)

(b) Loss of $1,000 ($18,000 − $17,000)   [Section 10.8]

10.24 Company Q trades an old asset with book value of $7,000 for a new one and also pays $5,000 in cash. The FMV of the old asset is $9,000; the *list price* of the new one is $16,000.

(a) What is the FMV of the new asset? Why?

(b) How much gain or loss should Company Q recognize on this exchange? Assume that the assets are similar.

SOLUTION

(a) $14,000 ($9,000 + $5,000). The list price is ignored.

(b) The gain of $2,000 ($9,000 − $7,000) is *not* recognized.   [Section 10.8]

Costs Incurred Subsequent to Acquisition

10.25 Company R incurs the following expenditures for its delivery truck:

1. Installation of brand new engine, $4,000. This will lengthen the truck's life by 3 years.

2. Replacement of old air conditioner with a brand new one, $1,500. (The old one did not work on Mondays and Thursdays and would automatically shut off on Sundays when the temperature reached 71°F.)

3. Oil change and lubrication, $60.

   (a) Should these items be capitalized or expensed?

   (b) Prepare a journal entry for each.

SOLUTION

(a) Items 1 and 2 should be capitalized; item 3 should be expensed.

(b) For item 1:

Accumulated Depreciation	4,000	
Cash		4,000

For item 2:

Truck	1,500	
Cash		1,500

For item 3:

Repair and Maintenance Expense	60	
Cash		60

[Section 10.9]

Sales of Plant Assets

10.26 Company S purchases a machine for $10,000 on January 1, 19X1. The machine is expected to have a 10-year life and no salvage value. Prepare the journal entry for each of the following independent cases involving the machine's disposal on January 1, 19X5.

(a) The machine is sold for $6,000.

(b) The machine is sold for $5,200.

(c) The machine is sold for $6,400.

(d) The machine is abandoned.

SOLUTION

The T-accounts appear as follows:

Machine	Accumulated Depreciation
10,000	1,000
	1,000
	1,000
	1,000

(a)   Cash   6,000
                             Accumulated Depreciation   4,000
                                    Machine   10,000

(b)   Cash   5,200
                             Accumulated Depreciation   4,000
                             Loss on Sale   800
                                    Machine   10,000

(c)   Cash   6,400
                             Accumulated Depreciation   4,000
                                    Machine   10,000
                                    Gain on Sale   400

(d)   Accumulated Depreciation   4,000
                             Loss on Disposal   6,000
                                    Machine   10,000   [Section 10.10]

10.27 Company T purchased a machine on January 1, 19X1, for $10,000. The machine has a 9-year life
with a $1,000 salvage value. On July 1, 19X4, the machine is disposed of.
    Prepare an entry if the disposal price is $6,700.

SOLUTION

                             Cash   6,700
                             Accumulated Depreciation   3,500
                                    Machine   10,000
                                    Gain on Disposal   200   [Section 10.10]

Involuntary Conversions

10.28 Company U has land with a book value of $20,000. The federal government, exercising its right
of eminent domain, purchases the land from Company U for its FMV of $25,000. Prepare the
journal entry.

SOLUTION

         Cash   25,000
                 Land   20,000
                 Gain on Involuntary Conversion (extraordinary)   5,000
                                                                              [Section 10.11]

Supplementary Problems

General

10.29 Company V purchases a machine for $4,000. It incurs installation costs of $100, delivery charges of $80,
testing costs of $75, and interest on a loan of $200. Prepare the necessary entries for these costs.

Land

10.30 Company W purchases land for $95,000 and incurs the following costs: draining, $1,000; attorney's fees, $500; title search, $1,400; and fence construction, $800. Prepare the necessary entries.

Buildings

10.31 Company X constructs its own building and incurs the following costs: bricks, $40,000; construction labor, $70,000; heat and power, $20,000; fixed overhead, $4,000.

(a) Determine the cost of this building.

(b) Would your answer to part (a) change if an outside construction company charged $127,000? Why?

Lump-Sum Purchases; Issuance of Stock for Plant Assets

10.32 A package consisting of building and land is bought at a lump-sum price of $70,000. The FMV of the building and land is $60,000 and $20,000, respectively. Allocate the cost to each item and prepare a journal entry.

10.33 Company F issues 80 shares of its $80-par common stock for a machine. Prepare a journal entry for each of the following independent cases:

(a) The FMV of the machine is $14,000.

(b) The FMV of the stock is $12,000.

Deferred Payment Contracts

10.34 On January 1, 19X1, Company H purchases a machine for a $50,000, five-year, non-interest-bearing note. The note is to be paid in five equal annual installments of $10,000 each, beginning on December 31, 19X1. Assume that the FMV of the machine is $48,000.

(a) Prepare the journal entry for the purchase.

(b) Prepare the annual amortization entry under the straight-line method.

(c) Prepare the annual entry for each installment.

10.35 Assume the same information as in Problem 10.34, except that the FMV of the machine is unknown, and the imputed rate is 10%. Prepare the entry for the purchase and the first year's amortization. Use the effective interest method.

Donations

10.36 Company I receives a building as a donation and spends $5,000 making it ready for use. At the time of the donation, the building had a FMV of $95,000. Prepare the entry for the donation and the $5,000 expenditure.

10.37 Company J donates a building to charity. The FMV and book value are $48,000 and $55,000, respectively. Prepare the required entries.

Exchanges of Plant Assets

10.38 Company K exchanges an old asset for a new, dissimilar one. The old asset had a book value of $30,000 (cost, $40,000; accumulated depreciation, $10,000) and a FMV of $35,000. In addition, Company K also paid $4,000 cash.

(a) How much gain or loss would Company K recognize on this exchange?

(b) At what amount should Company K record the new asset?

(c) Prepare the required journal entry.

10.39 How would your answers to Problem 10.38 change if the assets were *similar*?

10.40 Company L trades land with a book value of $60,000 and a FMV of $53,000 for a machine, and also pays cash of $2,000. Prepare an entry for this exchange.

10.41 Assume the same information as in Problem 10.40, except that the exchange is for a similar asset. Would your entry be any different? If not, why not?

10.42 Company M trades an old machine (cost, $16,000; accumulated depreciation, $10,000) for a new one, and receives $5,000 in cash. Assume that the machines are dissimilar and the FMV of the old machine is $9,000. Prepare the journal entry.

10.43 Assume the same information as in Problem 10.42, except that the machines are *similar*, and the FMV of the new machine is $4,000.

(a) Is there a gain or a loss in this situation?

(b) If there is a gain, how much would be recognized?

(c) Prepare the required journal entry.

10.44 Company N trades in an old machine (FMV, $35,000; cost, $50,000; accumulated depreciation, $20,000) for a new machine with a FMV of $28,000. It also receives cash of $7,000.

(a) If the assets are dissimilar, how much gain should be recognized?

(b) How much gain should be recognized if the assets are similar?

10.45 Prepare the journal entry for the transaction in Problem 10.44 if:

(a) The assets are dissimilar.

(b) The assets are similar.

10.46 Company O trades in an old asset with a book value of $10,000 for a new one and pays $8,000 in cash. The FMV of the old one is $12,000; the *list price* of the new one is $25,000.

(a) What is the FMV of the new asset? Why?

(b) How much gain or loss should Company O recognize on this exchange if:

1. The assets are similar.

2. The assets are dissimilar.

Costs Incurred Subsequent to Acquisition

10.47 Company R incurs the following costs relating to several of its plant assets.

(a) $10,000 to add a room to its plant headquarters.

(b) $2,000 to air condition the vice president's office.

(c) $300 for oil changes to seven of the company's vehicles.

(d) $500 for miscellaneous minor repairs to the company garage.

(e) $700 to add a major part to one of the production machines. This will increase the machine's life by 3 years.

Prepare a journal entry for each of these expenditures.

Sales of Plant Assets

10.48 Company S purchases a machine for $6,000 on July 1, 19X1. The machine is expected to have a 5-year life and a $1,000 salvage value. On December 31, 19X4, Company S disposes of the machine. Prepare the necessary journal entry for each of the following cases.

(a) The disposal price is $2,500.

(b) The disposal price is $2,200.

(c) The disposal price is $2,900.

Involuntary Conversions

10.49 On December 31, 19X5, a building owned by Company T burns to the ground. The building was purchased on January 1, 19X1, for $51,000 and was expected to have a 50-year life and a $1,000 salvage value. The building was covered under a $50,000 insurance policy with a $10,000 deductible. Prepare the required journal entry. Assume that the insurance company has committed itself to make the required insurance reimbursement.

Appendix 10A

Capitalization of Interest

We mentioned in the chapter text that interest costs incurred to finance the *purchase* of plant assets should not be capitalized (i.e., debited to the asset) but instead debited to Interest Expense. If, however, plant assets are *constructed* rather than *purchased*, *some* of the interest *is* capitalized, starting with the first construction expenditure and ending when the asset is substantially complete.

Only *plant* assets qualify for interest capitalization. Inventories that are routinely manufactured in large quantities for resale purposes do not qualify for interest capitalization.

The amount of interest to be capitalized is determined by multiplying the *weighted-average accumulated expenditures* by the appropriate interest rate. The result is called the *avoidable interest.* Capitalization is limited to the *lower* of the avoidable interest versus the *actual interest.*

EXAMPLE 1

If the avoidable interest is $10,000 and the actual interest is $11,000, then only $10,000 is capitalized and the remaining $1,000 is expensed.

Conversely, if the avoidable interest is $10,000 and the actual interest is only $9,000, only $9,000 is capitalized.

How do we determine the "weighted-average" accumulated expenditures? If the construction expenditures are incurred evenly throughout the year, we simply take the beginning-of-year accumulated expenditures, add to it the end-of-year accumulated expenditures, and divide by 2. If, however, the expenditures are incurred unevenly throughout the year, we must take a weighted average.

EXAMPLE 2

A company began construction of a building on January 1, 19X1 (thus the accumulated expenditures at year-beginning were zero). By December 31, it had spent $200,000. The average is (0 + $200,000) ÷ 2 = $100,000 (assuming that the expenditures were incurred evenly during the year).

EXAMPLE 3

Let's continue with the previous example. By December 31, 19X2, the *total* accumulated expenditures are $500,000. The average for 19X2 is ($200,00 + $500,000) ÷ 2 = $350,000.

EXAMPLE 4

Company Red incurred the following expenditures for construction of a building during 19X1: January 1, $100,000; July 1, $240,000; October 1, $290,000. Since the expenditures were incurred unevenly, we must use a weighted average calculation, as follows:

Jan. 1–June 30	$100,000 × 6	$ 600,000
July 1–Sept. 30	340,000* × 3	1,020,000
Oct. 1–Dec. 31	630,000[†] × 3	1,890,000
		$3,510,000

*($100,000 + $240,000)
[†]($100,000 + $240,000 + $290,000)

We now divide the total of $3,510,000 by 12 to arrive at the weighted average of $292,500 for the year.

Once we determine the weighted-average accumulated expenditures, we multiply this amount by the appropriate interest rate to determine the capitalized interest. For the portion of the weighted-average accumulated expenditures that is less than or equal to any amount *specifically* borrowed to finance the construction, we use the interest rate incurred on that borrowing; for any remaining portion, we use the *average* rate incurred on all other debt outstanding during the period. Let's look at how we calculate the average rate.

EXAMPLE 5

Company Red has the following debt outstanding during 19X1:

$$\begin{array}{ll}
\$100,000\ @\ 10\%\ \text{interest (interest} = \$10,000) \\
\underline{\quad 400,000}\ @\ 6\%\ \text{interest (interest} = \underline{\quad 24,000)} \\
\$500,000 \qquad\qquad\qquad\qquad\qquad\quad \$34,000
\end{array}$$

$$\text{Average rate} = \frac{\text{total interest}}{\text{total principle}} = \frac{\$34,000}{\$500,000} = 6.8\%$$

EXAMPLE 6

Company Green's weighted-average accumulated expenditures for 19X1 is $500,000. Its outstanding debt during 19X1 consists of the following:

$$\begin{array}{ll}
\text{Specific Construction Debt: } \$400,000\ @\ 10\%;\ \text{Interest} = \$40,000 \\
\text{General Bonds Payable: } \$300,000\ @\ 8\%;\ \text{Interest} \quad = \underline{\quad 24,000} \\
\text{Total } actual \text{ interest} \qquad\qquad\qquad\qquad\qquad\qquad = \$64,000
\end{array}$$

For $400,000 of the $500,000 accumulated expenditures, we use the 10% rate incurred for the specific construction debt; for the remaining $100,000, we use the 8% rate incurred for the bonds. Thus the avoidable interest is:

$$\begin{array}{l}
\$400,000 \times 10\% = \$40,000 \\
\ 100,000 \times 8\% \ \ = \underline{\quad 8,000} \\
\qquad\qquad\qquad\quad\ \ \$48,000
\end{array}$$

Since the avoidable interest ($48,000) is less than the actual interest ($64,000), we capitalize the 48,000 and the entry is:

Plant Asset	48,000	
Interest Expense	16,000	
Cash		64,000

Now let's look at an example that ties together all these concepts.

EXAMPLE 7

Gold Corporation incurs construction expenditures evenly throughout the year. On January 1, 19X1, its accumulated expenditures were $200,000; at December 31, 19X1, they were $400,000. Thus the weighted average is $300,000.

During 19X1, Gold had the following debt outstanding during the entire year:

Specific Construction Debt	$200,000 @ 10%	= $20,000
Bond Payable	$300,000 @ 8%	= $24,000
Note Payable	400,000 @ 6%	= 24,000
Total Non-construction Debt and Interest:	$700,000	$48,000

Thus the average interest rate on non-construction debt is:

$$\frac{\$48,000}{\$700,000} = 6.86\% \quad \text{(rounded)}$$

For $200,000 of the $300,000 accumulated expenditures, we use the specific construction debt rate of 10%; for the remaining $100,000, we use the average non-construction rate of 6.8%. Thus the avoidable interest is:

$$\$200,000 \times 10\% = \$20,000$$
$$\$100,000 \times 6.8\% = \underline{6,800}$$
$$\$26,800$$

Since this is less than the actual interest of $68,000 ($20,000 + $48,000), it is the amount to be capitalized. The journal entry, therefore, is:

Plant Asset	26,800	
Interest Expense	41,200	
Cash		68,000

Rapid Review

1. Interest incurred on the _____ of plant assets may be capitalized, while interest incurred on the _____ of plant assets may not.

2. The amount to be capitalized is the lower of the _____ interest versus the _____ interest.

3. To determine the capitalized interest, we multiply the appropriate interest rate by the weighted-average _____.

4. If at the beginning of the year a company had already spent $50,000 on construction, and by year-end its total spending was $90,000, then its average for the year is _____ (assuming that spending is done evenly throughout the year).

Answers: **1.** construction; purchase **2.** avoidable; actual **3.** accumulated expenditures **4.** $70,000

Solved Problems

10A.1 Determine the amount of interest to capitalize if:

    (*a*)   Avoidable interest = $5,000; actual interest = $4,700.

    (*b*)   Avoidable interest = $3,000; actual interest = $3,300.

SOLUTION

(*a*)　$4,700　　　(*b*)　$3,000

10A.2 Determine the weighted-average accumulated expenditures if at year-beginning and at year-end the accumulated amounts were $90,000 and $160,000, respectively.

SOLUTION

($160,000 + $90,000) ÷ 2 = $125,000

10A.3 Gold Corp. incurred the following construction expenditures during 19X1, when it began construction of a building: January 1, $20,000; April 1, $60,000; June 1, $50,000; October 1, $70,000.

Determine the weighted-average accumulated expenditures for 19X1.

SOLUTION

Jan. 1–Mar. 31:	$20,000 × 3 = $	60,000
Apr. 1–May 31:	$80,000 × 2 =	160,000
June 1–Sept. 30:	$130,000 × 4 =	520,000
Oct. 1–Dec. 31:	$200,000 × 3 =	600,000
		$1,340,000
	÷ 12 = $	111,667 (rounded)

10A.4 Green Corp. has the following outstanding debt during the entire year:

1. $40,000 bond payable, 9%
2. $90,000 notes payable, 5%

Determine the average interest rate for the year.

SOLUTION

Bond interest = 40,000 × 9% = $3,600
Note interest = 90,000 × 5% = 4,500
$8,100

$$\text{Average interest} = \frac{\$8,100}{\$40,000 + \$90,000} = 6.23\%$$

10A.5 Copper Corporation incurs construction expenditures evenly during 19X1. At January 1 and December 31, its accumulated expenditures were $0 and $200,000, respectively. During 19X1, Copper Corporation had the following debt outstanding all year:

Specific Construction Debt	$80,000 @ 10%
General Bond Payable	40,000 @ 12%
General Note Payable	60,000 @ 14%

Determine the amount of interest capitalization for 19X1.

SOLUTION

Weighted-average accumulated expenditures:

$$\frac{0 + \$200,000}{2} = \$100,000$$

Average interest rate on nonspecific construction debt:

$$\frac{(\$40,000 \times 12\%) + (\$60,000 \times 14\%)}{\$40,000 + \$60,000} = 13.2\%$$

Interest capitalization:

$$
\begin{array}{lll}
\$\ 80,000 \times 10\% & = \$\ 8,000 & \text{(specific construction debt rate)} \\
\underline{\ \ \ \ 20,000} \times 13.2\% & = \underline{\ \ \ 2,640} & \\
\$100,000 & \ \ \ \ \$10,640 &
\end{array}
$$

10A.6 For Problem 10A.5, prepare a journal entry for the total interest incurred.

SOLUTION

Total interest incurred:

$$(80,000 \times 0.10) + (\$40,000 \times 0.12) + (\$60,000 \times 0.14) = \$21,200$$

Plant Asset	10,640	
Interest Expense	10,560	
Cash		21,200

Chapter 11

Depreciation and Depletion

11.1 INTRODUCTION

The wearing down of plant assets is referred to as *depreciation*; the wearing down (consumption) of natural resources (coal, oil, timber) is referred to as *depletion*. We shall discuss depreciation first.

Depreciation, as defined by the accounting profession, is the allocation of an asset's cost to expense in a systematic and rational manner, over the periods expected to benefit from the use of the asset.

Under the matching principle which we discussed earlier in this book, expenses should be matched to and recognized in the same period as their related revenues. Therefore, plant assets—which produce revenue over several periods—must have their expense (depreciation) gradually recognized and allocated over those periods as well.

Depreciation is an attempt at *cost allocation* rather than *asset valuation*. Even in those situations where an asset's fair market value has *increased*, depreciation recognition is still necessary.

Assets depreciate because of physical factors and economic factors. *Physical factors* consist of the physical wear and tear and deterioration of the asset as the asset is used over time. *Economic factors* consist primarily of market conditions that cause an asset to become obsolete. The asset may be in perfect *physical* shape, but if other assets are produced in the marketplace that are faster and more efficient, it becomes economically impractical to continue using this asset, and early disposal becomes a necessity.

Most plant assets do not depreciate completely—they can be sold as scrap at the end of their useful lives. The ending value is referred to as *scrap value*, *salvage value*, or *residual value*.

Thus, the amount an asset will depreciate is its original cost less its salvage value, and this is referred to as the *depreciable base*.

EXAMPLE 1

An asset cost $5,000 and has a salvage value of $1,000. Its depreciable base, therefore, is $4,000.

11.2 DEPRECIATION METHODS: STRAIGHT-LINE METHOD; ACTIVITY METHOD

Two commonly used methods to calculate depreciation are the straight-line method and the activity method. They both fulfill the "systematic and rational" criteria set forth by the accounting profession in its definition of depreciation.

Under the *straight-line method*, depreciation is a function of time: Equal time periods are assigned equal amounts of depreciation no matter how much the asset is used each period. The formula for this method is:

$$\text{Depreciation} = \frac{\text{cost} - \text{salvage value}}{\text{asset life}}$$

EXAMPLE 2

Let's use the following data for all our examples involving depreciation:

$$\text{Machine cost} = \$1,000$$
$$\text{Salvage value} = 100 \quad (\text{depreciable base} = \$900)$$
$$\text{Life} = 3 \text{ years}$$

If the machine was purchased on January 1, 19X1, the annual depreciation for 19X1, 19X2, and 19X3 is:

$$\frac{\$1,000 - \$100}{3} = \$300$$

If the asset was not purchased on January 1, then we must prorate the first and last year's depreciation, based on the number of months used in those periods. Many companies use the following convention: If an asset is purchased before the 15th of the month, it is considered purchased at the beginning of *this* month; if it is purchased on the 15th or afterward, it is considered purchased at the beginning of the *next* month. Thus, if Green Company purchases one asset on March 12, it is considered to have been purchased on March 1, while if it purchases another asset on March 18, that one is considered to be purchased on April 1.

EXAMPLE 3

Let's continue with the same data of the previous example but assume that the machine was purchased on September 1, 19X1. Thus in 19X1 the machine was used for only 4 months of the year ($\frac{4}{12}$). The depreciation for all periods is:

$$\begin{aligned}
&\text{19X1 (Sept.–Dec.):} && \$300 \times \tfrac{4}{12} = \$100 \\
&\text{19X2 (all year):} && \qquad\quad\ = 300 \\
&\text{19X3 (all year):} && \qquad\quad\ = 300 \\
&\text{19X4 (Jan.–Aug.):} && \$300 \times \tfrac{8}{12} = 200
\end{aligned}$$

The straight-line method has an advantage in that it is easy to compute. A disadvantage, however, is that all years are assigned the same amount of depreciation, regardless of how many units are produced. According to the matching principle, those years with more production should be assigned more depreciation, since they usually produce more revenue.

The *activity method* of depreciation bases depreciation on activity rather than time. The more activity during the year, the more depreciation is taken; the less activity, the less depreciation is taken. The formula for the activity method is:

$$\frac{\text{Cost} - \text{salvage value}}{\text{Capacity in units}}$$

Capacity in units can be measured in units of output (units produced), or in units of input (machine hours). Let's look at an example.

EXAMPLE 4

Let's continue with the data of the previous examples, where a machine with a salvage value of $100 and a 3-year life was purchased for $1,000. Assume that the machine has an estimated capacity of 900 units and this year 350 units were produced. The depreciation calculation is:

$$\frac{\$1,000 - \$100}{900 \text{ units}} = \$1 \text{ per unit}$$

Thus this year's depreciation is $350 \times \$1 = \$350$.

EXAMPLE 5

In Example 4, capacity was measured in units of output. Alternatively, it can be measured in units of input. If we assume that the machine under consideration can be used for 1,800 hours, then depreciation per hour is:

$$\frac{\$1,000 - \$100}{1,800} = \$0.50 \text{ per hour}$$

If this year the machine was used 700 hours, depreciation is $700 \times \$0.50 = \$350$.

An advantage of the activity method is that it perfectly applies the matching principle, as follows:

More activity → more revenue recognition → more depreciation expense

Less activity → less revenue recognition → less depreciation expense

There are several disadvantages, however. For one, this method requires an estimate of the machine's capacity, which is not always an easy task. Secondly, the economic aspect of depreciation—obsolescence—is not a function of activity, but of time.

11.3   SUM-OF-THE-YEARS'-DIGITS (SYD) AND DECLINING-BALANCE METHODS

Some methods are called *accelerated* methods because they take high depreciation during the early years of an asset's life and low depreciation during the later years. We shall discuss the *sum-of-the-years'-digits* (SYD) method first.

Under the SYD method, depreciation is determined by the use of an annual fraction whose denominator will be the same each year, but whose numerator will change. The denominator is the sum of the digits that constitute the life of the asset; the numerator is the digits in reverse. This fraction is then multiplied by the depreciable base.

EXAMPLE 6

The denominator for a machine with a life of 3 years (digits 1, 2, and 3) is $1 + 2 + 3 = 6$. The numerator for year 1 is 3; for year 2 it is 2; for year 3 it is 1. Thus the fractions are $\frac{3}{6}$, $\frac{2}{6}$, and $\frac{1}{6}$ for years 1, 2, and 3, respectively.

EXAMPLE 7

A machine with a life of 4 years has a constant denominator of 10 $(1 + 2 + 3 + 4)$. The digits in reverse are 4, 3, 2, and 1. Thus the fractions per year are:

$$\text{Year 1: } \tfrac{4}{10} \qquad \text{Year 3: } \tfrac{2}{10}$$
$$\text{Year 2: } \tfrac{3}{10} \qquad \text{Year 4: } \tfrac{1}{10}$$

EXAMPLE 8

Let's continue with our machine that cost $1,000 and has a salvage value and life of $100 and 3 years, respectively. The constant denominator is 6 $(1 + 2 + 3)$; the numerators are 3, 2, and 1. Thus, if the machine was purchased on January 1, 19X1, the annual depreciation is:

$$19X1: \qquad \tfrac{3}{6} \times \$900 = \$450$$
$$19X2: \qquad \tfrac{2}{6} \times \$900 = \ \ 300$$
$$19X3: \qquad \tfrac{1}{6} \times \$900 = \ \ 150$$

If an asset has a short life, it is easy to calculate the denominator by adding up the years' digits manually. But what if it has a long life, such as 25 years? Is it actually necessary to add up 25 digits? Fortunately, it is not. The famous mathematician Gauss gave us a quick formula with which we can quickly add up the sum of a series of numbers. The formula is:

$$S = \frac{N(N + 1)}{2}$$

where S represents the sum, and N represents the life of the asset. Let's see how this works.

EXAMPLE 9

A machine with a life of 3 years has a sum of 6, calculated as follows:

$$S = \frac{N(N + 1)}{2}$$

$$= \frac{3(3 + 1)}{2} = 6$$

A machine with a 25-year live has a sum of 325, calculated as follows:

$$S = \frac{N(N + 1)}{2}$$

$$= \frac{25(25 + 1)}{2} = 325$$

If an asset is purchased sometime *during* the year instead of on January 1, the depreciation calculation under SYD must be prorated, and some years will require the use of *two* fractions instead of the usual *one*. This is illustrated in the next example.

EXAMPLE 10

Assume again that we are dealing with a machine that cost $1,000 and has a salvage value and life of $100 and 3 years, respectively. But now let's assume that it was purchased on September 1, 19X1, instead of on January 1. Thus, during 19X1 the machine was used just 4 months ($\frac{4}{12}$ of the year). As you recall, the denominator for a 3-year life is 6; the numerators are 3, 2, and 1, respectively. Thus, for 19X1, depreciation is $\frac{3}{6} \times \$900 \times \frac{4}{12} = \$150$. Notice that the depreciation is prorated by $\frac{4}{12}$ because the machine was in use for only four-twelfths of the year (September–December).

Now let's go to 19X2. It might seem that we now immediately begin using the new fraction, $\frac{2}{6}$. However, this is incorrect. Each fraction must be used a full 12 months before we can proceed to the next one. Since the fraction $\frac{3}{6}$ was used only for 4 months in 19X1, it must be used for another 8 months in 19X2. Therefore, the 19X2 depreciation is arrived at via two calculations:

$$\frac{3}{6} \times \$900 \times \frac{8}{12} = \$300$$

and

$$\frac{2}{6} \times \$900 \times \frac{4}{12} = 100$$

Thus the total depreciation for 19X2 is $400.

EXAMPLE 11

Let's continue with the previous example. For 19X3 we still must use the fraction $\frac{2}{6}$ for another 8 months. Thus the calculation is:

$$\frac{2}{6} \times \$900 \times \frac{8}{12} = \$200$$

and

$$\frac{1}{6} \times \$900 \times \frac{4}{12} = 50 \qquad \text{(total depreciation is \$250)}$$

For 19X4, the machine will be used 8 months (January–August), and depreciation is:

$$\frac{1}{6} \times \$900 \times \frac{8}{12} = \$100$$

We now go to the *declining-balance method*. Under this method, the depreciation rate will be either $1\frac{1}{2}$ times or double the straight-line rate. We will assume double the rate ("double" declining balance) throughout this chapter.

Thus, if an asset has a 5-year life, it will depreciate by one-fifth every year under straight-line depreciation. For double-declining-balance depreciation (DDB) however, the depreciation is *double* that, or two-fifths.

EXAMPLE 12

A machine with a 6-year life will depreciate by one-sixth every year under straight-line, and double that, two-sixths, under DDB.

It is important to note that under the declining-balance method, salvage value is *not* subtracted as it was under the other methods. Thus, care must be taken in the latter years of the asset's life not to accidentally depreciate the salvage.

There is another important difference between this method and the other methods. Those methods use the depreciable base (cost − salvage value) in the calculations; DDB uses *book value* (cost − accumulated depreciation).

The annual depreciation is calculated as follows:

$$\text{Depreciation} = \text{fixed fraction} \times \text{book value}$$

Let's look at an example.

EXAMPLE 13

We continue with our machine that was purchased for $1,000 with a salvage value of $100 and a life of 3 years. For straight-line purposes, the machine will depreciate one-third per year; therefore, for DDB purposes, the fixed fraction is $\frac{2}{3}$. The calculations are:

Year	Cost	Accumulated Depreciation	Book Value		Fixed Fraction		Depreciation
19X1	$1,000	0	$1,000	$\times$	$\frac{2}{3}$	$=$	$667
19X2	1,000	$667	333	$\times$	$\frac{2}{3}$	$=$	222
19X3	1,000	889 ($667 + $222)	111				

At this point, the book value is $111. If we now multiply this by $\frac{2}{3}$, depreciation will be $74, and the new book value will be $37 ($111 − $74). But this cannot be allowed, since the salvage value is $100. Therefore, in order to avoid cutting into the salvage value, depreciation will be only $11—the amount needed to reduce the book value from $111 to the salvage value of $100.

Notice that throughout the calculations, *book value* was used (instead of the depreciable base), and salvage value was *not* subtracted.

In Example 13, care had to be taken in the last period not to *overdepreciate*. In some cases, care must be taken not to *underpreciate*, as we will see in the next example.

EXAMPLE 14

A machine with a 4-year life and a salvage value of $200 has a book value of $500 after 3 years. If we blindly multiply the fraction $\frac{2}{4}$ by $500 in year 4, depreciation of $250 will be taken, with a resulting book value of $250 ($500 − $250). Since salvage value is only $200, however, we must take depreciation of $300 ($500 book value − $200 salvage value).

If an asset is purchased *during* the period instead of on January 1, then depreciation for the first year must be reduced, as illustrated in the next example.

EXAMPLE 15

Assume that our $1,000 machine with a salvage value of $100 and a life of 3 years is purchased on September 1, 19X1. Thus, during 19X1, the machine was owned for only $\frac{4}{12}$ of the year. The calculations are:

Year	Cost	Accumulated Depreciation	Book Value	Fixed Fraction	Depreciation
19X1 (4 months)	$1,000	0	$1,000	$\times \frac{2}{3} \times \frac{4}{12}$	= $222 (rounded)
19X2	1,000	$222	778	$\times \frac{2}{3}$	= 519 (rounded)
19X3	1,000	741 ($222 + $519)	259		

In 19X3 we cannot multiply the book value of $259 by $\frac{2}{3}$ because that would cut into the salvage value. Instead, depreciation will be $159 ($259 book value − $100 salvage value). No depreciation will be taken in 19X4.

11.4 GROUP AND COMPOSITE DEPRECIATION

Companies with many plant assets often do not want to bother recording depreciation for each one, but instead, depreciate them as a group. If the assets are similar in nature, the collection is referred to as a *group*; if the assets are dissimilar, the collection is a *composite*. The depreciation for either a group or a composite uses an average for the entire collection and depreciates on that basis.

Let's look at an example.

EXAMPLE 16

Diversified Corporation has three types of plant assets. Their costs, salvage values, useful lives, and straight-line depreciation (by type) are as follows:

Type	Cost	Salvage Value	Depreciable Base	Useful Life	Yearly Depreciation
1	$ 40,000	$1,000	$ 39,000	10 years	$3,900
2	50,000	2,000	48,000	20 years	2,400
3	20,000	3,000	17,000	5 years	3,400
	$110,000		$104,000		$9,700

We now compute a depreciation rate for the entire group, as follows:

$$\text{Depreciation rate} = \frac{\text{yearly depreciation}}{\text{original cost}} = \frac{\$9,700}{\$110,000} = 8.82\% \quad \text{(rounded)}$$

We also compute a composite (group) life, as follows:

$$\text{Composite (group) life} = \frac{\text{depreciable base}}{\text{yearly depreciation}} = \frac{\$104,000}{\$9,700} = 10.72 \text{ years} \quad \text{(rounded)}$$

Thus, these assets will be assigned yearly depreciation of $9,700, which is 8.82% of their cost, and at this rate, it will take 10.72 years to depreciate them down to their salvage value.

We saw in Chapter 10 that when plant assets are disposed of, a gain or loss may occur, and will be recognized. For example, if a machine with cost and accumulated depreciation of $10,000 and $6,000, respectively (book value = $4,000) is sold for $3,000, there is a *recognized* loss of $1,000. Conversely, if it is sold for $5,000, there is a *recognized* gain of $1,000. The entries for both of these cases are:

Loss Situation:			*Gain Situation:*		
Cash	3,000		Cash	5,000	
Loss	1,000		Accumulated Depreciation	6,000	
Accumulated Depreciation	6,000		Machine		10,000
Machine		10,000	Gain		1,000

Under the group and composite depreciation method, however, no gains or losses are recognized; amounts needed to balance the journal entry are "buried" in the debit to Accumulated Depreciation.

This practice is justified on the grounds that some assets will be sold *before* they reach the composite life (which will usually result in a gain), while others will be sold *after* they reach the composite life (which will usually result in a loss). Thus, the gains and losses would offset each other anyway.

EXAMPLE 17

In Example 16, if one of the type 1 assets that cost $7,000 is sold for $5,000, the entry is:

Cash	5,000	
Accumulated Depreciation	2,000	
Machine		7,000

Notice that no loss or gain is recognized; the Accumulated Depreciation debit is simply "plugged" to balance the entry.

11.5   DEPRECIATION: MISCELLANEOUS ISSUES

Because of rapid changes in technology, plant assets may suddenly experience a dramatic decline in value. This is referred to as an *impairment*. In some cases, the impairment may be total; in others, only partial.

The FASB is currently discussing the accounting implications of impairments. At this time the most common practice is to recognize the impairment by debiting a loss account and crediting Accumulated Depreciation for the amount of the impairment. The loss is *not* considered to be extraordinary, since such losses occur frequently.

EXAMPLE 18

Advance Tech Corp. has a computer with cost and accumulated depreciation of $30,000 and $5,000, respectively, and thus a book value of $25,000. A competitor begins marketing a more sophisticated and efficient computer which makes Advance Tech's computer obsolete, nonmarketable, and salable only for scrap at $1,000. Thus a loss of $24,000 has been incurred ($25,000 − $1,000), and the following entry is made:

Loss Due to Equipment Obsolescence	24,000	
Accumulated Depreciation		24,000

We have been discussing depreciation from the point of view of *financial accounting*—accounting used for preparation of the financial statements. For *tax purposes*, however, companies must follow the rules set forth in the Tax Reform Act of 1986, which divides plant assets into several categories and prescribes the depreciation method to be used for each category. The Act also assumes salvage value to be zero, and assigns a tax life to plant assets that is usually shorter than the economic life. These features are unacceptable for financial accounting.

Thus companies will often use a different depreciation method, asset life, and salvage value for financial statement purposes than they use for tax purposes. These differences require special journal entries, which are discussed in *Intermediate Accounting II* of this series.

One other miscellaneous issue is that of the required accounting treatment for a change in the estimate of an asset's life or salvage value. This topic was discussed in Chapter 2.

11.6   DEPLETION OF NATURAL RESOURCES

There are three types of costs incurred in acquiring and preparing various natural resources (coal, oil, timber, etc.) for use:

1. *Purchase price*—amounts paid to the seller for the natural resource.

2. *Exploration costs*—amounts paid to *find* the natural resource (usually associated with oil).

3. *Development costs*—amounts paid to prepare the resource site for mining. These include drilling costs, extraction costs, and the construction of tunnels, shafts, and wells.

We mentioned in previous chapters that the cost of an asset is the purchase price plus all costs necessary to make the asset ready for use. The same rule applies to natural resources: The cost of such resources includes all three costs mentioned.

EXAMPLE 19

Oil Corp. purchases a coal mine and pays the seller $110,000. It also incurs $30,000 in exploration costs and $70,000 in development costs. The journal entry is:

Coal Mine	210,000	
Cash		210,000

If equipment is purchased for use in the mining process, the cost is *not* added to the cost of the natural resource. Thus, in Example 19, if equipment was purchased for $5,000, the entry would be a debit to Equipment rather than to Coal Mine.

If such equipment has other, alternative uses, it should be depreciated over its useful life. If not, it should be depreciated over its own life, or the life of the natural resource, whichever is shorter.

Natural resources become physically consumed with time. This process is referred to as *depletion* and is analogous to the depeciation of plant assets. Generally, the activity method is used, and the depletion rate is computed as follows:

$$\text{Depletion rate} = \frac{\text{cost of natural resource} - \text{salvage value}}{\text{estimated capacity in units}}$$

Each year the company makes the following journal entry:

Depletion Expense	xx	
Accumulated Depletion		xx

If costs must be incurred to prepare the barren land for resale once the natural resource has been removed, these costs reduce the salvage value.

EXAMPLE 20

Land is purchased that contains a coal mine. The coal mine is completely exhausted over time, and the company now wishes to sell the land for $10,000. However, no buyer will pay this price unless the coal mine is filled and covered—a process that will cost $2,000. The salvage value is therefore only $8,000.

EXAMPLE 21

Black Coal Corp. purchases land containing a coal mine for $50,000 and incurs exploration and development costs of $10,000 and $20,000, respectively. The salvage value of the land is $6,000, but $1,000 must be spent to make is salable. If geologists estimate that the coal mine contains 10,000 tons, the depletion rate is:

$$\frac{\$50,000 + \$10,000 + \$20,000 - \$5,000^*}{\$10,000} = \$7.50 \text{ per ton}$$

$$^*(\$6,000 - \$1,000)$$

EXAMPLE 22

In Example 21, if Black Coal Corp. mines and sells 2,000 tons during the first year, the depletion is $2,000 \times \$7.50 = \$15,000$ and the entry is:

Depletion Expense	15,000	
Accumulated Depletion		15,000

On the balance sheet, the coal mine would be presented as follows:

Coal Mine	$80,000*
− Accumulated Depletion	−15,000
Net Asset	$65,000

*(50,000 + 10,000 + 20,000)

On the income statement, depletion expense is part of the cost of producing the product, and therefore part of the cost of goods sold to be subtracted from sales in arriving at gross profit.

Summary

1. The wearing down of plant assets is referred to as *depreciation*; the wearing down (consumption) of natural resources is referred to as *depletion*.

2. Depreciation is the allocation of an asset's cost to expense in a systematic and rational manner over the periods expected to benefit from the use of the asset. Thus depreciation recognition is required even if an asset's fair market value has increased.

3. Assets will depreciate for their cost less salvage value. This amount is known as the *depreciable base*.

4. Four commonly used depreciation methods are: *straight-line*, *activity*, *sum-of-the-years'-digits* (SYD) and *double-declining-balance* (DDB). The last method differs from the first three in that salvage value is *not* subtracted and *book value* is used in the computations, rather than the depreciable base. Care must therefore be taken under this method to avoid cutting into the salvage value during the latter years of the asset.

5. Assets purchased before the 15th of the month are considered to be purchased at the beginning of the month; assets purchased on the 15th or later are considered to be purchased on the first day of the next month.

6. The formula for straight-line depreciation is:

$$\frac{\text{Cost} - \text{salvage value}}{\text{Asset life}}$$

The formula for the activity method is:

$$\frac{\text{Cost} - \text{salvage value}}{\text{Capacity in units or hours}}$$

The formula for the sum-of-the years'-digits method is:

$$(\text{Cost} - \text{salvage}) \times \text{varying fraction}$$

The denominator of this fraction is the sum of the years' digits and remains constant. The numerator is the years' digits in reverse, and this changes from year to year. The formula for double-declining-balance depreciation is:

$$\text{Book value} \times \text{fixed fraction}$$

The fixed fraction is double the fraction used under straight-line.

7. To quickly determine the sum of an asset's years, use the following formula:

$$S = \frac{N(N + 1)}{2}$$

where S represents the sum and N represents the asset's life.

8. Companies with many plant assets may use either group or composite depreciation. *Group depreciation* is used for a collection of similar assets; *composite depreciation* is used for dissimilar assets.

9. The depreciation rate for both these methods is

$$\frac{\text{Yearly depreciation}}{\text{Original cost}}$$

while the composite (group) life is

$$\frac{\text{Depreciable base}}{\text{Yearly depreciation}}$$

10. Under the group and composite depreciation methods, gains and losses are *not* recognized upon asset disposals.

11. If an asset suffers a sudden, permanent decline in value due to technological change, a loss should be recognized by the following entry:

Loss Due to Obsolescence	xxx	
Accumulated Depreciation		xxx

The loss is *not* considered to be extraordinary.

12. The three costs incurred in acquiring and developing natural resources are: purchase price, exploration costs, and development costs. All three are debited to the natural resource and become subject to depletion.

13. The depletion rate is determined as follows:

$$\frac{\text{Cost} - \text{salvage value}}{\text{Estimated capacity in units}}$$

14. If costs must be incurred to prepare the barren land for resale once the natural resource has been removed, these costs reduce the salvage value.

Rapid Review

1. Consumption of natural resources is referred to as _____.

2. The depreciation method selected must be systematic and _____.

3. Cost minus salvage value is called the _____.

4. The method that does *not* subtract salvage is _____.

5. Natural resources are depleted via the _____ method.

6. The _____ method uses a different fraction each year.

7. The formula for determining the sum of a series of numbers is _____.

8. Companies that have many similar assets may depreciate them under the _____ method.

9. Sudden permanent declines in asset values are called _____.

10. The three costs incurred for natural resources are _____, _____, and _____.

Answers: **1.** depletion **2.** rational **3.** depreciable base **4.** DDB **5.** activity **6.** SYD **7.** $S = N(N + 1)/2$ **8.** group **9.** impairments **10.** purchase price; exploration costs; development costs

Solved Problems

Depreciation Methods: Straight-Line Method; Activity Method

11.1 Blue Corp. purchased a machine for $2,600 with a $200 salvage value and a 4-year life. The machine has a production capacity of 4,800 units and was purchased on January 1, 19X1.

(*a*) Determine annual depreciation under the straight-line method.

(*b*) Determine annual depreciation under the activity method.

Assume that production for 19X1–19X4 was: 19X1, 2,000 units; 19X2, 1,200 units; 19X3, 1,000 units; 19X4, 600 units.

SOLUTION

(*a*) $\dfrac{\$2,600 - \$200}{4} = \$600$ for each year

(*b*) $\dfrac{\$2,600 - \$200}{4,800} = \$0.50$ per unit

$$19X1: \quad \$0.50 \times 2,000 = \$1,000$$
$$19X2: \quad \$0.50 \times 1,200 = \$600$$
$$19X3: \quad \$0.50 \times 1,000 = \$500$$
$$19X4: \quad \$0.50 \times 600 = \$300 \qquad \text{[Section 11.2]}$$

11.2　Assume the same information as in Problem 11.1, except that the machine was purchased on October 1. Determine depreciation for each year under the straight-line method.

SOLUTION

The depreciation for each *whole* year is $600.

$$19X1 \text{ (Oct.–Dec.):} \quad \$600 \times \tfrac{3}{12} = \$150$$
$$19X2 \text{ (full year):} \qquad \qquad \qquad 600$$
$$19X3 \text{ (full year):} \qquad \qquad \qquad 600$$
$$19X4 \text{ (full year):} \qquad \qquad \qquad 600$$
$$19X5 \text{ (Jan.–Sept.):} \quad \$600 \times \tfrac{9}{12} = 450 \qquad \text{[Section 11.2]}$$

11.3　On January 1, 19X1, Green Corporation purchased a $2,200 machine with a $100 salvage value and a 3-year life. The machine has a capacity of 1,050 units and produced the following: 19X1, 500 units; 19X2, 300 units; 19X3, 150 units; 19X4, 100 units.

(*a*)　Determine the annual depreciation under the straight-line method.

(*b*)　Determine the annual depreciation under the activity method.

SOLUTION

(*a*)　$\dfrac{\$2,200 - \$100}{3} = \$700$

(*b*)　$\dfrac{\$2,200 - \$100}{1,050} = \$2 \text{ per unit}$

$$19X1: \ 500 \times \$2 = \$1,000$$
$$19X2: \ 300 \times \$2 = 600$$
$$19X3: \ 150 \times \$2 = 300$$
$$19X4: \ 100 \times \$2 = 200 \qquad \text{[Section 11.2]}$$

11.4　Black Corp. purchases a machine for $2,900 with a $100 salvage value and a capacity of 1,000 hours. Each unit of output requires $1\frac{1}{2}$ hours of input. During 19X1 and 19X2 the machine produces 200 and 100 units, respectively. Determine depreciation for each year.

SOLUTION

$$\frac{\$2,900 - \$100}{1,000} = \$2.80 \text{ per hour}$$

$$19X1: \ 200 \text{ units} \times 1\tfrac{1}{2} = 300 \text{ hours}$$
$$\times \underline{\$2.80}$$
$$\underline{\$840}$$

$$19X2: \ 100 \text{ units} \times 1\tfrac{1}{2} = 150 \text{ hours}$$
$$\times \underline{\$2.80}$$
$$\underline{\$420} \qquad \text{[Section 11.2]}$$

Sum-of-the-Years'-Digits (SYD) and Declining-Balance Methods

11.5   Determine the numerators and denominators to be used for each of the following assets, under the SYD method:

(*a*)   10-year life

(*b*)   8-year life

(*c*)   12-year life

SOLUTION

(*a*)   The numerators are 10, 9, 8, 7, 6, 5, 4, 3, 2, 1. The denominator is:

$$S = \frac{10(10 + 1)}{2} = 55$$

(*b*)   The numerators are 8, 7, 6, 5, 4, 3, 2, 1. The denominator is:

$$S = \frac{8(8 + 1)}{2} = 36$$

(*c*)   The numerators are: 12, 11, 10, 9, 8, 7, 6, 5, 4, 3, 2, 1. The denominator is:

$$S = \frac{12(12 + 1)}{2} = 78$$ [Section 11.3]

11.6   A machine with a 3-year life and salvage value of $100 is purchased for $6,100 on January 1, 19X1. Determine the annual depreciation under SYD.

SOLUTION

19X1: $\frac{3}{6} \times \$6,000 = \$3,000$ (the depreciable base is $6,100 - \$100 = \$6,000$)
19X2: $\frac{2}{6} \times \$6,000 = \ 2,000$
19X3: $\frac{1}{6} \times \$6,000 = \ 1,000$ [Section 11.3]

11.7   Assume the same information as in Problem 11.6, except that the machine was purchased on July 1, 19X1. Determine depreciation for each year under the SYD method.

SOLUTION

19X1 (July–Dec.): $\frac{3}{6} \times \$6,000 \times \frac{6}{12} = \underline{\underline{\$1,500}}$

19X2 (all year): $\frac{3}{6} \times \$6,000 \times \frac{6}{12} = \$1,500$
                           $\frac{2}{6} \times \$6,000 \times \frac{6}{12} = \$1,000$
                                        Total $= \underline{\underline{\$2,500}}$

19X3 (all year): $\frac{2}{6} \times \$6,000 \times \frac{6}{12} = \$1,000$
                           $\frac{1}{6} \times \$6,000 \times \frac{6}{12} = \ \ \ 500$
                                        Total $= \underline{\underline{\$1,500}}$

19X4 (Jan.–June): $\frac{1}{6} \times \$6,000 \times \frac{6}{12} = \underline{\underline{\$\ \ 500}}$ [Section 11.3]

11.8   Red Corp. purchases a machine for $4,200 on January 1, 19X1. The machine has a 4-year life and a salvage value of $200. Determine depreciation for each year under SYD.

SOLUTION

$$19X1:\ \tfrac{4}{10} \times \$4{,}000 = \$1{,}600$$
$$19X2:\ \tfrac{3}{10} \times \$4{,}000 = \ 1{,}200$$
$$19X3:\ \tfrac{2}{10} \times \$4{,}000 = \ \ \ 800$$
$$19X4:\ \tfrac{1}{10} \times \$4{,}000 = \ \ \ 400 \qquad\qquad \text{[Section 11.3]}$$

11.9 Assume the same information as in Problem 11.8, except that the machine was purchased on October 1. Determine depreciation for each period under SYD.

SOLUTION

$$19X1:\ \tfrac{4}{10} \times \$4{,}000 \times \tfrac{3}{12} = \underline{\$\ \ \ 400}$$

$$19X2:\ \tfrac{4}{10} \times \$4{,}000 \times \tfrac{9}{12} = \$1{,}200$$
$$\tfrac{3}{10} \times \$4{,}000 \times \tfrac{3}{12} = \underline{+\ \ 300}$$
$$\phantom{19X2:\ \ \tfrac{3}{10} \times \$4{,}000 \times \tfrac{3}{12} = }\$1{,}500$$

$$19X3:\ \tfrac{3}{10} \times \$4{,}000 \times \tfrac{9}{12} = \$\ \ 900$$
$$\tfrac{2}{10} \times \$4{,}000 \times \tfrac{3}{12} = \underline{+\ \ 200}$$
$$\phantom{19X3:\ \ \tfrac{2}{10} \times \$4{,}000 \times \tfrac{3}{12} = }\$1{,}100$$

$$19X4:\ \tfrac{2}{10} \times \$4{,}000 \times \tfrac{9}{12} = \$\ \ 600$$
$$\tfrac{1}{10} \times \$4{,}000 \times \tfrac{3}{12} = \underline{+\ \ 100}$$
$$\phantom{19X4:\ \ \tfrac{1}{10} \times \$4{,}000 \times \tfrac{3}{12} = }\$\ \ 700$$

$$19X5:\ \tfrac{1}{10} \times \$4{,}000 \times \tfrac{9}{12} = \$\ \ 300 \qquad \text{(Jan.–Sept.)} \qquad \text{[Section 11.3]}$$

11.10 Orange Corp. purchases a machine on January 1, 19X1, for $6,000. The machine has a life of 4 years and a salvage value of $200. Determine depreciation for each year under DDB.

SOLUTION

Recall that annual depreciation under DDB is determined by multiplying the book value by a fixed fraction. In this case, the fixed fraction is $\tfrac{2}{4}$.

$$19X1:\ \tfrac{2}{4} \times \$6{,}000 = \$3{,}000$$
$$19X2:\ \tfrac{2}{4} \times \$3{,}000 = \ 1{,}500 \qquad \text{(Book value} = \$6{,}000 - \$3{,}000)$$
$$19X3:\ \tfrac{2}{4} \times \$1{,}500 = \ \ \ 750 \qquad \text{(Book value} = \$6{,}000 - \$3{,}000 - \$1{,}500)$$

19X4: Since book value is now $750 ($6,000 − $3,000 − $1,500 − $750) and the salvage value is $200, the depreciation is $550.   [Section 11.3]

11.11 Assume the same information as in Problem 11.10, except that the machine was purchased on September 1, 19X1. Determine depreciation for each period under DDB.

SOLUTION

$$19X1:\ \tfrac{2}{4} \times \$6{,}000 \times \tfrac{4}{12} = \$1{,}000 \qquad \text{(Sept.–Dec.)}$$
$$19X2:\ \tfrac{2}{4} \times \$5{,}000 \ \ \ \ \ \ = \ 2{,}500 \qquad (\$6{,}000 - \$1{,}000)$$
$$19X3:\ \tfrac{2}{4} \times \$2{,}500 \ \ \ \ \ \ = \ 1{,}250 \qquad (\$6{,}000 - \$1{,}000 - \$2{,}500)$$
$$19X4:\ \tfrac{2}{4} \times \$1{,}250 \ \ \ \ \ \ = \ \ \ 625 \qquad (\$6{,}000 - \$1{,}000 - \$2{,}500 - \$1{,}250)$$

19X5 (Jan.–Aug.): Since book value is now $625 ($6,000 − $1,000 − $2,500 − $1,250 − $625) and salvage value is $200, depreciation is 425.

[Section 11.3]

11.12 White Corp. purchases a machine on January 1, 19X1, for $3,000 with a life of 3 years and a salvage value of $150. Determine depreciation for each year under DDB.

SOLUTION

The fixed fraction is $\frac{2}{3}$.

19X1: $\frac{2}{3} \times \$3,000 = \$2,000$
19X2: $\frac{2}{3} \times \$1,000 = \quad 667$ (rounded)   ($3,000 − $2,000)
19X3: Since book value is now $333 ($3,000 − $2,000 − $667) and salvage value is $150, depreciation is the difference, or $183.   [Section 11.3]

11.13 Assume the same information as in Problem 11.12, except that the machine was purchased on July 1, 19X1. Determine depreciation for each period under DDB.

SOLUTION

19X1: $\frac{2}{3} \times \$3,000 \times \frac{6}{12} = \$1,000$ (July–Dec.)
19X2: $\frac{2}{3} \times \$2,000 \quad = \quad 1,333$ (rounded)   ($3,000 − $1,000)
19X3: $\frac{2}{3} \times \quad \$667 \quad = \quad 445$ (rounded)   ($3,000 − $1,000 − $1,333)
19X4 (Jan.–June): Since book value is now $222 ($667 − $445) and salvage value is $150, depreciation is the difference, or $72.   [Section 11.3]

11.14 Determine the fixed fraction to be used under the DDB method for each of the following asset lives:

(*a*)   6 years

(*b*)   8 years

(*c*)   10 years

SOLUTION

(*a*) $\frac{2}{6}$ (*b*) $\frac{2}{8}$ (*c*) $\frac{2}{10}$ [Section 11.3]

Group and Composite Depreciation

11.15 Blue Corp. has three types of similar machines with the following costs, salvage values, and lives, respectively:

Type A: $50,000, $10,000, 4 years
Type B: $20,000, $ 2,000, 6 years
Type C: $30,000, $ 3,000, 3 years

Determine the depreciation rate and composite life for these groups.

SOLUTION

Type	Cost	Salvage	Depreciable Base	Life	Yearly Depreciation
A	$ 50,000	$10,000	$40,000	4 years	$10,000
B	20,000	2,000	18,000	6 years	3,000
C	30,000	3,000	27,000	3 years	9,000
	$100,000		$85,000		$22,000

$$\text{Depreciation rate} = \frac{\$22,000}{\$100,000} = 22\%$$

$$\text{Composite life} = \frac{\$85,000}{\$22,000} = 3.86 \text{ years} \qquad \text{(rounded)} \qquad [\text{Section } 11.4]$$

11.16 Suppose that Blue Corp. in Problem 11.15 disposed of one of the machines that cost $7,000 for $9,000. Prepare an entry for the disposal.

SOLUTION

Cash	9,000	
Accumulated Depreciation	2,000	
Machine		7,000 [Section 11.4]

11.17 Amber Corp. has two types of similar machines with the following costs, salvage values, and lives, respectively:

Type 1: $4,000, $500, 5 years

Type 2: $8,000, $800, 8 years

Determine the depreciation rate and composite life for these groups.

SOLUTION

Type	Cost	Salvage	Depreciable Base	Life	Yearly Depreciation
1	$ 4,000	$500	$ 3,500	5 years	$ 700
2	8,000	800	7,200	8 years	900
	$12,000		$10,700		$1,600

$$\text{Depreciation rate} = \frac{\$1,600}{\$12,000} = 13.33\% \qquad \text{(rounded)}$$

$$\text{Composite Life} = \frac{\$10,700}{\$1,600} = 6.69 \text{ years} \qquad \text{(rounded)} \qquad [\text{Section } 11.4]$$

11.18 Suppose that Amber Corp. of Problem 11.17 disposes of a machine with cost of $2,000 for a price of $1,800. Prepare the necessary entry.

SOLUTION

Cash	1,800	
Accumulated Depreciation	200	
Machine		2,000 [Section 11.4]

Depreciation: Miscellaneous Issues

11.19 White Corp. has a machine that cost $18,000 and has accumulated depreciation of $5,000. Suddenly, the machine suffers a permanent impairment and is now worth only $2,000. Prepare a journal entry for the impairment.

SOLUTION

Loss Due to Equipment Obsolescence	11,000	
Accumulated Depreciation		11,000*
*(Book value of $13,000 minus $2,000)		[Section 11.5]

Depletion of Natural Resources

11.20 Mining Corp. purchases land containing a coal mine for $20,000. It pays $2,000 and $5,000 in exploration and development costs, respectively. Prepare the entry needed for these transactions.

SOLUTION

Coal Mine	27,000		
Cash		27,000	[Section 11.6]

11.21 Assume that the mine in Problem 11.20 is estimated to have a capacity of 12,500 tons of coal. After the mine is totally depleted, the barren land will be salable for $3,000, provided that $1,000 is spent on restoring the land.

(a)   Find the depletion rate.

(b)   Prepare an entry for depletion during 19X1 if 4,000 tons of coal were mined and sold.

SOLUTION

(a)   Depletion rate $= \dfrac{\$27,000 - (\$3,000 - \$1,000)}{12,500 \text{ tons}} = \$2$ per ton

(b) $4,000 \times \$2 = \$8,000$

Depletion Expense	8,000		
Accumulated Depletion		8,000	[Section 11.6]

11.22 Green Corp. purchases land containing oil for $50,000, and spends $5,000 on exploration costs. It is estimated that the land will have a salvage value of $4,000. The total capacity of the land is expected to be 3,000 barrels.

In addition to the land, Green buys heavy machinery for $5,100 to be used in the pumping process. The machinery has a life of 5 years, a salvage value of $100, and will have alternate uses after the land is depleted.

(a)   Prepare the entries for the purchase of the land, the exploration costs, and the purchase of the machinery.

(b)   Determine the depletion rate.

(c)   Prepare the entries for depletion and depreciation. Assume that 1,000 barrels were pumped and sold this year.

SOLUTION

(a)

Oil Well	55,000		
Cash		55,000	
Machinery	5,100		
Cash		5,100	

(b)   Depletion rate $= \dfrac{\$55,000 - \$4,000}{3,000} = \$17$ per barrel

(c)

Depletion Expense	17,000		
Accumulated Depletion		17,000	
Depreciation Expense	1,000		
Accumulated Depreciation		1,000	[Section 11.6]

Supplementary Problems

Depreciation Methods: Straight-Line Method; Activity Method

11.23 On January 1, 19X1, White Corp. purchased a machine for $3,800 with a $400 salvage value and a 4-year life. After the machine's life is over, White will have to spend $200 to make the machine salable.

   The machine has a production capacity of 900 units, and production for 19X1–19X4 was as follows: 19X1, 400 units; 19X2, 200 units; 19X3, 100 units; 19X4, 200 units.

   (*a*) Determine the annual depreciation under the straight-line method.

   (*b*) Determine the annual depreciation under the activity method.

11.24 Assume the same information as in Problem 11.23, except that the machine was purchased on July 1, 19X1. Determine the depreciation for each period under the straight-line method.

11.25 Green Corp. purchases a machine for $7,600 with a $300 salvage value and a capacity of 2,000 hours. Each unit of output requires 2 hours of input. During 19X1 and 19X2, the machine produces 350 units and 200 units, respectively. Determine depreciation for each year.

Sum-of-Years'-Digits (SYD) and Declining-Balance Methods

11.26 Determine the numerators and denominators to be used for each of the following asset lives under the SYD method.

   (*a*) 11 years

   (*b*) 7 years

   (*c*) 6 years

11.27 A machine with a 4-year life and salvage value of $500 is purchased on January 1, 19X1, for $8,500. Determine the annual depreciation under SYD.

11.28 Assume the same information as in Problem 11.27, except that the machine was purchased on July 1, 19X1. Determine depreciation for each period under SYD.

11.29 Pink Corp. purchases a machine for $8,400 on October 1, 19X1. The machine has a 4-year life and a salvage value of $400. Determine the annual depreciation under SYD.

11.30 Orange Corp. purchases a machine on January 1, 19X1, for $9,000. The machine has a 3-year life and a $600 salvage value. Determine depreciation for each year under DDB.

11.31 Assume the same information as in Problem 11.30, except that the machine was purchased on July 1, 19X1. Determine depreciation for each period under DDB.

11.32 White Corp. purchases a machine on October 1, 19X1, for $14,000. The machine has a 4-year life and a salvage value of $1,500. Determine depreciation for each period under DDB.

11.33 Determine the fixed fraction to be used under the DDB method for each of the following asset lives:

   (*a*) 12 years

   (*b*) 7 years

   (*c*) 13 years

Group and Composite Depreciation

11.34 Gold Corp. has three classes of dissimilar machines with the following costs, salvage values, and lives, respectively:

> Class A: $40,000, $ 5,000, 5 years
>
> Class B: 80,000, 10,000, 10 years
>
> Class C: 50,000,   8,000, 7 years

Determine the depreciation rate and composite life for these classes.

11.35 Suppose that in Problem 11.34, a machine with a cost of $7,000 is sold for $5,000. Prepare the journal entry for the sale.

Depreciation: Miscellaneous Issues

11.36 Black Corp. has a machine that cost $12,000 and has accumulated depreciation of $4,000. Due to market conditions, the machine suffers a sudden impairment and is now worth only $1,000. Prepare the required journal entry if:

(a) The impairment is considered permanent.

(b) The impairment is *not* considered permanent.

Depletion of Natural Resources

11.37 Tan Corp. purchases land containing a coal mine for $30,000 and pays $3,000 and $6,000 in exploration and development costs, respectively. Prepare the necessary entry.

11.38 Assume that geologists estimate that the mine in Problem 11.37 has a 13,000-ton capacity, and that the land will have a salvage value of $2,000.

(a) Find the depletion rate.

(b) Prepare an entry for the depletion of 19X1 if 3,000 tons of coal are mined and sold.

Chapter 12

Intangible Assets

12.1 INTRODUCTION

Intangible assets are assets that have no physical substance (they can neither be seen nor touched) and carry a high degree of uncertainty regarding future benefits because of their indefinite lives and tendency to experience downward fluctuations in value. Examples of intangibles include patents, copyrights, trademarks, leasehold improvements, organization costs, franchises, and goodwill. These items are not physical in nature; they merely represent *rights* to future benefits.

It should be noted that receivables are *not* classified as intangible assets, even though they have no physical substance. Mere lack of physical substance is not sufficient to warrant classification as an intangible; a high degree of uncertainty regarding future benefits must be present as well.

Intangible assets are recorded at purchase price plus any other fees necessary for their acquisition, such as brokers' fees, legal fees, and government registration fees.

EXAMPLE 1

Company A purchases a patent from Company B for $30,000 and pays a broker's fee and legal fee of $500 and $1,000, respectively. The entry would be a debit to Patent and a credit to Cash for $31,500.

If a company purchases an intangible asset by issuing stock, the asset is recorded at its *own* fair market value, or the fair market value of the *stock*, whichever is more clear. Similarly, if the intangible asset was purchased as part of a package deal (a *basket purchase*), the total cost is allocated to the various items in the package according to their respective fair market values. These concepts were discussed in previous chapters.

Intangible assets, like tangible assets, do not live forever but gradually wear down with time. This process was called depreciation for tangible assets; for intangibles it is referred to as *amortization*. The journal entry consists of a debit to Amortization Expense and a credit to either Accumulated Amortization or directly to the asset itself.

While the various methods used for depreciation may also be used for amortization, the custom is to use the straight-line method. The accounting profession has ruled that for intangibles whose life is unknown, the *maximum* period allowed for amortization is 40 years.

EXAMPLE 2

Company B has two intangible assets. The first has an indefinite life, while the second has a *definite* life of 35 years. The first asset should be amortized over 40 years or less; the second should be amortized over 35 years.

12.2 PATENTS; COPYRIGHTS; TRADEMARKS AND TRADENAMES

Patents, which are granted by the U.S. Patent Office, give the holder the right to use, manufacture, and sell a product or process for 17 years, without interference by others. They may be acquired directly from the U.S. Patent Office, or purchased from other holders.

The cost of a patent, which includes registration fees, purchase price, broker fees, and attorney fees, should be debited to the account Patents. If the patent is purchased directly from the U.S. Patent Office, it provides legal protection for 17 years and thus should be amortized over that period. If, however, it is purchased from another holder who has already held it for some time, it should be amortized over its remaining legal life.

EXAMPLE 3

Company C purchases a patent from Company D, which acquired it 4 years ago from the U.S. Patent Office. If Company C paid $10,000 for the patent and incurred a $3,000 legal fee for the purchase, the total of $13,000 should be amortized over 13 years (17 minus 4). The annual entry is:

Amortization Expense	1,000*	
Patents (or Accumulated Amortization)		1,000*
*($13,000 ÷ 13)		

If the actual life of a patent is deemed to be shorter than its legal life because of competition from other products, the shorter period should be used for amortization.

EXAMPLE 4

Company D acquires a patent from its holder for $5,000. The patent's remaining *legal* life is 8 years, but it is not expected to have any value after 5 years. The amortization period is 5 years, and the annual amortization is $1,000 ($5,000 ÷ 5).

Cost incurred in *successfully* defending a patent in court against legal challenges should be debited to the Patents account—they are considered an additional cost of the patent. *Unsuccessful* costs of a patent defense, however, should be expensed and the unamortized patent cost should be completely amortized, since the patent will provide no future protection.

EXAMPLE 5

Company E purchases a patent for $8,000 and debits the Patents account for this amount. The patent is estimated to provide benefits for the next 9 years. Immediately after the purchase, the patent is challenged in court and *successfully* defended at a cost of $1,000. This amount should also be debited to Patents, and the entire $9,000 should be amortized at $1,000 ($9,000 ÷ 9) per year.

EXAMPLE 6

Assume the same information as in Example 5, except that the patent defense was *unsuccessful*. The $1,000 court cost should be debited to Legal Fee Expense; the $8,000 patent cost should be instantly amortized, as follows:

Amortization Expense	8,000	
Patents		8,000

Copyrights give authors, painters, and other artists the exclusive right to reproduce and sell their works. The right is given for the life of the creator plus 50 years.

The cost of acquiring a copyright is debited to the Copyrights account. Since the life of the copyright is indefinite, the maximum amortization period allowed is 40 years.

EXAMPLE 7

Company E purchases a copyright from its creator for $40,000. It debits Copyrights and credits Cash for $40,000, and amortizes it annually via the following entry:

Amortization Expense	1,000*	
Copyrights (or Accumulated Amortization)		1,000*
*($40,000 ÷ 40)		

Company E may, if it so decides, use a shorter period than 40 years.

Trademarks and *tradenames* are symbols and names, respectively, that are used to identify a company or product. These are acquired from the U.S. Patent Office and are renewable for an indefinite number of 20-year periods.

If the trademark or tradename is purchased from another party, the purchase price is debited to the trademark/tradename account. If it is self-developed, all costs involved in its creation go into this account. These costs include design fees, consulting fees, registration fees, attorney fees, legal defense fees, and others.

Since the life of trademarks and tradenames is indefinite, the 40-year maximum applies.

EXAMPLE 8

Company F developed a trademark for its product. Its development costs were:

Design Fees	$ 500	Registration Fees (Patent Office)	$ 25
Attorney Fees	1,000	Consulting Fees	475

The journal entry to record the trademark is:

Trademarks	2,000	
Cash		2,000

The annual amortization entry is:

Amortization Expense	50*	
Trademarks		50*

*($2,000 ÷ 40)

12.3   LEASEHOLD IMPROVEMENTS; ORGANIZATION COSTS; FRANCHISES

Leasehold improvements are improvements made by a tenant to rental property. These revert without charge to the landlord, upon expiration of the lease. Some consider these costs to be a *tangible* asset because they have physical substance. Others, however, feel that because they revert to the landlord, they are more of a "right" than a physical asset, and thus should be considered intangible. We will follow this latter approach.

The cost of leasehold improvements should be debited to Leasehold Improvements and amortized over the life of the lease or the life of the improvements, whichever is shorter. If the lease contains an option for renewal and it is probable that the option will be exercised, then the amortization period should be the *total* life of the lease (including the option period) or the life of the improvements, whichever is shorter.

EXAMPLE 9

Company G leases two buildings and makes improvements in each that are expected to last 20 years. The lease life of the first building is 18 years; the lease life of the second is 22 years. The first building's improvements should be amortized over 18 years; the second building's improvements should be amortized over 20 years.

Organization costs are costs incurred in creating a corporation. Examples are legal fees, underwriter's fees, and state registration fees. These costs are debited to the account Organization Costs and are subject to the 40-year maximum amortization life. Since for tax purposes companies amortize these costs over 5 years, it has become customary to do the same for financial statement purposes as well.

Some accountants feel that operating losses incurred in the start-up of a business should be capitalized (debited to an asset account) rather than expensed, because they are an unavoidable cost of starting a business. The FASB, however, disagrees with this view on the grounds that these costs have no future benefit and thus do not satisfy the definition of an asset.

EXAMPLE 10

Company H spends $5,000 in legal fees and $2,000 in state registration fees in organizing itself as a corporation. It also incurs $15,000 in operating losses during its first year of operations. The legal and underwriting fees are debited to the intangible asset Organization Costs and amortized over the 40-year maximum period (or 5 years). The operating losses, however, are immediately expensed.

The right to sell a certain product in a specific geographic area is called a *franchise*. Burger King, McDonald's, and Carvel are examples of companies that use a franchise system.

Franchises are acquired by making an initial lump-sum payment to the franchisor for the right to sell the product and use the product name. This cost is debited to the intangible asset Franchises and then gradually amortized. If the franchise life is unlimited, the 40-year maximum rule applies; if it is limited, the amortization period is the life of the franchise. If, in addition to the initial lump-sum fee, an annual fee is also required, this fee is immediately expensed.

EXAMPLE 11

Company I purchases a franchise which gives it the exclusive right to sell Delicious Ice Cream in Monsey, New York, for 10 years. There is an initial lump-sum fee of $20,000 and an annual fee of $1,000. The entries are:

	Franchise	20,000	
	Cash		20,000
Annually:	Amortization Expense	2,000*	
	Franchise		2,000*
	*($20,000 ÷ 10)		
Annually:	Franchise Expense	1,000	
	Cash		1,000

12.4 GOODWILL

Suppose there is a very successful grocery store in your neighborhood with tangible assets (groceries, land, etc.) that have market values of $100,000 and liabilities of $20,000, thus having a net market value of $80,000. This store has a huge annual sales volume because of its strategic location, good salespeople, excellent reputation, and superior management.

Suppose you were to walk by one day and offer to buy the store for the $80,000 market value. You would take the assets, agree to pay the liabilities, and the store would become yours. Do you think the owners would agree to sell you the store for this price? The answer is: definitely not!

Why not? Because this store is not a mere collection of assets and liabilities—it is much more than that. It is a successful business; it is a "machine" that produces huge annual amounts of net income; it is more than the sum of its individual asset parts. And it takes a great deal of time and effort to create a successful store like this one. Thus the price you pay must cover not only the physical assets (minus the liabilities); it must also include something extra for the intangible factor—the successful, established business. This factor is called *goodwill*.

Therefore, if you and the seller eventually agree on a price of, say, $110,000, then $80,000 of this ($100,000 − $20,000) is being paid for the *tangible* assets (minus liabilities), while the remaining $30,000 is being paid for the *intangible* asset, goodwill. Thus goodwill is defined in the following way:

$$\text{Goodwill} = \text{price paid} - \text{FMV of Net Assets}$$

where FMV of net assets is the fair market value of the assets minus liabilities.

It should be noted that it is the *fair market value* of the net assets that we are concerned with, not the *book value*. Book values are often outdated and undervalued, and therefore irrelevant in negotiating the purchase price.

EXAMPLE 12

Company J purchases the net assets of Company K, whose book values and fair market values are as follows:

	FMV	Book Value
Accounts Receivable (net)	$ 8,000*	$10,000
Merchandise Inventory	30,000	20,000
Building	90,000	80,000
Bonds Payable	(30,000)	(30,000)
Net Assets	$98,000	$80,000

*Management feels the book value of $10,000 should be reduced by $2,000 to reflect estimated bad debts.

As a result of negotiations, Companies J and K agree on a purchase price of $120,000. Since the FMV of the net assets is $98,000, the difference of $22,000 represents goodwill. Therefore, Company J makes the following journal entry to record the purchase:

Accounts Receivable	8,000	
Merchandise Inventory	30,000	
Building	90,000	
Goodwill	22,000	
Bonds Payable		30,000
Cash		120,000

Notice that book values are ignored in the entry and in the computation of goodwill.

Goodwill, like other intangible assets, should be amortized over its estimated life by a debit to Amortization Expense and a credit to Goodwill (or Accumulated Amortization). Since the life is indefinite, the 40-year maximum rule applies, and the straight-line method is usually used.

Occasionally a company may be sold for *less* than the FMV of its net assets, resulting in *negative* goodwill (also called "badwill"). This type of situation is discussed in *Advanced Accounting* of this series.

Goodwill may be recorded *only if a purchase takes place*, because at that time we have an *objective* assessment of its value—the negotiated, arms'-length purchase price. It is not permissible to record goodwill in the absence of a purchase, merely because one "feels" that goodwill exists.

EXAMPLE 13

The controller of Company L wakes up one morning and decides that the company is worth $150,000, which is $40,000 more than the $110,000 FMV of the net assets. She wishes to make an entry debiting Goodwill and crediting Capital for $40,000. This is a violation of GAAP.

We have seen that when a buyer and a seller negotiate a purchase price, the amount paid over and above the FMV of the net assets is for goodwill. But what factors are taken into consideration in arriving at the purchase price? Is the price solely a function of the parties' respective negotiating abilities? The answer is no.

A commonly used approach is to project the company's future average annual earnings (based on recent earnings of approximately 5 years), compare these earnings to those of other companies in the same industry, and then take the present value of the excess. The procedure is summarized as follows:

1. Determine the company's average annual earnings for the past 5 years or so. Make sure to remove any extraordinary or unusual gains or losses, since these are not expected to recur.

2. Determine the FMV of the company's net assets.

3. Multiply this value by the normal rate of return for the industry.

4. Compare the result of step 1 to the result of step 3. If the amount in step 1 is greater, take the excess and discount it either indefinitely or over a specific number of periods. The result is the goodwill.

Let's look at an example.

EXAMPLE 14

The net assets of Company M have a fair market value and book value of $70,000 and $50,000, respectively. During the past 5 years, *total* earnings of Company M were $200,000, but these included an extraordinary gain of $30,000 and an extraordinary loss of $10,000. These must be removed, resulting in total earnings of $180,000 ($200,000 − $30,000 + $10,000). Thus the average earnings over 5 years are $180,000 ÷ 5 = $36,000, and these are projected for several years into the future.

EXAMPLE 15

Let's continue with the previous example and assume that the normal rate of return for the industry is 35%. Thus, on assets with a fair market value of $70,000, most companies would earn $24,500 ($70,000 × 35%; notice that *book* values are ignored). Since this company earned $36,000, there are excess earnings of $11,500.

We now take the present value of this amount over several years at a chosen interest rate. Both the number of years and the rate are determined by hard bargaining at the negotiation table.

Suppose the parties agree on a 5-year period at a rate of 10%. According to the tables in the Appendix to this book, the present value of an ordinary annuity at 10% for 5 periods is 3.791 and when multiplied by $11,500, the result is $43,597. *This is the goodwill*, and it represents the amount to be paid for Company M over and above the fair market value of the net assets. Thus the total purchase price will be $113,597 ($70,000 + $43,597).

EXAMPLE 16

In Example 15, the annuity of $11,500 may alternatively be discounted over an "indefinite" number of years rather than over a specific, limited number. Since there is no row in the present value tables for "indefinite," how is this done? The answer is: Take the annuity and divide it by the interest rate (the mathematical reasons behind this procedure are beyond the scope of our discussion). Thus $11,500 ÷ 0.10 is $115,000, and this is the goodwill.

EXAMPLE 17

The present value of $4,000 discounted indefinitely at 15% is calculated as $4,000 ÷ 0.15 = $26,667.

In some cases, the parties involved will base goodwill on *undiscounted* future excess earnings. Thus, in the previous case, if the companies, as a result of negotiation, agreed to use 5 years of *undiscounted* excess earnings, the goodwill would be $57,500 ($11,500 × 5) and the purchase price, $127,500 ($70,000 + $57,500).

12.5 RESEARCH AND DEVELOPMENT COSTS

Companies spend large amounts of money on the research and development of new products. In the past, many companies would debit an asset account for these costs on the grounds that the costs were expected to bring future economic benefits and thus fulfilled the definition of an asset. Many times, however, no product evolves and the money spent goes to waste. Therefore, the FASB ruled in 1973 that all *research and development costs* (R&D) should be expensed in the period incurred.

The FASB has defined research and development costs in the following way:

Research: planned search or critical investigation aimed at the discovery of new knowledge with the hope that such knowledge will be useful in developing a new product or service, or in bringing about a significant improvement to an existing product or service.

Development: the translation of research findings or other knowledge into a plan or design for a new product or service, or for a significant improvement to an existing product or service. It includes the conceptual formulation, design and testing of product alternatives, construction of prototypes, and operation of pilot plants. It does *not* include routine or periodic alterations to existing products, production lines, and other ongoing operations, nor does it include market research or market testing activities.

Thus, based on the previous definitions, the following are examples of R&D activities:

Laboratory research aimed at discovery of new knowledge

Searching for applications of new research findings

Nonroutine modification of a product or process design

Design, construction, and testing of prototypes and models

Design of tools, jigs, molds, and dies involving new technology

Design, construction, and operation of a pilot plant

Engineering activity required to advance the design of a product to the manufacturing stage

The following are *not* considered R&D activities:

Engineering follow-through in an early phase of commercial production

Quality control during commercial production, including routine testing

Troubleshooting during production

Routine, ongoing efforts to refine or improve an existing product

Periodic design changes to existing products

Routine design of tools, jigs, molds, and dies.

Legal work on patent registration (these are debited to the patent)

EXAMPLE 18

Company N spends money on the following activities:

1. Design of tools and jigs involving new technology
2. Routine design of tools and jigs
3. Modification of a product design (nonroutine)
4. Routine effort to refine an existing product

Activities 1 and 3 are considered R&D; activities 2 and 4 are not.

If materials, equipment, or intangibles are purchased to be used for R&D activities and they have no alternative future use, they should immediately be expensed, as discussed. However, if they do have an alternative use, even if only for future R&D activities, they should be capitalized and gradually depreciated (or amortized if intangible). The annual depreciation and amortization are classified as R&D Expense.

EXAMPLE 19

Company O purchases three machines for an R&D project. Machine A cannot be used for any other project; machine B can be used for other R&D projects, while machine C can be used for other projects not involving R&D. Machine A should be immediately expensed; machines B and C should be capitalized.

If one company does R&D activities for another under a contractual arrangement for which it is to be reimbursed, these costs should, naturally, be debited to a receivable instead of to expense.

EXAMPLE 20

Company P does R&D activities for Science Corp. and bills Science Corp. $10,000. For Company P this is a receivable, and Accounts Receivable is debited. For Science Corp. this is an expense, and R&D Expense is debited.

12.6 DEFERRED CHARGES

Deferred charges includes several intangibles such as plant rearrangement costs and organization costs.

Plant rearrangement costs are costs incurred in rearranging the layout of machinery in the factory in order to promote efficiency. Since this will yield future economic benefits, the cost is considered an asset, rather than an expense, and is thus capitalized over the future periods expected to benefit. If the number of future periods is unclear, then the 40-year maximum rule should be applied.

EXAMPLE 21

Company Q spends $5,000 on rearranging its machinery. Its entry is:

$$
\begin{array}{lcc}
\text{Rearrangement Costs} & 5,000 & \\
\qquad \text{Cash} & & 5,000 \\
\end{array}
$$

Another asset included under the deferred charges classification is long-term prepayments of insurance. The portion of the prepayment that will expire within 1 year is classified as a current asset; the remainder is a deferred charge.

EXAMPLE 22

Company R purchases a 5-year insurance policy on December 31, 19X1, for $5,000 and prepays the entire amount. On the December 31, 19X1, balance sheet, $1,000 is classified as a current asset, while the remaining $4,000 falls under the deferred charge classification.

12.7 COMPUTER SOFTWARE COSTS

According to FASB *Statement No. 86*, costs incurred in developing computer software for sale or lease to others are considered R&D (and therefore expensed) until *technological feasibility* has been established. Costs incurred subsequent to this point are capitalized.

Technological feasibility is established upon completion of a detailed program design or working model. Therefore, all costs involved in planning, designing, and coding activities that are needed to establish that the product can be produced to meet its design specifications should be expensed.

Once technological feasibility *has* been established and costs are capitalized, they need to be gradually amortized. The annual amortization should be the *greater* of straight-line amortization versus amortization calculated by applying a ratio of current revenue divided by total revenue. This latter method is called the *percentage-of-revenue approach*.

EXAMPLE 23

Company S incurs software costs beyond the point of technological feasibility in the amount of $100,000. The expected life is 5 years; therefore straight-line amortization is $20,000.

This year Company S earned $1,000,000 from sales of the software, and expects to make *total* sales of

$4,000,000. Thus, under the percentage-of-revenue approach, one-quarter is amortized ($1,000,000 ÷ $4,000,000 = $\frac{1}{4}$), yielding $25,000 ($\frac{1}{4} \times$ $100,000). Since this is more than the straight-line result, this is the amount we choose.

If the net realizable value of capitalized software costs falls below its unamortized cost, the software should be written down.

EXAMPLE 24

Company T has computer software costs of $100,000 which are being amortized over 5 years. Two years have gone by; thus the unamortized cost is $60,000. Because of rapid changes in the market, this software can now be sold for only $45,000. It therefore needs to be written down by $15,000.

Summary

1. *Intangible assets* are assets that have no physical substance *and* carry a high degree of uncertainty regarding their future economic benefits. Examples include patents, copyrights, trademarks, leasehold improvements, organization costs, franchises, and goodwill.

2. Intangibles are recorded at purchase price plus any other fees incurred for their acquisition. These include brokers' fees, legal fees, and registration fees.

3. The wearing-down of intangible assets is referred to as *amortization*. The custom is to use the straight-line method and a *maximum* life of 40 years.

4. The cost of a *patent* should be debited to the Patents account and amortized over the legal life of 17 years, or its useful life if that is less.

5. Costs incurred in *successfully* defending a patent against legal challenges should be debited to the Patents account and amortized over the remaining life of the patent. *Unsuccessful* costs of defending a patent should be expensed, and the original patent cost should be immediately written down to zero, since the patent no longer provides any legal protection.

6. *Copyrights* provide protection for the life of the author plus 50 years. However, the maximum amortization period is limited to 40 years, as mentioned earlier. Similarly, while *trademarks* and *tradenames* may be renewed indefinitely, they are also subject to the 40-year maximum rule.

7. *Leasehold improvements* are improvements made by a tenant to rental property which revert to the landlord upon expiration of the lease. Their cost should be debited to the Leasehold Improvements account and amortized over the life of the improvements, or the life of the lease, whichever is shorter. If the lease contains a renewal option and it is probable that the option will be exercised, then the amortization period should extend over the total life of the lease (including the renewal period) or the life of the improvements, whichever is shorter.

8. *Organization costs* are costs incurred in creating a corporation, such as legal fees, underwriter's fees, and state registration fees. These costs are debited to the Organization Costs account and are subject to the 40-year rule. The custom, however, is to amortize them over 5 years.

9. The FASB has ruled that operating losses incurred in the start-up of a business should be immediately expensed, since they bring no future benefits.

10. Initial lump-sum payments paid for a *franchise* are capitalized and then gradually amortized over the franchise life. If the franchise life is unlimited, the 40-year rule applies.

11. If, in addition to the initial fee, an annual franchise fee is also required, this fee should be immediately expensed.

12. *Goodwill* is measured by the excess of the price paid for a business over and above the fair market value of the net assets (assets minus liabilities). The book values of the net assets are ignored in all computations.

13. Goodwill, like other intangible assets, is gradually amortized over time, with a maximum life of 40 years. The straight-line method is usually the method selected.

14. For all intangible assets, the amortization entry consists of a debit to Amortization Expense and a credit to Accumulated Amortization. Some credit the asset account directly.

15. The procedure for estimating the amount to be paid for goodwill involves the following steps:

    (*a*) Determine the company's average annual earnings for the past 5 years or so. Make sure to remove any extraordinary or unusual gains or losses, since these are not expected to recur.

    (*b*) Determine the fair market value of the company's net assets.

    (*c*) Multiply this value by the normal rate of return for the industry.

    (*d*) Compare the result of step 1 to the result of step 3. If the result of step 1 is greater, take the excess and discount it either indefinitely, or over a specific number of periods. The result is the goodwill.

16. To determine the present value of an annuity at a given rate *i* over an "indefinite" number of periods, simply divide the annuity by *i*.

17. The FASB has ruled that *research and development* (R&D) costs should be expensed immediately as incurred.

18. Broadly speaking, costs incurred in the search for knowledge or, in the translation of knowledge into a plan or design for a new product, are considered R&D and expensed. Costs incurred after the product has reached the commercial production stage are not considered R&D and are capitalized.

19. Materials or equipment purchased for R&D activities that have alternative future use should be capitalized. These alternative uses may even be future R&D projects.

20. R&D activities done for other companies under contractual arrangements requiring reimbursement should be debited to Accounts Receivable, not expensed.

21. *Deferred charges* include organization costs, plant rearrangement costs, and long-term prepayments of insurance. *Plant rearrangement costs* are incurred in rearranging the factory layout to promote factory efficiency. These should be capitalized and gradually amortized over the maximum 40 year life.

22. *Long-term prepayments of insurance* are presented on the balance sheet in two parts: The portion that will expire over the next year is a current asset; the remainder is a deferred charge.

23. Costs incurred in developing computer software for sale or lease are expensed if technological feasibility has not yet been established. Subsequent costs incurred are capitalized and gradually amortized using either the straight-line method or the percentage-of-revenue method, whichever provides the larger amortization.

24. Capitalized computer software costs should be written down to net realizable value if this is below unamortized costs.

Rapid Review

1. Assets that have no physical substance and carry a high degree of uncertainty regarding future benefits are called _____.

2. The wearing-down process for these assets is called _____.

3. The maximum period over which intangible assets may be kept on the books is _____.

4. Costs incurred in successfully defending a patent are debited to _____.

5. _____ provide protection for a creative work.

6. Improvements made to rented property are referred to as _____.

7. These improvements should be amortized over the life of the _____ or _____, whichever is _____.

8. Costs incurred in creating a corporation are called _____.

9. Operating losses incurred in the start-up of a business should immediately be _____.

10. The right to sell a certain product in a specific geographic area is called a _____.

11. The assets of a business minus the liabilities are called _____.

12. Goodwill is measured by the excess of the _____ over and above the _____.

13. The present value of a $3,000 annuity discounted "indefinitely" at 14% is _____.

14. Research and development costs should be immediately _____.

15. If equipment purchased for R&D activities has alternative future uses, it should be _____.

16. R&D activities done for others under contractual arrangements should be debited to _____.

17. Plant rearrangement costs are an example of a _____.

18. Long-term insurance prepayments represent both a _____ and a _____.

19. Computer software development costs should be expensed until the point of _____ has been established.

20. The two methods of amortizing computer software costs are the _____ method and the _____ method.

21. The method to be chosen is the one providing the _____ amount.

Answers: **1.** intangibles **2.** amortization **3.** 40 years **4.** Patents **5.** Copyrights **6.** leasehold improvements **7.** improvements; lease; shorter **8.** organization costs **9.** expensed **10.** franchise **11.** net assets **12.** purchase price; fair market value **13.** $21,429 (rounded) **14.** expensed **15.** capitalized **16.** Accounts Receivable **17.** deferred charge **18.** current asset; deferred charge **19.** technological feasibility **20.** straight-line; percentage-of-revenue **21.** greater

Solved Problems

Patents; Copyrights; Trademarks and Tradenames

12.1 Company A purchases a patent from Brown Corp. for a price of $10,000 and incurs legal fees and consulting fees related to the purchase in the amounts of $4,000 and $6,000, respectively. The patent's remaining legal life is 15 years, but because of market competition, its useful life is estimated to be only 10 years.

(*a*) Prepare the entry for the patent acquisition.

(*b*) Prepare the annual amortization entry.

SOLUTION

(*a*)	Patents	20,000	
	Cash		20,000

(*b*)	Amortization Expense	2,000	
	Accumulated Amortization (or Patents)		2,000 [Section 12.2]

12.2 Company B purchases a patent for $50,000 with a remaining life of 17 years. One year after the purchase, it incurs a $10,000 legal fee in *successfully* defending the patent in court. Prepare the necessary entries for:

(*a*) The acquisition of the patent

(*b*) The amortization during the first year

(*c*) The $10,000 legal fee

(*d*) The amortization for years 2 through 17

SOLUTION

(a)   Patents   50,000
                              Cash   50,000

(b)   Amortization Expense   2,941*
                              Accumulated Amortization   2,941*
                         *($50,000 ÷ 17, rounded)

(c)   Patents   10,000
                              Cash   10,000

(d)   Amortization Expense   3,566*
                              Accumulated Amortization   3,566*
                         *[$2,941 + ($10,000 ÷ 16)]   [Section 12.2]

12.3   Assume the same information as in Problem 12.2, except that the patent defense is unsuccessful. Prepare the entries for parts (c) and (d).

SOLUTION

(c)   Legal Fee Expense   10,000
                              Cash   10,000

(d)   Since the patent is now worthless, the entire remaining book value of $47,059 ($50,000 − $2,941) should be amortized, as follows:

                       Amortization Expense   47,059
                              Accumulated Amortization   47,059   [Section 12.2]

12.4   Company C purchases a copyright for $30,000 and incurs legal fees of $5,000 related to the purchase. What is the amount of the annual amortization? Assume that the maximum period is used.

SOLUTION

       $875   ($35,000 ÷ 40 years).   [Section 12.2]

Leasehold Improvements; Organization Costs; Franchises

12.5   Company D enters into a 25-year lease agreement, with an option to renew for an additional 5 years. Immediately upon signing the lease, Company D improves the leased property by spending $5,000 on several major repairs. The improvements are expected to last 28 years.

(a)   Prepare the entry for the leasehold improvements.

(b)   Determine the annual amortization if it is probable that the renewal option will be exercised.

(c)   Determine the annual amortization if renewal is *not* probable.

SOLUTION

(a)   Leasehold Improvements   5,000
                                      Cash   5,000

(b) $5,000 ÷ 28 years = $178.57
(c) $5,000 ÷ 25 years = $200   [Section 12.3]

12.6   Company D incurs $7,000 in underwriter and state registration fees while being organized as a corporation. In addition, it incurs $20,000 in losses during its first year of business.

(a)   How are the organization fees recorded?

(b)   What should the annual amortization amount be?

(c)   How are the $20,000 losses treated?

SOLUTION

(a)   Debited to the asset account, Organization Costs.

(b)   If the maximum 40-year period is used, the amortization is $175 ($7,000 ÷ 40); if the 5-year customary period is used, it is $1,400 ($7,000 ÷ 5).

(c)   They are immediately expensed.   [Section 12.3]

12.7   Company E pays a franchise fee of $90,000 to enable it to sell Good Product for the next 30 years. In addition, it is required to pay an annual fee of $1,000.

(a)   Prepare an entry for the initial $90,000 franchise fee and the annual amortization.

(b)   Prepare an entry for the $1,000 annual fee.

SOLUTION

(a)   Franchise   90,000
                                      Cash   90,000
                             Amortization Expense   3,000*
                                      Accumulated Amortization   3,000*
                                  *($90,000 ÷ 30)

(b)   Franchise Expense   1,000
                                      Cash   1,000   [Section 12.3]

Goodwill

12.8   Company F has assets and liabilities with fair market values of $50,000 and $10,000, respectively, and it is purchased for $90,000.

(a)   What is the value of Company F's net assets?

(b)   How much goodwill is implied in the purchase price?

(c)   Prepare an entry for the purchase.

(d)   Prepare the annual amortization entry (assume that the life of the goodwill is unknown).

SOLUTION

(a) $40,000 ($50,000 − $10,000)

(b) $50,000 ($90,000 − $40,000)

(c)	Assets	50,000	
	Goodwill	50,000	
	Liabilities		10,000
	Cash		90,000

(d)	Amortization Expense	1,250*	
	Accumulated Amortization		1,250*
	*($50,000 ÷ 40 years)		[Section 12.4]

12.9 Company G has the following assets and liabilities:

	Book Value	Fair Market Value
Accounts Receivable	$ 50,000	$ 40,000
Machinery	10,000	30,000
Building	55,000	85,000
Bonds Payable	(12,000)	(12,000)

(a) Before calculations for goodwill are made, what value should a purchaser assign to Company G?

(b) Assume that a purchaser pays $175,000. How much is the goodwill, if any?

(c) What entry should the purchaser make if the price is $175,000?

SOLUTION

(a) $143,000 (fair market value of assets − fair market value of liabilities)

(b) $32,000 ($175,000 − $143,000)

(c)	Accounts Receivable	40,000		
	Machinery	30,000		
	Building	85,000		
	Goodwill	32,000		
	Bonds Payable		12,000	
	Cash		175,000	[Section 12.4]

12.10 During the past 5 years, Company G had *total* earnings of $100,000 which included an extraordinary gain of $10,000 and an extraordinary loss of $4,000. What is Company G's *average* annual earnings for these 5 years?

SOLUTION

($100,000 − $10,000 + $4,000) ÷ 5 years = $18,800   [Section 12.4]

12.11 Company H averaged $60,000 in annual earnings over the past 5 years. The fair market value of its net assets has been, on average, $600,000; the book value, $480,000. The normal rate of return for this industry is 8%.

(a)   How much in excess earnings has Company H been earning annually compared to others in the same industry?

(b)   If the excess is to be discounted at 10% for an "indefinite" time period, how much will goodwill be?

(c)   If the excess is to be discounted for 7 years at 10%, find the goodwill.

(d)   If the excess earnings are expected to last for the next 7 years but are *not* to be discounted, find the goodwill.

SOLUTION

(a)

Industry Earnings ($600,000 × 8%):	$48,000
Company H Earnings:	60,000
Excess Company H Earnings:	$12,000

(b) $12,000 ÷ 0.10 = $120,000

(c)   4.868 × $12,000 = $58,416

(d) $12,000 × 7 = $84,000   [Section 12.4]

12.12 Find the present value of the following:

(a) $5,000 at 10%, discounted "indefinitely"

(b) $8,000 at 14%, discounted "indefinitely"

(c) $20,000 at 16%, discounted "indefinitely"

SOLUTION

(a) $5,000 ÷ 0.10 = $50,000

(b) $8,000 ÷ 0.14 = $57,143 (rounded)

(c) $20,000 ÷ 0.16 = $125,000   [Section 12.4]

12.13 Company I has the following assets and liabilities on December 31, 19X8:

	Fair Market Value	Book Value
Machinery	$ 20,000	$ 30,000
Building	70,000	68,000
Accounts Receivable	10,000	8,000
Accounts Payable	(15,000)	(15,000)

During the past 5 years, Company I earned a *total* net income of $100,000. This included an extraordinary gain of $7,000 and an extraordinary loss of $9,000. The industry in which Company I operates has an average annual rate of return on its assets of 18%.

(a)   What is the value of Company I before calculating goodwill?

(b)   What net earnings has Company I averaged over 5 years?

(c)   What *excess* annual net earnings has Company I averaged compared to the rest of the industry?

SOLUTION

(a) $85,000 ($20,000 + $70,000 + $10,000 − $15,000)

(b) $20,400 ($100,000 − $7,000 + $9,000) ÷ 5 years

(c)

Company I Earnings	$20,400
Industry Earnings ($85,000 × 0.18)	15,300
Company I Excess Earnings	$ 5,100

[Section 12.4]

12.14 Let's continue with the previous problem.

(a) If excess annual earnings are to be discounted "indefinitely" at 15%, determine the goodwill and purchase price, and prepare a journal entry for the purchase.

(b) If the excess annual earnings are to be discounted for 4 years at 16%, determine the goodwill and purchase price.

SOLUTION

(a) Goodwill = $5,100 ÷ 0.15
         = $34,000
Purchase price = $85,000 FMV + $34,000 goodwill
         = $119,000

Journal entry:

Machinery	20,000	
Building	70,000	
Accounts Receivable	10,000	
Goodwill	34,000	
Accounts Payable		15,000
Cash		119,000

(b) Goodwill = $5,100 × 2.798
         = $14,270   (rounded)
Purchase price = $85,000 + $14,270
         = $99,270

[Section 12.4]

Research and Development Costs

12.15 Company J incurs the following costs:

(a) Construction of a building to be used for both R&D projects and other projects

(b) Purchase of a machine to be used exclusively for the creation of a prototype for a new product

(c) Salaries of researchers working to apply research findings to develop a new surgical procedure

(d) Same as the previous case, except that the salaries are billable to Science Corp.

(e) Legal fees to obtain a patent on a new heart machine

(f) Market research fees to determine selling price of a new product

(g) Costs of testing a prototype

(h) Engineering costs incurred to advance a prototype to the full production stage

(i) Cost of routine design of tools and jigs

Determine for each of the above if it is to be capitalized or expensed.

SOLUTION

(a)	Capitalize	(f)	Expense (selling expense)
(b)	Expense (R&D)	(g)	Expense (R&D)
(c)	Expense (R&D)	(h)	Expense (R&D)
(d)	Capitalize (A/R)	(i)	Capitalize
(e)	Capitalize (Patents)		

[Section 12.5]

12.16 Company K purchases a building for $100,000 which is to be used to create a prototype for a new type of hydrogen bomb. Once the prototype is completed, the building will have to be burned down because of high radiation levels. During the period of bomb construction, the salaries of Company K's scientists are billable to the U.S. government on a cost-plus-profit basis. The total billed this period was $5,000.

Prepare entries for the above transactions.

SOLUTION

R&D Expense	100,000	
Cash		100,000

Accounts Receivable	5,000		
Cash		5,000	[Section 12.5]

Deferred Charges

12.17 Company L spends $120,000 on rearranging its factory machinery. Prepare an entry for this transaction and for the annual amortization. Assume that the life of the future benefits to be obtained from the rearrangement is unknown.

SOLUTION

Plant Rearrangement Costs	120,000	
Cash		120,000

Amortization Expense	3,000*		
Accumulated Amortization		3,000*	[Section 12.6]
*($120,000 ÷ 40)			

12.18 On July 1, 19X1, Company M purchases a 4-year life insurance policy for which it prepays the total premium of $4,000. Show how this policy would be presented on the December 31, 19X1, balance sheet.

SOLUTION

Of this policy, $500 has expired [($4,000/4) × 1/2]; $3,500 remains.

Current Assets:		
Prepaid Insurance:	$1,000*	
Deferred Charges:		
Long-Term Prepaid Insurance:	$2,500	[Section 12.6]

*The portion that will expire over the next year.

Computer Software Costs

12.19 Company N spends $5,000 in determining the technological feasibility of certain computer software. After the point of technological feasibility has been established, it spends another $20,000 in completing the software's production. Prepare journal entries for each of these transactions.

SOLUTION

R&D Expense	5,000	
Cash		5,000

Computer Software	20,000		
Cash		20,000	[Section 12.7]

12.20 Company O has capitalized $100,000 of computer software costs incurred after the establishment of technological feasibility. The software is expected to last 5 years and bring in total revenue of $500,000; this year's revenue portion is expected to be $200,000. Determine the amortization for this year.

SOLUTION

Straight-Line Amortization: $100,000 \div 5$ years $= \$20,000$

Percentage-of-Revenue Amortization: $\dfrac{\$200,000}{\$500,000} \times 100,000 = \$40,000$

We choose the larger figure, $40,000.   [Section 12.7]

12.21 Company P has unamortized computer software costs of $25,000.

   (*a*)   If the software's net realizable value is $28,000, prepare a journal entry, if needed.

   (*b*)   If the net realizable value is $21,000, prepare a journal entry, if needed.

SOLUTION

(*a*)   No entry needed

(*b*)	Amortization Expense	4,000	
	Accumulated Amortization		4,000 [Section 12.7]

Supplementary Problems

Patents; Copyrights; Trademarks and Tradenames

12.22 Company Q purchases a patent from Blue Corp. for $25,000 and incurs legal fees of $1,000 related to the purchase. The patent's remaining legal life is $16\frac{1}{2}$ years, but its useful life is estimated to be only 10 years.

     In addition to the patent, Company Q also purchases a copyright for $80,000 and spends $2,000 on legal fees.

   (*a*)   Prepare the entry for the acquisition of the patent and the copyright.

   (*b*)   Prepare the annual amortization entry for each.

12.23 Company R purchases a patent for $30,000 with a remaining life of 15 years. Two years after the purchase, the patent is challenged in court and Company R has to pay $5,000 in legal fees to defend the patent.

    (a) Prepare the entry for the acquisition of the patent and the annual amortization during the first 2 years.

    (b) Assume that the patent defense is successful. Prepare the entry for the legal costs incurred and for the annual amortization for years 3 through 15.

12.24 Assume the same information as in Problem 12.23, except that the patent defense is unsuccessful. Prepare the entry for the legal costs and the annual amortization for years 3 through 15.

Leasehold Improvements

12.25 Company S enters into a 20-year lease agreement with a renewal option for 7 years. Immediately after the lease is signed, Company S spends $10,000 on leasehold improvements. These improvements are expected to last 25 years.

    (a) Prepare the entry for the leasehold improvements.

    (b) Determine the annual amortization if it is probable that the renewal option will be exercised.

    (c) If the renewal is *not* probable, determine the annual amortization.

Goodwill

12.26 Company T has assets and liabilities with fair market values of $20,000 and $4,000, respectively; the respective book values are $18,000 and $3,000. Diversified Corp. purchases Company T for $25,000.

    (a) Before calculating goodwill, what value did Diversified assign to Company T?

    (b) How much did Diversified pay for goodwill?

    (c) Prepare entries for the purchase and the annual amortization of goodwill. Assume that the life of the goodwill is estimated at 9 years.

12.27 Company V has the following assets and liabilities:

	Book Value	Fair Market Value
Merchandise	$10,000	$ 9,000
Machinery	20,000	25,000
Land	40,000	60,000
Accounts Payable	5,000	5,000

    (a) Before calculating goodwill, what value should a purchaser assign to Company V?

    (b) If a purchaser pays $100,000 for Company V, prepare the entry for the purchase.

12.28 Company W averaged $80,000 in annual earnings during the past 5 years. The fair market value of its net assets is $500,000; the book value is $450,000. The normal rate of return for this particular industry is 10%.

    (a) How much in excess earnings has Company W been earning annually compared to others in the same industry?

    (b) If the excess is to be discounted "indefinitely" at 12%, what will goodwill be?

    (c) If the excess is to be discounted for 5 years at 12%, what will goodwill be?

12.29 Find the present value of the following:

    (a) $10,000 discounted at 8%, "indefinitely"

    (b) $30,000 discounted at 10%, "indefinitely"

12.30 Company X has the following assets and liabilities:

	Fair Market Value	Book Value
Accounts Receivable	$ 12,000	$ 9,000
Building	50,000	45,000
Land	20,000	35,000
Accounts Payable	(5,000)	(5,000)
Bond Payable	(10,000)	(8,000)

During the past 5 years, Company X earned a total net income of $120,000. This included extraordinary gains of $10,000 and extraordinary losses of $7,000. The industry in which Company X operates has an average annual return on assets of 19%.

(*a*)   What net income has Company X averaged over 5 years?

(*b*)   How much excess annual net income has Company X averaged compared to the rest of the industry?

12.31 Let's continue with the previous problem.

(*a*)   If excess annual net income is to be discounted "indefinitely" at 19%, determine the goodwill and purchase price, and prepare a journal entry for the purchase.

(*b*)   If excess annual net income is to be discounted at 19% for 5 years, determine the goodwill and the purchase price.

Computer Software

12.32 Company Y produces computer software, and spends $3,000 on a particular software item to establish its technological feasibility. After this point, it spends another $8,000 to complete the production and manufacture of the software. Prepare journal entries for both the $3,000 and the $8,000.

12.33 Company Z has capitalized $40,000 of software costs incurred after establishing technological feasibility. The software is expected to last 5 years and bring in *total* revenues of $60,000; this year's revenue portion is expected to be $10,000. Determine the amortization for this year.

Chapter 13

Current Liabilities

13.1 INTRODUCTION

The FASB has defined liabilities as probable future sacrifices of economic benefits arising from present obligations, to transfer assets to other entities in the future, as a result of past transactions. In other words, a *liability* is a *present obligation* to transfer assets in the future, and the transaction that created this obligation *has already occurred*.

The FASB has defined *current liabilities* as obligations to be paid either out of current assets or the creation of other current liabilities, and that will be paid within 1 year *or* the operating cycle, whichever is longer (the terms *current assets* and *operating cycle* were defined in Chapter 3). This chapter will discuss numerous examples of current liabilities.

We saw in previous chapters that liabilities are measured and reported at their *present value*, not at their face value. This practice, however, is not followed for *current* liabilities, since the short time period involved makes the face value not significantly different from the present value.

EXAMPLE 1

Blue Company has an operating cycle of 14 months and a liability payable in 13 months. Green Company has an operating cycle of 9 months and a liability payable in 11 months. For both Blue and Green, the liability is considered current, since it is payable within the longer of the operating cycle or 1 year.

EXAMPLE 2

Gold Corporation has a liability that must be paid in 8 months, and will be paid out of a sinking fund. Since a sinking fund is not considered a current asset, the liability is not considered current.

13.2 ACCOUNTS PAYABLE AND NOTES PAYABLE

A typical example of a current liability is accounts payable, also known as trade accounts payable. These are *oral* promises to pay others for goods and services and usually do not bear interest.

In contrast, notes payable are *written* promises to pay others and they usually *are* interest-bearing. Thus an entry must be paid each period to recognize the related interest expense.

On bank loans, the bank will often deduct the interest in advance, rather than requiring annual, physical interest payments. This is called *discounting* a note payable. Let's look at an example.

EXAMPLE 3

On October 1, 19X1, Copper Corporation borrows $10,000 from the bank and signs a note promising to pay in 1 year. The bank discounts the note at 10%. It thus "chops off" $1,000 and gives Copper only $9,000. The entry on October 1 is:

Cash	9,000	
Discount on Note	1,000	
Notes Payable		10,000

Copper does not debit interest expense at this time, because interest is generated with the passage of time and no time has yet passed. Instead, it debits the discount account, which is a contra to Notes Payable. At this point, Copper owes only $9,000. As time passes, however, interest will start to pile up and gradually "puff up" the payable to the full $10,000, which will be paid at maturity.

On December 31, 19X1, an entry must be made to recognize 3-months of accrued interest. To make things simple, let's use straight-line amortization. Thus the monthly amortization is $83.33 ($1,000 ÷ 12) and the entry is:

Interest Expense	250*	
Discount on Note		250*
*($83.33 × 3)		

The 19X1 income statement reports interest expense of $250; the balance sheet shows a current liability, as follows:

Notes Payable	$10,000
Less Discount ($1,000 − $250)	(750)
Net Payable	$ 9,250

The accrued interest has "puffed up" the balance from the original $9,000 to $9,250.

The maturing portion of long-term debt is considered a current liability. Thus, if a $10,000 loan is payable in installments of $1,000 for each of the next 10 years, this year's $1,000 installment is considered current, while the remaining $9,000 is noncurrent.

Companies occasionally "refinance" their short-term liabilities. This means that they "roll over" the liability from short-term status to long-term status, by getting permission from the creditor to extend the payment deadline. In this case, the liability should, naturally, be reclassified on the balance sheet from current to long-term status.

But what happens if the company merely *intends* to refinance, but has not yet done so? Should reclassification be required? The accounting profession has stated that the following *two* conditions need to be met:

1. The company *intends* to refinance; and
2. The company has the *ability* to refinance.

Financing "ability" may be demonstrated by *either*:

(a) Entering into a financing agreement that permits the company to refinance if it so decides; or

(b) Actually refinancing the liability after the balance sheet date, but before the balance sheet is issued.

EXAMPLE 4

White Corporation intends to refinance a current liability and enters into a finance agreement on December 28, 19X1, permitting it to refinance at any time during the next 10 months. By the time it issues its balance sheet on March 1, 19X2, it has *not yet* done so.

Black Corporation intends to refinance, but has not signed any agreement by December 31, 19X1. However, before it issues its statements on March 1, 19X2, it actually goes ahead and does the refinancing.

Both White and Black Corporations would reclassify their liabilities from current to long-term, since both intent and ability to refinance were present.

13.3 DIVIDENDS PAYABLE, RETURNABLE DEPOSITS, AND SALES TAXES

Dividends payable in cash become a liability to the corporation when declared by the board of directors and are considered current since they usually are paid within the year (often within 3 months). Dividends payable in a corporation's own stock (stock dividends), however, are not even considered to be a liability, because they are revocable by the board of directors. They should, instead, be classified as part of stockholders' equity.

Accumulated but *undeclared* dividends on cumulative preferred stock ("dividends in arrears") are *not* a liability, since the corporation has no obligation to pay them until a formal declaration is made by the board of directors. Nevertheless, they should be disclosed in the footnotes.

Deposits received from customers which must be returned are a liability to the company. The status of this liability—whether current or long-term—depends on the expected return date.

EXAMPLE 5

On June 15, 19X1, Bell Telephone receives a $50 deposit from a customer for the installation of a telephone. The customer is entitled to a return of the deposit on June 15, 19X2, if the telephone is returned undamaged. The entry by Bell Telephone on June 15, 19X1, is:

Cash	50	
Liability on Customer Deposit		50

This liability will be shown as *current* on the December 31, 19X1, balance sheet, since it must be paid within 12 months.

Companies that issue gift certificates for cash, which are redeemable in services or merchandise, should debit Cash and credit the liability, Unearned Revenue. Since the redemptions usually take place within 1 year or the operating cycle, the liability is current.

Upon redemption, the liability account is debited and a revenue account is credited.

In many states and cities, businesses are required to charge sales tax on retail sales. The business collects the tax from the customer and must then remit the money to the government. Since the remittance usually takes place within 30 to 60 days, the liability to the government is a current one.

EXAMPLE 6

Green Corp. makes sales of $100, on which it collects 8% sales tax. The entry is:

Cash	108	
Sales		100
Sales Tax Payable		8

Upon remittance of the $8 to the government, Green's entry is:

Sales Tax Payable	8	
Cash		8

EXAMPLE 7

Brown Corp. credits the sales account for the *entire* amount received from the customer—including the sales tax. During 19X1, the credits to the sales account amounted to a total of $1,000. At year-end, Brown must determine how much sales tax it owes. Assume a sales tax rate of 5%.

To solve this problem, let x = sales. Thus,

$$x + 0.05x = \$1,000 \quad \text{(sales + tax = total)}$$
$$1.05x = \$1,000$$
$$x = \$952.38$$

Since sales = $952.38, the tax must be $47.62 ($1,000 − $952.38). Brown's original entry was:

```
          Cash                1,000
                Sales                    1,000
```

The year-end adjusting entry is:

```
          Sales                        47.62
                Sales Tax Payable                  47.62
```

13.4 PAYROLL-RELATED TAXES

As we know all too well, what we earn (gross pay) is not what we take home (net pay), because federal, state, and city income taxes, plus Social Security taxes, are withheld. These are current liabilities of the employer, who must remit them to various government agencies.

Withholdings for federal, state, and city *income* taxes are based on tables; withholdings for Social Security use set rates. This tax has two components: the Federal Insurance Contribution Act (FICA) component and the Medicare component. For 1994, the FICA component used a 6.2% tax rate on gross salary, limited to a ceiling of $57,600 gross, while the Medicare component used a 1.45% rate, with no ceiling. Thus the total Social Security tax was 7.65%.

EXAMPLE 8

John Brown earned $60,000 during 19X4. His FICA tax is 6.2% of $57,600, which equals $3,571.20, while his Medicare tax, which is not subject to a ceiling, is 1.45% of $60,000, which equals $870. His total Social Security tax is thus $4,441.20.

EXAMPLE 9

Gold Corp. incurred $50,000 of gross salaries during 19X4. The federal and state income tax withholdings, based on the tables, were $15,000 and $7,000, respectively, while Social Security tax was $3,825. The entry to accrue the salaries is:

```
     Salaries Expense                    50,000
           Federal Income Tax Payable              15,000
           State Income Tax Payable                 7,000
           Social Security Tax Payable              3,825
           Salaries Payable                        24,175
```

Salaries Expense is debited at *gross*; Salaries Payable is credited at *net*; the various payables are all *current* liabilities.

Upon remittance of the various taxes to their respective government agencies, Gold makes the following entry:

```
     Federal Income Tax Payable      15,000
     State Income Tax Payable         7,000
     Social Security Tax Payable      3,825
           Cash                                    25,825
```

In addition to the above taxes, which are *withheld from the employee*, the *employer* must also pay several taxes *out of his or her own pocket*. These taxes are: Social Security, federal unemployment insurance, and state unemployment insurance, and are referred to as *payroll taxes*.

For the Social Security tax, the employer must match the withholding from the employee. Thus a total of 15.3% will be remitted to the government—7.65% withheld from the employee and another 7.65% paid by the employer.

For unemployment insurance, the rates for federal and state purposes are 0.8% and 5.4%, respectively, with a $7,000 gross salary ceiling.

EXAMPLE 10

By March 15, 19X1, Meir Fischer had earned $6,000, and his gross salary for the period March 16–March 30 is $1,500. His employer's Social Security tax will be $114.75 (7.65% × 1,500); the federal unemployment insurance is $8, while the state unemployment insurance is $54. Note that the latter computations are based on $1,000, not $1,500, because of the $7,000 ceiling.

The entry for these taxes is:

Payroll Tax Expense	176.75	
Social Security Tax Payable		114.75
Federal Unemployment Insurance Payable		8.00
State Unemployment Insurance Payable		54.00

13.5 BONUSES

Companies often give bonuses to their employees as a reward for superior performance. The entry to accrue a bonus is:

Bonus Expense	XXX	
Bonus Payable		XXX

Since bonuses are an expense, they reduce the income and also the income tax.

EXAMPLE 11

Red Corp. has the following information for 19X1:

Revenue	$30,000
Various Expenses	10,000
Bonus Expense	5,000
Tax Rate	20%

Without the bonus, Red's income before tax would have been $20,000 ($30,000 − $10,000) and its tax $4,000 ($20,000 × 20%). Because of the bonus, its income before tax is only $15,000 and its tax is $3,000 ($15,000 × 20%).

Since bonuses affect the income and the tax, they may be calculated in several different ways, as follows:

1. The bonus is a percentage of income *before* subtracting the bonus and *before* subtracting tax.
2. The bonus is a percentage of income *after* subtracting the bonus but *before* subtracting tax.
3. The bonus is a percentage of income *after* subtracting the bonus and *after* subtracting the tax.

EXAMPLE 12

Green Corp's income *before* bonus and tax is $100,000. Let's assume a bonus rate of 10% and a tax rate of 20%.

If the bonus, B, is based on income *before* the bonus and *before* tax, the bonus calculation is simple:
$$B = 0.10(\$100,000)$$
$$= \$10,000$$

If the bonus is based on income *after* the bonus but *before* tax, the calculation is:
$$B = 0.10(\$100,000 - B)$$
$$B = \$10,000 - 0.10B$$
$$1.10B = \$10,000$$
$$B = \$9,091 \quad \text{(rounded)}$$

EXAMPLE 13

Let's continue with the information in Example 12. Assume that the bonus is based on income *after* the bonus and *after* tax. In this case, we need to determine the tax in order to determine the bonus, but in order to determine the bonus, we first need to determine the tax. So how do we begin?

The answer is: We use simultaneous equations. Let T = tax and B = bonus. Then

$$B = 0.10(\$100,000 - B - T)$$
$$T = 0.20(\$100,000 - B)$$

We now substitute for T in the first equation:

$$B = 0.10[\$100,000 - B - 0.20(\$100,000 - B)]$$
$$B = 0.10(\$100,000 - B - \$20,000 + 0.20B)$$
$$B = \$10,000 - 0.10B - \$2,000 + 0.02B$$
$$B = \$8,000 - 0.08B$$
$$1.08B = \$8,000$$
$$B = \$7,407 \qquad \text{(rounded)}$$

13.6   CONTINGENT LIABILITIES—DEFINED

According to the FASB, a *contingency* is an existing situation or condition which may give rise to a future gain (gain contingency) or future loss (loss contingency). At the moment, however, it is uncertain as to whether or not the gain or loss will materialize. We will focus on loss contingencies.

The FASB has identified three degrees of uncertainty: remote, reasonably possible (stronger than remote), and probable (stronger than reasonably possible). If the contingent loss is *both probable* and *estimable*, an entry should be made debiting an expense or loss account and crediting a liability, and both the expense and the liability appear in the statements.

If the estimate is not one amount but a range of amounts, and one amount within the range appears to be a better estimate than the others, then *that* amount should be accrued. If, however, no amount within the range is a better estimate, then the lowest amount within the range is accrued and the highest is merely disclosed in the footnotes.

EXAMPLE 14

Green Corp. has a contingent liability which is probable and estimated to be within the $1,000–$4,000 range, with $2,800 the most likely outcome. Thus this is the amount to be accrued.

If, however, no one particular amount can be estimated, Green would accrue $1,000 and disclose in the footnotes the potential of $4,000.

If the contingency is *either* probable *or* estimable, but not both, then footnote disclosure, rather than accrual, is the required approach, provided that the contingency is at least reasonably possible.

13.7   CONTINGENT LIABILITIES—EXAMPLES

One example of a contingent liability is a pending lawsuit against the company. This should be recorded if probable and estimable via the following entry:

Estimated Loss on Lawsuit	XXX	
Estimated Liability on Lawsuit		XXX

A classic example of a contingent liability is estimated future warranty costs to be paid by the company to correct product defects. Since these are usually estimable and probable, they should be accrued in the period of the sale—as per the matching principle—rather than at the time of actual payment. Let's look at an example.

EXAMPLE 15

During 19X1, Black Corp. sells 100 machines and guarantees their performance for the next 3 years. Based on prior experience, Black estimates that future warranty costs will average $50 per machine and be incurred gradually over the 3-year period immediately following the sale. By December 31, 19X1, Black has already spent $2,000 on repairing defective machines. The entries are:

Warranty Expense	2,000	
Cash		2,000

Estimated Warranty Expense	3,000*	
Estimated Warranty Liability		3,000*
*[(100 machines × $50) − $2,000]		

Since the future costs are probable and estimable, they must be recognized *in their entirety* during the year of sale, rather than later.

For 19X1, Black Corp.'s income statement will show warranty expense of $5,000 ($2,000 + $3,000), while its balance sheet will report a liability of $3,000.

Sometimes a warranty is sold to the customer separately from the product. The product will usually have a 1- or 2-year automatic warranty, with an option to purchase an additional, extended warranty beyond that period. The proceeds from the sale of the warranty should be credited to Unearned Revenue, since the seller may have to perform future services under the warranty. As time passes, warranty revenue will gradually be recognized. This is illustrated in the next example.

EXAMPLE 16

Car Corp. sells a car for $15,000. The car comes with an automatic 3-year warranty. The customer purchases an additional, extended warranty for $300 to cover years 4–6. At the time of sale, Car's entries are:

Cash	15,300	
Sales		15,000
Unearned Warranty Revenue		300

Starting with year 4, Car makes the following annual entry:

Unearned Warranty Revenue	100	
Warranty Revenue		100*
*($300 ÷ 3)		

If Car pays out any money during the warranty period to cover repairs, it debits Warranty Expense and credits Cash.

Many companies offer special "deals" to their customers upon the return of boxtops or labels. These are called *premiums*. Since the future obligation is both probable and estimable, it should be accrued in the year of sale via a debit to Premium Expense and a credit to a liability. Any mailing costs incurred increases the premium expense.

EXAMPLE 17

Wonder Cereal Company offers its customers a rubber duck for 50¢ plus 10 boxtops. The ducks cost Wonder 75¢ each; thus Wonder loses 25¢ cents on each duck purchased. During 19X1, Wonder engages in the following transactions:

1. A purchase of 1,000 ducks at 75¢ each
2. Sales of 8,000 boxes of cereal
3. Receipt of 3,000 boxtops from customers

Wonder estimates that 70% of the boxtops will be returned (8,000 × 0.70 = 5,600 boxtops). The entries for 19X1 are:

For the Duck Purchases:

Ducks	750*	
Cash		750*

*(1,000 × $0.75)

For the Sale of Cereal:

Cash	XXX	
Sales		XXX

For the Receipt of the Boxtops:

Cash	150*	
Premium Expense	75	
Ducks		225[†]

*3,000 boxtops ÷ 10 = 300 ducks; 300 ducks × $0.50 = $150.
[†]300 ducks × $0.75 = $225.

The ducks cost $225, while the cash received was only $150. Thus the expense is $75. To record the contingent liability on December 31, the entry is:

Premium Expense	65	
Estimated Premium Liability		65*
*Estimated Return of Boxtops (8,000 × $0.70)		5,600
Boxtops Already Returned		−3,000
Future Expected Boxtops		2,600
Divide by 10		÷10
Future Ducks to Be Mailed		260
Expense per Duck ($0.75 − $0.50)		×$0.25
Total Expense		$65

The 19X1 balance sheet will show a $65 liability; the 19X1 income statement will show premium expense of $140 ($75 + $65).

Summary

1. A *liability* is a present obligation to transfer assets or services in the future as a result of past transactions.

2. *Current liabilities* are liabilities that will be paid out of current assets or the creation of other current liabilities, and will be paid within 1 year or the operating cycle, whichever is longer.

3. Current liabilities are measured and reported at face value rather than present value.

4. *Discounting* a note payable refers to the standard bank practice of deducting the interest from the original loan proceeds, rather than requiring annual, physical interest payments.

5. The process of changing a liability from short-term to long-term by having the creditor extend the payment date is referred to as *refinancing*. If this occurs, the liability should be reclassified on the balance sheet to long-term status.

6. If refinancing has not yet actually taken place but the company has *both* the *ability* and the *intent* to do so, reclassification is required.

7. Financing ability is demonstrated by either:

   (a) Entering into a finance agreement permitting the company to refinance if it so desires; or

   (b) Actually refinancing the liability after the balance sheet date, but before the balance sheet is issued.

8. Cash dividends payable are a current liability when declared; stock dividends payable are not a liability at all, but an element of stockholders' equity.

9. Dividends in arrears on cumulative preferred stock are not a liability until declared. Nevertheless, they should be disclosed in the footnotes.

10. Upon receipt of cash for the issuance of gift certificates, Cash should be debited and Unearned Revenue credited. Since the redemptions usually take place within a short time period, the liability is a current one.

11. Federal, state, city, and Social Security taxes withheld from employees are a current liability of the employer, who must remit these taxes to the various government agencies.

12. The Social Security tax has two components: FICA, which uses a 6.2% rate; and Medicare, which uses 1.45%.

13. The entry for the payroll involves a debit to Salaries Expense at the gross amount, a credit to Salaries Payable at the net amount, and several credits to liability accounts for the withholdings.

14. In addition to the withholdings, the employer must pay several taxes out of his or her own pocket. These taxes, referred to as *payroll taxes*, include additional Social Security tax, federal unemployment insurance, and state unemployment insurance.

15. *Bonuses* are an expense and thus reduce income and income tax. The entry is:

$$\text{Bonus Expense} \qquad \text{xxx}$$
$$\text{Bonus Payable} \qquad\qquad \text{xxx}$$

16. Bonuses may be based on income *before* subtracting bonus and tax, or *after* subtracting bonus and tax.

17. A *loss contingency* is an existing situation or condition which *may* give rise to a future loss. If the contingency is both probable and estimable, it should be accrued and reported as a liability. If, however, only one of these conditions has been fulfilled, the contingency should merely be disclosed in the footnotes, but not accrued. Disclosure is required only if the contingency is at least reasonably possible (not merely remote).

18. Examples of contingent liabilities include pending lawsuits, estimated future warranty costs, and premium expense relating to special company offers. All of these should be recorded via debit to an expense account and a credit to an estimated liability.

Rapid Review

1. A present obligation to transfer assets in the future is called a _____.

2. Current liabilities must be paid within 1 year or the _____.

3. A written promise to pay another party is referred to as a _____.

4. The process of deducting the interest in advance on a note is called _____.

5. Transferring a liability from short-term status to long-term status is known as _____.

6. Accumulated but undeclared dividends on preferred stock are called _____.

7. The above-mentioned dividends are not a liability but an element of _____.

8. The *total* rate for both components of the Social Security tax is _____.

9. Salary expense is debited at _____, while salaries payable are credited at _____.

10. Taxes payable out of the employer's own pocket are called _____.

11. These taxes consist of Social Security and _____.

12. Possible future liabilities are referred to as _____ liabilities.

13. It is required to accrue a future liability if the liability is both _____ and _____.

14. For a future liability to require footnote disclosure, it must be at least _____.

15. Special deals offered to customers upon the return of boxtops or labels are called _____.

Answers: **1.** liability **2.** operating cycle **3.** note payable **4.** discounting **5.** refinancing **6.** dividends in arrears **7.** stockholders' equity **8.** 7.65% **9.** gross; net **10.** payroll taxes **11.** unemployment insurance **12.** contingent **13.** probable; estimable **14.** reasonably possible **15.** premiums

Solved Problems

Introduction

13.1 Company A has an operating cycle of 15 months and a liability payable in 14 months, while Company B, with an operating cycle of 11 months, has a liability payable in 13 months. Determine for each company if the liability is considered current.

SOLUTION

Company A: current
Company B: noncurrent

[Section 13.1]

Accounts Payable and Notes Payable

13.2 On July 1, 19X1, Company C signs a 1-year, $5,000 note, which the bank discounts at 10%. Prepare the necessary entries on July 31 and on December 31.

SOLUTION

July 1	Cash	4,500	
	Discount on Note	500*	
	Note Payable		5,000
	*(10% of $5,000)		
Dec. 31	Interest Expense	250*	
	Discount on Note		250*
	*($500 × $\frac{1}{2}$ year)		

[Section 13.2]

13.3 For Problem 13.2, prepare the balance sheet presentation for the note on December 31, 19X1.

SOLUTION

Notes Payable	$5,000
Less Discount ($500 − $250)	(250)
Net Payable	$4,750

[Section 13.2]

13.4 On December 29, 19X1, Company D enters into a finance agreement to refinance its current liabilities. Although Company D intends to refinance, it has not done so by the date its statements are issued—April 10, 19X2.

Company E intends to refinance a current liability on December 31, 19X1, but does not actually do so until April 1, 19X2, which is 10 days *before* its statements are issued.

Company F also intends to refinance, but does not enter into an agreement until January 10, 19X2, and actually refinances on May 5, 19X2—a week *after* its statements are issued.

Determine for each company whether reclassification on the December 31, 19X1, balance sheet is permitted.

SOLUTION

Company D—yes. Both intent and ability are present.
Company E—yes. Again, both intent and ability are present.
Company F—no. Intent is present, but not ability.

[Section 13.2]

Dividends Payable, Returnable Deposits, and Sales Taxes

13.5 Determine which of the following is considered a current liability, as of December 31, 19X1.

(a) Cash dividends payable of $5,000 due on March 15, 19X2.

(b) Stock dividends payable of $7,000, due April 15, 19X2.

(c) Dividends in arrears on cumulative preferred stock for $3,000.

(d) Customer deposits of $8,000, expected to be returned in May.

If an item is not a current liability, state its proper classification.

SOLUTION

$13,000 ($5,000 + $8,000). The stock dividend payable is an element of stockholders' equity, while the dividends in arrears require footnote disclosure only.   [Section 13.3]

13.6   Company G sells gift certificates of $5,000 that are redeemable in services. During 19X1, $3,000 of certificates were redeemed. Prepare the entries for these transactions.

SOLUTION

Cash	5,000	
Unearned Revenue		5,000
Unearned Revenue	3,000	
Service Revenue		3,000

[Section 13.3]

13.7   Company H sells goods of $500, to which it adds an 8% sales tax. Prepare the entry for the sale.

SOLUTION

Cash	540	
Sales		500
Sales Tax Payable		40

[Section 13.3]

13.8   Company J sold goods on which it charged an 8% sales tax and included the entire amount of $972 in sales, via the following entry:

Cash	972	
Sales		972

Prepare the necessary adjusting entry.

SOLUTION

Sales	72*	
Sales Tax Payable		72*

*Let x = sales
$x + 0.08x = \$972$
$1.08x = \$972$
$x = \$900$
$0.08x = \$72$ = sales tax   [Section 13.3]

Payroll-Related Taxes

13.9   Shuki Yaefat earned $75,000 during 19X1. Determine his FICA and Medicare tax.

SOLUTION

FICA = $57,600 ceiling × 6.2% = $3,571.20
Medicare = $75,000 × 1.45% = $1,087.50   [Section 13.4]

13.10   Company K incurred $40,000 of salaries during 19X1. The federal, state, and Social Security withholdings were $8,000, $6,000, and $3,060, respectively. Prepare the entry for this payroll.

SOLUTION

Salaries Expense	40,000	
Federal Income Tax Payable		8,000
State Income Tax Payable		6,000
Social Security Tax Payable		3,060
Salaries Payable		22,940

[Section 13.4]

13.11 Green Corp. has one employee, who earned $55,000 this year. Prepare Green's entry for its payroll tax.

SOLUTION

Payroll Tax Expense	4,641.50	
Social Security Tax Payable		4,207.50*
Federal Unemployment Insurance Payable		56.00†
State Unemployment Insurance Payable		378.00‡

*Social Security = $55,000 \times 7.65\% = \$4,207.50$.
†Federal Unemployment = $7,000 \times 0.8\% = \$56.00$.
‡State Unemployment = $7,000 \times 5.4\% = \$378.00$.

[Section 13.4]

Bonuses

13.12 White Corp. has income of $70,000 before bonus and tax. Assume a bonus percentage of 20% and ignore taxes. Calculate the bonus if:

(a)   The bonus is based on income *before* the bonus.

(b)   The bonus is based on income *after* the bonus.

SOLUTION

(a) $B = 0.20(\$70,000)$
       $= \$14,000$

(b) $B = 0.20(\$70,000 - B)$
         $B = \$14,000 - 0.20B$
   $1.20B = \$14,000$
         $B = \$11,667$ (rounded)

[Section 13.5]

13.13 Company L earned income of $30,000 during 19X1. Its tax rate and bonus percentage are each 20%. Determine the bonus if:

(a)   The bonus is based on income *after* the bonus but *before* taxes.

(b)   The bonus is based on income *after* the bonus and *after* tax.

SOLUTION

(a) $B = 0.20(\$30,000 - B)$
           $= \$6,000 - 0.20B$
   $1.20B = \$6,000$
         $B = \$5,000$

(b) $B = 0.20(\$30,000 - B - T)$
           $T = 0.20(\$30,000 - B)$
           $B = 0.20[\$30,000 - B - 0.20(\$30,000 - B)]$ (substituting in the first equation)
           $B = 0.20(\$30,000 - B - \$6,000 + 0.20B)$
           $B = \$6,000 - 0.20B - \$1,200 + 0.04B$
           $B = \$4,800 - 0.16B$
      $1.16B = \$4,800$
           $B = \$4,134$ (rounded)   [Section 13.5]

Contingent Liabilities—Defined

13.14 Company M has the following contingent liabilities.

(a) An estimated $7,000 loss from a pending lawsuit. The attorney for Company M considers the loss to be probable.

(b) An estimated warranty cost of $1,000. The attorney considers this loss to be reasonably possible.

(c) Another lawsuit with an estimated loss of $25,000. The attorney considers the loss to be remote, since the suit is based on a frivolous claim.

Determine the proper accounting treatment for each of these contingencies.

SOLUTION

(a) Accrue via an entry debiting an expense and crediting a liability and report on the financial statements as such.

(b) Disclose in the footnotes.

(c) Ignore.   [Section 13.6]

13.15 Brown Corp. has two contingent liabilities, which are each probable and estimable. The first liability is estimated to be in the $10,000–$20,000 range, with no single number in this range considered more likely than any other number. The second liability is in the same range, but $14,000 is considered most likely. Determine the proper accounting treatment for each liability.

SOLUTION

The first liability will be accrued at $10,000 and the footnotes will disclose the $20,000 maximum potential liability. The second liability will be accrued at $14,000; no disclosure will be made of the $20,000.   [Section 13.6]

Contingent Liabilities—Examples

13.16 Green Corp. sells 50 machines during 19X1. It expects to incur warranty costs of $10 per machine during the 5-year warranty period. Thus far in 19X1, it has already spent $200 to repair several machines.

(a) Prepare the entry for the actual warranty costs thus far.

(b) Prepare the December 31, 19X1, adjusting entry.

(c) Determine warranty expense for the year.

SOLUTION

(a)	Warranty Expense	200	
	Cash		200
(b)	Estimated Warranty Expense	300*	
	Estimated Warranty Liability		300*

*(50 machines × $10) − $200 already recognized.

(c) $500 ($200 + $300)   [Section 13.7]

13.17 Truck Corp. sells a truck for $25,000. The truck comes with a basic 3-year warranty and an additional 2-year extended warranty, for which the customer pays an extra $300. During 19X1, Truck pays out $150 in repairs required under the basic warranty.

(a)   Prepare the entry for the sale of the truck and the extended warranty.

(b)   Prepare the entry for the $150 repair.

(c)   Prepare the annual entry to recognize revenue from the sale of the extended warranty.

SOLUTION

(a)	Cash	25,300	
	Sales		25,000
	Unearned Revenue		300
(b)	Warranty Expense	150	
	Cash		150

(c)   In 19X4:

Unearned Warranty Revenue	150*	
Warranty Revenue		150*

*($300 ÷ 2 years)   [Section 13.7]

13.18 Sweet Cereal Corp. offers its customers a baseball card for 10 boxtops. The cards cost Sweet Corp. 20¢ each. During 19X1, Sweet Corp. engaged in the following transactions:

(a)   A purchase of 1,500 cards

(b)   Sales of 7,000 boxes of cereal at $3.00 each

(c)   Receipt of 4,000 boxtops from customers

    Prepare entries for the above information.

SOLUTION

(a)	Cards	300*	
	Cash		300*

*(1,500 × $0.20)

(b)	Cash	21,000	
	Sales		21,000
(c)	Premium Expense	80*	
	Cards		80*

*4,000 boxtops ÷ 10 =   400 cards
                 ×$0.20
                 $80

[Section 13.7]

13.19 For Problem 13.18, determine the contingent liability on December 31 and prepare an entry. Assume Sweet estimates that 70% of the boxtops will be returned.

SOLUTION

Premium Expense	18*	
Estimated Premium Liability		18*
*Estimated Return of Boxtops (7,000 × 70%)	4,900	
Boxtops Already Returned	−4,000	
Future Expected Returns	900	
Divide by 10	÷10	
Future Cards to Be Mailed	90	
Expense per Card	$0.20	
Total Future Contingent Expense	$18	[Section 13.7]

Supplementary Problems

Introduction

13.20 Company P has an operating cycle of 16 months and a liability payable in 17 months. Company Q has an operating cycle of 10 months and a liability payable in 11 months. Determine if each of these liabilities is considered current.

Accounts Payable and Notes Payable

13.21 On July 1, 19X1, Company R signs a 20-year, $40,000 note, which the bank discounts at 10%. Prepare the required entries for July 1, 19X1, December 31, 19X1, and July 1, 19X2.

13.22 For the note in Problem 13.21, show the balance sheet on December 31, 19X1, and determine interest expense for 19X1.

Dividends Payable, Returnable Deposits, and Sales Taxes

13.23 On December 31, 19X1, Company S has a cash dividend payable and a stock dividend payable. Are these considered current liabilities? If not, how should they be classified?

13.24 During 19X1, Company T sells gift certificates of $12,000 redeemable in dental services. During the last 3 months of 19X1, $4,000 of these certificates are redeemed. Prepare the entries for these transactions.

13.25 Company V sold goods on which it charged a 5% sales tax and included the entire amount received in the sales account. Its entry was:

Cash	525	
Sales		525

Prepare an adjusting entry.

Payroll Related Taxes

13.26 Company W has one employee, who earned $49,000 during 19X1. Prepare the entry to record the payroll tax.

Bonuses

13.27 Green Corp. has income of $50,000 before bonus and tax. Assume a bonus percentage of 10% and ignore taxes. Calculate the bonus if:

(a) The bonus is based on income *before* the bonus.

(b) The bonus is based on income *after* the bonus.

13.28 Assume the same information as in Problem 13.27, and that the tax rate is 20%. Determine the bonus if:

(a) The bonus is based on income *after* the bonus but *before* tax.

(b) The bonus is based on income *after* the bonus and *after* tax.

Contingent Liabilities—Examples

13.29 Blue Corp. sells 80 machines during 19X1, which it guarantees for 4 years. Blue expects to incur warranty costs of $15 per machine during the warranty period. In 19X1 thus far, it has spent $300 on repairs.

(a) Prepare the entry for the actual warranty costs incurred in 19X1.

(b) Prepare the December 31, 19X1, adjusting entry.

(c) Determine warranty expense for 19X1.

13.30 Sugar Cocoa Corp. offers its customers a chocolate bar for 10 boxtops returned, plus 25¢. The bars cost Sugar Cocoa 65¢ each. During 19X1, Sugar Cocoa engaged in the following transactions:

(a) A purchase of 2,000 chocolate bars

(b) Sales of 10,000 boxes of cocoa at $4.00 each

(c) Receipt of 3,000 boxtops and 300 quarters

It is estimated that 70% of the boxtops will be redeemed. Prepare all the required entries, including the contingent liability.

Examination IV

Chapters 10, 11, 12, 13

A. True–False Questions. Place the letter T or F next to the question.

1. _____ Delivery charges on the purchase of a machine are debited to Delivery Expense.

2. _____ Land improvements with a limited life should be debited to the Land account.

3. _____ Interest cost incurred in borrowing money to *purchase* a building is considered interest expense.

4. _____ For construction of a building, variable overhead incurred is debited to Building; fixed overhead is debited to Expense.

5. _____ The cost of a package purchase is allocated to each item in the package according to the ratio of fair market values.

6. _____ For purchases involving a non-interest-bearing note, the asset purchased is debited at the fair market value, if this is known.

7. _____ Donated assets received are credited to Donated Capital.

8. _____ When assets are donated to others and the fair market value is greater than the book value, a gain is recognized.

9. _____ For dissimilar assets, *both* gains and losses are recognized upon exchange.

10. _____ For similar assets, no gains are recognized by the party paying cash.

11. _____ Major repairs that increase the quality of an asset are debited to Accumulated Depreciation.

12. _____ An asset's cost minus its accumulated depreciation is known as its depreciable base.

13. _____ The sum-of-the-years'-digits method is an example of an accelerated method of depreciation.

14. _____ To calculate a sum of years, the formula you would use is:

$$S = \frac{N(N-1)}{2}$$

15. _____ The double-declining-balance method does not subtract salvage value in its calculations.

16. _____ The depreciation of several dissimilar assets as one large group is called composite depreciation.

17. _____ Depletion refers to the using up of natural resources.

18. _____ Assets with no physical substance are referred to as nonphysical assets.

19. _____ Depletion refers to the using up of tangible assets.

20. _____ The maximum life for intangibles is 40 years.

21. _____ Costs incurred in creating an organization are called start-up costs.

22. _____ The start-up costs are usually amortized over a 5-year period.

23. _____ A company's fair market value, over and above its physical assets, is called goodwill.

24. _____ R&D costs are capitalized and gradually expensed.

25. _____ Liabilities payable within 1 year are called long-term liabilities.

26. _____ The process of rolling over a short-term liability to a long-term liability is called refinancing.

27. _____ Dividends in arrears are a short-term liability.

28. _____ Social Security taxes are paid by both employer and employee.

29. _____ Contingent liabilities must be accrued if both estimable and reasonably possible.

B. Completion Questions. Fill in the blanks.

30. Another name for plant and equipment is _____.

31. For building construction, all costs incurred from _____ until completion are debited to the building.

32. Idle buildings should be classified as _____.

33. If stock is issued for a machine, the machine should be debited for its own fair market value or the FMV of the _____, whichever is more _____.

34. For deferred payment contracts, the "hidden" interest is calculated using the _____ rate.

35. Donations given or received are called _____ transfers.

36. For dissimilar assets, the new asset is debited at the _____ of the old asset, plus any cash _____, minus any cash _____.

37. If an expenditure increases the asset life, it should be debited to _____.

38. When a plant asset is sold and the cash received is less than book value, a _____ is recognized.

39. The depreciation method selected should be systematic and _____.

40. Assets depreciate because of both economic and _____ factors.

41. Another name for scrap value is _____ value.

42. Under the straight-line method, depreciation is a function of _____.

43. The denominator (for sum-of-the-years'-digits purposes) of a machine with an 80-year life is _____.

44. A depreciation method that does not subtract salvage is _____.

45. Sudden, dramatic declines in an asset's value are called _____.

46. Costs of obtaining natural resources include purchase price, _____, and _____.

47. Assets without physical substance are called _____ assets.

48. The exclusive right to manufacture a product is called a _____.

49. The "using up" of intangibles is referred to as _____ and the maximum period allowed is _____ years.

50. Improvements made by a tenant to rented property are called _____.

51. The above-mentioned improvements should be amortized over their own life or the life of the rental, whichever is _____.

52. It is the custom to amortize organization costs over _____ years.

53. The right to sell a product in a specific area is known as a _____.

54. To discount an annuity over an "indefinite" number of periods, divide the annuity by the _____.

55. Plant rearrangement costs are an example of a _____.

56. Computer software costs should be capitalized if incurred subsequent to establishing _____.

57. Current liabilities are not reported at present value but at _____ value.

58. Dividends payable become a liability when _____.

59. The Social Security tax rate is _____.

60. Salaries Expense is debited at _____ while Salaries Payable is credited at _____.

61. Taxes paid out of the pocket of the employer are called _____ taxes.

62. Liabilities that may happen but have not yet happened are called _____ liabilities.

63. Special deals that companies make for the return of boxtops are called _____ .

C. Problems

64. Company A exchanges an old machine for a new machine and pays $5,000 in cash. The old machine had a cost of $30,000 and accumulated depreciation of $23,000, and its fair market value was $9,000.

    (a) Determine the gain or loss on the exchange.

    (b) Prepare an entry if the machines are (i) dissimilar, (ii) similar.

65. Company B purchases a machine on July 1, 19X1, for $30,000. The machine is expected to have a 3-year life and a $3,000 salvage value. Determine the depreciation for 19X1, 19X2, 19X3, and 19X4 under:

    (a) Straight-line

    (b) Sum-of-the-years'-digits

    (c) Double-declining-balance

66. Company C purchases Sunshine Corp. for $60,000. The assets and liabilities of Sunshine consist of the following:

	Book Value	Fair Market Value
Accounts Receivable	$ 5,000	$ 4,000
Merchandise	7,000	8,000
Building	50,000	70,000
Patent	3,000	1,000
Note Payable	25,000	25,000

    Prepare an entry for the purchase.

67. Company D gives its employees a bonus equal to 10% of its income. The income is $60,000 and the tax rate is 10%. Determine the bonus if:

    (a) The bonus is based on income *after* the bonus but *before* taxes.

    (b) The bonus is based on income *after* the bonus and *after* taxes.

Answers to Examination IV

A. True–False Questions

1. F 2. F 3. T 4. F 5. T 6. T 7. F 8. T 9. T 10. T 11. F 12. F 13. T
14. F 15. T 16. T 17. T 18. F 19. F 20. T 21. F 22. T 23. T 24. F 25. F
26. T 27. F 28. T 29. F

B. Completion Questions

30. fixed assets 31. excavation 32. investments 33. stock; clear 34. imputed 35. nonreciprocal
36. fair market value; given; received 37. Accumulated Depreciation 38. loss 39. rational

40. physical **41.** salvage **42.** time **43.** 3,240 **44.** double-declining balance **45.** impairments **46.** exploration costs; development costs **47.** intangible **48.** patent **49.** depletion; 40 **50.** leasehold improvements **51.** shorter **52.** 5 **53.** franchise **54.** interest rate **55.** deferred charge **56.** technological feasibility **57.** face **58.** declared **59.** 7.65% **60.** gross; net **61.** payroll **62.** contingent **63.** premiums

C. Problems

64. (*a*)   Gain of $2,000 (FMV of 9,000 − book value of 7,000)

(*b*)

If dissimilar:

New Machine	14,000	
Accumulated Depreciation	23,000	
Old Machine		30,000
Cash		5,000
Gain on Exchange		2,000

If similar:

New Machine	12,000	
Accumulated Depreciation	23,000	
Old Machine		30,000
Cash		5,000

65. (*a*)   The annual depreciation is $9,000.

For 19X1: $9,000 × $\frac{1}{2}$ year = $4,500

For 19X2: $9,000

For 19X3: $9,000

For 19X4: $9,000 × $\frac{1}{2}$ year = $4,500

(*b*)   The denominator will always be 6.

For 19X1: $\frac{3}{6}$ × $27,000 × $\frac{1}{2}$ year   <u>$ 6,750</u>

For 19X2: $\frac{3}{6}$ × $27,000 × $\frac{1}{2}$ = $6,750

        +$\frac{2}{6}$ × $27,000 × $\frac{1}{2}$ = <u>4,500</u>

Total 19X2 $11,250

For 19X3: $\frac{2}{6}$ × $27,000 × $\frac{1}{2}$ = $4,500

        +$\frac{1}{6}$ × $27,000 × $\frac{1}{2}$ = <u>2,250</u>

Total 19X3 $ 6,750

For 19X4: $\frac{1}{6}$ × $27,000 × $\frac{1}{2}$ = $ 2,250

(*c*)   The DDB rate is twice the straight-line rate of $\frac{1}{3}$, which yields $\frac{2}{3}$.

For 19X1: $30,000 × $\frac{2}{3}$ × $\frac{1}{2}$ year = $10,000

For 19X2: 20,000 × $\frac{2}{3}$ = 13,333   (rounded)

For 19X3: Book value is now   = $ 6,667 ($30,000 − $10,000 − $13,333)

To get this down to the salvage of $3,000 requires depreciation of $3,667.

66.

Accounts Receivable	4,000	
Merchandise	8,000	
Building	70,000	
Patent	1,000	
Goodwill	2,000	
Note Payable		25,000
Cash		60,000

67. (*a*)
$$B = 0.10(\$60,000 - B)$$
$$= \$6,000 - 0.10B$$
$$1.10B = \$6,000$$
$$B = \$5,455 \quad \text{(rounded)}$$

(*b*)
$$B = 0.10(\$60,000 - B - T)$$
$$T = 0.10(\$60,000 - B)$$
$$B = 0.10[\$60,000 - B - 0.10(\$60,000 - B)]$$
$$= 0.10(\$60,000 - B - \$6,000 + 0.10B)$$
$$= \$6,000 - 0.10B - \$600 + 0.01B$$
$$= \$5,400 - 0.09B$$
$$1.09B = \$5,400$$
$$B = \$4,954 \quad \text{(rounded)}$$

Appendix: Interest Tables

TABLE 1 Future Value of $1

Periods	0.5%	1%	1.5%	2%	3%	4%	5%	6%	7%	8%	9%	10%	12%	14%	16%	18%	20%
1	1.005	1.010	1.015	1.020	1.030	1.040	1.050	1.060	1.070	1.080	1.090	1.100	1.120	1.140	1.160	1.180	1.200
2	1.010	1.020	1.030	1.040	1.061	1.082	1.103	1.124	1.145	1.166	1.188	1.210	1.254	1.300	1.346	1.392	1.440
3	1.015	1.030	1.046	1.061	1.093	1.125	1.158	1.191	1.225	1.260	1.295	1.331	1.405	1.482	1.561	1.643	1.728
4	1.020	1.041	1.061	1.082	1.126	1.170	1.216	1.262	1.311	1.360	1.412	1.464	1.574	1.689	1.811	1.939	2.074
5	1.025	1.051	1.077	1.104	1.159	1.217	1.276	1.338	1.403	1.469	1.539	1.611	1.762	1.925	2.100	2.288	2.488
6	1.030	1.062	1.093	1.126	1.194	1.265	1.340	1.419	1.501	1.587	1.677	1.772	1.974	2.195	2.436	2.700	2.986
7	1.036	1.072	1.110	1.149	1.230	1.316	1.407	1.504	1.606	1.714	1.828	1.949	2.211	2.502	2.826	3.185	3.583
8	1.041	1.083	1.126	1.172	1.267	1.369	1.477	1.594	1.718	1.851	1.993	2.144	2.476	2.853	3.278	3.759	4.300
9	1.046	1.094	1.143	1.195	1.305	1.423	1.551	1.689	1.838	1.999	2.172	2.358	2.773	3.252	3.803	4.435	5.160
10	1.051	1.105	1.161	1.219	1.344	1.480	1.629	1.791	1.967	2.159	2.367	2.594	3.106	3.707	4.411	5.234	6.192
11	1.056	1.116	1.178	1.243	1.384	1.539	1.710	1.898	2.105	2.332	2.580	2.853	3.479	4.226	5.117	6.176	7.430
12	1.062	1.127	1.196	1.268	1.426	1.601	1.796	2.012	2.252	2.518	2.813	3.138	3.896	4.818	5.936	7.288	8.916
13	1.067	1.138	1.214	1.294	1.469	1.665	1.886	2.133	2.410	2.720	3.066	3.452	4.363	5.492	6.886	8.599	10.699
14	1.072	1.149	1.232	1.319	1.513	1.732	1.980	2.261	2.579	2.937	3.342	3.797	4.887	6.261	7.988	10.147	12.839
15	1.078	1.161	1.250	1.346	1.558	1.801	2.079	2.397	2.759	3.172	3.642	4.177	5.474	7.138	9.266	11.974	15.407
16	1.083	1.173	1.269	1.373	1.605	1.873	2.183	2.540	2.952	3.426	3.970	4.595	6.130	8.137	10.748	14.129	18.488
18	1.094	1.196	1.307	1.428	1.702	2.026	2.407	2.854	3.380	3.996	4.717	5.560	7.690	10.575	14.463	19.673	26.623
20	1.105	1.220	1.347	1.486	1.806	2.191	2.653	3.207	3.870	4.661	5.604	6.727	9.646	13.743	19.461	27.393	38.338
22	1.116	1.245	1.388	1.546	1.916	2.370	2.925	3.604	4.430	5.437	6.659	8.140	12.100	17.861	26.186	38.142	55.206
24	1.127	1.270	1.430	1.608	2.033	2.563	3.225	4.049	5.072	6.341	7.911	9.850	15.179	23.212	35.236	53.109	79.497
26	1.138	1.295	1.473	1.673	2.157	2.772	3.556	4.549	5.807	7.396	9.399	11.918	19.040	30.167	47.414	73.949	114.475
28	1.150	1.321	1.517	1.741	2.288	2.999	3.920	5.112	6.649	8.627	11.167	14.421	23.884	39.204	63.800	102.967	164.845
30	1.161	1.348	1.563	1.811	2.427	3.243	4.322	5.743	7.612	10.063	13.268	17.449	29.960	50.950	85.850	143.371	237.376
32	1.173	1.375	1.610	1.885	2.575	3.508	4.765	6.453	8.715	11.737	15.763	21.114	37.582	66.215	115.520	199.629	341.822
34	1.185	1.403	1.659	1.961	2.732	3.794	5.253	7.251	9.978	13.690	18.728	25.548	47.143	86.053	155.443	277.964	492.224
36	1.197	1.431	1.709	2.040	2.898	4.104	5.792	8.147	11.424	15.968	22.251	30.913	59.136	111.834	209.164	387.037	708.802
40	1.221	1.489	1.814	2.208	3.262	4.801	7.040	10.286	14.974	21.725	31.409	45.259	93.051	188.884	378.721	750.378	1469.722
44	1.245	1.549	1.925	2.390	3.671	5.617	8.557	12.985	19.628	29.556	44.337	66.264	146.418	319.017	685.727	1454.817	3047.718
48	1.270	1.612	2.043	2.587	4.132	6.571	10.401	16.394	25.729	40.211	62.585	97.017	230.391	538.807	1241.605	2820.567	6319.749

Reprinted with the permission of the NAA.

TABLE 2   Present Value of $1

Periods	0.5%	1%	1.5%	2%	3%	4%	5%	6%	7%	8%	9%	10%	12%	14%	16%	18%	20%
1	0.995	0.990	0.985	0.980	0.971	0.962	0.952	0.943	0.935	0.926	0.917	0.909	0.893	0.877	0.862	0.847	0.833
2	0.990	0.980	0.971	0.961	0.943	0.925	0.907	0.890	0.873	0.857	0.842	0.826	0.797	0.769	0.743	0.718	0.694
3	0.985	0.971	0.956	0.942	0.915	0.889	0.864	0.840	0.816	0.794	0.772	0.751	0.712	0.675	0.641	0.609	0.579
4	0.980	0.961	0.942	0.924	0.888	0.855	0.823	0.792	0.763	0.735	0.708	0.683	0.636	0.592	0.552	0.516	0.482
5	0.975	0.951	0.928	0.906	0.863	0.822	0.784	0.747	0.713	0.681	0.650	0.621	0.567	0.519	0.476	0.437	0.402
6	0.971	0.942	0.915	0.888	0.837	0.790	0.746	0.705	0.666	0.630	0.596	0.564	0.507	0.456	0.410	0.370	0.335
7	0.966	0.933	0.901	0.871	0.813	0.760	0.711	0.665	0.623	0.583	0.547	0.513	0.452	0.400	0.354	0.314	0.279
8	0.961	0.923	0.888	0.853	0.789	0.731	0.677	0.627	0.582	0.540	0.502	0.467	0.404	0.351	0.305	0.266	0.233
9	0.956	0.914	0.875	0.837	0.766	0.703	0.645	0.592	0.544	0.500	0.460	0.424	0.361	0.308	0.263	0.225	0.194
10	0.951	0.905	0.862	0.820	0.744	0.676	0.614	0.558	0.508	0.463	0.422	0.386	0.322	0.270	0.227	0.191	0.162
11	0.947	0.896	0.849	0.804	0.722	0.650	0.585	0.527	0.475	0.429	0.388	0.350	0.287	0.237	0.195	0.162	0.135
12	0.942	0.887	0.836	0.788	0.701	0.625	0.557	0.497	0.444	0.397	0.356	0.319	0.257	0.208	0.168	0.137	0.112
13	0.937	0.879	0.824	0.773	0.681	0.601	0.530	0.469	0.415	0.368	0.326	0.290	0.229	0.182	0.145	0.116	0.093
14	0.933	0.870	0.812	0.758	0.661	0.577	0.505	0.442	0.388	0.340	0.299	0.263	0.205	0.160	0.125	0.099	0.078
15	0.928	0.861	0.800	0.743	0.642	0.555	0.481	0.417	0.362	0.315	0.275	0.239	0.183	0.140	0.108	0.084	0.065
16	0.923	0.853	0.788	0.728	0.623	0.534	0.458	0.394	0.339	0.292	0.252	0.218	0.163	0.123	0.093	0.071	0.054
18	0.914	0.836	0.765	0.700	0.587	0.494	0.416	0.350	0.296	0.250	0.212	0.180	0.130	0.095	0.069	0.051	0.038
20	0.905	0.820	0.742	0.673	0.554	0.456	0.377	0.312	0.258	0.215	0.178	0.149	0.104	0.073	0.051	0.037	0.026
22	0.896	0.803	0.721	0.647	0.522	0.422	0.342	0.278	0.226	0.184	0.150	0.123	0.083	0.056	0.038	0.026	0.018
24	0.887	0.788	0.700	0.622	0.492	0.390	0.310	0.247	0.197	0.158	0.126	0.102	0.066	0.043	0.028	0.019	0.013
26	0.878	0.772	0.679	0.598	0.464	0.361	0.281	0.220	0.172	0.135	0.106	0.084	0.053	0.033	0.021	0.014	0.009
28	0.870	0.757	0.659	0.574	0.437	0.333	0.255	0.196	0.150	0.116	0.090	0.069	0.042	0.026	0.016	0.010	0.006
30	0.861	0.742	0.640	0.552	0.412	0.308	0.231	0.174	0.131	0.099	0.075	0.057	0.033	0.020	0.012	0.007	0.004
32	0.852	0.727	0.621	0.531	0.388	0.285	0.210	0.155	0.115	0.085	0.063	0.047	0.027	0.015	0.009	0.005	0.003
34	0.844	0.713	0.603	0.510	0.366	0.264	0.190	0.138	0.100	0.073	0.053	0.039	0.021	0.012	0.006	0.004	0.002
36	0.836	0.699	0.585	0.490	0.345	0.244	0.173	0.123	0.088	0.063	0.045	0.032	0.017	0.009	0.005	0.003	0.001
40	0.819	0.672	0.551	0.453	0.307	0.208	0.142	0.097	0.067	0.046	0.032	0.022	0.011	0.005	0.003	0.001	0.001
44	0.803	0.645	0.519	0.418	0.272	0.178	0.117	0.077	0.051	0.034	0.023	0.015	0.007	0.003	0.001	0.001	<.001
48	0.787	0.620	0.489	0.387	0.242	0.152	0.096	0.061	0.039	0.025	0.016	0.010	0.004	0.002	0.001	<.001	<.001

Reprinted with the permission of the NAA.

TABLE 3 Future Value of an Ordinary Annuity of $1

Periods	0.5%	1%	1.5%	2%	3%	4%	5%	6%	7%	8%	9%	10%	12%	14%	16%	18%	20%
1	1.000	1.000	1.000	1.000	1.000	1.000	1.000	1.000	1.000	1.000	1.000	1.000	1.000	1.000	1.000	1.000	1.000
2	2.005	2.010	2.015	2.020	2.030	2.040	2.050	2.060	2.070	2.080	2.090	2.100	2.120	2.140	2.160	2.180	2.200
3	3.105	3.030	3.045	3.060	3.091	3.122	3.153	3.184	3.215	3.246	3.278	3.310	3.374	3.440	3.506	3.572	3.640
4	4.030	4.060	4.091	4.122	4.184	4.246	4.310	4.375	4.440	4.506	4.573	4.641	4.779	4.921	5.066	5.215	5.368
5	5.050	5.101	5.152	5.204	5.309	5.416	5.526	5.637	5.751	5.867	5.985	6.105	6.353	6.610	6.877	7.154	7.442
6	6.076	6.152	6.230	6.308	6.468	6.633	6.802	6.975	7.153	7.336	7.523	7.716	8.115	8.536	8.977	9.442	9.930
7	7.106	7.214	7.323	7.434	7.662	7.898	8.142	8.394	8.654	8.923	9.200	9.487	10.089	10.730	11.414	12.142	12.916
8	8.141	8.286	8.433	8.583	8.892	9.214	9.549	9.897	10.260	10.637	11.028	11.436	12.300	13.233	14.240	15.327	16.499
9	9.182	9.369	9.559	9.755	10.159	10.583	11.027	11.491	11.978	12.488	13.021	13.579	14.776	16.085	17.519	19.086	20.799
10	10.228	10.462	10.703	10.950	11.464	12.006	12.578	13.181	13.816	14.487	15.193	15.937	17.549	19.337	21.321	23.521	25.959
11	11.279	11.567	11.863	12.169	12.808	13.486	14.207	14.972	15.784	16.645	17.560	18.531	20.655	23.045	25.733	28.755	32.150
12	12.336	12.683	13.041	13.412	14.192	15.026	15.917	16.870	17.888	18.977	20.141	21.384	24.133	27.271	30.850	34.931	39.581
13	13.397	13.809	14.237	14.680	15.618	16.627	17.713	18.882	20.141	21.495	22.953	24.523	28.029	32.089	36.786	42.219	48.497
14	14.464	14.947	15.450	15.974	17.086	18.292	19.599	21.015	22.550	24.215	26.019	27.975	32.393	37.581	43.672	50.818	59.196
15	15.537	16.097	16.682	17.293	18.599	20.024	21.579	23.276	25.129	27.152	29.361	31.772	37.280	43.842	51.660	60.965	72.035
16	16.614	17.258	17.932	18.639	20.157	21.825	23.657	25.673	27.888	30.324	33.003	35.950	42.753	50.980	60.925	72.939	87.442
18	18.786	19.615	20.489	21.412	23.414	25.645	28.132	30.906	33.999	37.450	41.301	45.599	55.750	68.394	84.141	103.740	128.117
20	20.979	22.019	23.124	24.297	26.870	29.778	33.066	36.786	40.995	45.762	51.160	57.275	72.052	91.025	115.380	146.628	186.688
22	23.194	24.472	25.838	27.299	30.537	34.248	38.505	43.392	49.006	55.457	62.873	71.403	92.503	120.436	157.415	206.345	271.031
24	25.432	26.973	28.634	30.422	34.426	39.083	44.502	50.816	58.177	66.765	76.790	88.497	118.155	158.659	213.978	289.494	392.484
26	27.692	29.526	31.514	33.671	38.553	44.312	51.113	59.156	68.676	79.954	93.324	109.182	150.334	208.333	290.088	405.272	567.377
28	29.975	32.129	34.481	37.051	42.931	49.968	58.403	68.528	80.698	95.339	112.968	134.210	190.699	272.889	392.503	566.481	819.223
30	32.280	34.785	37.539	40.568	47.575	56.085	66.439	79.058	94.461	113.283	136.308	164.494	241.333	356.787	530.312	790.948	1181.882
32	34.609	37.494	40.688	44.227	52.503	62.701	75.299	90.890	110.218	134.214	164.037	201.138	304.848	465.820	715.747	1103.496	1704.109
34	36.961	40.258	43.933	48.034	57.730	69.858	85.067	104.184	128.259	158.627	196.982	245.477	384.521	607.520	965.270	1538.688	2456.118
36	39.336	43.077	47.276	51.994	63.276	77.598	95.836	119.121	148.913	187.102	236.125	299.127	484.463	791.673	1301.027	2144.649	3539.009
40	44.159	48.886	54.268	60.402	75.401	95.026	120.800	154.762	199.635	259.057	337.882	442.593	767.091	1342.025	2360.757	4163.213	7343.858
44	49.079	54.932	61.689	69.503	89.048	115.413	151.143	199.758	266.121	356.950	481.522	652.641	1211.813	2271.548	4279.546	8076.760	15233.592
48	54.098	61.223	69.565	79.354	104.408	139.263	188.025	256.565	353.270	490.132	684.280	960.172	1911.590	3841.475	7753.782	15664.259	31593.744

Reprinted with the permission of the NAA.

TABLE 4 Present Value of an Ordinary Annuity of $1

Periods	0.5%	1%	1.5%	2%	3%	4%	5%	6%	7%	8%	9%	10%	12%	14%	16%	18%	20%
1	0.995	0.990	0.985	0.980	0.971	0.962	0.952	0.943	0.935	0.926	0.917	0.909	0.893	0.877	0.862	0.847	0.833
2	1.985	1.970	1.956	1.942	1.913	1.886	1.859	1.833	1.808	1.783	1.759	1.736	1.690	1.647	1.605	1.566	1.528
3	2.970	2.941	2.912	2.884	2.829	2.775	2.723	2.673	2.624	2.577	2.531	2.487	2.402	2.322	2.246	2.174	2.106
4	3.950	3.902	3.854	3.808	3.717	3.630	3.546	3.465	3.387	3.312	3.240	3.170	3.037	2.914	2.798	2.690	2.589
5	4.926	4.853	4.783	4.713	4.580	4.452	4.329	4.212	4.100	3.993	3.890	3.791	3.605	3.433	3.274	3.127	2.991
6	5.896	5.795	5.697	5.601	5.417	5.242	5.076	4.917	4.767	4.623	4.486	4.355	4.111	3.889	3.685	3.498	3.326
7	6.862	6.728	6.598	6.472	6.230	6.002	5.786	5.582	5.389	5.206	5.033	4.868	4.564	4.288	4.039	3.812	3.605
8	7.823	7.652	7.486	7.325	7.020	6.733	6.463	6.210	5.971	5.747	5.535	5.335	4.968	4.639	4.344	4.078	3.837
9	8.779	8.566	8.361	8.162	7.786	7.435	7.108	6.802	6.515	6.247	5.995	5.759	5.328	4.946	4.607	4.303	4.031
10	9.730	9.471	9.222	8.983	8.530	8.111	7.722	7.360	7.024	6.710	6.418	6.145	5.650	5.216	4.833	4.494	4.192
11	10.677	10.368	10.071	9.787	9.253	8.760	8.306	7.887	7.499	7.139	6.805	6.495	5.937?	5.453	5.029	4.656	4.327
12	11.619	11.255	10.908	10.575	9.954	9.385	8.863	8.384	7.943	7.536	7.161	6.814	6.194	5.660	5.197	4.793	4.439
13	12.556	12.134	11.732	11.348	10.635	9.986	9.394	8.853	8.358	7.904	7.487	7.103	6.424	5.842	5.342	4.910	4.533
14	13.489	13.004	12.543	12.106	11.296	10.563	9.899	9.295	8.745	8.244	7.786	7.367	6.628	6.002	5.468	5.008	4.611
15	14.417	13.865	13.343	12.849	11.938	11.118	10.380	9.712	9.108	8.559	8.061	7.606	6.811	6.142	5.575	5.092	4.675
16	15.340	14.718	14.131	13.578	12.561	11.652	10.838	10.106	9.447	8.851	8.313	7.824	6.974	6.265	5.668	5.162	4.730
18	17.173	16.398	15.673	14.992	13.754	12.659	11.690	10.828	10.059	9.372	8.756	8.201	7.250	6.467	5.818	5.273	4.812
20	18.987	18.046	17.169	16.351	14.877	13.590	12.462	11.470	10.594	9.818	9.129	8.514	7.469	6.623	5.929	5.353	4.870
22	20.784	19.660	18.621	17.658	15.937	14.451	13.163	12.042	11.061	10.201	9.442	8.772	7.645	6.743	6.011	5.410	4.909
24	22.563	21.243	20.030	18.914	16.936	15.247	13.799	12.550	11.469	10.529	9.707	8.985	7.784	6.835	6.073	5.451	4.937
26	24.324	22.795	21.399	20.121	17.877	15.983	14.375	13.003	11.826	10.810	9.929	9.161	7.896	6.906	6.118	5.480	4.956
28	26.068	24.316	22.727	21.281	18.764	16.663	14.898	13.406	12.137	11.051	10.116	9.307	7.984	6.961	6.152	5.502	4.970
30	27.794	25.808	24.016	22.396	19.600	17.292	15.372	13.765	12.409	11.258	10.274	9.427	8.055	7.003	6.177	5.517	4.979
32	29.503	27.270	25.267	23.468	20.389	17.874	15.803	14.084	12.647	11.435	10.406	9.526	8.112	7.035	6.196	5.528	4.985
34	31.196	28.703	26.482	24.499	21.132	18.411	16.193	14.368	12.854	11.587	10.518	9.609	8.157	7.060	6.210	5.536	4.990
36	32.871	30.108	27.661	25.489	21.832	18.908	16.547	14.621	13.035	11.717	10.612	9.677	8.192	7.079	6.220	5.541	4.993
40	36.172	32.835	29.916	27.355	23.115	19.793	17.159	15.046	13.332	11.925	10.757	9.779	8.244	7.105	6.233	5.548	4.997
44	39.408	35.455	32.041	29.080	24.254	20.549	17.663	15.383	13.558	12.077	10.861	9.849	8.276	7.120	6.241	5.552	4.998
48	42.580	37.974	34.043	30.673	25.267	21.195	18.077	15.650	13.730	12.189	10.934	9.897	8.297	7.130	6.245	5.554	4.999

Reprinted with the permission of the NAA.

Index

SCHAUM'S OUTLINES
IN
ACCOUNTING, BUSINESS, & ECONOMICS

Ask for these books at your local bookstore or check the appropriate box(es) and mail with the coupon on the back of this page to McGraw-Hill, Inc.

☐ **Bookkeeping and Accounting, 3/ed**
order code 037593-3/$12.95

☐ **Business Law**
order code 069062-6/$12.95

☐ **Business Mathematics**
order code 037212-8/$12.95

☐ **Business Statistics, 2/ed**
order code 033533-8/$12.95

☐ **Calculus for Business, Economics, & the Social Sciences**
order code 017673-6/$12.95

☐ **Contemporary Mathematics of Finance**
order code 008146-8/$11.95

☐ **Cost Accounting, 3/ed**
order code 011026-3/$13.95

☐ **Financial Accounting**
order code 057304-2/$12.95

☐ **Intermediate Accounting I, 2/ed**
order code 010204-x/$12.95

☐ **Intermediate Accounting II**
order code 019483-1/$12.95

☐ **International Economics, 3/ed**
order code 054538-3/$11.95

☐ **Investments**
order code 021807-2/$12.95

☐ **Macroeconomic Theory, 2/ed**
order code 017051-7/$12.95

☐ **Managerial Accounting**
order code 057305-0/$13.95

☐ **Managerial Economics**
order code 054513-8/$12.95

☐ **Managerial Finance**
order code 057306-9/$13.95

☐ **Introduction to Mathematical Economics, 2/ed**
order code 017674-4/$12.95

☐ **Mathematical Methods for Business & Economics**
order code 017697-3/$12.95

☐ **Microeconomic Theory, 3/ed**
order code 054515-4/$12.95

☐ **Operations Management**
order code 042726-7/$12.95

☐ **Personal Finance**
order code 057559-2/$12.95

☐ **Principles of Accounting I, 4/ed**
order code 037278-0/$12.95

☐ **Principles of Accounting II, 4/ed**
order code 037589-5/$12.95

☐ **Principles of Economics**
order code 054487-5/$11.95

☐ **Statistics and Econometrics**
order code 054505-7/$10.95

NAME_____

(please print)

ADDRESS_____

CITY_____ STATE_____ ZIP_____

ENCLOSED IS ☐ A CHECK   ☐ MASTERCARD   ☐ VISA   ☐ AMEX   (✓ ONE)

ACCOUNT # _____ EXP. DATE _____

SIGNATURE _____

PLEASE ADD $1.25 (SHIPPING/HANDLING) AND LOCAL SALES TAX.

MAKE CHECKS PAYABLE TO MCGRAW-HILL., INC. PRICES SUBJECT TO CHANGE
WITHOUT NOTICE AND MAY VARY OUTSIDE U.S. FOR THIS INFORMATION, WRITE
TO MCGRAW-HILL OR CALL THE 800 NUMBER.

McGraw Hill

PLEASE SEND
COMPLETED FORM TO:

MCGRAW-HILL, INC.
ORDER PROCESSING S-1
PRINCETON ROAD
HIGHTSTOWN, NJ 08520

OR CALL:
1-800-338-3987